REACTION TO COLONIALISM

Northern Province of Zambia: administrative boundaries, 1970

REACTION TO COLONIALISM

A prelude to the politics of
independence in northern Zambia
1893–1939

by

HENRY S. MEEBELO

Foreword by
His Excellency Dr Kenneth D. Kaunda
President of the Republic of Zambia

PUBLISHED FOR
THE INSTITUTE FOR AFRICAN STUDIES
UNIVERSITY OF ZAMBIA
BY
MANCHESTER UNIVERSITY PRESS
1971

© 1971 UNIVERSITY OF ZAMBIA
Published by the University of Manchester at
THE UNIVERSITY PRESS
316–324 Oxford Road, Manchester M13 9NR

ISBN 0 7190 1028 4 (hard covers)
0 7190 1029 2 (paperback)

Distributed in the USA by
HUMANITIES PRESS INC
303 Park Avenue South, New York, N.Y. 10010

Printed in Great Britain by
Butler & Tanner Ltd, Frome and London

161342

CONTENTS

FOREWORD

BY HIS EXCELLENCY DR KENNETH D. KAUNDA,

PRESIDENT OF THE REPUBLIC OF ZAMBIA

Very little is written about the reaction of the people of Zambia to the advent of foreign rule. Reading various history books describing the discontent of the people of this country, an impression has many a time been conveyed that only in highly populated industrial areas on the Copperbelt and elsewhere along the line of rail was there an indication of a reaction against foreign domination. Deductions have been made as to the reasons why a protest movement grew up in areas like the Copperbelt. An impression is given that the protest movement on the Copperbelt was not so much due to the people's dislike for foreign rule as to the struggle for better jobs, better salaries and better social conditions, so that the clash between the foreigners and the indigenous people of Zambia is portrayed as the result of economic factors.

This thesis, however, clearly indicates that the protest movement, the refusal of the people to accept foreign rule, and their struggle to rid themselves of foreign rulers, existed long before the copper mines were born and long before the line of rail brought masses of populations to what are now urban centres.

This is, therefore, more than a doctoral thesis. It is a description of the early part of the struggle to keep away foreign rule. It is a candid essay on the refusal of a people to be dominated. It is a proud story, for it confirms that the struggle for Zambia's independence is long and bitter and that the losses sustained by people when they were completely colonised have been more than made up by the successes of the new generation of leaders who, working in concert, have helped to mould Zambia in its present form.

For students of history this is an exciting discovery and a fascinating study in the techniques of divide and rule used by the colonisers to bring the rest of the country to heel. For politicians it is a study in the heroic efforts made by a people to resist domination by another and shows that the greatest enemy of society may not be an outsider but a member of the society who knows its strength and weaknesses.

This is, indeed, an exciting story and it is an honour for me to write this foreword. It is a book I certainly commend not only to professional historians but to politicians and non-politicians alike. It is a tremendous contribution to the history of this nation.

State House, Lusaka
9 June 1970

PREFACE

The *esse* or the force of African nationalism in Malawi, writes one historian of the formation and character of the Nyasaland National Congress in the 1940's, 'was not the product of an imported exotic plant; it sprang from a natural, indigenous growth with its roots deep in the past'.[1] Gray's observation is as apposite to the bellicose mood of African nationalism in Zambia as it is to Malawi's African politics during the same period. Just as the Nyasaland National Congress was formed out of a congeries of Native Welfare Associations in 1944,[2] so also was Zambia's first African nationalist party—the Northern Rhodesia African Congress—which came into being in 1948, a child of a Federation of Welfare Societies that had been formed two years before.[3] In both countries these Welfare Organisations had, for many years before World War II, been the power-house of African politics.

At a casual glance, Welfare Societies in Zambia would seem to be the only coalescence of African political thinking and activity linking post-war nationalist agitation with political developments before the war. But a closer look at the trend of events before World War II would reveal intense political activity, which suggests a wider and variegated background to the nationalist politics of the post-war years. For although the immediate social circumstances that had led to the formation of Welfare Societies, most of which mushroomed in the early 1930's, are important causal factors that must constantly be kept in view by students of the political history of modern Zambia, these societies owed their genesis perhaps as much to what had gone on before between the ruled (Africans) and the rulers (Europeans) as to the prevailing circumstances of the day. The founders of Welfare Societies were able to draw not only on their own experiences since colonial rule was thrust upon them, but also on the successes or failures of older 'cells' of African opposition to European rule, in order to form a more effective resistance movement.

[1] Richard Gray, *The Two Nations* (London: Oxford University Press, 1960), p. 344.　　[2] *Ibid.*, p. 142.
[3] Richard Hall, *Zambia* (London: Pall Mall Press, 1965), p. 125.

History, one might say, is an unbroken stream of events flowing sometimes quietly, sometimes in billows, and at times cascading over cataracts of crowded happenings; and so the tidal wave of belligerent nationalism in post-war Northern Rhodesia was the estuary of an ever-flowing river of African political thinking and activity which came running down the years, having as its source the inception of colonial rule. Thus, it is important, in order to understand fully African politics in general and, in particular, the turbulent nationalist politics in Northern Rhodesia after the Second World War, to pay some attention to the older, if less well organised, forms of African political expression, from the time colonial rule was established three-quarters of a century ago. As the Russian scholar A. B. Davidson has observed, it is difficult to understand the modern African liberation movement without reference to the various forms of African resistance to European rule in the past.[4]

This study seeks to make some contribution in this respect by attempting, on a regional basis, to trace the development and assess the nature of African political consciousness under white rule in the Northern Province of modern Zambia. African reactions, be they individual or collective, to various 'white–black' contact situations and to measures introduced by the colonial authorities are examined in some detail, as they are, in their own way, manifestations of African nationalism, if only in its nascent stages. Inevitably, in this context, at a time when illiteracy was endemic and political outlook parochial among the people of the Northern Province and this part of Africa as a whole, the term 'nationalism' may well be considered a misnomer, as it acquires a shade of meaning which is somewhat different from that which it normally carries, say, in reference to nineteenth-century Europe or post-war Africa. But this would seem to be a difference only in degree rather than in kind of a phenomenon that is basically the same, but which is varied by differing levels of social development.

In undertaking this type of investigation, I was motivated by certain deeply felt needs. Quite apart from the need to provide a historical background to post-war African politics in Northern

---

[4] Cited in T. O. Ranger, 'Connexions between "primary resistance" movements and modern mass nationalism in East and Central Africa, Part I', *Journal of African History*, Vol. IX, No. 3 (1968), pp. 437–439.

Rhodesia—even though only on a limited front—there is an obvious gap to be filled in the early political history of most newly independent African States. So far, most of the historiography on Central Africa, for example, appears to suffer from an imbalance which tends to distort the picture of events during the early days of colonial rule. The history of Central Africa is, for the most part, still the story of European settlement and enterprise. The role of the African people in the new colonial order seems secondary, and is mentioned only in so far as it impinges on orderly white enterprise, as if European activity was the prime mover of things in all situations. The part played in the political evolution of this part of Africa by early African political pressure groups has, as one anthropologist has observed, yet to be fully explored.[5]

A fair amount of work has, of course, been done to redress this imbalance. Richard Gray's *The Two Nations*, Philip Mason's *The Birth of a Dilemma*, Robert I. Rotberg's *The Rise of Nationalism in Central Africa*, Richard Hall's *Zambia*, Terence Ranger's *Revolt in Southern Rhodesia*, *The Zambesian Past*, a symposium edited by Eric Stokes and Richard Brown, and the more recent studies in *Aspects of Central African History* edited by Terence Ranger, are indeed valuable guides into what is still largely Central African history's *terra incognita*. However, a lot more remains to be done before historians will be in a position to see, in its true perspective, the role played by Africans in the political and economic vicissitudes of colonial Africa. It would not, for example, be possible to understand fully the reasons behind the B.S.A.C. Administration's decision in 1909 to rescind its long-standing order which forbade *mitanda* or garden villages in the Northern Province of Zambia, or why the newly established Imperial Government reduced the poll tax in 1925 from ten shillings to seven shillings and sixpence, without knowledge of the attitudes or reactions of the African people to these measures. Thus, because the political history of a people is essentially the story of the interaction of the activities and thinking of its rulers with those of the ruled, a history of Zambia based solely or mainly on colonial policies and measures or on European activities is necessarily unbalanced, and an equipoise must therefore be sought in unravelling the untold

[5] J. van Velsen, 'Some early pressure groups in Malawi', *The Zambesian Past: Studies in Central African History*, ed. E. Stokes and R. Brown (Manchester University Press, 1966), p. 407.

story of African participation in the country's politico-economic development.

The choice of the Northern Province as the area of this investigation is of no particular significance. Indeed, except for the fact that, like the Western (formerly Barotse) Province and the Eastern Province, the Northern Province was one of the first areas in Zambia to be opened up by the forces of colonialism, and therefore affords a longer span of white–black contact for extensive examination, the choice could have fallen on any other province or area. However, for obvious reasons of convenience, it has had to be taken as a geographical unit—a unit which, during the seventy years of British rule, once comprised three separate administrative units (or districts, as provinces were called before 1930), and which at another time were fused into two districts, the two forming in 1933 what was then called the Northern Province, comprising the modern Northern Province, the Luapula Province and the Serenje District of the Central Province of today. After the Second World War, in 1947, the modern Northern Province, which is the ambit of this study, came into being.[6] It would not have been possible to limit this study to any single ethnic group, since the tribes of the province, as elsewhere in Zambia, had so intermingled and district boundaries had been so drawn by the colonial authorities that one tribe could be found in two or more districts in the province, and a district could have as many as six tribes or sub-tribes within its boundaries.[7] The Bemba, for example, were found in Kasama, Abercorn, Chinsali, Mpika, Luwingu and Mporokoso districts. It would thus be impossible to study their reactions to European rule without reference to the attitudes of their neighbours, with whom they may have co-operated or differed in their opposition to alien rule.

[6] *African Affairs Annual Report for the Year 1947* (Lusaka: Government Printer), pp. 7, 17.

[7] It is, in fact, said that in Zambia, where there are some seventy-three tribes speaking about thirty different dialects, so much intermixture of tribes had taken place under colonial rule that it was difficult to distinguish even approximately the boundaries of tribal areas and that such a situation had bedevilled the creation of Native Reserves, into which various tribal groups were forced to move by the colonial authorities. See Lord Hailey, *Native Administration in the British African Territories*, Part II (London: H.M.S.O., 1950), p. 18; *Report of the Commission appointed to enquire into the Financial and Economic Position of Northern Rhodesia* (1938), p. 177.

This study has drawn on a variety of materials. In addition to the literature that has been cited already, certain other works have provided important background information for the theme of the study. Works like Marshall Hole's *The Making of Rhodesia*, Sir Harry Johnston's *British Central Africa*, Roland Oliver's *Sir Harry Johnston and the Scramble for Africa*, C. Gouldsbury and H. Sheane's *The Great Plateau of Northern Rhodesia*, Stephen Mpashi's *Abapatili Bafika ku Babemba*, Andrew Roberts' thesis, 'A political history of the Bemba (North-eastern Zambia) to 1900', which will soon be published, and *The Story of the Northern Rhodesia Regiment*, edited by W. V. Brelsford, are, as it were, an illuminating commentary on the establishment of white rule in ths part of Central Africa, just as Lewis Gann's *A History of Northern Rhodesia* is, like the other works mentioned earlier on, a pathfinder for research workers in the field of economic and political developments in Zambia.

It is, however, upon archival materials that this study rests heavily. These range from District Tour Reports, Quarterly and Annual Reports to confidential correspondence between various centres in the Northern Province and the country's capital, and they are deposited in the Zambia National Archives in Lusaka. All documentary references, therefore, are, unless stated otherwise, to the Zambia National Archives in Lusaka. It must be pointed out, however, that these records are not at all continuous for all areas; there are gaps here and there which make it a little difficult to discern much concatenation in the trend of events in the area, and to see the reactions of the various ethnic groups as parts of a single whole. As will be seen from the study itself, there is a constant change of the *dramatis personae*: sometimes the Bemba hold the stage; sometimes it is the Bisa or the Namwanga or some other group, depending upon what the available sources cover. This inadequacy of the sources tends to make the story of African reaction to colonial rule in the Northern Province read rather more like a series of disparate episodes than a continuum of initiatives and reactions, and it is one of the obvious weaknesses of this study.

Apart from studying official records in the Archives, opportunity was taken to consult various publications and manuscripts at the Institute of Social Research of the University of Zambia, formerly known as the Rhodes-Livingstone Institute. Later, in

July and August 1967, I spent a month in the Northern Province collecting oral evidence, in an endeavour to gain additional insights into the questions posed by official records. Thanks to the District Secretaries who were in charge of the seven districts I visited and to whom I had given advance notice of my research tour, I was able to make easy contacts with people who, from the administrators' thorough knowledge of their own districts, were considered to be very knowledgeable about events during the period under study. It turned out, however, that, except for those of them who were literate, the eye-witness accounts of some of the informants about certain events were often too generalised to be of great value. But educated informants, like Donald Siwale, gave very useful information, although it is a matter for regret that their oral evidence was not backed by their own or other Africans' recorded accounts of the events they were recounting.

This lack of African written sources, and the hazy and sometimes unreliable reminiscences of eye-witnesses of the march of events in these early years of colonial rule, are some of the problems with which students of Zambia's political history will have to live. No doubt a prolonged stay in the province would have elicited more information; but lack of financial support for the exercise, which I had to undertake entirely at my own expense, made this impossible. It now remains for other history research workers to pick up the threads of the enquiry from where I left them, as I believe greater use could still be made of oral evidence than has been possible in this study.

There was, however, something that was more rewarding about my visit to the Northern Province. Although it was not possible for me to have access to the diaries and other records of mission stations like Mwenzo under the Free Church of Scotland and Kawimbe under the London Missionary Society because they have been sent out of Zambia—I was fortunate to have been allowed to consult a few White Fathers' Mission diaries covering the oldest mission stations at Mambwe and Kayambi, and also the later one at Chilonga. These give a fairly good account of the reactions of the Mambwe and the Bemba to European influence, missionary as well as official, from 1891 to 1914. They are all written in French and the Rt. Rev. Adolphus Fürstenberg, the Bishop of Mbala (Abercorn), in whose archives they are deposited, was kind enough to have the relevant entries translated for me. It is unfortunate, however, that the diaries relating to Chilubula and Malole, among others, were sent to Rome a few years ago, reportedly for photostating. Their removal has created a regrettable, if temporary, gap in the annals of Zambia.

The foregoing review of the source materials for this study should surely be indicative of another important but inevitable weakness of the study itself. It is clear that, because information from African sources, in either written or oral form, is scant, by far the greater part of this enquiry relies upon non-African evidence in trying to find answers to most questions. With such 'hearsay evidence' one is, in effect, examining African reactions to colonial rule through the spectacles of the colonial authorities and not by looking directly at the actors themselves. Such evidence is, not unnaturally, replete with the dangers of under-estimation or exaggeration.

This study was originally prepared as a thesis for the degree of Doctor of Philosophy of the University of London and is published in substantially unchanged form. Many more persons than I can list here have, in one way or another, been of great assistance to me in the course of my research and in the preparation of the study itself, and I am deeply indebted to them all. I would, however, like to record my special gratitude to Professor J. D. Omer-Cooper of the University of Zambia for the encouragement he gave me throughout my research and for the various arrangements which he made with the University authorities to afford me certain services which made my work easier; to the Director of Government Archives, Lusaka, and his staff for their inexhaustible patience and help; to Mr John Mashambe, an Inspector of Schools in Zambia's Ministry of Education, and himself a member of Bemba royalty, who, in discussions, taught me more about the Northern Province than I could have otherwise known; to the Rt. Rev. Adolphus Fürstenberg, the Bishop of Mbala, for giving me permission to consult the White Fathers' Mission diaries in his archives; to Mrs G. Martin of Martin's Secretarial Services, Lusaka, for having carried out the arduous task of typing various drafts of the study so patiently and diligently; and to Mr Stephen Mpashi, a well-known Zambian author, who drew my attention to possible sources of non-official materials during my research.

My intellectual debt in the preparation of the study itself is real and great, and I would therefore like to express my deepest gratitude to Mr Ian Henderson, Dr Andrew Roberts and Professor J. van Velsen of the University of Zambia and to Professor T. O. Ranger, and Dr K. J. McCracken, formerly of the University College, Dar-es-Salaam, for having read the book in its thesis form. Their seasoned observations and advice were invaluable. Finally, my wife Mary, who suffered the loneliness and distraction which attends research, deserves the warmest thanks of all.

Henry S. Meebelo

Lusaka
April 1970

ABBREVIATIONS

A.N.W.A.	Abercorn Native Welfare Association
B.S.A.C.	British South Africa Company
D.C.	District Commissioner
D.O.	District Officer
K.N.W.A.	Kasama Native Welfare Association
L.M.S.	London Missionary Society
L.N.W.A.	Livingstone Native Welfare Association
Lu.N.W.A.	Luanshya Native Welfare Association
M.W.A.	Mwenzo Welfare Association
N.C.	Native Commissioner
N.N.W.A.	Ndola Native Welfare Association
N.R.Ex.Co.	Northern Rhodesia Executive Council
N.R.J.	*Northern Rhodesia Journal*
P.C.	Provincial Commissioner
R.L.J.	*Rhodes-Livingstone Journal*
S.N.A.	Secretary for Native Affairs

CHAPTER I

THE NORTHERN PROVINCE AND ITS PEOPLES
ON THE EVE OF EUROPEAN RULE

When in February 1867 Chitimukulu Chitapankwa made David Livingstone stay three weeks at his court in the hope that, with some pestering, the Scottish missionary would give away all the European-made goods in his possession, the Bemba king hardly imagined that his people would one day hate to see a whiteman in their midst, or even near the borders of their country. Nor did he ever suspect that Livingstone was only a forerunner of many more whitemen of the same persuasion who would come and destroy the very foundations upon which Bemba power was based. Livingstone himself had but praise for the 'crocodile king';[1] he was 'good-natured', wrote the doctor about Chitapankwa, 'and our intercourse is a laughing one'.[2] Sixteen years after Livingstone's visit, Chitapankwa was again to accord to another whiteman, Giraud, what the Frenchman himself later called a 'splendid reception'.[3]

Yet for ten years after the death of Chitapankwa in 1883, no European was to be received by any Bemba chief,[4] and the Bemba became known to Europeans visiting this part of Central Africa as a fierce and intractable people. Sir Harry Johnston, writing to Hugh Charles Marshall in 1893, informing him of his appointment as the Magistrate and Collector for Tanganyika District, an area to the north of Bembaland, covering the country of the Lungu, the Tabwa, the Mambwe and the Namwanga, warned the young officer that the area to which he was being transferred was 'one of the most difficult posts to occupy in the whole of British Central Africa'. While in Abercorn, the administrative centre of his new district, Marshall—Johnston wrote—would come face to face with the much-dreaded Bemba, with whom he should, all the same, enter into friendly relations. Marshall was enjoined to pursue a waiting policy: he should seek to gain the friendship of neighbouring tribes while at the same time watching his opportunity to enter into negotiations with the Bemba. He was, moreover, to exercise tact in his dealings with this warlike people, otherwise, Johnston warned, there would be open friction with the crocodile kings, which it would not be possible to contain, because for quite some time there would be no reinforcements from Nyasaland to swell Marshall's small police force of half a dozen Sikhs and a handful of Nyasaland Tonga, which, in the meantime, he was advised to augment by enlisting local tribesmen who would take refuge at Abercorn from the ravages of Bemba raids.[5]

What was it that brought about so radical a change in the attitude of the Bemba towards Europeans, and made the new Chitimukulu, Sampa Kapalakasha, the most hostile of all contemporary Bemba rulers to the cautious advance of the Johnston Administration[6]—an attitude which stood in sharp contrast to that of his predecessor? Contemporary Bemba belief is said to have attributed the cause of this revulsion against whitemen to Giraud, who was suspected of having bewitched or poisoned Chitapankwa because the king fell ill and died soon after the Frenchman's visit.[7] But this may well have been little more than an allegorical explanation for a phenomenon whose 'real' causes lay elsewhere. It is necessary therefore to try and identify these causes, because not only do they put Bemba intractability in its true perspective, but they also explain the way in which non-Bemba tribes received European rule.

Ever since their arrival in the country from *Kola* or *Buluba* in the Congo about the end of the seventeenth century or the beginning of the eighteenth century,[8] the Bemba had been engaged in incessant wars of conquest with other tribes of the Northern Province, establishing chieftainships wherever they thought necessary, and creating new ones in the process.[9] They occupied Bisa country north of the Chambeshi and conquered parts of the Chinsali District which had been in Bisa hands,[10] and under Chitimukulu Chitapankwa in the latter half of the nineteenth century they conquered the Lungu under Zombe, the Mambwe under Nsokolo and the Namwanga under Chikanamulilo, taking slaves and cattle as they went.[11] These military successes, and the territorial expansion that went with them, owed much of their impetus to the trade in guns and other commodities with the Arabs which greatly increased the wealth and the military resources of Bemba chiefs.[12]

By the time the first missionaries and colonial officials arrived in the country in the late 1880's and the early 1890's respectively, Bemba hegemony had been established over the surrounding tribes, and the preoccupation of the crocodile kings then was merely to maintain this ascendancy and to exploit the material as well as the human resources of their 'empire'. They continually raided their neighbours for grain and livestock, as well as for slaves, whom they sold to the Arabs for guns, gunpowder and various items of merchandise. Indeed, it is said that the Bemba took little trouble to grow enough food for themselves but depended on raiding neighbouring tribes for most of their requirements, often boasting that Mambwe country, for example, was their grain store.[13] Even after more than a decade of white rule the Bemba were still wont to boast, as the two Administration officials, Gouldsbury and Sheane, observed whilst in the country, that 'they do not know how to hoe, that their own trade was war, and that subject tribes supplied their various wants'—the Senga bringing in tobacco, the Bisa fish and salt, while the Iwa and the Namwanga brought in hoes, livestock and grain.[14] But it would not be true to say that these raids of the Bemba on other tribes were actuated solely by the warlike tradition of this tribe. Quite apart from this, there were other factors which combined to make raids an 'institutionalised' activity, in the sense that raiding became an established way of life of the Bemba. One of these factors is ecological, and it had a lot to do with the mode of life not only of the Bemba but also of their neighbours, and consequently determined inter-tribal relations quite considerably.

The Northern Province of Zambia (formerly Northern Rhodesia), which is the compass of this study, is a land mass covering an area of 62,880 square miles,[15] and lies between the upper reaches of the Luangwa in the east and Lake Mweru in the west, covering the whole of the Chambeshi River basin and parts of the Bangweulu swamps in the south, as well as the plateau to the south of Lake Tanganyika. A study of a soils map of the area will show that most of the province consists of infertile leached laterite soils, most of the patches of fertile land being found in the Abercorn, Isoka and Mporokoso Districts. Apart from soil infertility, the province has also suffered from another curse of nature: the tse-tse fly. Most of this area, especially the central parts, which are occupied mostly by the Bemba, is infested with tse-tse fly, and it can be assumed that the position was not any better even sixty or eighty years ago, judging from the apparently unabated tse-tse infestation of the province over the last thirty years.[16]

Living in such a harsh environment was not without difficulties for the people of the Northern Province, and the ecology of the area shaped their livelihood and, through it, the course of African history in this part of Zambia. In later years, when European settlement in the various parts of Northern Rhodesia was an economic proposition uppermost in the minds of colonial officials, the Northern Province, as will be shown later in this study, attracted very few white settlers, and this lack of a white settler farming community, such as the one that was to be found in the Southern Province, for example, and which absorbed some of the country's labour force, restricted the labour market in the Northern Province, and was one of the factors that gave rise to labour migration and its attendant problems. But on the eve of European rule the Northern Province's poor soils and tse-tse fly infestation were perhaps even of more crucial significance to the people of the area, as the people could not earn a living outside the province's subsistence economy. Apart from hunting, fishing and picking wild fruit, the people of the Northern Province, like most African peoples on the continent, depended on the soil for their livelihood, and in order to make up for the infertility of the soil at their level of technological development they practised shifting cultivation, of which there were two main varieties.[17] The first one was the more common method of stumping, or cutting down tree trunks waist-high, which was more characteristic of people like the Namwanga, the Mambwe and the Bisa.[18] The second method, locally known as *Chitemene*, in which trees were pollarded and branches heaped together, dried and burned to provide an ash bed in which the fingermillet was planted, was more characteristic of the Bemba, although it seems that this method was also extensively used by other neighbouring tribes.[19]

By these methods the people of the Northern Province grew various crops, and of these the finger millet was the commonest. The Senga, the Iwa and the Namwanga also grew tobacco, while the Bisa produced cotton, as a result of which they were great weavers of cotton cloths—an industry which, in addition to iron works and hides, made them successful traders.[20] Apart from such agricultural products, those tribes which lived in tse-tse-free areas reared livestock: the Mambwe, the Lungu and the Namwanga to the north and north-east, as well as the Bisa around the Bangweulu swamps in the south, were breeders of cattle, sheep and goats.[21] But the Bemba, who mainly occupied the tse-tse fly infested areas of the Northern Province, hardly reared any livestock. Even as late as the 1930's, Audrey Richards could still find that neither chiefs nor commoners owned more than a few goats or sheep.[22] Against this background it seems clear why the Bemba, traditionally a warlike and essentially a non-pastoral people, practising a type of shifting cultivation on relatively poor land which could scarcely afford them all their food requirements, often raided their neighbours for cattle and grain. An expansionist Bemba State, backed by guns and perpetually animated by the wealth which its rulers had amassed in the course of their commercial intercourse with the Arabs, sought to thrive on the economic and human resources of the surrounding tribes.

But it would not be correct to explain the recurrence of Bemba raids only in terms of the parlous economic position of the tribe. The Bemba raided neighbouring tribes not only for grain and livestock, but also for slaves, whom they sold to the Arabs for guns, cloth, beads and other goods. By the time European rule was established in the country towards the close of the last century, the Arabs seem to have gained tremendous influence in the Northern Province, establishing settlements which provided a ready market for slaves and became an ever-present incentive to Bemba raids.[23] It is said, for example, that the Arab *tembe* or stockaded village under Kapandansalu, built close to that of Chibale, a Senga chief in the upper Luangwa valley, became 'a great slave market'.[24] Thus it would seem that the Bemba were implicated in the slave trade, and their involvement in this human traffic was, as Roberts puts it, 'a crucial factor in shaping their general attitude to European advance. It may be that Bemba dependence on the trade in slaves and ivory was far enough advanced to render them highly susceptible to interference with it.[25] Such a reaction from a people living in a country where there was little else to take the place of slaves as the country's main export was to be expected. Unlike the people of West Africa, who had gold, palm oil and spices to fall back upon as commercial substitutes for the slave trade, the Bemba had no other commodity in which to trade with the outside world at the same lucrative level. Even ivory, which was second in importance to the trade in slaves, seems to have grown scarce, owing to the decline in the elephant population, which had been thinned by decades of uncontrolled hunting. As early as 1879 Joseph Thomson could notice, for example, that in the country between Lake Tanganyika and the east coast elephants had practically disappeared and that there were none in Mambwe country.[26] Fourteen years later, Lieutenant Crawshay, an official in Johnston's Administration, reported that 'ivory is becoming a very rare commodity in the hitherto sought districts of Senga and Luwemba'.[27]

With the trade in ivory on the wane, the slave trade became of even greater importance to the Bemba. The anti-slave trade activities of the African Lakes Company in Nyasaland and in the eastern parts of the Northern Province—in the course of which it was engaged in a desperate struggle against the Arabs to defend the local African populations; it opened stations at Mwenzo and near Lake Tanganyika and embarked on the construction of the Stevenson Road in 1881 from the northern tip of Lake Nyasa to the southern end of Lake Tanganyika in order to promote 'legitimate trade'[28]—could not be looked on with indifference by the crocodile kings. The position caused them even greater concern when the London Missionary Society, which since 1877 had been struggling against numerous odds to found a mission station in the area around the southern end of Lake Tanganyika,[29] finally established itself in Mambwe country at Nyamukolo in 1884 and at Fwambo in 1887.[30] For the L.M.S. mission stations, like those of the White Fathers, who arrived in the country in 1891 and established their first station at Mambwe Mwela,[31] and like the administrative posts that were established at Chiengi in 1892 and at Abercorn in 1893,[32] became a threat to the time-honoured freedom of the Bemba to raid their subject-tribes. It was probably this increasing interference with their trade in slaves and their hitherto unfettered tradition of raiding their neighbours for grain and livestock, rather than the allegation against Giraud, which made the Bemba seal off the borders of their country to European penetration for many years.

It is difficult to estimate accurately the effects of Bemba raids and wars of conquest on neighbouring tribes. But the picture painted by a few accounts of the state of affairs in the country at the time seems quite a grim one. Livingstone, who passed through the Northern Province early in 1867, observed that the Bisa, a matrilineal tribe like the Bemba, which was living in the southern parts of the province, were, as he put it, 'dependants of the Babemba, reduced . . . to a miserable jungly state'.[33] They were, he went on to say,

poor dependants of the Babemba, or rather their slaves, who cultivated little . . . so as to prevent their conquerors from taking away more than a small share . . . This tribe is engaged in the slave-trade, and the evil effects are seen in their depopulated country and utter distrust of everyone.[34]

The Lungu, a patrilineal group living to the north of the Bemba, also seem to have been in a 'jungly state' as a result of Bemba raids. Even after more than ten years of British rule they had no paramount chief, as the tribe was rent by family feuds and clan dissensions resulting from Bemba raids, which inhibited all attempts at cohesion.[35] Compared with the plight of the Lungu, the Mambwe, another patrilineal tribe to the north-east of the Bemba, were perhaps a more miserable lot. It is said that the Mambwe had suffered so severely from the depredations of the Bemba that they were only saved from extermination by the arrival, in the first instance, of the London Missionary Society and, later, of the Administration.[36] But this, however, would seem to be an overstatement of the state of affairs in the country. What appears likely is that the Mambwe, in their ceaseless and desperate attempts to evade the ever-recurring Bemba raids, became an increasingly migratory people. Three months after their arrival in Mambwe country in 1891, the White Fathers noted, with a strain of dismay, that owing to Bemba raids the Mambwe had gone to live in areas as far away from their homeland as the shores of Lake Nyasa:

The Amambwe were living formerly much more to the West. They were pushed away by the Babemba, and still now, they have to suffer so much from their traditional enemies that they do not dare to cultivate their fields and many migrate far away up to the shores of the Nyassa. If they are assured they will find protection with the mission, they will all come to live near it.[37]

It is probably for this reason that Gouldsbury and Sheane thought that the Mambwe were on the verge of extinction, and it is probably for the same reason that the White Fathers, on arrival in

Mambwe country, formed the impression that 'Umambwe seems a small country with only about ten villages'.[38]

The effects of Bemba raids on neighbouring tribes went far beyond the social turmoil to which they gave rise. Perhaps more than any other single factor, they determined the response of these other tribes to European intrusion and made them look to the white missionaries and the officials of the Administration for protection against the Bemba. Thus, a congeries of over a dozen tribes, mutually hostile and enfeebled by decades of tribal wars and raids, saw, with almost universal diffidence, the gradual establishment of white mission stations in their midst, and the piecemeal occupation of their country by a financially and administratively ill-equipped British Administration in Nyasaland. With the exception of the Bemba, who put up 'armed recalcitrance' here and there in order to safeguard their 'empire' and the economic interests that were part and parcel of their hegemony, the rest of the tribes—the Unga, the Ambo, the Namwanga, the Iwa, the Mambwe, the Lungu, the Tabwa, the Bisa and others —received white rule with a kind of fatalistic resignation. After colonial rule was finally established in the Northern Province, some of these tribes sought to undo what the crocodile kings had done by their wars of conquest: they claimed back territories and chieftainships which they had lost during the Bemba wars and raids, and refuted claims of suzerainty over them by their Bemba overlords. This became a problem which taxed the attention of the Administration in the 1920's, and which assumed even greater complexity with the introduction of Indirect Rule in the 1930's.

What has been said so far in these introductory pages on the state of African societies in this part of Central Africa on the eve of colonial rule might give one the impression that the Bemba State was a monolithic, highly centralised and militarised polity, capable of withstanding the buffets of Western imperialism, which was sweeping the African continent. But in fact Bemba society seems to have been too ill-prepared to repulse any thrustful European advance. Although chiefs could raise armies to fight or raid surrounding tribes—such as the army seen by Otto Genthe at Chief Chikwanda's court in 1898, consisting of about six hundred men[39]—the Bemba do not seem to have had any general military organisation[40] at all comparable to the closely knit regimental organisation of the Zulu,[41] or the highly centralised military system of their offshoot, the Ndebele.[42] In times of peace the only sign of Bemba military power was the presence at each big court of one or two captains (*abashika*), who performed ritual functions which were connected with war magic.[43]

This lack of a general and co-ordinated military organisation, which in the end proved fatal for Bemba resistance to European occupation, appears to have been one of the weaknesses inherent in the Bemba polity itself—a polity which one authority has, with considerable justification, called 'a stratified federation', because, as he puts it, 'its diverse ranks of rulers were drawn from different strata of the kingdom'.[44] The Bemba kingdom was, as it still is even today, divided into districts (*ifyalo*) and each district (*icalo*) was as much a geographical unit as it was a political entity, having a definite boundary and name dating from historical times, and ruled over by a chief with a fixed title.[45] For example, the district under Chief Mwamba was known as Ituna; that under Nkolemfumu was called Miti and Chief Nkula's was known as Ichinga. Even the king, Chitimukulu, had his own *icalo*—Lubemba—over which he ruled, in addition to being overlord of the whole Bemba country.[46] There were different categories of chieftainships, of varying importance. Holders of prominent chiefly posts like the Mwambaship, the Nkolemfumuship, the Nkulaship, the Chikwandaship and the Mpepoship, were promoted from lower ranks to greater chieftainships of the kingship, depending upon their genealogical seniority.[47] Chieftainships such as those of Nkweto, Chimbola, Mwaba and Mfungo were, like the aforementioned, also held by members of the royal clan, the *bena ng' andu*, but they were provincial posts to which succession was localised.[48] The other category of chieftainships belonged to 'sons' of *bena ng' andu* chiefs, like Makasa and Mporokoso, who succeeded to positions of 'perpetual sonship'.[49] Although the king was ritually supreme over all his chiefs, because he had superior relics at the shrine of his capital and because his priest-councillors (*bakabilo*) had greater ritual powers than the *bakabilo* of his vassals,[50] politically he seems to have exercised little control over them. Each chief enjoyed a measure of internal autonomy and none could be said to have been a satellite of Chitimukulu. As Andrew Roberts aptly sums up the position:

the Bemba polity in the late nineteenth century consisted of the flexible ties [of kinship] linking chieftainships in a correspondingly fluid pattern

of subordination. There was still no system of centralised administration through which Chitimukulu could exert authority throughout
Bemba country. In terms of effective executive power, Chitimukulu
was at best *primus interpares*. Each Chief in his own territory (*icalo*) was
more or less autonomous in matters of administration, depending on
the prevailing constellation of alliances and antagonisms throughout
Bemba country. For the subordinate titles were not ranked in any
formal hierarchy by which their rights and responsibilities might have
been defined in relation to the centre and to each other.[51]

These fissionary tendencies in the Bemba body politic seem to
have been aggravated by the economic situation in the country.
Lewis Gann has observed that, unlike in the Western Province,
among the Lozi, where there was regional economic specialisation
and therefore a certain measure of economic interdependence,
which contributed to political cohesion, in Bembaland each *icalo*
produced much the same goods, and this lack of economic
diversification and the consequential absence of economic interdependence denied the Bemba polity of one possible unifying
factor.[52] To what extent Gann's observation is true, in view of the
fact that Bemba economic life was mainly sustained by raids on
neighbouring tribes, it is difficult to say. But one thing appears
more likely: external trade in slaves and ivory with the Arabs
seems to have had a negative effect on the tendency towards unity
in the Bemba polity.[53] For it increased the wealth and therefore
the power of all chiefs, and not just Chitimukulu alone, and this
tended to make certain chiefs grow more and more powerful,
much to the detriment of the king's authority. Thus, as Roberts
says, 'the circulation of goods continued to be a matter of greater
political than economic significance'.[54]

It seems unlikely, therefore, that under such a loose administration, bedevilled by the competing economic interests of the traditional rulers, the Bemba would have mobilised a 'national' army
to stem the advancing tide of white rule. Eric Stokes and Richard
Brown, citing, as an example, the rise to political supremacy of
Chitimukulu Chitapankwa during the Ngoni wars in the latter
half of the nineteenth century, have advanced the view that the
power of the Bemba king 'varied in proportion to the external
danger'.[55] This does not seem to be a valid observation, because
on its own it does not explain why, given as a fact the point that

feuds and civil wars were a political malaise endemic in Bemba society,[56] Chitimukulu Sampa or his successor, Makumba, failed, as will be shown in the next chapter, to raise a 'national' army to ward off European intrusion, as Chitapankwa had done against the Ngoni. And yet the reign of both kings witnessed, at an increasing rate, the European occupation of the Northern Province, which, according to Roberts, was 'the gravest external threat that the Bemba had yet faced'.[57]

Clearly, neither Sampa's nor Makumba's power can be said to have 'varied in proportion to the external danger'. Quite apart from the state of affairs in the Bemba polity itself, it seems more likely that the power of the Bemba king varied according to his calibre—his ability to wield power by exploiting the weaknesses of his dissident vassals and at the same time winning their confidence and allegiance. For, as Roberts says, political cohesion in the Bemba State was 'dangerously dependent on the personalities of its office-holders'.[58] That probably accounts for Chitapankwa's successful reign. Although after forcibly taking over the Chitimukuluship in the early 1860's from his somewhat dumb and lean-witted maternal uncle, Bwembya, he was for some time a sickly king, Mutale Chitapankwa soon became perhaps the greatest of the later Chitimukulus, and probably the greatest consolidator of the Bemba kingdom.[59] He considerably extended the size of Bemba country during the twenty-one years that he was king,[60] which, at the time of his death in 1883, had spread over an area of about 30,000 square miles, with a population of about 100,000.[61] Popular and resourceful, he used to lead Chiefs Mwamba Chileshe Kapalaula and Makasa Chipemba on raiding missions to Lungu and Mambwe country,[62] and maintained a personal and intimate relationship with his brother, Mwamba Chileshe Kapalaula, which played down the rivalry inherent in the two powerful positions. It is said that, in spite of spates of tension between them, they never fought and they continued to exchange presents.[63] This close relationship between the Chitimukuluship and the Mwambaship gave unity to the kingdom; but it was unity of a delicate and transient nature which crumbled when the two brothers died in 1883.[64] Coming, as they did, at the time when the clouds of European occupation were gathering on the horizon, the deaths must have been a shock to the whole Bemba body politic, and it is probably as a result of their occurrence in a fast-changing political situation that the Bemba, shocked into an increased sense of insecurity, sought to keep Europeans out of their country.

When Chitimukulu Chitapankwa died, Sampa Mulenga Kapalakasha, who was at the time Nkula, acceded to the Chitimukuluship, the putative successor, Mwamba Chileshe Kapalaula, having died earlier. Unlike Chitapankwa, who, according to Livingstone, was a 'good-natured' man, with a 'fat, jolly face',[65] and who because of his power and popularity had moulded the Bemba into a fairly united people, the new Chitimukulu was essentially an egotist, who cared more for his own welfare than for that of his people. Even before he was made Nkula, he fought and defeated Shichansa Chitupi, who was then Nkula, in order to take over the chieftainship. It was only through Chitimukulu Chitapankwa's military intervention that he relinquished the position and fled into the hills in the Ibwe area. Because of this selfish act Sampa earned himself such unpopularity in the country that few people wanted him to be the successor to Chitapankwa.[66]

It was probably on the strength of Sampa's unpopularity and not so much because the late Chitimukulu Chitapankwa was his father, that Chief Makasa Chipemba took the unprecedented action of removing the late king's cattle and property to his capital, Kabisha, a few days before Sampa acceded to the Chitimukuluship. The result, however, of Makasa's uncustomary action was to provoke an endless feud between the two men. The new Chitimukulu, immediately on assuming his office, marched on Makasa to retrieve the 'stolen' property, which it was his right to inherit. Sampa was, however, repulsed and, in humiliation, he withdrew to a new village near Malashe. Makasa was forced to return the herd of cattle and property only after Sampa, in revenge, had fought Makasa's son, Luombe, burning his village and taking away his cattle. This animosity between the king and his perpetual son lingered on even after Makasa Chipemba's death. Mukuka, who succeeded Chipemba, inherited the Chitimukulu-Makasa feud as well. Sampa, who, like Mwambe Mubanga Chipoya, was notorious for mutilating with rare facility any supposed offender, once went to Makasa Mukuka's capital and, in cold blood, killed three of the latter's people. It was due to this perpetual state of animosity between the two men that Makasa later defied his overlord Chitimukulu by receiving Bishop Dupont in 1895, at a time when, by decree of the Bemba king, no whiteman was allowed to enter Bemba country.[67]

Chitimukulu Sampa does not seem to have seen the need for co-operation between himself and his chiefs in the kingdom. He was never on good terms even with Mwamba Mubanga Chipoya, the most powerful of Bemba chiefs at the time. The cause of their life-long feud is not clear. But it seems likely that their enmity had its beginnings in the dispute between the late Chitimukulu Chitapankwa and Sampa, whilst he was Nkula, as to who should have succeeded Mwamba Kapalaula. For, while Chitapankwa pressed the claims of Mubanga Chipoya to the Mwambaship, Nkula Sampa was supporting another nephew, Chanika.[68] However, whatever the cause of their age-old misunderstanding was, these vendettas led to frequent bloody battles between uncle and nephew which resulted in the nephew extending his sway at the expense of his uncle, Chitimukulu. Mwamba Chipoya took over large areas of Chitimukulu's country, Lubemba, and the feud continued until the death of Sampa in 1896.

What happened after the death of Sampa regarding succession to the Chitimukuluship is clouded with uncertainty. According to François Tanguy, when Sampa died the people wanted Mwamba Mubanga Chipoya to be Chitimukulu, because Chimfwembe Makumba, the putative heir, was too old. But Mwamba Chipoya refused the offer, because it was taboo for him to accede to the kingship while his uncle, Makumba, the rightful heir, was still alive. Moreover, Mwamba preferred to remain in his own province, Ituna, which was at any rate larger than that of Chitimukulu.[69] This is a view to which Chitimukulu Musenga subscribed. The late Paramount recalled that Mwamba Mubanga Chipoya refused to accept the kingship which the people offered him because they felt that, as Mwamba was the most powerful Bemba chief, he should become Chitimukulu. Mubanga Chipoya preferred to have Makumba made Chitimukulu instead.[70]

However, while Tanguy and Chitimukulu Musenga portray Mwamba Chipoya as having been a modest man, making no claim to the Chitimukuluship rendered vacant by the death of

Sampa, Brelsford, once a District Officer among the Bemba people, depicts him as a man still possessed by the old compulsive ambition that used to drive him to fight the late Chitimukulu Sampa to gain political ascendancy over the head of state. According to Brelsford, after the death of Sampa, Mwamba Chipoya announced his intention to take over the Chitimukulu-ship and warned the weak Chimfwembe Makumba, who was the rightful heir, to keep away, which he did. However, before Chipoya was in a position to move to Chitimukulu's capital, Makumba and Chief Chikwanda marched to the capital and took away the late Chitimukulu's wives. But Chipoya in time caught up with the raiding party and killed most of them. Chikwanda managed to escape to his salt pans in Mpika, but Makumba was captured and tortured by Mwamba Chipoya, who released him to assume the Chitimukuluship only when Makumba was show-ing signs of dying.[71] Robert Young, who was at the time Assistant Collector in the Chambeshi District east of Bemba country, also wrote that Mwamba, 'who was then the strong man of the Awemba', wished to become the Chitimukulu, but he was too frightened of the whitemen's power on the periphery of Bemba country to force his way to that position.[72] According to Roberts, Mwamba Chipoya had coveted the Chitimukuluship but was deterred from seizing it by certain ominous events—attacks on people by a lion, a snake and a crocodile—which were believed to be the spirit of Bwembya avenging his dethronement by Chitapankwa, and also by the notion that Makumba, the putative heir, was a sickly old man whom he could dominate.[73]

There is something to be said for either view. It is possible, as Brelsford, Roberts and Young argue, that Mwamba Chipoya tried to seize the Chitimukuluship. If he had forced his way to the kingship, his action would have been supported by precedent, because Chitapankwa, for example, became Chitimukulu not in accordance with the Bemba customary law of succession to the Chitimukuluship, but by force. Mwamba Chipoya may very well have wanted to be Chitimukulu, in order to combine his long-standing political ascendancy over the whole country with the spiritual leadership of the Bemba nation, which rested only with the Chitimukuluship. On the other hand, however, he may have been modest and circumspect enough to avoid a succession crisis in the face of the gathering power of the whiteman on the horizon of Bembaland. After all, Mwamba had all the political power that he could ever hope to wield in the land: his *icalo* was larger than that of the king, and his position, save in the ritual and spiritual sense, was *de facto*, although not by tradition, equivalent to that of Chitimukulu.[74] Because Mwamba was so powerful, Audrey Richards has suggested that had European rule not been established at the time, and had it not been for the reverence which the Bemba felt for the superior relics at the shrines of the king's capital and the ritual powers of his *bakabilo*, Chipoya would have seceded from the federal State.[75] But it seems unlikely that Mwamba would have taken such a step, however powerful he may have felt himself to be. Secession, in the context of the web of kinship relationships linking various chieftainships, could only have been meaningful through migration, and migration, at the time when the imperial frontier was closing in on the Northern Province, would have been suicidal for Mwamba. At any rate, as Werbner observes, Mwamba stood to gain more in maintaining his influence within the Kingdom than in severing his ties with it.[76]

Whatever the actual circumstances surrounding Makumba's accession to the Chitimukuluship were, there is no doubt that for two decades or so before the advent of colonial rule in the Northern Province the Bemba polity was in the throes of civil war, in which the tribe's main chieftainships, including the Chitimukuluship itself, were involved in incessant family feuds and power struggles, at the expense of the unity for which Chitapankwa had laid a solid foundation. Chimfwembe Makumba thus acceded to a Chitimukuluship which, although still rich in spiritual authority and political symbolism, was bankrupt of the force of political authority such as Chitapankwa had wielded and Mubanga Chipoya's Mwambaship later assumed. Divided, the crocodile kings remained precariously perched on the Bemba social pyramid over a nation that was losing a sense of direction and unity, and over a welter of subject tribes who, with this increasingly apparent Bemba disunity and with the gradual European intrusion in their territories, were becoming increasingly defiant and hostile to the ruler tribe.

Yet in spite of this disunity among the Northern Province's tribal societies, it was not until after the submission of the Bemba to white rule when their most powerful chief—Mwamba

Mubanga Chipoya—died in 1898, that colonial authority asserted itself over the whole province. That it took more than a decade from the beginning of the 'scramble', before British rule was finally and firmly established over the region, was due not only to the state of affairs in the area but also to the general attitude of the official mind of imperialism towards Central Africa, and in particular to these regions. For the response of the African people in the Northern Province to the establishment of colonial rule seems to have been influenced as much by the nature of European intrusion itself as by the social and political conditions prevailing in the area on the eve of white rule. The seemingly slow pace at which the imperial frontier closed in on the Northern Province seems, however, to have been influenced less by the state of affairs in the region than by the thinking of the imperial policy makers in London, Blantyre and Cape Town, as they played away at the chessboard of power politics, in a world that was startled by a sudden and epoch-making intensification of European rivalries in a continent which had hitherto offered little attraction to Western imperialism.

Although Johnston seemed to think that Bemba country was 'a very rich and populous one',[77] it came very low on Britain's scale of priorities for the extension of empire in Central Africa. Unlike Matebeleland and Mashonaland, which, with their fabled mineral wealth, had attracted fortune-seekers into settling in these areas, northern Zambesia, even as late as 1888, was considered by Her Majesty's Government as 'pestilential and useless to empire'.[78] Britain was quite happy to limit her colonial commitments to southern Zambesia, which, in addition to its economic attractions, served as a very strategic area in her 'encirclement policy' stance against the Transvaal *voortrekkers'* challenge to her imperial supremacy, as long as Portugal promised to keep out of the Nyasa region, which had been occupied by British missionaries, and provided also that this northern Zambesian policy received the support of the colonial governments in South Africa.

This grim picture of Northern Rhodesia's economic potential and, in the words of Roland Oliver, 'the [unfavourable] state of public opinion and the parsimony of Parliament . . .' in Britain,[79] combined to make British colonial policy in northern Zambesia one of prevarication and temporisation. Even repeated and pathetic appeals for official intervention and assistance by the

African Lakes Company and British missionaries in the Nyasa region and the Northern Province, who were engaged in a desperate struggle against the Arab slave traders to protect the native population, did not receive favourable response until the end of the 1880's.[80]

It was not until the integrity and security of British interests in the Nyasa region and Zambesia as a whole seemed threatened by the Portuguese, after the Lisbon Anglo–Portuguese negotiations on the fate of northern Zambesia, that Britain realised that the Portuguese were in no mood to negotiate the future of a country which they wished to take by imprescriptible right. It was only then that Her Majesty's Government decided to keep Portugal out of Central Africa, including northern Zambesia which London had earlier been prepared to see fall within Lisbon's sphere of influence.[81] British annexation of northern Zambesia then became imperative. This, together with the granting of the charter to Rhodes' British South Africa Company in 1889, and his financial offer to the British government for the administration of North-eastern Rhodesia, galvanised a hesitant and parsimonious Conservative government into taking immediate steps for the annexation of these territories. To Sir Harry Johnston, the Chartered Company's intervention in the acquisition of North-eastern Rhodesia seemed like an act of special providence in a situation that was becoming increasingly untenable. He later wrote to Rhodes commending him for his timely and salutary action:

All that time [before 1889] affairs in what is now called British Central Africa were rather at a deadlock. The Foreign Office and the Colonial Office then and now entertained much the same ideas that you and I held about the necessity of extending the British Empire within reasonable limits over countries not yet taken up by other European powers, to provide new markets for our manufacturers and afford further scope for British enterprise . . . If I am right, you are the more to be lauded inasmuch as . . . when the Government, though wishing to save this country from the Portuguese and the Germans and secure it for England, yet had not a penny to spend on it, you stepped forward and said 'Make this extension of British supremacy, and I will find the money to administer the new territories.' It seemed to me as though this offer on your part changed the situation at once . . .

Within a week of its being made new instructions were drawn up for me at the Foreign Office, and an entirely new scheme of policy developed of which the direct result has been the establishment of British supremacy over British Central Africa . . . [82]

Thus came into being a country to which, as a sheer act of faith, Johnston gave the promising name of British Central Africa, 'on the principle that it is disastrous to a dog's interest to give him a bad name.[83]

Rhodes' offer led to an agreement between the British government and his company in 1891, by which the Chartered Company's field of operations was extended to North-eastern Rhodesia, the powers of government remaining for the time being with Her Majesty's Commissioner for Nyasaland, Sir Harry Johnston, who would be in receipt of £10,000 per annum from the Company until the end of 1895, as a contribution towards the maintenance of a police force. This grant was to be supplemented from time to time to meet part of the expenses relating to the general administration of the country.

However, in spite of these grants-in-aid to the Johnston Administration by the British South Africa Company, the North-eastern Rhodesian part of British Central Africa was to remain largely unpacified even after it was declared a protectorate in 1893–94.[84] While the recalcitrant Yao in the Lake Malawi area continued their slave raids on the surrounding tribes, Johnston felt it incumbent upon him to bring law and order to these troubled parts of Nyasaland, before attempting to bring North-eastern Rhodesia closer within the compass of his administration. The amphibious warfare into which Johnston had thrown his meagre financial and human resources was too expensive an affair for an administration which had hardly found its feet, and it is not surprising therefore that 'it was in debt and in danger'.[85] Not even with the annual subsidies received from Rhodes' company was Johnston able to maintain an optimum force of Sikhs, Zanzibaris and local tribesmen which he required for the suppression of the slave trade and for reprisals against recalcitrant chiefs. It was therefore by force of circumstances, if he appeared to pester Rhodes in trying to ensure that the latter did not default or delay in paying the promised grants.

Once the Commissioner for Nyasaland was moved to write to

the Chartered Company's tycoons, warning that any reduction in his administration's expenditure, as a result of the Company's failure to honour its promises of more funds, while Makanjira and other malcontents in the Lake area remained a threat to law and order, would entail the withdrawal of all Company officials from the Northern Province, as there would be no funds for their maintenance in the circumstances. He pointed out mournfully that if the Company were to instruct him to effect such a withdrawal, the consequences to the Company's interests and to the welfare of the native peoples in the area of such an action would be dire:

Before taking this step [the withdrawal of officials] however, I would advise you to consider the serious consequences which would result from retrograde action on the upper Congo and the south end of Tanganyika, all the money you have up to date invested in those parts for the erection of buildings and the development of the country will be thrown away and the natives whom we have now accustomed to look to us for protection will be thrown once more on the tender mercies of the Arabs or the Belgians.[86]

Thus the Nyasaland situation, with its financial complications, combined perhaps with Johnston's own turn of mind—that of an 'intellectual and opportunist, [and] not [a] congenital or romantic'[87] imperialist—to make the British imperial frontier's advance into the Northern Province a piecemeal process. For the four years that the Johnston Administration was in charge of Northeastern Rhodesia it was barely able to open four administrative stations at places in the Northern Province it deemed strategic. The first station, opened in 1890 at Chiengi, on the north-eastern corner of Lake Mweru, was abandoned a year later. Another station was opened in 1891 at Kalunguisi, which was first known as Rhodesia, and before Hugh Marshall came to open Abercorn in 1893 as his Tanganyika District Headquarters, a station had been opened at Choma, almost half-way between Lakes Tanganyika and Mweru.[88] Besides these, only the trading posts opened by the African Lakes Company at Chiengi, Abercorn and Ikawa, and Scottish mission stations in the Mambwe and Namwanga country gave physical expression to British presence in the Northern Province.

It is intriguing, as Hole observes, that Rhodes, who was wont to take rapid action in imperial matters, should, instead of taking over North-eastern Rhodesia at once, have played 'a waiting game while such heavy demands were being made upon his Company's funds, largely for the benefit of the adjoining protectorate . . .'[89] The gusto with which he had adopted and publicised Johnston's idea of a Cape-to-Cairo British empire, and the zest with which he had sought to have his Company chartered, seemed to have deserted him. If the economic unattractiveness of Northern Rhodesia, and the local missionaries' opposition to Company rule, had some influence on Rhodes' dilatory policy towards northern Zambesia, his Company's commitments in Mashonaland and Matebeleland and their attendant financial strains did certainly weigh heavily on his sense of direction and priorities. No direct administrative involvement by the Company was possible in the Northern Province, as long as southern Zambesia remained the focal point of its investments and attention. That this was in fact the position is amply illustrated in a letter from the Company's secretary in Cape Town to Sir Harry Johnston:

As you have truly observed, our energies are being severely taxed to meet the many calls upon the purse of the Company, and for this reason we shall be glad if you will draw upon us for as small sums as possible. . . . At the same time Mr. Rhodes has no wish to abandon what you have already done in the region of Lake Mweru, and while maintaining that, trusts to you to remember the financial obligations the Company had already incurred. Once, however, that we show a production of gold from Mashonaland or Matabeleland, as we hope to do this year, our financial burdens as a Company would be greatly lightened, and we could then well afford to let you bring this region around Lake Mweru and the Luapula into closer touch with your Administration in Zomba.[90]

This financial strain on the Company's purse was, moreover, accentuated by two other factors. Partly as a somewhat instinctive reaction to the politico-religious troubles in Uganda, and partly as translation into fact of his dream of a Cape-to-Cairo British empire, Rhodes embarked on the costly project of constructing the transcontinental telegraph line.[91] While the construction of the line was in progress, the Company was unfortunately facing a rebellion in Matebeleland, which further aggravated its financial position. It is not very surprising, therefore, that the Chartered

Company preferred to leave the running of North-eastern Rhodesia's affairs under the Johnston Administration at less than £15,000 per annum rather than take direct responsibility over a territory whose administration, let alone development, would, in those most unpropitious circumstances, have cost the Company several thousand pounds more.[92] It was only after the situation in Southern Rhodesia was contained, and Whitehall was showing some unease over the insolvent Johnston Administration's continued involvement in the conduct of affairs in North-eastern Rhodesia, that the British South Africa Company assumed the reins of government in these regions, and proceeded to complete the process of occupying the country, which had proceeded in a rather 'leap-frog' fashion over the years. It is against this temporising British imperial advance into these regions, as distinct from the resolute and compulsive European intrusion in southern Zambesia,[93] for example, that the reactions of the warring native populations of the Northern Province of Zambia to the coming of European rule must be examined.

NOTES

[1] The term 'crocodile king' is derived from the name of the Bemba royal clan—*Bena ng'andu*, which means 'people of the crocodile'—to which most of the important chiefs belong. It seems to have made its first appearance in the literature on the Bemba in C. Gouldsbury and H. Sheane, *The Great Plateau of Northern Rhodesia* (London: Edward Arnold, 1911), p. 16.

[2] David Livingstone, *The Last Journals of David Livingstone in Central Africa*, ed. H. Waller (London: John Murray, 1874), Vol. I, p. 190.

[3] Gouldsbury and Sheane, *op. cit.*, p. 17.

[4] Chief Mporokoso, for example, refused a visit by Lt Crawshay, an official of the British Central Africa Administration in 1892. W. Thomas of the London Missionary Society station at Kambole, who visited Chief Ponde in 1894, and the White Fathers who visited Chief Makasa in the same year were probably the first white men to be received by any Bemba chief of importance since the days of Giraud; see Andrew Roberts, 'A political history of the Bemba (North-eastern Zambia) to 1900' (Wisconsin University, Ph.D. Thesis, 1966), p. 267.

[5] Johnston to Marshall, 26 July 1893, Abercorn District Note Book, p. 208, KSU 1/1.

[6] Andrew Roberts, *loc. cit.*

[7] R. A. Young, 'Awemba history as I have heard it', MS, n.d., Lusaka Archives; Gouldsbury and Sheane, *loc. cit.*; Roberts, *op. cit.*, pp. 256–257.

[8] Andrew Roberts, 'Chronology of the Bemba', *J. Afr. Hist.*, XI (1970), pp. 11, 221–40; see also Ann Tweedie, 'Towards a history of the Bemba from oral sources', *The Zambesian Past: Studies in Central African History*, ed. E. Stokes and R. Brown (Manchester University Press, 1966), pp. 197, 218–219.

[9] *Ibid.*

[10] F. M. Thomas, *Historical Notes on the Bisa Tribe of Northern Rhodesia*, R.L.J., Comm. 8 (1958), p. 35.

[11] F. Tanguy, *Imilandu Ya Babemba* (4th ed., Lusaka: O.U.P., 1966), pp. 56–58; see also Roberts, 'A political history of the Bemba'.

[12] Andrew Roberts, 'The nineteenth century in Zambia', *Aspects of Central African History*, ed. T. O. Ranger (London, Ibadan and Nairobi: Heinemann, 1968), p. 83; Tweedie, *op. cit.*, p. 219.

[13] Chinsali District Note Book, p. 231, KT Q2; Stephen A. Mpashi, *Abapatili Bafika ku Babemba* (Lusaka: O.U.P., 1966), pp. 8, 17. Mpashi's book is based on oral sources and on the White Fathers' mission books.

[14] Gouldsbury and Sheane, *op. cit.*, p. 11.

[15] Lord Hailey, *Native Administration in British African Territories*, Part II (H.M.S.O., 1950), p. 136.

[16] Audrey Richards, during a research tour of the province in the early 1930's, noted that only a third of the area was free from the fly; see Richards, *Land, Labour and Diet in Northern Rhodesia* (London: O.U.P., 1939), p. 18. In the 1940's it was estimated that half of Chinsali and Kasama Districts had tse-tse fly, while a quarter of Isoka and parts of Abercorn were also infested; see Lord Hailey, *loc. cit.*

[17] For a detailed discussion of these methods of cultivation in the Northern Province and the cultivation 'calendar', see Richards, *op. cit.*, pp. 288–328.

[18] *Ibid.*, p. 288.

[19] Gouldsbury early this century wrote that *Chitemene* was 'almost universal throughout these parts'; see C. Gouldsbury, *An African Year* (London: Edward Arnold, 1912), p. 208. Visiting the province some twenty years later, Richards also formed the same impression; *op. cit.*, p. 18.

[20] Gouldsbury and Sheane, *op. cit.*, pp. 12–14, 24.

[21] *Ibid.*, Gouldsbury, *An African Year*, p. 104.

[22] Richards, *op. cit.*, p. 18.

[23] For an interesting discussion of Arab and Swahili settlements and their influence in the Northern Province, see Andrew Roberts, 'A political history of the Bemba', pp. 233–248; cf. Thomas, *op. cit.*, pp. 22–28.

[24] Roberts, 'A political history of the Bemba', p. 240.

[25] *Ibid.*, p. 249.

[26] *Ibid.*, p. 236.

[27] Quoted in *ibid.*, p. 264.

[28] 'Historical notes of events relating to occupation of Tanganyika District of Northern Rhodesia', ZP 1/3/1.

[29] *Ibid.*; Peter Bolink, *Towards Church Union in Zambia* (Sneek: T. Wever-Francker, 1967), pp. 33–38.

[30] Bolink, *op. cit.*, pp. 33–38.

[31] Old Mambwe Mission Diary, 19 July 1891.

[32] 'Historical notes', *loc. cit.*

[33] Livingstone, *op. cit.*, p. 170.

[34] *Ibid.*, p. 175.

[35] Gouldsbury, *op. cit.*, p. 104; Gouldsbury and Sheane, *op. cit.*, p. 12.

[36] Gouldsbury and Sheane, p. 11.

[37] Old Mambwe Mission Diary, 27 October 1891.

[38] *Ibid.*, 28 August 1891.

[39] E. Stokes and R. Brown, 'Editors' Introduction', *The Zambesian Past*, p. XXVIII, n. 2.

[40] Audrey Richards, 'The political system of the Bemba tribe—North-eastern Rhodesia', *African Political Systems*, ed. M. Fortes and E. E. Evans-Pritchard (London: O.U.P., 1940), p. 108.

[41] Max Gluckman, 'The Kingdom of the Zulu of South Africa', *African Political Systems*, pp. 31–32.

[42] T. O. Ranger, *Revolt in Southern Rhodesia, 1896–7* (London: Heinemann, 1967), p. 33.

[43] Richards, 'The political system of the Bemba', p. 108.

[44] Richard P. Werbner, 'Federal administration, rank, and civil strife among Bemba royals and nobles', *Africa*, Vol. XXXVII, No. 1 (January 1967), p. 23.

[45] Richards, 'The political system of the Bemba tribe', p. 91.

[46] *Ibid.*

[47] Roberts, 'A political history of the Bemba', p. xiv.

[48] *Ibid.*; Werbner, *op. cit.*, p. 24.

[49] Roberts, 'A political history of the Bemba', p. xiv.

[50] Werbner, *op. cit.*, p. 38; for a discussion of the functions of the *bakabilo* see Richards, 'The political system of the Bemba tribe', pp. 99–112.

[51] Roberts, 'A political history of the Bemba', p. 221; cf. Werbner, *op. cit.*, pp. 22–23.

[52] L. H. Gann, *The Birth of a Plural Society: the Development of Northern Rhodesia under the British South Africa Company, 1894–1914* (Manchester University Press, 1958), pp. 25–26.

[53] Roberts, 'A political history of the Bemba', p. 248.

[54] *Ibid.*

[55] Stokes and Brown, *op. cit.*, p. xxvii.

[56] Werbner, *op. cit.*, p. 23; Roberts, 'A political history of the Bemba', p. 221.

[57] Roberts, 'A political history of the Bemba', p. 272.

[58] *Ibid.*

[59] Werbner, *op. cit.*, p. 34.

[60] W. V. Brelsford, *The Succession of Bemba Chiefs: a Guide for District Officers* (Lusaka: Government Printer, 1948), p. 6.

[61] Roberts, 'A political history of the Bemba', p. 217.

[62] Tanguy, *op, cit.*, pp. 56–58.

[63] Roberts, 'A political history of the Bemba', p 251.

[64] *Ibid.*

[65] Livingstone, *op. cit.*, p. 190.

[66] Tanguy, *op. cit.*, p. 65; according to Roberts, 'A political history of the Bemba', p. 251, although Kapalakasha was accepted as successor by the *bakabilo*, he was refused recognition by several chiefs.

[67] Tanguy, *op. cit.*, p. 72.

[68] Brelsford, *op. cit.*, p. 7; cf. Roberts, 'A political history of the Bemba', p. 252.

[69] Tanguy, *op. cit.*, p. 74.

[70] Interview with Paramount Chief Chitimukulu Musenga, 3rd August 1967, Chitimukulu's village, Kasama. Chitimukulu Musenga died on 27 October 1969.

[71] Brelsford, *op. cit.*, pp. 7–8.

[72] Young, *loc. cit.*; see also Chinsali District Note Book, p. 231.

[73] Roberts, 'A political history of the Bemba', p. 277.

[74] Audrey Richards, 'The life of Bwembya, a native of Northern Rhodesia', *Ten Africans*, ed. Margery Perham (London: Faber and Faber, 1936), p. 21.

[75] Richards, 'Social mechanisms for the transfer of political rights in some African tribes', *Journal of the Royal Anthropological Institute*, XC (1960), p. 147.

[76] Werbner, *op. cit.*, p. 39.

[77] Johnston to H. C. Marshall, 26 July 1893, Abercorn District Note Book, p. 208, KSU1/1.

[78] Ronald Robinson, John Gallagher and Alice Denny, *Africa and the Victorians* (New York: St Martins Press, 1961), pp. 225–226.

[79] Roland Oliver, *Sir Harry Johnston and the Scramble for Africa* (London: Chatto & Windus, 1959), p. 140.

[80] 'Historical notes', *loc. cit.*

[81] Robinson, Gallagher and Alice Denny, *op. cit.*, pp. 226–227.

[82] Johnston to Rhodes, 8 October 1893, F.O. 2.55, cited in Oliver, *op. cit.*, pp. 153–154.

[83] Sir Harry H. Johnston, *British Central Africa* (London: Methuen & Co., 1896), pp. vii.

[84] A. J. Wills, *An Introduction to the History of Central Africa* (London: O.U.P., 1967), p. 181.

[85] Oliver, *op. cit.*, p. 228.

[86] Johnston to Harris, 9 December 1893, cited in *ibid.*, p. 240.

[87] Oliver, *op. cit.*, p. 17.

[88] Michael Gelfand, *Northern Rhodesia in the Days of the Charter* (Oxford: Basil Blackwell, 1961), pp. 82–83.

[89] Hugh Marshall Hole, *The Making of Rhodesia* (London: Macmillan & Co., 1926), p. 383.

[90] Harris to Johnston, 10 March 1894, B.S.A.C. papers, cited in Oliver, *op. cit.*, p. 242.

[91] Hugh Marshall Hole, *op. cit.*, pp. 383–384.

[92] Oliver, *op. cit.*, p. 246.

[93] R. Brown, 'Aspects of the scramble for Matabeleland', *The Zambesian Past*, p. 63.

CHAPTER II

BLACK MEETS WHITE

I. AFRICAN COMMUNITIES AND THE COMING OF EUROPEAN MISSIONARIES AND ADMINISTRATORS

The reactions of the African people to European intrusion at the end of the last century, writes one historian of the British occupation of East Africa, were largely influenced by 'the nature and prosperity of their economic life, the past history of their relations with other tribes, and their experiences of alien influences of Arabs, Christian missionaries, and European travellers ...'[1] Hemphill's postulate is of a much wider application than its context would suggest and it seems particularly pertinent to African response to the 'scramble' in the Northern Province of Zambia.

When, in the middle of 1895, the British South Africa Company assumed the reins of government in North-eastern Rhodesia, the Northern Province as a whole had behind it more than four decades of Arab influence,[2] and anything up to a decade of Christian missionary and European private enterprise in the areas inhabited by the Iwa, the Namwanga, the Mambwe, the Lungu and the Tabwa. In August 1878 the first party of missionaries sent by the London Missionary Society to evangelise these regions arrived in the area and tried unsuccessfully to establish a station near Lake Tanganyika's southern end.[3] It was followed during the next six years by five other parties, the last of which ultimately managed to establish a station at Nyamukolo in 1884 and three years later at Fwambo.[4] Assisted with transport facilities by the Livingstonia Central Africa Company (later renamed the African Lakes Company), which was founded in 1877[5] by Scottish missions to combat the slave trade by promoting legitimate trade, the missionaries set out against innumerable vicissitudes to Christianise the local people—the Tabwa, the Lungu and the Mambwe. In the meantime, the company itself was, in spite of its meagre resources, endeavouring to fight the slave trade by bartering European-manufactured goods for ivory and other local products. With its trading posts at Ikawa and Chiengi,[6] and another

25

one at Mambwe Mwela, a place which was in 1891 to become the site for the first mission station of the White Fathers,[7] it sent out its officials to buy such commodities with whatever merchandise they could offer. By the end of the 1880's, according to one eye-witness account, European traders were a common sight in what were later to be known as Abercorn and Ikawa Divisions.[8] However, as pointed out earlier, with the decline in the supply of ivory, which seems to have been the only commodity that could sustain legitimate trade as a reasonably viable enterprise, this attempt at peaceful abolition of the slave trade was doomed to failure.[9]

As the L.M.S. missionaries were trying to settle down to their difficult task of evangelising the local population, the White Fathers arrived at Mambwe Mwela (Old Mambwe) in July 1891 from Karema, in German East Africa,[10] to set up their first mission station, from which they later moved into Bemba country. Three years later the Livingstonia Mission established a station at Mwenzo, a site which was believed to possess several strategic advantages, one of them being its propinquity to the 'warlike and dreaded Awemba'.[11] Thus, by the time the British South Africa Company took over the administration of North-eastern Rhodesia from the Johnston Administration in 1895, Christianity was already planted in the Northern Province and all that remained was for it to strike root and spread to all parts of the province, paving the way for colonial rule as it did so. An examination of the reactions of the local population to the advent of the Christian missionaries and, subsequently, colonial rule, will be the task of this chapter.

In a discussion of the manner in which Christianity spread in Africa, one African writer has argued that it 'advanced with the sword, a case of gin or paper treaties in one hand and the Bible in the other'.[12] Osei's observation no doubt holds true in respect of certain parts of Africa. It is known, for example, that when in 1881 three Portuguese Catholic missionaries arrived in the Congo they were accompanied by a military and a naval officer and had with them presents and a letter from the king of Portugal to the king of Kongo; and a Portuguese gunboat was to be sent every month to watch over their interests.[13] But this does not seem to have been the case in the Northern Province. Apart from the rigorous role which the missionaries played, in the absence of white Administration authorities, to enforce Western values and

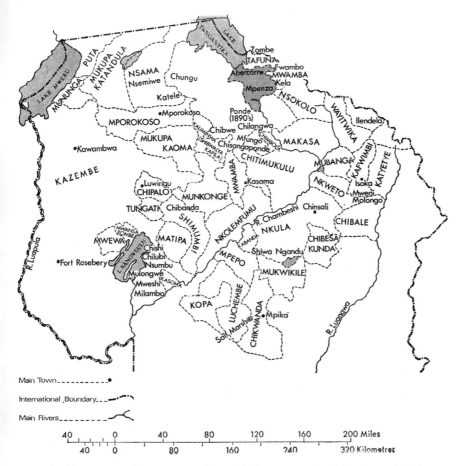

Chiefdoms in north-eastern Northern Rhodesia recognised by the colonial administration *c.* 1950. Only those European areas mentioned in the text are shown—shaded)

Christian moral standards, and to maintain law and order among 'their people', as they thought fit, and in the course of which they had recourse to the use of force,[14] there was hardly any occasion when they established a mission station by force of arms. Nor do they seem to have distributed spirituous liquors or to have waved paper treaties in the face of African traditional rulers in order to establish themselves. Their most potent means of gaining influence was the protection and the European manufactured goods which they seemed to offer the people.

Perhaps nowhere in the Northern Province was the role of European missionaries as protectors better appreciated than among the non-Bemba tribes, who were living in constant fear of Bemba and Arab raids. Only a few months after Fwambo mission station was established in 1887 there was an Arab raid;[15] five years later, after having been in the country for a year, the White Fathers at Old Mambwe reported that the Bemba had raided Zombe's village near Abercorn;[16] and in 1895 there was fighting between the Bemba and the Lungu around the new L.M.S. mission station at Kambole.[17] Thus perennial victims of Bemba raids as the Lungu, the Mambwe and other surrounding tribes were, they naturally welcomed the white intruders as their protectors. It is said, for example, that when the Welsh congregationalist David Jones opened Fwambo mission station in 1887, the local Lungu and Mambwe welcomed him, but they made it clear that they would not listen to his sermons or work for him until he had built a stockade round the station and demonstrated his ability to protect them against Bemba and Arab raids.[18] However, Jones did not react immediately to these demands, and for the three years that he remained unmoved both Fwambo and Nyamukolo suffered from a scarcity of labour, and their churches and schools remained empty.[19] But when, in 1890, fortifications were constructed round the mission stations, some of the people came to live on mission land and attended prayers, either of their own volition or in accordance with regulations made by the missionaries.[20] In 1892, a year after the station at Fwambo had moved to Kawimbe, there were some eighty African houses around the mission at the new site, and the same pattern prevailed at the other two L.M.S. mission stations, one of which, Kambole, became a refugee camp during the Bemba–Lungu war of 1895.[21]

Like the L.M.S. mission stations, the White Fathers' Old

Mambwe mission also became a sanctuary for the terror-stricken Mambwe. In September 1892 the Fathers reported that 'the fear of being attacked by the Babemba brings a new village of Bamambwe near the Mission. They borrow guns and ammunitions to protect themselves'.[22] Before this, a prominent Mambwe chief—Chief Mpande—had established himself on the outskirts of the mission station.[23] The White Fathers felt themselves not only under a moral obligation, but also bound by the Johnston Administration, to give protection to the local population against their traditional enemies, the Bemba, and the Arab slave traders who were harrying the country. In January 1893 Sir Harry Johnston granted the missionaries permission to acquire all types of arms and ammunition, so that they might protect not only themselves, but also the Mambwe and other weaker tribes against possible attacks by the Bemba and the Arabs, and they were enjoined, as far as possible, to group the local population around their mission station in order to ensure maximum safety for the people.[24] Of course, as pointed out earlier, even before this instruction was given by Johnston, some of the local people had already come to live near the mission station for their own protection. The mission, moreover, became a home for the destitute and the orphaned. In May 1894, for example, there were forty-six orphans of varying ages being looked after by the missionaries,[25] and ten months later this number more than trebled to one hundred and thirty-four.[26]

The apparent readiness with which the other tribes acquiesced in European rule was thus a revulsion against the Bemba. That this was so was a point which was echoed a few years later by Robert Young, the Assistant Collector at Mirongo *Boma*, which was opened in August 1897 near the Luangwa valley to check Bemba raids on neighbouring tribes—the Bisa and the Senga. Looking back a few months after the station was established, Young declared: 'All the surrounding natives were very pleased that the station was built, as it saved them from the ever-recurring raids of the Awemba.'[27] This may well have been too simplistic an assessment of a situation in which reactions to European intrusion were probably more varied than one can suppose. But it nevertheless serves to emphasise the fact that the other tribes of the Northern Province generally received the whiteman with a degree of equanimity and relief. Even though it is stated from a different standpoint, Donald Siwale's eye-witness account of African reactions to European advance lends support to this view. According to Siwale, there was practically no armed resistance by most tribes to the coming of the Europeans, because on the one hand Africans regarded whitemen, from the look of the colour of their skin, as a weak race, and on the other because Europeans did not appear as enemies of the African people.[28] The White Fathers of Kayambi mission station who visited Bisa country for a month in 1898 reported that their 'reception was everywhere favourable'.[29] All this evidence throws some light on the march of events in what was a very complex social situation. But whether the behaviour of some non-Bemba chiefs in the area, who, with a startling apparent lack of any political scruples, 'sold' their entire territories and all rights pertaining thereto for a few European-made goods, could be explained in similar terms is quite another matter.

Chief Chikanamulilo of the Namwanga, in a transaction to which Alfred Sharpe and one Matope, a Nyasaland African from Bandawe, were witnesses in January 1891, ceded his territory and all the rights which he and his people exercised over it to the African Lakes Company merely, as the document of agreement to which he appended his thumbprint stated, 'in consideration of goods to the value of £50 sterling paid to me by John Lowe Nicoll [the company's representative]'.[30] Six months later Mangwe Kafola, a Mambwe chief, entered into a similar agreement with the company, again with John Nicoll as the company's agent in a deed of sale in which Chief Kafola agreed 'in the presence of my people [to] cede, transfer, assign and make over absolutely and for all time coming to the said African Lakes Company' all Mwambe country under his charge. The deed of sale, which made no reference to the price paid for the land, transferred to the African Lakes Company all game reserves, mining rights, governing rights, taxes and 'privileges of whatever sort or kind may be connected with the territory referred to'.[31] The Mwambe paramount chief—Mwene Mambwe Nsokolo—'earnestly desirous that the benefits of civilisation should further be established to me and my people, and in consideration of the payment this day made to me in goods and merchandise by John Lowe Nicoll' executed a similar transaction with the company two years later —in September 1893.[32]

D

The atmosphere in which the Nicoll concessions were extracted remains unknown in the absence of evidence from African sources, either written or oral. But one cannot but be intrigued by the seeming readiness and recklessness with which those Mambwe and Namwanga chiefs felt able to give away their lands and, by implication, their very chiefdoms and chieftaincies, in a society where a chief was not so much the owner as the custodian of the land. No doubt the unquenchable thirst for European goods that had permeated African society, and which it was the privilege mostly of royalty and the tribal oligarchy to slake, had influenced the chiefs. But as guardians of the people, they seem to have lost sight of their traditional responsibilities, as if, without selling their territories 'the benefits of civilisation' would never again have come their way. They seem to have forgotten that in the African society, as one Nigerian chief later put it, 'land belongs to a vast family, of which many are dead, few are living, and countless members are still unborn'.[33]

It is possible, on the other hand, that all these transactions were executed in ignorance of their legal, social and political implications by the chiefs. As one District Officer commented on a similar phenomenon in Malawi during the same period:

They [the chiefs] could not possibly have understood the meaning or functions of a commercial firm and they could not have realised that the agreement that they made was a sale, and that by this act they disinherited their tribe and deprived posterity of the right to their lands.[34]

Thus Stewart Burton and Adam M'Culloch, witnesses to the Mangwe Kafola agreement, may have satisfied the African Lakes Company officials and the Johnston Administration in Zomba by merely affirming that they had 'truly and honestly translated the terms of this agreement to the vendor in Kimambwe language and that he has signed the said agreement in full understanding of its purpose'.[35] But it seems doubtful whether these agreements in fact carried the same political importance and the same sense of legal commitment in the minds of the African chiefs as they did in the thinking of the concessionaires. Running through all of them were trappings of the English law of contract, which, among a people where land was never bought or sold, was at best, a misplaced analogy.

While John Nicoll was thus committing the Isoka chiefs to

these dubious undertakings, Hugh Charles Marshall, the first Magistrate and Collector of Tanganyika District, arrived in Abercorn, the headquarters. Soon after his arrival, Marshall, wanting to get the feel of the political atmosphere in the area, decided to visit the nearest chief, Fwambo, of the Mambwe. According to Moses Sikazwe, a message was sent to the chief warning him of the collector's intended visit and pointing out to him that, unlike the other whitemen in the country, who were missionaries, Marshall was an administrator, with the authority and the means to contain any ugly situation in the area. Wondering what kind of a person this new whiteman was, and incensed by Marshall's veiled threat to punish any recalcitrant chief, Chief Fwambo ordered his people to come armed to the *indaba* which Marshall was to address, so that the whiteman might know that Fwambo and his men were a fighting people with whom Marshall would have to reckon. Arriving at the chief's capital in the company of Dr Carson, who was a missionary at the London Missionary Society's Kawimbe mission station, Marshall was greeted by a crowd armed with axes, spears, bows and arrows, and deliberately worked into a fighting mood. But after a mock battle staged by Marshall's police, Sikazwe goes on to say, 'Fwambo and his people were so frightened that they began clapping hands, acknowledging Marshall and his men as superior and submitting to his administration'.[36]

In the absence of a documentary account of this episode, it seems difficult to give much weight to this show of intractability by Fwambo and his people. However, taking into account the fact that Fwambo and another Mambwe chief, Kela, were the only chiefs in the area who had held out against the Bemba before the coming of the Europeans,[37] it seems probable that, in defence of this measure of independence and security which he appears to have enjoyed, Fwambo could have been driven into such a display of recalcitrance towards European encroachment. As it happens, the incident is perhaps the only known instance of resistance to the establishment of European rule among the non-Bemba tribes of Tanganyika District. All in all, because of missionary influence, the fear of the Bemba, and the economic benefits derived from their early contacts with European traders, the Namwanga, the Mambwe, the Lungu and others do not appear to have shown any opposition to the establishment of colonial rule. It was only the Bemba, with something to lose—their empire and a flourishing trade in slaves and guns—who, in spite of internal dissensions, showed protracted and aggressive antagonism to the establishment of white rule. Indeed, one could say of the Bemba rulers, as Eric Stokes and Richard Brown have argued in respect of the 'fissiparous matrilocal' 'caravan States' of the Yao of eastern Malawi, that 'the total loss of wealth and prestige which threatened them as warrior chiefs when once caught within the confines of colonial rule . . . acted as a constant spur to their resolution'.[38]

That the Bemba were not in a mood to make friends with whitemen must have been made rudely obvious to Marshall when, soon after his visit to Chief Fwambo, he made overtures to one of their chiefs, Ponde, and to the priest Chimba. Seeing in European merchandise a bait with which to entice an intractable but acquisitive people, Marshall sent bales of cloth as gifts to Chimba and Ponde. But, contrary to his expectation, the cloth was rejected and returned to him by the two men, who informed Marshall that they would not accept calico of such poor quality from him, an 'impolite Arab', when they could easily have obtained better material elsewhere by selling slaves.[39] A year earlier, in 1892, another Bemba chief, Mporokoso, a 'perpetual son' of Chief Mwamba, had refused to receive Lieutenant Crawshay, an Administration official, at his court.[40]

Perhaps the most intransigent of all Bemba rulers in the face of European intrusion was the king himself—Chitimukulu Sampa Kapalakasha. He had given orders to all his vassals that no white-man should be allowed to enter Bemba country. According to one of his vassals, Chief Makasa Mukuka, Sampa's resolute anti-European stand was the result of strong Arab influence at the king's court. The Arabs, said Makasa in an interview with the White Fathers early in 1895, had strongly advised the king against allowing whitemen in his country because their very presence in the kingdom spelt doom for his lucrative trade in slaves.[41] There is little doubt that the Arabs exercised considerable influence at many a royal court in Bemba country; Makasa himself was found surrounded by Arab slave traders when the White Fathers visited him early in 1894.[42] However, it may well be that Arab influence at Sampa's court was exaggerated, and the Arabs were made scapegoats for the difficult situation in which the Bemba head of state found himself in the face of European advance. For it must have been clear to Sampa, even without the advice of his Arab trading partners, that the missionaries and the Administration officials were, by their very anti-slave trade activities, a menace to the sovereignty and territorial integrity of his kingdom. He may well have recognised, as King Lobengula of the Matabele in a similar situation confessed a few years earlier, that raids and, in his case, their concomitant, the slave trade, were 'indispensably necessary to the preservation of his power and the political existence of his people'.[43]

The White Fathers, as well as the L.M.S. missionaries, were well aware of Chitimukulu Sampa's hostility to white encroachment. But at the same time they were probably conversant with the economic situation in Bemba country and the competing economic interests of its rulers, and they seized on these factors to gain entry into Bemba country and to worm their way through the country right up to the centre of the Bemba polity.

Early in 1894 there was a locust visitation in the Northern Province, as a result of which the country was hit by famine.[44] The L.M.S. missionaries at Kambole saw in this a God-sent opportunity to make overtures to Chitimukulu Sampa himself, having contacted his 'son', Chief Chungu, the previous year.[45] Through Chief Ponde they offered gifts to the king and promised to feed the starving Bemba population if they were allowed into his country. Ponde, on receiving the message and the gifts, decided to take them personally to Sampa, who accepted them but refused to see W. Thomas, one of the white missionaries at Kambole.[46] According to Rothberg, Sampa wanted to see James Hemans, a black West Indian,[47] who came to the country in 1888 and, according to Gann, was 'an able, forceful and even violent man', 'tolerant of native customs and was accused of being too lenient towards their immoral habits'.[48] Sampa was 'hostile'[49] to the white missionaries and Rothberg claims that Sampa stated his preference for Hemans in words which are tinged with a race-consciousness on the defensive, and distrustful of whitemen:

I do not want to see the white man just now. I want the one who is of my colour and who can speak so that I might understand him, to come and see me. I will hear whatever he has to say and I will go by his words. He will be my friend.[50]

According to Roberts, however, Rothberg is mistaken in attributing these words to Sampa, for Hemans reported that it was Ponde who had said them. Since Hemans did not himself visit Ponde, and since neither Thomas nor Hemans visited Sampa, the evidence on this point should be treated with some reserve.[51] Indeed, even the very fact that the source of Sampa's alleged preference for Hemans is a letter written by Hemans himself,[52] throws into doubt its authenticity, especially if one takes into account Hemans' own negrophile disposition and his unhappy relations with his white colleagues.[53] But this does not in any way detract from the fact that Chitimukulu Sampa was anti-white, which is the point that Rothberg purports to demonstrate. Soon after Ponde left his capital, Sampa sent orders that Thomas and his party, who were at Ponde's court, should be killed. Their lives were only saved by Ponde's refusal to cooperate in the conspiracy on the pretext that such action would provoke massive retribution by the whiteman.[54] It was probably due to Sampa's unbending anti-European policies that Ponde could not allow Thomas to settle in his village but instead invited Hemans to his capital and sent him a small tusk of ivory as a token of goodwill.[55]

This early attempt by the L.M.S. to gain a foothold in Bemba country was apparently not followed up, presumably because of the Bemba–Lungu war of 1895, which turned Kambole mission station into a refugee centre for numbers of Lungu tribesmen.[56] It was not until 1900, after the Bemba were pacified, that the Society felt able to move into Bemba country and establish a school near Chief Mporokoso's village which in 1908 became known as Kashinda Mission.[57] Thus with such inactivity on the part of the London Missionary Society and with the Livingstonia Mission plagued by manpower and financial problems, as a result of which it was unable to open its first mission station in Bemba country (Lubwa) until 1904,[58] the task of opening up Sampa's country for Christianity, and for white rule, now rested with the White Fathers.

2. THE SUBMISSION OF THE BEMBA

On 15 October 1893 the White Fathers decided to abandon Old Mambwe mission station because the heavy traffic of caravans carrying slaves which used to pass through the station from Lunda and Bemba country to the east coast made missionary work difficult.[59] They felt that if they were to make any progress in evangelising the people they would have to move away from the distractions and interference of what was not only an international highway but also a busy slave trade route. Their plan was, as they put it, 'to penetrate as soon as possible into the Bemba country'.[60]

The decision probably constituted a turning point in the history of Bemba submission to European rule. For from that time the White Fathers embarked on the subtle psychological campaign of 'lavishly distributing presents, by which they gained influence over Makasa, who agreed to the setting up of a Kayambi mission station in his country in direct defiance of his overlord Chitimukulu',[61] and by which they also won over other Bemba chiefs. That this buying over of the Bemba rulers was a deliberate instrument of policy was clearly stated from the very start by the White Fathers themselves when they were planning their first onset on a Bemba minor chief living near the mission station:

To prepare the ground in view of moving the Bemba country, a present has been sent to Kitika, a nearby Bemba chief; in return a goat is sent to the Fathers, which means the gift has been received favourably.[62]

When a few days later two Fathers visited Chitika they were warmly received.[63] Thus their first attempt at buying over Bemba chiefs was successful, and subsequent attempts were to be attended with even greater success. Chitika's compromising reaction was only the beginning of a process by which Bemba chiefs were, one after another, to fall prey to the twin forces of religion and commerce, which were in the Northern Province, as elsewhere in Africa, the forerunners of colonialism. With these economic blandishments, with the quiet tact and diplomacy with which they approached Bemba royalty, and with the 'capacity ... to persevere [which] was closely related to a mentality which sanctified death by equating it with martyrdom' so characteristic of contemporary missionaries,[64] the White Fathers won success after success. This, perhaps more than any other single factor, explains to a great extent the relatively peaceful submission of the Bemba to white rule.

After their visit to Chitika, Van Oost and Depaillat proceeded to Mipini, Makasa's capital, where they were also warmly received, in spite of the presence in the capital of some Arabs who were buying slaves. Makasa Mukuka gave the white missionaries a present—a slave girl.[65] For the Fathers this warm welcome was a good omen, and they went back to Old Mambwe with a ray of hope of penetrating Bemba country. However, probably because of the famine that was ravaging the country, as a result of a locust visitation in the month that followed the Fathers' visit to Mipini, they found themselves unable to visit Makasa again until a year later.[66] In the meantime the future seemed bleak. Four months after their visit to Makasa's capital the White Fathers decided that if moving into Bemba country was going to prove impossible their mission station would then be transferred to Lake Rukwa in German East Africa.[67] However, before such action was taken every attempt would be made to move the mission into Bemba country.

Their second visit to Mipini, in January 1895, was less encouraging than the first one. In spite of the long hours they spent with Chief Makasa, trying to obtain his agreement to the establishment of a mission station in his country, the chief could not be persuaded to grant them permission, because, he informed the missionaries, Chitimukulu Sampa Kapalakasha had decreed that no whitemen should come to live in Bemba country.[68] Sampa had already heard of the White Fathers' visit the previous year, and had subsequently sent a message to Makasa, warning him against the danger of allowing whitemen into his province, Mpanda. Chitimukulu pointed out to his 'son' that it was usually through Mpanda that enemy tribes had in the past invaded Bemba country, giving the Ngoni as an example; and he enjoined Makasa to exercise particular vigilance over any whiteman coming to his capital.[69]

Makasa himself was quite willing to receive the missionaries in his province; but Chitimukulu Sampa's attitude made it impossible and unwise for him to do so. He told the visiting missionaries that a party of messengers sent by a Mr Palmer, an agent of the African Lakes Company living at a depot near Mwenzo, had, together with his own men, been massacred at Sampa's court.[70] Whether Palmer's messengers were actually massacred or made to drink poison (umwafi) on the king's orders, as Chief Mporokoso claimed,[71] seems unclear. But in whichever way the men met their deaths, the story seems an eloquent illustration of Sampa's strong animus against whitemen and of the fact that he was prepared to put to death even some of his own people who were assisting white intruders in their resolve to penetrate Bemba country. 'Kitiamkulu' Mporokoso is said to have asserted, in his explanation of the killings, that he 'was then angry with the white people'.[72]

Since his accession to the Chitimukuluship, Sampa had been fanning anti-white feeling among his people, for example, by repeating the old story that his predecessor, Chitapankwa, had been bewitched by a white man, Giraud.[73] Makumba, his successor, was to use the same allegation to attempt to seal off his country from European intrusion.[74] But as pointed out earlier, the Giraud story was probably more of an allegory than anything else. The whiteman was said to be dangerous, not so much because his presence in the country spelt actual death for the king, but because white influence was synonymous with the prohibition of the slave trade, and such prohibition brought in its trail economic ruin for the slave-trading chiefs. Perhaps nobody realised better Chitimukulu Sampa's apprehension in this connection than a chief like Makasa who had actually experienced European influence since the arrival in Mambwe and Namwanga country of European missionaries. It may well be that Makasa himself held the same fears about white intrusion as it affected the Bemba ruler's trade in slaves. But it seems the long-standing hostility between the two men made Makasa assume a 'relatively favourable attitude to the advent of European missionaries',[75] and subsequently admit the White Fathers into his country in order to strengthen his position.[76]

However, in the middle of 1895 Sampa found it possible, even though only temporarily, to agree to the setting up of a White Fathers' mission station in Makasa's country.[77] The reason for this change of heart is not clear. But it seems possible that, with the mounting colonial pressures on the periphery of his country, and having heard about the White Fathers' good work in Mambwe country, Chitimukulu probably saw in these men of God allies against the white Administration which was threatening the sovereignty and integrity of Bembaland. For Joseph, an African convert who was sent by the White Fathers in 1895 to investigate discreetly the relations between Makasa and Sampa, found that

Chitimukulu had few warriors and that, in the words of Andrew Roberts, 'his mood was so capricious that war and peace were equally likely',[78] and early in 1896 he had to ask the White Fathers to intercede for him in a quarrel with the Administration.[79] But for whatever reason Sampa agreed to the establishment of a White Fathers' mission station in Mpanda, the Paramount's favourable reaction to the proposal made Makasa invite the missionaries to go and choose a site for the new station. He told the Fathers that they could build a mission station in the country he had taken from the Mambwe which, he said, was not useful, as the Mambwe were under British rule.[80]

This arrangement was confirmed when, in June of the same year, Bishop Lechaptois, from Karema, and Father Joseph Dupont, who had succeeded the late Father Van Oost as Superior of Old Mambwe mission, visited Makasa. The chief, who, accompanied by a hundred warriors, honoured the white visitors by meeting them one full day's walk from his capital,[81] reiterated his willingness to have a mission station in his country.[82] The visitors were pleased with this renewed protestation of friendship on Makasa's part, and what was even more encouraging to them was the popular enthusiasm shown for the intended establishment of a mission station in these parts of Bemba country, which had been depopulated by tribal wars and famine.[83] The people seemed happy to hear that the White Fathers intended setting up a mission station and that Chief Makasa had agreed. For them, the presence in their midst of such an institution meant greater security, and those of their numbers who had fled their homes informed the visiting missionaries that they would be happy to go back to their old villages as soon as the mission station was established.[84] It was therefore not without reason that Dupont, on his return to Old Mambwe, immediately sought permission from the British authorities at Abercorn to set up the first mission station in Bemba country.

Dupont's hopes were, however, to prove ill-timed. Unfamiliar with the mechanics of the Bemba political system, the missionaries do not seem to have known where the centre of power lay in the Bemba polity and consequently placed undue reliance on Makasa, apparently taking his avowed fear of Chitimukulu as sheer escapism. It was probably because they realised that Makasa's undertaking with the missionaries was something not to be relied

upon that the government officials at Abercorn hesitantly agreed
to the White Fathers establishing a mission station in Bemba
country and warned them that the Administration would take no
responsibility for their safety whilst in Bemba country, as there
was no army for such an undertaking.[85] Hardly more than a week
after Lechaptois and Dupont left Makasa's capital, the chief sent
word to Dupont asking him to postpone his departure for Mipini
because Chitimukulu had withdrawn his permission for the
establishment of a mission station in Makasa's country.[86] Chitimukulu Sampa Kapalakasha, on informing Makasa of the revoca-
tion of his earlier decision, warned that should he (Makasa) act
contrary to the new instructions, the Paramount would levy war
on him; he told Makasa that if the White Fathers wanted any
such favour from him as head of state they would have to give
him the salute that slaves and his own people gave him.[87] Implicit
in these words was a demand by Chitimukulu that the French
missionaries should send 'gifts of friendship' to him and not to
Makasa, as they had done hitherto. A minor chief, Sampa
probably thought, was being exalted and showered with presents
while he, the king of the land, from whom authority issued, got
nothing in return for his offer to the white missionaries. Chitimukulu may well have also felt that with the missionaries constantly
calling on Makasa the latter was wielding too much power, which,
in the context of the strained relations between the two men,
would have placed the authority of the Chitimukuluship in
jeopardy.[88]

Makasa's mind was torn between obeying his overlord and
allowing the missionaries to establish a mission in his country.
To obey Chitimukulu's instructions would have meant that he
was going to lose the 'benefits of civilisation', which he was
already enjoying as a result of his contact with the missionaries.
On the other hand, if he did not take his overlord's instructions
he would have earned himself the wrath of the Paramount, with
all its bloody consequences. After making a close study of the
situation, Makasa chose the latter, and sent a message to the
White Fathers assuring them that, in spite of Chitimukulu's
rescinding of the earlier arrangements, he was still desirous of
having a mission station established in his province and urged
them to proceed to do so.[89] They would, however, he said, have
to bring 'many guns' with them in order to protect him in the

event of an attack by Chitimukulu. But, fearing lest establishing a mission station in Bemba country by force would spark off a conflagration, the White Fathers decided to wait.[90]

The waiting was not long, however. Only a few days elapsed before Father Dupont and Brother Anthony were on their way to Makasa's court.[91] In the meantime they were finding great difficulty in recruiting carriers for what seemed to be a hazardous expedition. Still morbidly afraid of their traditional enemies, the Mambwe were very reluctant to enrol for the trip to Bemba country. Dupont had to gather some fifteen Mambwe chiefs and, 'over a roasted bull', persuade them to trust some of their men to his protection. But even the number of men he was able to raise in this manner dwindled to a few score when it was learnt that Chitimukulu was mobilising an army.[92]

When on 11 July 1895 Dupont and Anthony set off for Mipini, Makasa's capital, with their frightened Mambwe porters, they were resigned to whatever treatment the chief would mete out to them. Leaving Brother Anthony and the porters just outside the capital, Dupont went ahead to Makasa's court, where he found that Makasa and his people had changed from the hospitable lot he knew to hostile men. The gates of the palisade were barricaded against him, while rifles were poking their muzzles through holes in the paling. Looking through the slits of the stockade he could see a group of men armed with guns, axes, spears, bows and arrows. His attempts to talk to them were greeted with words of abuse and yells of defiance. As he went round the palisade looking for an opening through which to enter, the armed men inside the stockade 'followed him step by step, threatening him all the time, especially when he came to a place where fifty human heads were stuck on poles'.[93] His attempts at befriending the people in the rest of the village met with equally hostile reaction. Men and women shouted abuse at him, and threatened him with spears and axes.[94]

Frustrated, but by no means completely discouraged, Dupont went to join Brother Anthony and the rest of the group at the camp they had put up just outside Makasa's capital. He later sent a messenger, accompanied by two warriors, to Makasa, to ask if he could see the chief. The emissaries returned to the camp amidst some ten Bemba warriors who were angrily talking to them,[95] and who later looked Dupont up and down and inspected

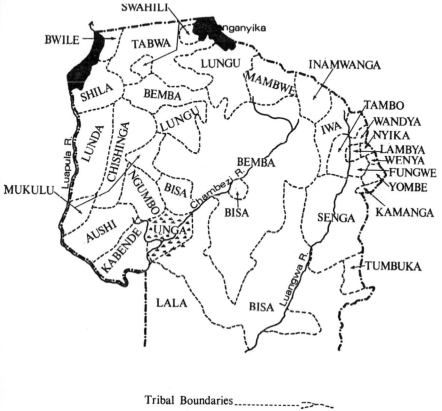

SWAHILI

BWILE

TABWA

nganyika

LUNGU

INAMWANGA

SHILA

BEMBA

MAMBWE

TAMBO

LUNGU

IWA

WANDYA

NYIKA

LUNDA

CHISHINGA

LAMBYA

WENYA

MUKULU

Luapula R.

NGUMBO

BISA

BEMBA

Chambezi R.

FUNGWE

YOMBE

AUSHI

KABENDE

UNGA

BISA

SENGA

KAMANGA

LALA

BISA

Luangwa R.

TUMBUKA

Tribal Boundaries . . . .

Important Rivers . . . .

50   0   50   100   150 Miles

50   0   100   200 Kilometres

Broad outline of the tribal divisions in the Northern Province

his entire escort.[96] The warriors, however, subsequently took Dupont and Anthony to Makasa. The two whitemen were shepherded into the palisade, the gate being open only enough to allow them to slip in sideways. Inside were other warriors who surrounded the missionaries, shouting all the time. As Dupont and Anthony were entering the second palisade a huge sentryman snatched away Dupont's walking-stick, angrily saying: 'No armed man goes into the king's presence.'[97]

Makasa's attitude had, surprisingly, taken a negative turn. The compromise solution he had suggested to the Fathers in regard to Chitimukulu's withdrawal of the permission for the establishment of a mission station in his country no longer seemed an issue worth raising with the missionaries again. The chief was an angry and disillusioned man. In the early part of his conversation with the two white visitors he refused to listen to what Dupont was trying to say. All that he could say to the missionaries was that they should go back to Old Mambwe at once because he did not want them and because Chitimukulu was threatening to come and fight him if they stayed.[98] A new idea appears to have entered Makasa's mind. It was now not simply a question of Chitimukulu refusing the chief permission to allow the missionaries in his country; Makasa himself apparently did not want them either. Dupont had to exercise a lot of tact and patience even to persuade the chief to allow him and his party to stay on for the night, as it was too late in the day for them to start off for Old Mambwe Mission. As the Mambwe porters entered the palisade for shelter, they were trembling with fear and 'stood, like men mesmerised, gazing at the heads on poles, while the Babemba gathered round them, saying: "Tomorrow at sunrise we shall be glad to see your heads there too".'[99]

It appeared to the missionaries that Makasa's decision to have nothing to do with them was irrevocable. In the middle of the night he sent one of his generals, called Nsunsu, to Dupont's tent with instructions to inform the priest that the short-lived friendly relations between him and the chief had been severed. Laying an elephant's tusk on Dupont's bed, Nsunsu broke the news to the clergyman, telling him that if he and his party failed to leave early the following day, anything that might befall them would be Dupont's sole responsibility.[100] When the people in the village heard that the chief had told the missionaries to go away, women acclaimed the decision with ululations, while men, brandishing their spears, sang:

> You there, you there,
> We warn you to run.
> If you have no ears, if you have no ears,
> Your heads will not be on your necks tomorrow,
> But will grow on those poles over there.[101]

The following morning, however, this strong tide of anti-white feeling abated. After offering the first mass ever to be said in Bemba country, Dupont, in what appears to have been a deliberate display of missionary magnanimity, treated a woman who had a wound on her leg. It is said that the people around were so impressed by this act of charity that they no longer talked about putting the missionaries' heads on spikes. Even Makasa was flabbergasted by the event, as much as he was the day before when Dupont, alone and unarmed, walked into his hostile Bemba warriors.[102] Perhaps because of this apparently frail intractability of Makasa's Bemba, 'Motomoto', as Dupont was nicknamed by the local people, decided to stay at Mipini and face Chitimukulu if he dared attack Makasa.

Dupont's decision not to return to Old Mambwe provoked another critical situation. When the news spread in Makasa's capital that the whitemen were staying, there were cries of 'War! There will be war! The Kitimukulu is on the way. He is already killing our chief. The white men are as good as dead.'[103] The people began cutting down trees to close the road to the village, while war drums throbbed in the background.[104] In the meantime Chitimukulu Sampa was attacking some of Makasa's villages, carrying away some women and children,[105] and had begun marching on Makasa's capital, when he turned back. It is not known why Sampa retreated. According to Howell, it was because his scouts had informed him that Makasa was adequately protected by the White Fathers;[106] Roberts is of the view that probably Sampa was not serious in his intention to attack Makasa,[107] and Gouldsbury and Sheane formed the impression that the reasons behind the retreat were just inexplicable.[108] But by this time Makasa had been won over by Motomoto, who had sent the chief presents of amity. The White Fathers had come to stay and by the end of July work began on the new mission

station at Kayambi, a short distance from Mipini. The chief himself led three hundred of his people to help in the mission-
building.[109] Thus Kayambi mission was established 'after threats
of war and other difficulties',[110] and to Chitimukulu Sampa the
presence of whitemen in Bemba country now seemed a *fait
accompli*.

But Sampa even at this late hour found it impossible to acquiesce
in such a situation. He commissioned four of his warriors to
assassinate Dupont, the Fathers' intrepid leader, in an ambush, but
the men failed because they got frightened out of their reputed
bravery when they saw Dupont shoot down a flying guinea fowl
with effortless ease.[111] Having failed to drive the missionaries out
of his country through the assassination of their leader, Sampa, at
the end of the same year—in December, 1895—invited Makasa
and the White Fathers to his capital in order 'to talk about some
important affairs'.[112] What these 'important affairs' were is yet to
be discovered. It may be that the king wanted advice and support
from Makasa and the White Fathers in the wake of what the
missionaries thought were 'strong rumours in the country that the
English will declare war on Chiti to punish him for his ravages
in the country'.[113] But even if this was the case, the sudden change
in his hostile attitude must have startled his adversaries. Was it
a genuine hand of friendship that Chitimukulu was stretching? Or
was he wooing his enemies into a snare? These were probably
a few of the questions that crossed the minds of the invited
guests. Indeed, the fact that they all declined the invitation suggests that they had some qualms about Kapalakasha's intentions. The missionaries reported that Makasa was afraid to go to
Chitimukulu's capital and that they too had to postpone such a
visit because 'nobody is certain about the Senior Chief's intentions'.[114]

However, in spite of this rebuff, Sampa did not give up the
idea of having his 'son' and the missionaries in his capital. At the
end of March 1896 he sent another delegation to Kayambi and
Mipini. He wanted Dupont at his capital so that the priest might
intercede for him with the English administrators, whom he
believed to be preparing to invade his country, and with the
missionary must go his two 'sons', Makasa and Chipukula. The
invitation was again turned down, with the two chiefs saying:
'Chitimukulu has killed all his sons and wants to kill us too.

E

We will not go.'[115] When, a week later, Sampa repeated his
appeal, Makasa and Chipukula once again declined, and Dupont
informed the king that, although he was quite willing to visit his
court and mediate in his quarrel with the Administration, he
could only do so after Sampa had returned the rifles which he
had stolen from the Administration, and which were the cause
of the friction between Chitimukulu and the Administration
officials.[116] Having failed to get the missionaries to his court,
Sampa seems to have felt that the only hope he had of warding off
the Administration officials, who were threatening to levy war
on his country ,was to form a united front with his chiefs to fight
the whiteman. He is said to have sent out messages to Mwamba
Mubanga Chipoya and to Makasa Mukuka, inviting the two
chiefs to his capital, where all three would offer sacrifice to their
apical ancestors for guidance and support in a war against the
whiteman.[117]

Neither Mwamba nor Makasa went to the Paramount's capital.
The time-honoured enmity between the king and the two chiefs
may have influenced their decision not to answer Chitimukulu's
call. Moreover, Makasa, on whom the White Fathers had gained
great influence, was advised by Dupont to keep clear of Chitimukulu's intrigue because a war with the British was an extremely
hazardous affair.[118]

After this series of fiascos in his stratagem, Chitimukulu Sampa
Kapalakasha died in May 1896, a disappointed old man.[119] His
death upset the precarious equilibrium of the Bemba polity. For
although in his reign the Bemba were hardly a united people,
their internal politics, as Roberts points out, appear to have derived
some measure of coherence and stability from the very fact that
he was isolated both from the leading Bemba chiefs and from the
Europeans in the Northern Province.[120] The situation was rendered even more critical by the fact that Nkula Mutale Shichansa
had died towards the end of 1895, and the Nkulaship, one of the
most important five offices in the Bemba kingdom, was still
vacant.[121] Now a tribe without a head, the Bemba became increasingly susceptible to the pressures of European intrusion. It
will be recalled that even soon after the establishment of the White
Fathers' mission station at Kayambi in the latter part of 1895, the
late Chitimukulu Sampa Kapalakasha, had shown signs of growing concern at European encroachment, especially about the

white Administration officials in neighbouring tribal areas, who were believed to be preparing for an invasion of his country. It seems appropriate at this juncture to have a cursory look at the colonial pressures which were building up on the borders of Bembaland in order to see, in their proper perspective, the White Fathers' subsequent penetration of the Bemba's *terra incognita* and the spectrum of the Bemba oligarchy's reactions to such penetration and, later, to the establishment of white rule in the country.

When Depaillat and Van Oost visited Chitika and Makasa in January 1894, European activity in the Northern Province was still confined to the areas bordering Bemba country in the north and north-east, and this was to remain the position over the following four years. But even though European activity was to be confined to the periphery of Bembaland, the encirclement of the Bemba, which began with the arrival of the first missionaries more than a decade before and was completed with the establishment of Mirongo *Boma* in 1897 by Robert Young, had brought changes in the Northern Province's social complex, the awareness of which was beginning to crystallise even in the minds of the Bemba. With their raiding grounds drastically reduced by the presence and the restraining activities of European missionaries and Administration officials in the province, and with the flow of arms and other goods from the Arab slave traders dammed by the Administration, the intractable Bemba rulers were gradually feeling the pinch of what seem to have been fairly effective 'economic sanctions' against their State. Although, even in the face of this constriction, they remained adamantly hostile to Europeans visiting them,[122] the effects on the Bemba polity of this encirclement seemed encouraging to the Administration authorities. As early as January 1896 John Bell, the Collector for Chambeshi District, was moved to write that there were indications that, as a result of these pressures put on the Bemba, the 'Awemba question', as he called it, could be settled peacefully. He went on to say that he had detected some willingness among some Bemba chiefs to come to terms with the whiteman, which in his view, was partly caused by famine in Bemba country on the one hand, and, on the other, by the defeat and execution of the Arab chief Mlozi at Karonga a few months before, which shook the Bemba's faith in the Arabs and resulted in increasing their fear of the whiteman's power.[123] Bell's views on the effect on the Bemba of Mlozi's execution were no doubt based on the official belief that Arab–Bemba relations were closely knit. Soon after the execution of the Arab chief, Sir Harry Johnston wrote to Rhodes: 'the Bemba raids were, in my opinion, directly due to the instigation and co-operation of the Arabs under Mlozi, and will probably cease of themselves now that Mlozi is hanged'.[124]

In the same despatch Bell reported that the Bemba oligarchy was, in the changing situation, split into a number of factions in regard to its attitude towards Europeans. There were, he said, those Bemba rulers who welcomed the whiteman because they appreciated the good work he was doing; and there was a second faction which was willing to come to terms with the whiteman but feared that its members would be expelled from their country if they did so. Then there was the third group—a group of extremists—'obstinate pigheaded and hostile, who will require forcible treatment'. But this, according to Bell, was a minority faction which should not determine the overall method that the Administration would apply to bring Bemba country under effective European control; at any event, Bell said, the Bemba 'as a people . . . are far and away the finest race in between Nyasa and Mweru and would be an acquisition in many ways'.[125]

That the Bemba should have been a divided nation in the face of gradual European encroachment on their dominions should be readily understandable. The endemic feuds among the chiefs; the work of white missionaries in neighbouring tribal areas, which was slowly being appreciated by the Bemba, as Makasa's attitude towards the White Fathers indicated; the slow but effective process of economic strangulation to which the Bemba polity was subjected by the white Administration's encirclement, all combined to split the rulers of these people. There was a crisis of confidence among the Bemba rulers which spelt doom for the country's future. The choice before the traditional authorities was a difficult one. They had either to capitulate or fight in defence of their independence. The first course was clearly unthinkable to a people with a proud history, while the latter was impossible for a nation whose leaders were immersed in feuds and civil wars. It is in the light of this painful dilemma that the behaviour of some of the chiefs and headmen should be looked at. Mubanga, a subordinate chief, of Chitimukulu, for example, gives this impression of a ruling class caught up in a bog of indecision and inaction. He is said to have professed to be pro-white, and in demonstration of his avowedly friendly attitude towards Europeans he sent Collector John Bell a herd of cattle while the latter was on a tour of the Chambeshi District. But even after this gesture of amity Mubanga, when asked to go and see Bell at his camp, responded to the invitation, in the Collector's own words, 'belatedly and unwillingly'. Bell regarded him as a 'very sensible man but not particularly plausible—and evidently between two stools—Kitimukulu and the whiteman'.[126]

The 'leadership crisis' indeed seems to have spread far and wide in Bembaland. On this same occasion, when Mubanga reluctantly went to Bell's camp he is reported to have informed the touring white officials that he (Mubanga) and other chiefs—Chewe, Kalulu, Makasa, Chipukula, Nkula and possibly Mwamba—were planning to hold an *indaba* to discuss the 'whiteman's *mlandu* [problem]'.[127] It seems that the meeting was called by Chitimukulu Sampa and was the direct result of Mlozi's defeat.[128] Whether in fact it did take place is not quite clear. But the very fact that it was ever contemplated should be illustrative of the difficult situation in which the Bemba leadership found itself.

Bell's approach to the so-called 'Awemba question' appears to have been pragmatic. But in the absence of some kind of opinion survey upon which his observations should have been based in order to make them more meaningful, it seems doubtful whether in fact Bemba opinion was as divided as he reported it to be. Nor did his hopes that the hostile clique he identified would not influence the Administration's method of dealing with the Bemba question come true—because, as later events showed, some sort of military action was found necessary.

The activities of Company officials in the adjoining areas, however, continued to be a nightmare to the men holding the reins of power in Bembaland. They took great exception to the fact that whitemen had found it possible to establish themselves in neighbouring territory when their (the Bemba's) allies, the Arabs, should have repulsed the white intruders. There were a number of Arabs living in the Luangwa valley, the main entry point through which Europeans had come into the Northern Province from Nyasaland, and the Bemba thought it unbelievable that the Arabs should have just sat back and let the whiteman through.

The question was asked whether, in view of their neutrality, the Arabs were for or against the Bemba. Thus the Bemba chief Nkula was prompted to send his men to the village of Chief Chibale of the Senga tribe, where some Arabs were living, to find out from them why they had allowed the whiteman to enter the country. Much to their chagrin, Nkula's emissaries were told that the Arabs were friends of the Europeans. This provoked Nkula's men into a fight in which many of them were killed, with the Arabs suffering no losses.[129]

It seems ironical that the Arabs, who no doubt wished to continue their slave trade with the Bemba, should have found it necessary to connive at European penetration of the country. It is possible, however, that the encounters that the Arabs had had with European authorities in East Africa and, even more recently, in Nyasaland, in which their chief, Mlozi, was captured and subsequently executed, were still too fresh in their minds for them to contemplate mounting what might well have been another futile onslaught on the whiteman. The prevailing military diffidence among the Bemba themselves was probably another factor that made the Arabs doubt the wisdom of fighting Europeans. Unless the Bemba were prepared to wage war against the white Administration, it seemed foolhardy for the Arabs to go to war on their own initiative, without any guarantee that the indigenous people would be in the battlefront to fight for their country.

The Arabs, however, came to realise later that the 'neutrality' they were assuming in the Anglo-Bemba confrontation would cost them Bemba friendship. They consequently sought to maintain their existing friendship with the Bemba by fanning the latter's hostility towards the Administration. Their influence at Mwamba's and Chitimukulu's courts became so great that Bell feared that trouble was likely to erupt at any moment. He therefore wrote to Major Forbes, the Administrator for North-eastern Rhodesia, for more guns and ammunition. Writing with a strain of some urgency, Bell reported that although lately the Bemba had been orderly, he had a presentiment that Chitimukulu would soon start raiding 'caravans going to the white man' because Arabs had told him that he was no longer getting a regular supply of guns and other goods, owing to the fact that the whiteman was raiding Arab caravans bringing these supplies into Bemba country. Moreover, Chitimukulu and Mwamba were more and more coming under Arab influence against Europeans and, because the Arabs knew that the whiteman was living in scattered communities and that the Administration had only ten Martini rifles, Bell feared that the Bemba and the Arabs would easily win any war if they took the initiative.[130]

Either the situation was deteriorating frightfully or Bell was being unduly pessimistic. In the same month when he asked Blantyre for arms and ammunition he had intercepted an Arab caravan on the Chozi river, north-east of Bemba country, and in the fighting that ensued three coast men and two Ruga-Ruga were killed, Bell himself sustaining no losses apart from one of his men, who was wounded. He seemed to see danger in the local men he had drafted into his police force for this expedition, doubting their morale and their efficiency in handling guns. He wrote later of his experiences during the expedition:

I had my Makua and Atonga Police and a few [local] natives. Keeping control of the latter was too awful. Never again will I go out with native warriors and cap guns. My insurance policy doesn't run to it.[131]

It was therefore with great reluctance that a few months later, in June 1896, Bell again took out a few local warriors to intercept an Arab caravan which was leaving Bemba country for the east coast. He hunted the caravan down and found the Arabs at a village late at night. But because he had 'only a number of uncontrollable natives' at his disposal, he postponed an encounter with the slavers until the following morning, during which he was able to free fifty slaves.[132]

As Arab caravan routes were being throttled by colonial officials in neighbouring territory, fewer and fewer goods were reaching the crocodile kings, and this growing scarcity in the supply of European consumer goods accentuated the economic competition among the Bemba rulers which was already an important political factor in the kingdom. There was a strong inclination among the chiefs to look to the White Fathers as an alternative, or supplementary, source of supply, and Kayambi mission station, like the Livingstonia mission station at Njuyu among the Malawi Ngoni,[133] became a factor in the rivalry between various Bemba chiefs, and Makasa, like the Malawi Ngoni chief, Chipatula, in relation to the Scottish mission observation post at Kaningina,[134] tried hard to exploit the friendship of the White Fathers at

Kayambi as support for his own position *vis-à-vis* other Bemba chiefs. Commenting on Makasa's attitude and actions in this connection just before the death of Chitimukulu Sampa Kapalakasha, Howell writes:

Of the three great Chiefs [Chitimukulu, Mwamba and Makasa], Makasa was, of course, the most sympathetic, but he was watching carefully lest the other two should permit the Fathers to work in their provinces. After all, these white men were living on his land, and he thought that he alone should profit by their works of charity and presents. When the missionaries were about to explore Kitimukulu's province, he at once furnished guides to whom he gave secret instructions to lose them. That incident sums up his attitude.[135]

When in June 1896 he decided to move his village nearer the Chambeshi river, Makasa insisted that the mission should also move with him, and when the White Fathers refused he ordered his people to have nothing to do with them and unsuccessfully demanded that the missionaries pay him ransom for a number of their converts whom he had seized and detained as 'slaves'.[136] Makasa may appear to have gone too far in trying to exploit his friendly relations with the missionaries. But his actions only emphasise the importance of the economic and political role which the White Fathers had come to play in Bembaland. Mwamba Mubanga Chipoya and the new Chitimukulu, Chimfwembe Makumba, were, as will be shown, to show the same reliance on the French missionaries in the end.

When Chitimukulu Sampa Kapalakasha died the stage was left clear for Mwamba Mubanga Chipoya, the most powerful of all Bemba chiefs, to assume even more authority in the country. He took up the old problem of the Anglo-Bemba conflict with the White Fathers, as Sampa had done earlier on, and asked them to intercede for him with the Administration in an attempt to avert a possible war between himself and government officials.[137] Father Dupont consequently sent a delegation to Ikawa *Boma* to plead with the collector there for peace between the Administration and Mwamba, and as a result the government officials abandoned 'their plan to punish Mwamba'.[138] But, while these negotiations were going on, Mwamba seems to have been making secret preparations for war against the Administration in which Makasa would also take part.[139] However, Makasa, probably aware of the military inadequacy of his people *vis-à-vis* the Administration police, doubted the wisdom of a war against the whitemen. He did not, however, dismiss the proposition outright as he had done when the same idea was put to him by the late Chitimukulu Sampa, but his unwillingness to be party to such a scheme and his dependence on the White Fathers give his actions an ambivalent appearance. He warned Dupont to be on his guard in view of Mwamba's intentions, but at the same time, in order to appear to Mwamba to be an enemy of the white missionaries, he had his principal wife whipped in public for accepting a piece of meat as a present from the missionaries.[140] Owing to the non-committed stance Makasa had taken, Mwamba felt a definite decision should be reached as to whether or not the Bemba should go to war. To settle the question once and for all, it is said that the two chiefs had recourse to a sorcerer, who put a hen to ordeal by poison. If the hen died, they would submit to British rule; if it lived they would fight the whiteman. 'The good hen,' as Howell has pithily put it, 'had the sense to die' and the Bemba chiefs gave up their persistent attempts to drive the whiteman out of the Northern Province.[141]

It would not, of course, be true to say that this change of heart was due solely to the verdict of the chicken ordeal. What appears to have been the cause of the change was a realisation among most Bemba chiefs that even though they were loath to be under European rule, they should nonetheless accept the fact that the whiteman had come to stay. It was probably this realisation and the material benefits which they derived from their contacts with white missionaries which made some of them take the initiative of inviting the White Fathers to set up mission stations in their respective provinces. At the funeral of Chief Makasa's classificatory sister in July 1896, for example, Chiefs Mwamba, Chikwanda and Changala refused to support Ponde, who insulted Makasa and the White Fathers for betraying the integrity and sovereignty of the Bemba State by their activities. But instead they commended Makasa for allowing the missionaries to establish themselves in his country and openly invited the White Fathers to do the same in their respective countries.[142] In December of the same year Mwamba sent presents to the missionaries at Kayambi, thanking them for their successful mediation between him and the Administration, as a result of which an Anglo-Bemba war was averted.[143] In the same month, he sent gifts to three different groups of Europeans living in the province: the White Fathers at Kayambi, the African Lakes Company officials at Mwenzo and the office of the Collector of Chambeshi District at Ikawa, so that any one of these establishments which returned the best gift to the chief would be rated as the best friend.[144] Each one of them returned a gift of one kind or another. However, the unfortunate coincidence that some Englishmen from either Mwenzo or Ikawa had asked Mwamba for women during a visit to his court made the chief so angry that he lost sight of the value of the gifts he had received from Mwenzo and Ikawa and decided that the two groups were not worthy of his friendship. He picked on the White Fathers as his best friends, and accordingly proceeded to invite them to visit him at his capital.[145]

Like the new *modus vivendi* which Mwamba and Makasa had adopted after the 'chicken ordeal verdict', Mwamba's decision to have nothing to do with the European civil authorities and to enter into closer relations with the missionaries cannot be explained solely in terms of the allegedly lewd conduct at his court of the unnamed Englishmen from Mwenzo or Ikawa. His decision was more probably based on some kind of political balance sheet, which took into account the merits and demerits of aligning himself with one side or the other, having accepted the inevitability of white presence in the country. This was possibly one of the occasions when the Bemba rulers had to distinguish between one group of Europeans and another, all of whom were usually considered pernicious; in such situations the choice fell on the less reprehensible whites, and in the case of Mwamba this meant the missionaries. In order to understand better the forces that slowly drove Mwamba and his overlord, Chitimukulu, into the hands of the White Fathers, it is necessary at this point to pay some attention to the latest developments both within and on the periphery of Bemba country since John Bell's anti-slave trade expeditions in the early part of 1896.

Although Bell had reported to Major Forbes in January 1896 that Mlozi's defeat had an 'excellent effect' on the few Bemba in his district, and that they were consequently 'very quiet and submissive',[146] he was later to report that trouble was imminent in the interior of Bemba country. Chitimukulu Sampa Kapalakasha had died in May 1896, and it seemed to Bell that the succession dispute which was gathering strength would end in an armed clash between the contenders for the paramountcy. His assistant, Robert Young, who visited Bemba country early in the following year, indeed reported that Mwamba Mubanga Chipoya was planning to seize the Chitimukuluship and that Chiefs Nkula, Ponde and others were behind him, while a few others were opposed to the idea and would, if necessary, ask Bell for help against Mwamba.[148] Bell saw in this succession dispute a golden opportunity for the Administration to intervene and prick the 'Bemba bubble' once and for all. Writing to Major Patrick Forbes, he asked the Administrator to allow him to 'step in, nominate and back up my own man'. This, argued Bell, was possible, provided he was given more arms with which to contain any awkward situation that might arise.[149] Forbes' reaction to this recommendation is not known; but Bell never intervened at all, and in 1898 Chimfwembe Makumba, whom on request from the Bemba Forbes had recognised as rightful heir, acceded to the Chitimukuluship in accordance with the Bemba customary law of succession to the paramountcy.[150] Presumably the support that Makumba is said to have sought from Ikawa during the succession dispute made Mwamba Chipoya give up his intention to seize the Chitimukuluship. Mwamba, according to Robert Young, sent a gift of ivory to Bell, pleading for peaceful coexistence with the whiteman.[151]

Before this, 'Bobo' Young had, on instructions from Bell, visited Mwamba's court to ascertain from the chief the possibility of setting up a station in Bemba country. His own account of the visit gives the impression of a people whose attitude was a mixture of complete disregard for a whiteman on the one hand and an absorbing liking for his consumer goods on the other. On his way to Mwamba's court at Chikutwe's village, Young was warned by the local people against the danger of visiting Mwamba, because the chief, they told him, did not want any whiteman in his country.[152] Impervious to all this admonition, however, Young proceeded to Mwamba's capital.

On his arrival at the court Young found Mwamba surrounded by his courtiers and a big crowd. The courtiers refused to allow Young to approach nearer to the chief than five or six yards and ordered him to sit on the ground, as all commoners and slaves did before this royal personage. But Young refused and 'just yelled good morning Mwamba'.[153] Probably partly because of this obviously discourteous conduct and partly because of Mwamba's somewhat deep-seated hatred of whitemen, Young was not given hospitable treatment at court. Kalimanshila, Mwamba's chief councillor, told Young that the chief was not prepared to listen to anything he had to say. Young then left for his camp, only to be sent for soon afterwards by the chief. On this occasion Mwamba, probably with the intention of belittling the visiting white official, merely asked Young what his name was and where he had come from, even though these particulars were known to him long before. Thereafter, Young withdrew to his camp, where he was later told that he would have no discussions with Mwamba unless he gave the chief some presents. As he had nothing to offer Mwamba, Young returned to Ikawa without achieving the object of his mission, notwithstanding the representations he had earlier made that he be allowed to see the chief and then send him the presents later.[154]

It is not clear, however, whether or not Young on this occasion discussed the possibility of establishing a station in Bemba country with Chief Mwamba. Elsewhere he states that during this visit to the chief's capital Mwamba refused him permission to set up a *boma* in the country, because Mwamba was under pressure from the Arabs and coast men who were then surrounding him.[155] Unless Young had paid more than one visit to Mwamba's court one would tend to take his account of the only visit cited as either confused or exaggerated. Not even an eye-witnesses' account of Young's visit sheds any more light on what actually transpired between the chief and the white visitor. Bwembya, one of Mwamba's grandchildren present at court during Young's visit, had this to say about the visit of the Chambeshi District Assistant Collector when he was interviewed forty years later by Audrey Richards:

He [Young] came to see Mwamba. He walked straight into Mwamba's presence with a little dog at his side. . . . He stood up in front of Mwamba and spoke his business. We were all staring at his face. He was not still after the manner of a chief, but he stood there twirling his moustache and looking quickly about him from right to left. But Mwamba remained silent and he looked straight in front with his eyes.[156]

If, as Young alleged, the Arabs had helped Mwamba frustrate the first attempt by the Administration to establish a station in Bemba country, they were also later on to mobilise and lead the Bemba into battle against the Administration and Chief Chibale's Senga people, whom the Bemba as well as their Arab allies considered to be catspaws of the whiteman. Four prominent Arab chiefs—Kapandansalu, Kopakopa, Chalauma and Mwanamatondo—whose *tembes* or stockaded villages were in the Luangwa valley, led an army of warriors from the areas of Chiefs Mwamba and Nkula to attack Chibale's village. On hearing about their advance, Chibale sent an urgent message to Ikawa *Boma* for help, on receipt of which Robert Young immediately set off for Chibale's with fifteen Nyasaland Tonga police. On arrival at the village, he tried to stave off violence by telling the raiders outside Chibale's *tembe* to withdraw. There was no response to his call, nor did the invaders show any sign of still wanting to attack Chibale. Soon afterwards Young returned to Ikawa, leaving his police behind with strict instructions not to shoot unless they were fired upon. It would appear from his early return to Ikawa that he had underrated the moral fibre and determination of the Bemba and regarded the position they had taken up near the village as no more than a case of vaingloriousness overleaping itself; 'it was all bounce of the Awemba', he said.[157] He never thought the Bemba would attack Chibale's village after his warning, even though as he was leaving for Ikawa they brandished their spears and pointed out their guns at him and called 'the white men dogs and the police women'.[158]

Yet only a day after Young's departure the Bemba and the Arabs began attacking Chibale's village and in the battle that ensued two Arabs and twenty three Bemba were killed, while neither Young's police nor Chibale's people suffered any losses. Later, Kapandansalu and Chalauma were taken prisoners.[159]

The Bemba and their allies lost. However, in spite of these relatively alarming casualties on their part they did not consider themselves vanquished after the Chibale armed clash. The Senga chief's village was again to be the scene of another clash between the allies and the Administration six months later, in October 1897.

Because of the conflict at Chibale's and because of incessant raids by the Bemba and the Arabs in the Luangwa valley, Charles

McKinnon, then Collector at Ikawa, sent Assistant Collector
Robert Young to open a new station as near to Chibale's village
as possible. Thus Mirongo *Boma* was established in August, 1897.
Although local tribes welcomed the establishment of the new
station because it would afford them protection from the Bemba
and Arab raiders, the nearest Bemba population—about twenty
miles away—did not receive the news with the same relief or
equanimity. On the contrary, they repeatedly sent messages to
Mirongo saying that 'the white man was to return at once to where
he came from or he and his people would be killed'.[160] At the
same time their Arab allies, also living approximately the same
distance from Mirongo, were professing friendship with Administration officials but in fact, as Young bitterly realised later, 'they
were trying to get the Awemba to attack the *Boma* which had
been made'.[161]

Hostilities were precipitated by the arrival of a large number
of Bemba warriors at the Arab strongholds in the Luangwa valley
and also by the arrival of some Bemba emissaries from Chief
Mwamba and Chief Nkula, who were sent to Chief Chibale to
tell him that if he would not go to Mwamba and explain why he
had brought whitemen to build a station at Mirongo they would
cut off his head and carry it off to Mwamba. Terrified by these
threats, Chibale immediately called for help from 'Bobo' Young
at Mirongo. In the meantime the Bemba and the Arabs besieged
his stockaded village. The arrival of Robert Young and his police
signalled the beginning of a battle that raged for five days, in the
course of which, according to Young, the Bemba-Arab league
lost eighteen to twenty lives, with about five wounded, while
Young's contingent and that of the Senga again suffered no
casualties.[162] Having suffered such heavy losses and hearing that
Collector Charles McKinnon and Assistant Collector John Drys-
dale were on their way from Ikawa to Chibale village with some
reinforcements, the Bemba beat a retreat, while the Arabs took
flight and crossed the Luangwa river to find refuge in the *tembe*
of another Arab—Mohammed bin Seya. As if in revenge for the
ill-treatment they had suffered at the hands of slave traders, 'the
local natives [wrote Young], seeing the Arabs fleeing, turned on
their former masters and slaughtered them wholesale'.[163]

The three Company Administration officials proceeded to the
villages which had been deserted by the Arabs and burnt them.

They then followed up the refugee Arabs across the Luangwa and attacked Mohammed bin Seya's *tembe*, capturing Kapandansalu, bin Seya himself and other Arabs. Kapandansalu, the Arab chief, was sentenced to death but died before his execution was due. With his death and with the fall of Mohammed bin Seya, the Arabs, who had been a terror to the Senga and other tribes in the vicinity of the Luangwa valley, and who had supplied the Bemba with guns and gunpowder, lost practically all the influence they had exercised over the people of these regions.[164]

After dealing this death-blow to Arab influence in the area east of the Chambeshi, McKinnon and his assistants turned on the Bemba and pursued them to Chief Nkula's village, where the Bemba made a strong stand but were overcome after two fights. McKinnon's expedition later broke up at Mwalule, the Bemba royal burial place, because the Bemba were, according to Young, then pacified and no longer sent messages to Mirongo telling whitemen to leave the country or die.[165] Indeed, Bemba resistance to colonial intrusion seemed to be petering out after these operations by McKinnon's military police, and to be giving way to a period of political confusion. As Gouldsbury and Sheane observed:

This little war [against the Bemba and the Arabs] had far-reaching results. External raids by the Awemba upon the surrounding tribes were checked, and the power of the Arab slavers was broken . . . The Wemba kings, being now confined within their own borders, turned, as if in rage, upon their own people, and inflicted upon them atrocious mutilations and other horrors, which previously they had reserved for their enemies alone. Dissension naturally followed, but the most cruel punishments were meted out to the rebels, and many of the Awemba were sold into slavery by their own chiefs.

All this paved the way for the acceptance of European domination.[166]

In the meantime there was a succession dispute as to who was going to be the Shimwalule, the hereditary undertaker or burial priest, who is one of the most important leaders of the Bemba. The holder of this important post in Bemba political and ritual life at the time was Chimbwi.[167] Before the burial of Chitimukulu Sampa Kapalakasha and Chief Nkula Mutale, who had died at the same time, Chimbwi Shinta had administered mortuary rites for Chitimukulu Chitapankwa and Mwamba *wa Milenge*,[168] and he was ordered by Mwamba Mubanga Chipoya to step down from the Shimwaluleship in favour of his (Chimbwi's) nephew, Nsofuyamutembo. It is not quite clear why Mwamba had sought to remove Chimbwi from the Shimwaluleship. According to one account, Mwamba Chipoya's action was an intrigue;[169] according to another, Mwamba wanted Chimbwi Shinta to relinquish his post because he had already buried a Chitimukulu, namely Chitapankwa, as well as Mwamba *wa Milenge*, and therefore could not continue to be a Shimwalule.[170] But, for whatever reasons Mwamba had sought the removal of the royal undertaker, Chimbwi himself was not impressed by the order. Taking advantage of the presence and influence of the B.S.A.C. Administration officials in nearby Bisa and Namwanga country, Chimbwi fled to Mirongo Boma to seek R. A. Young's support for retaining the Shimwaluleship, taking with him the important paraphernalia used in mortuary rites.[171] Young later went with Chimbwi to Mwalule to investigate the matter. Before he got there Nsofuyamutembo fled to Makasa's village, leaving Chimbwi to retain the priesthood.

Although a number of occasions are known when the Shimwaluleship was seized by aspirants to that position,[172] Chimbwi's case seems unique in the history of the Bemba. The sacrosanctity of probably the most important ritual office in Bembaland was violated by a self-centred man, who apparently enjoyed neither the support of any ruler nor the sympathy of the people. By deciding to retain the Shimwaluleship contrary to established custom, and by successfully courting the support of the European administration to retain a position for which he was no longer eligible, Chimbwi Shinta had given expression to the fissionary tendencies prevalent in the Bemba ruling class, which seem to have been on the increase since the establishment of white rule and European mission stations in areas adjacent to Bemba country.

While mighty chiefs like Mwamba were, as far as possible, steadfast in their uncompromising attitude towards European political influence, those, like Makasa, on the lower rungs of the chieftainship ladder and who wanted some measure of independence from their overlords tended to enlist the support of the white immigrants against the latter. And those like Shinta who, within the traditional framework of things, would have sunk into social and political oblivion evoked the support of the Administration to retain certain positions, rights and privileges to which they had no legitimate claim.

Shinta's case also exposed the military diffidence that was taking root among the Bemba since their defeat at Chibale. Nsofuyamutembo's flight was an act of no-confidence in the ability of his overlord Mwamba Chipoya to protect him from possible disciplinary action by Young. He may well have been right in thinking that flight was the only course open to him. For Mwamba in fact later failed to reinstate him. The army which the former sent under Kalimanshila to avenge Nsofuyamutembo's plight never crossed the Chambeshi, and Young later wrote, with an air of success, that 'since then there has been no trouble in this [Mirongo] Division'.[173] It is against this background of the Administration's police operations against the Bemba and the Arabs east of the Chambeshi that Mwamba's shifting stance in the face of European advance must be seen. As Young wrote of him after the last skirmish at Chibale's *tembe* and the mopping up operations that followed it, 'Mwamba was in a great state of fear after this and moved his head village further into his country away from the Chambeshi'.[174] These increasing colonial pressures, like the presence of the White Fathers in Bemba country, became a political factor of growing importance and, like the economic advantages which friendly relations with the White Fathers brought to Bemba chiefs, they influenced Mwamba's responses to the French missionaries' overtures to him for permission to establish a mission station in his country, Ituna. Indeed, his request to Dupont in December 1896 that the latter should mediate between him and the European Administration, to which reference was made earlier, seems indicative of his growing fear of these colonial pressures and his inclination towards the White Fathers for political survival. Early in 1897 he sent a message to Ikawa asking for peace.[175]

Mwamba's standing invitation seemed a source of inspiration to the White Fathers, who were irrevocably committed to their idea of penetrating Bemba country. Thus they wasted no time in seizing the opportunity to besiege the citadel of Bemba recalcitrance—Mwamba's country—and Dupont and another Father, Letort, soon set about preparing for the journey to Ituna. But, as was the case at Old Mambwe mission, during their preparations

F

to move the mission to Makasa's country the Fathers found it difficult to get the right number of porters for the journey, because Makasa's Bemba were loath to go to Ituma, where people still had their ears, hands and noses cut off with rare facility by Mwamba. Ultimately, however, in April 1897 the expedition set off 'with twenty strapping warriors and fifteen boys to act as pages for Bwana Moto-Moto at court'.[176]

Opinion appears to have been divided at court on whether or not Dupont and his party should be received by Mwamba. According to Andrew Roberts, some councillors, of whom Kalimanshila, the chief councillor and war-leader was one, did not want the Fathers to come to Ituna;[177] and according to Howell, Mwamba himself did not want to see the missionaries and had to be prevailed upon by Kalimanshila to receive them.[178] But whatever the exact spectrum of feelings was about the White Fathers' visit, Dupont's reception at Mwamba's court was far from cordial. Leaving Father Letort and most of the party at a camp near Mwamba's capital, Dupont, carried on a hammock, proceeded to Mafula (the chief's capital), where he found Mwamba surrounded by scores of his subjects and his army. By appearing before the powerful Bemba chief while perched on a hammock, Dupont caused great offence not only to Mwamba himself but also to his subjects, who regarded such conduct as impertinent. Two young men—Mwanakabolo and Nkungaela—therefore stepped out from the crowd and struck Dupont's hammock with axes, causing him to fall to the ground. And while he lay on the ground, Dupont was the subject of a volley of insults from Mwanakabolo, while the crowd threatened him with guns—a situation which could easily have resulted in bloodshed, but for Mwamba's personal intervention.[179]

The days that followed Dupont's arrival at Mafula were days of hard bargaining between the chief and the missionaries. Mwamba's attitude towards the White Fathers appears to have been influenced a great deal by materialistic considerations, and his stance changed as opportunities in this regard changed. From the beginning he insisted that Letort and the rest of Dupont's party should come to the capital before he could ever give permission to the missionaries to build a mission station in his country, because he wanted the merchandise which was in the possession of Letort's contingent.[180] When Letort and his group ultimately arrived at court and no goods seemed forthcoming, Mwamba took away the poles which he had earlier given the Fathers for the construction of a mission station, to which he had agreed early in May 1897.[181] He would, no doubt, have liked to drive out the Fathers from his country; but his love for the European manufactured goods in their possession made him want them to stay, if only for a short time. 'The king,' as Howell has observed, 'seemed unable to come to a decision. He both persecuted the priests and honoured them.'[182] Just like Lewanika, who had in 1883 made a party of Jesuit Fathers, led by Depelchin, stay several months at his capital and demanded that they should give him presents before he would allow them to occupy the land he had offered them two years before,[183] and, like the Lozi king, who had 'never missed an opportunity of asking for a gift—perhaps a candle, perhaps some coffee or medicines for his eye or head'—from François Coillard, whom he had invited to his capital in 1886,[184] so Mwamba, as Roberts puts it, 'played cat and mouse with Dupont for nearly two weeks',[185] and pestered the missionaries 'for plates, lanterns, candles—in fact for everything he could think of'.[186] For a fortnight he temporised and did not agree to the establishment of a mission station in his country until Dupont gave him his revolver, on which the chief had cast his eyes for quite some time.[187]

But no sooner had Mwamba given the Fathers permission to build a mission in Ituna than he withdrew it. It may be that the chief had used his strong bargaining position to get as many European consumer goods as the white visitors could give away, and once he got these he was apparently happy to leave matters lie until such time when he was once again in a position to exploit the missionaries' evangelistic zeal to the full, or when it seemed to him that he might lose their friendship to another chief. But the White Fathers ascribed Mwamba's changed attitude to Arab influence. It is said that while Dupont and his party were at court a caravan of Arab slavers arrived and told the chief that the English, Motomoto's friends, had robbed them while they were on their way to the court, and taken away the guns and ammunition which they were bringing for the chief. They told Mwamba not to trust whitemen, be they missionaries or Administration officials.[188] Dupont, they alleged, had in fact come to prepare an invasion of Ituna by his English friends.[189] So the

White Fathers went back to Kayambi with little to show as a reward for their arduous journey to Ituna or for their acrid experiences at Mwamba's court. Before they left his capital, the chief, with a pile of arrows beside him, angrily warned Dupont:

> Never will a white man have a house in my country. I did not kill you, as I ought, because our ancestors taught us not to kill travellers. But if you come back I shall receive you with these arrows.[190]

Back at Kayambi, the White Fathers were saddled with the problem of manpower shortage occasioned by the death from blackwater fever of two of their numbers within a period of five months—Father Guillet, on 14 July 1897, and Father Goestowers on 10 December.[191] Thus they commented in the diary that 'after the refusal of Mwamba and the death of the two Fathers, the foundation [of a mission station] at the centre of the Bemba country will be more difficult'.[192] However, a few months later in 1898, Dupont, who had been elevated to the rank of bishop for the 'Nyassa 'region in May the previous year,[193] and Father Delamarche, were able to visit the court of the new Chitimukulu Makumba, who received them warmly, embracing the two missionaries and begging them to establish a mission station in his country.[194] The Fathers, pleased with Chitimukulu's offer, went back to Kayambi to prepare for their new station. But they returned to the Paramount's court five months later only to find that the king had changed his mind. Chitimukulu Makumba, while professing friendship with the White Fathers, refused the missionaries food and told them to leave at once. The weak old king was apparently too afraid of Mwamba to let the whitemen stay in his country, Lubemba.[195]

If Mwamba had intimidated Chitimukulu into withdrawing his consent to the establishment of a mission station in Lubemba, it was not so much a question of Mwamba not wanting whitemen in Bemba country as a way of ensuring that the White Fathers would go back to his country, and become a sure source of his merchandise requirements. For, shortly after arriving back from his disappointing second visit to Chitimukulu's court, Dupont received a delegation from Ituna, headed by Chikutwe, one of Chitimukulu's councillors. Chikutwe, calling Chitimukulu a rascal for having ill-treated the missionaries, informed Dupont that Mwamba wanted the White Fathers to go to Ituna without delay and that the chief was prepared to give them land on which to build a station. Dupont, after the sad experiences he had at Mwamba's court the year before, was sceptical about the invitation. He told Chikutwe that unless and until Mwamba sent him 'presents of peace, an escort of honour, and men to carry our luggage', he would not go to Ituna.[196] It was, however, only a matter of days before Mwamba's messengers arrived at Kapili, where they waited for the missionaries with several carriers, an escort of fifty warriors, and presents of peace in the form of a cow and its calf.[197]

Chitimukulu Makumba naturally viewed these new developments with considerable concern. Apparently Makumba concluded that he had been out-manœuvred by Mwamba. Thus, when he heard that Dupont was camping near his capital en route to Mwamba's court, Chitimukulu sent his own children with a message to the bishop, mournfully alleging that 'Mwamba played me an evil trick. Am I not also a child of God? If you are not satisfied with Mwamba, come back to me and I will give you land. We shall govern the whole country between us.'[198] If these words were indicative of the king's disillusionment regarding Mwamba's political integrity, they also expressed Chitimukulu Makumba's determination to receive the missionaries in his country, irrespective of what Mwamba's reactions would be to such action.

Dupont's reception at Mwamba's court this time seems to have been very cordial indeed. Mwamba seems to have had a radical change of mind. No doubt the chief's ill-health had a lot to do with this change. He had been bed-ridden for some time, and it was probably the concern about the future of his country and of his own family that made him call in the White Fathers. For, in sharp contrast to his ambivalent and sometimes hostile attitude during Dupont's previous visit, Mwamba this time took great pains to assure the missionaries that it had never been his intention to kill Europeans. He asked the White Fathers to build a house so that everyone might see that he meant them no harm.[199]

Since Dupont's last visit the previous year, political pressure had been gathering around the royal court. Ponde, Mwamba Mubanga Chipoya's classificatory brother, had made known his intentions to seize the Mwambaship on the death of Mubanga Chipoya, and had therefore been suspected of having bewitched the ruling Mwamba in order to take over the chieftainship.[200]

Mwamba must have been very apprehensive of Ponde's intentions to take over the chieftainship, for this would have resulted
in the massacre of his wives and children as well as other innocent
people, and the bloodshed in the circumstances would have ex-
ceeded that which usually went with the ritual killings on the
death of a chief.[201] To forestall Ponde's designs and their consequential bloodbath, and in an effort to save his own life, the ailing
chief, according to the White Fathers, appointed Dupont his
successor.[202]

What Mwamba exactly said seems unclear. According to
Howell, the chief, 'as thin as a skeleton', whispered to Dupont:
'If you cure me I will give you half of my kingdom. If I die you
will be master of my country and prevent the massacre of my
people.'[203] A translation by Gouldsbury and Sheane of Dupont's
own testimony in French of what Mwamba said reads very much
the same:

> You have excellent remedies and can, no doubt, cure me; if you do,
> I will give you half of my country. On the other hand, if I die, I will
> give you the whole—and you will look after my wives, children and
> people, so that they may not be killed![204]

But it seems doubtful, even from the above quotations, whether
in fact Mwamba appointed Bishop Dupont as his successor. What
seems probable is that Dupont was only charged with the responsibility of protecting the dying chief's people and nothing more.
Chitimukulu Musenga's recollections seventy years later of the
circumstances in which Mwamba took Dupont in his confidence
are practically pertinent here:

> I, my mother, Mwango, and her sister, and Nkolemtumu Kanyanta
> were called in by the ailing chief, Mwamba, who was then with
> Dupont. The dying chief asked the bishop to protect us, in the event
> of succession troubles and murders, against his brothers—Ponde and
> Chikwanda—and keep the peace in his country, as the bishop, said
> the chief, was his friend and the people's protector. There was no
> question of Dupont having been made chief by Mwamba. He was
> merely asked to prevent the recurrence of traditional barbarities until
> a successor was found, and recognised by the Administration.[205]

One might regard Chitimukulu Musenga's testimony as dis-
torted and coloured by a natural desire to glorify the history of

his people, who have just emerged from colonial overrule. But an account in Bemba by a White Father, François Tanguy, who had access both to the mission papers and to oral tradition, would seem to lend support to the Paramount's recollections. According to Tanguy, Mwamba Mubanga Chipoya said to Dupont:

Nalafwa; naliishiba walitemwa Babemba; nakulubwile calo candi; abantu bakabutukila ukoli; ukabapokeko kuli Ponde. Uukampyana, ni Kanyanta, umwipwa wandi; te umbi iyoo; niwe wishi.[206]

From these words of Father Tanguy, it seems even clearer that Mwamba did no more than trust his country and people to Dupont's protection. By virtue of his having been Nkolemfumu, Kanyanta was to succeed Mubanga Chipoya as Mwamba,[207] the bishop only being the heir-apparent's 'father' who, in a society where both succession and inheritance are matrilineal, could not have succeeded to any chieftainship. Thus, if Dupont had assumed the role of a chief after Mwamba's death, it was because the people of Ituna—during these critical months, when by custom Kanyanta could not become Mwamba until after the burial of the late chief a year later—had, in the absence of an effective leader, to look to the missionaries for protection and direction.

Yet in spite of the apparently flimsy nature of the evidence in favour of his case, Dupont, previously a modest man, without any pretensions or apparent aspirations to political power, became more and more politically assertive. Although two days after Mwamba's death he wrote the Administrator for North-eastern Rhodesia that he had told 'a gathering of thirty-three chiefs that my work is to teach the people the law of God and not to rule any country',[208] the bishop seems to have been entertaining a sense of gratification and success at his new position in Bemba political and social life. Two days before the chief died, he wrote in his note book:

I am offered a vast country, one of the most thickly populated in Central Africa; a country into which representatives of European governments have not yet dared to penetrate. I came here with a lay brother not sure of what was awaiting me at the hands of these brigands. Now they have chosen me to be their king.[209]

Transported with this high sense of success as 'bishop-king' of Mwamba's country, Dupont did more than merely congratulate himself on being a worthy successor to one of the most important political positions among the Bemba. He tried to consolidate his new office by getting the local people to ratify Mwamba's 'will'. He made them append their signatures or thumbprints to what Rotberg has called 'a legalistic document of cession' which was written in French but explained in Bemba and Swahili to the signatories.[210] Translated, it read:

> We the undersigned ministers and officers of the King do hereby make known to all those whom it may concern that Mwamba . . . on his own initiative and by the wish of his people called His Lordship Monseigneur Joseph Dupont, Bishop of Thibar. . . . This same Mwamba in full possession of his faculties and liberty, in public and before us present, on the 12th day of October, 1898, has appointed . . . Dupont, the forementioned as his successor and heir and has given him the whole of his country with the rights of the soil, all his goods movable and immovable, real and personal . . . both the right of sovereignty over the whole country and territory and the special protection of his women and children.[211]

Even if one were to assume that Mwamba had ceded his country to Dupont in the same way that Namwanga and Mambwe chiefs had done to the African Lakes Company, the validity of the bishop's claim to the Mwambaship would still be doubtful. The document to which the chief's helpless and frightened councillors were signatories lacked the force of legality because, as Wills has commented on such concessions in general,

> land agreements with native chiefs could hardly be valid in any case, unless the chief were educated or had special advice, for the two parties would have quite different conceptions of the meaning of land ownership.[212]

Moreover, the chief himself was in the daze of a dying man, and he could hardly have been 'in full possession of his faculties and liberty', as the document of cession had it; furthermore, Dupont is said to have tried to bribe two rubber traders—Campbell-Hunter and Rabinek—into affixing their signatures to the document, but the two refused and reported his claim to the Administration.[213]

To question the validity of Dupont's claim to the Mwambaship is not, however, to deny the bishop's pacifying role in the leadership crisis of Ituna. As soon as news broke that Mwamba was dead, all women in the royal village, fearing that they might be ritual murder victims, 'slung their babies on their backs and, with the bigger children trotting at their heels', took refuge with the White Fathers at Milungu, and by mid-day on 24 October most of the soldiers at the court had deserted Kalimanshila to join the missionaries.[214] Dupont later controlled the activities of Kalimanshila, who, once Mwamba's right-hand man, was, to the applause of a gathering, preaching revolt against the ruling Crocodile clan, and he also intimidated Ponde into releasing the late chief's wives, whom Ponde had captured in a pillage of a few villages near Mwamba's capital.[215] When members of the royal clan who had seized Mwamba's cattle at Kabwe in Ituna were captured by the dead chief's warriors and brought to Dupont for retribution, the bishop surprised the people by merely ordering the offenders to return the cattle and pay a fine, instead of ordering their decapitation or mutilation, as was done under the old order.[216]

Thus, as Rotberg writes:

The Bishop's intervention, no matter how narrow in his motive, prevented bloodshed after Mwamba's death and precipitated the assumption of British rule in Bembaland much earlier than had been anticipated. For the first time, the British South Africa Company was permitted to assert its authority over the central plateau of Northeastern Rhodesia.[217]

But if Dupont's intervention merely precipitated the assumption of British rule in Bembaland, it was the leadership crisis in Ituna —the death of Mwamba Mubanga Chipoya in October 1898 and Ponde's unbending determination to succeed to the Mwambaship—which actually brought about the possibilities of British occupation of Bemba country. Indeed, it might be said, as Stokes and Brown have argued, that in Mwamba's death lay the *primum mobile* to the establishment of colonial rule among the Bemba. For his death and the succession dispute that ensued 'permitted the White Fathers and the Administration to step in and take over the country almost bloodlessly'.[218] Robert Young, who was still in the country at the time, also saw in Mwamba's death 'a good opportunity to occupy Mwamba's country and practically open the whole of Awemba country then closed to Europeans by the chiefs . . .'[219] But it must be pointed out that the receptive attitude of the common people was also an important factor in the European occupation of Bemba country. A previously resistive people now became ardent followers of the White Fathers. This political somersault should, perhaps, not be surprising. For the brutalities and mutilations which the people had suffered at the hands of their rulers[220] could hardly have made them remain rigidly or aggressively loyalist in the new situation. Moreover, the consequences of the throttling of the trade routes to the east coast and of the hemming in of Bemba country by the Administration, as a result of which the Bemba's traditional raiding grounds were sealed off, were felt particularly by the commoners. For in order to raise slaves for sale to the Arabs, chiefs had to raid their own people.[221] This naturally alienated the people, and if Kalimanshila had suddenly put on the appearance of a revolutionary he was probably merely taking advantage of this popular revulsion against the ruling clan in order to acquire a position of influence such as, or even stronger than, the one he had occupied under Mwamba.

Although Ponde had, in response to Dupont's threats, stopped pillaging the villages around Mafula, the late Mwamba's capital, he had not given up the idea of becoming the new Mwamba. He told McKinnon and Young, who later visited Ituna, that he intended to be Mwamba, and that he would not leave Ituna for his country in the Abercorn Division.[222] It was only after McKinnon had appealed to him to go back to Abercorn, so that the question of who was the rightful successor might be properly investigated by Administration, and after he was frightened at the sight of the Collector's Iwa and Senga contingent and the North Nyasa police, who were fixing bayonets on Young's orders, that Ponde withdrew and the officials took the opportunity to build the first station in Bemba country at Old Kasama.[223]

Ponde was quiet for some time. In the meantime Young, who had remained at Kasama with a contingent of thirty police to hold Lubemba, was making enquiries as to who was the rightful successor to Mwamba Mubanga Chipoya. The enquiry was inevitably a long and intricate process, but Ponde could not wait that long. Thinking 'he had Might and so must be Right', as Young put it, Ponde came back to Mwamba's country and built a village on top of a hill, with rocks all around the edge.[224] He was fortifying the village when he received a message from Young reminding him of what McKinnon had said to him a few weeks before. But Ponde simply ignored the warning, and told Young that he was Mwamba and intended to remain where he was.[225] Ponde's truculence, and that of his cousin, Mporokoso, made the Administration decide to marshal its military resources against what were the only obvious outcrops of resistance left among the Bemba.

However, Ponde's refusal to heed Young's warning was only an incident in a series of acts of defiance by this politically ambitious man. Early in 1898 he had rebuffed a police contingent which Marshall, the Collector at Abercorn, had sent to his court as a show of strength, and when later in the year William Johnstone, who was sent by Marshall on an inspection tour of Bemba country, came to his capital, Ponde refused to give Johnstone the meal, fowls and eggs which the latter asked for to feed his carriers. He challenged the touring official to a fight if the latter insisted on getting food supplies from his village.[226]

Johnstone was subjected to the same treatment when he called on Mporokoso. Having camped outside the chief's stockaded village, he sent his *capitao*—Chikungulu—to Mporokoso to ask for food supplies. But the chief refused to give Johnstone's party any food, and said that it was Johnstone who, as a commoner, should have given him food as tribute.[227]

It was as a result of such incidents, in addition to Ponde's ceaseless endeavours to seize the Mwambaship, that the Administration subsequently decided that a force should be sent to subdue the two recalcitrant chiefs. Collector McKinnon of Ikawa, with his two assistants, George Lyons and Jock Law, and with Andrew Law, Acting Collector at Abercorn and brother to Jock Law, converged at Kasama early in 1899, where Young joined them and 'with the usual contingent of various tribes, including Awemba out for loot, went up against Ponde'.[228] One of Ponde's men, whose daughter had been shot by the chief's nephew and whose compensation claim the chief had refused, led the party to a place from where it was possible to enter the stockaded village without any difficulty. After 'one or two skirmishes' with the Administration police, Ponde escaped.[229]

Ponde, evidently the most persistent trouble-maker as far as the

Administration was concerned, was defeated. That he should have been routed with such speed after many months of unrestrained resistance was probably due to his military unpreparedness and lack of popular support in his determination to seize the Mwamba-ship. For, as Robert Young once confessed, 'if Ponde had got time to finish the fortifications he began, it would have been impregnable to us'.[230]

After the defeat of Ponde, Andrew Law, with an African force, and accompanied by his two assistants, Hector Croad and William Johnstone, marched on Mporokoso's stockaded village. The party, however, met with such resistance that it had to retire.[231] Fighting could not begin until H. T. Harrington, Collector at Kalungwisi, joined the expedition with an additional eighty rifles.[232] But even then, for almost a whole day the battle raged, and the defenders, who were ably led by the Arabs under Nasaro bin Suliman, only took flight after heavy fire through the holes of the stockade from Harrington's contingent, and after Law's men had entered the palisade through the gate, which was still under construction.[233]

The defeat of Mporokoso in April 1899 marked the end of Bemba resistance to the establishment of white rule in the Northern Province. It had been erratic resistance, often lacking coherence and a sense of direction. Even at the eleventh hour, when it seemed clear that the survival of the Bemba nation demanded a united stand against European intrusion, the crocodile kings failed to sink their differences. Ponde and Mporokoso each fought a lone battle behind his stockade, when a joint army, judging from the strong stand the latter put up at his *tembe*, would probably have reduced the chances of victory which McKinnon and Andrew Law appear to have won with such speed. This lack of co-ordination in Bemba resistance to European encroachment revealed not only the weaknesses of the Bemba polity, but also, as Roberts points out, a lack of a concerted anti-white policy.[234] 'Bemba chiefs were making limited decisions about specific and immediate situations', sharing as their only general policy 'a rational reluctance to make irrevocable commitments for or against Europeans'.[235]

To the historian, the end of Bemba resistance to European encroachment may seem sheer 'pliant submission' by a formerly formidable people.[236] But to the Administration officials who were involved in the punitive expeditions against these people, it was not as easy as it seems today. Almost a decade passed from the time the first administrative posts were established in neighbouring areas before Bemba country was brought under Company rule. Robert Young later wrote that after the mopping up opcrations in Kazembe's country, following the defeat of Ponde and Mporokoso, members of the North Nyasa police 'had a rest and marched back to Nyasaland . . . and got *medals for the Awemba war*'.[237] Young himself was moved to ask Codrington, the new Administrator for North-eastern Rhodesia, for a medal of distinguished service in the so-called 'Awemba war', and justified his claim with an argument with which the Administrator is said to have agreed. He told Codrington rather impertinently:

Well, the Awemba did put up some little fights and chase Watson and his crowd back to Kalungwisi and that's more than any of your wild Ngoni did.[238]

Earlier, after the 'little war' against the Bemba at Chibale's village late in 1897 and the defeat of Kapandansalu and other Arabs in the Luangwa valley, Young had been recommended by McKinnon for an award of a Victoria Cross for his part in the expeditions.[239]

Throughout these years of pacification, resistance to European rule had been centred almost exclusively around the chiefs and their courts. The ordinary village people had been little more than interested but helpless bystanders. The final and effective establishment of colonial rule broke the power of the chiefs and saw the beginning of popular political assertion. A new era of mass resistance to white rule had begun.

NOTES

[1] Marie de Kiewiet Hemphill, 'The British sphere, 1884–1890', *History of East Africa*, ed. Roland Oliver and Gervasse Mathew (Oxford: Clarendon Press, 1963), p. 397.

[2] Cf. Roberts, 'A political history of the Bemba', p. 237.

[3] 'Historical Notes'; ZPI/3/1; Bolink, *op. cit.*, p. 37.

[4] 'Historical Notes'; Bolink, *op. cit.*, p. 38, gives the dates for the establishment of Nyamukolo and Fwambo as 1885 and 1889 respectively, and so does A. J. Hanna; *The Beginnings of Nyasaland and North-eastern Rhodesia, 1859–1895* (Oxford: Clarendon Press, 1956), pp. 46–47.

[5] 'Historical Notes'; Hanna gives the year as 1878; *op. cit.*, p. 20.

[6] Gelfand, *loc. cit.*

[7] Old Mambwe Mission Diary, 19 July 1891.

[8] Interview with Donald Siwale, 28 July 1967.

[9] Joseph Thomson had predicted in 1879 that in twenty years the elephant would be a rare animal, and said he could see nothing that would take the place of ivory as a staple export from the Northern Province; see Roberts, 'A political history of the Bemba', p. 264.

[10] Old Mambwe Mission Diary, 19 July 1891.

[11] W. Vernon Stone, 'The Livingstonia Mission and the Bemba', *The Bulletin of the Society for African Church History*, Vol. II, No. 4 (1968), p. 311.

[12] G. K. Osei, *The African: his antecedents, his genius and his destiny* (London: the African Publishing Society, 1967), p. 1.

[13] Ruth Slade Reardon, 'Catholics and Protestants in the Congo', *Christianity in Tropical Africa*, ed. C. G. Baeta (London: O.U.P., 1968), p. 84.

[14] For a discussion of the role of white missionaries as civil authorities in these early years, see Robert I. Rotberg, *Christian Missionaries and the Creation of Northern Rhodesia, 1880–1924* (Princeton University Press, 1965), pp. 57–66.

[15] John V. Taylor and Dorothea Lehmann, *Christians of the Copperbelt: the Growth of the Church in Northern Rhodesia* (London: S.C.M. Press, 1961), p. 19.

[16] Old Mambwe Mission Diary, 6 November 1892.

[17] Taylor and Lehmann, *op. cit.*, p. 13.

[18] Rotberg, *op. cit.*, p. 57.

[19] *Ibid.*

[20] *Ibid.*, pp. 57–58.

[21] Taylor and Lehmann, *op. cit.*, pp. 13, 19.

[22] Old Mambwe Mission Diary, 26 September 1892.

[23] *Ibid.*, 2 September 1892.

[24] *Ibid.*, 26 January 1893.

[25] *Ibid.*, 20 May 1894.

[26] *Ibid.*, 10 March 1895.

[27] Chinsali District Note Book, p. 241.

[28] Interview with Donald Siwale, 28 July 1967.

[29] Kayambi Mission Diary, 21 June 1898.

[30] B.S.A.C. land and mineral rights in North-eastern Rhodesia, NER A 3/8.

[31] *Ibid.*

[32] *Ibid.*

[33] Quoted in C. K. Meek, *Land, Law and Custom in the Colonies* (London: O.U.P., 1946), p. ii. A. J. Wills makes the same point in his discussion of land agreements in general at this time: *op. cit.*, p. 204.

[34] Cited in Robert I. Rotberg, 'The transformation of East Africa', *Twentieth-century Africa*, ed. P. J. M. McEwan (London: O.U.P., 1968), p. 342.

[35] B.S.A.C. land and mineral rights, NER A3/8.

[36] Interview with Moses Sikazwe, 29 July 1967.

[37] Roberts, 'A political history of the Bemba', p. 194.

[38] Stokes and Brown, *op. cit.*, p. xxxii. Stokes and Brown observe further that 'All over eastern and central Africa it was the warrior trading class repre-

sented by Arabs and Swahilis who had most to lose and who proved the least assimilable': *ibid.*

39 Interview with Moses Sikazwe.
40 Roberts, 'A political history of the Bemba', p. 267.
41 Old Mambwe Mission Diary, 23 February 1895.
42 *Ibid.*, 31 January 1894.
43 Quoted in Richard Brown, *op. cit.*, p. 67.
44 Old Mambwe Mission Diary, 2 February, 25 March and 17 April 1894.
45 Taylor and Lehmann, *op. cit.*, p. 13.
46 Roberts, 'A political history of the Bemba', p. 267.
47 Rotberg, *op. cit.*, pp. 159–60.
48 L. H. Gann, *A History of Northern Rhodesia: Early Days to 1953* (London: Chatto & Windus, 1964), p. 39.
49 Roberts, 'A political history of the Bemba', p. 267.
50 Hemans to Thomson, 3 July 1894, quoted in Rotberg, *loc. cit.*
51 Roberts, 'A political history of the Bemba', n. 63, p. 267.
52 Hemans to Thomson, 3 July 1894, quoted in Rotberg, *op. cit.*, pp. 159–160.
53 Rotberg, *loc. cit.*
54 Roberts, 'A political history of the Bemba', p. 267.
55 *Ibid.*
56 Taylor and Lehmann, *loc. cit.*; Bolink, *op. cit.*, p. 39.
57 Bolink, *op. cit.*, p. 41.
58 *Ibid.*, p. 29; Stone, *op. cit.*, p. 312.
59 Old Mambwe Mission Diary, 15 October 1893.
60 *Ibid.*
61 Stokes and Brown, *op. cit.*, p. xxix.
62 Old Mambwe Mission Diary, 19 January 1894.
63 *Ibid.*, 28 January 1894.
64 H. A. C. Cairns, *Prelude to Imperialism: British reactions to Central African Society, 1840–1890* (London: Routledge & Kegan Paul, 1965), p. 17.
65 Old Mambwe Mission Diary, 28 January 1894.
66 *Ibid.*, 10 January 1895.
67 *Ibid.*, 19 May 1894.
68 *Ibid.*, 10 January 1895.
69 Interview with Chitimukulu Musenga, 3 August 1967.
70 Old Mambwe Mission Diary, 10 January 1895.
71 Testimony by Mporokoso in an interview with Foulett Weatherley, an Administration official, cited in the *British Central Africa Gazette*, 15 September 1895, p. 6.
72 *Ibid.* In what appears to be another incident, messengers from Fife taking presents and friendly messages to Sampa were attacked by a party of Bemba men on the Chambeshi; *ibid.*, 1 April 1895, p. 2.
73 Young, *loc. cit.*
74 Tanguy, *op. cit.*, p. 75.
75 Roberts, 'A political history of the Bemba', p. 254.
76 *Idem*, 'The nineteenth century in Zambia', p. 90.
77 Old Mambwe Mission Diary, 15 June 1895.
78 Roberts, 'A political history of the Bemba', p. 270.

[79] Old Mambwe Mission Diary, 6 March 1896.

[80] *Ibid.*, 27 April 1895.

[81] A. E. Howell, *Bishop Dupont: the King of the Brigands* (Franklin, Pa.: News-Herald Printing Company, 1949), pp. 28–29. As Howell himself states on p. 3 of the book, *Bishop Dupont* is more or less a translation of Henry Pineau's *Evêque—Roi des Brigands* (Montreal and Quebec: Les Pères Blancs, 1944), which is based on contemporary sources, including Dupont's diaries. See Ann Tweedie, *op. cit.*, p. 222.

[82] Old Mambwe Mission Diary, 4–8 June 1895.

[83] *Ibid.*

[84] *Ibid.*

[85] Howell, *loc. cit.*; Mpashi, *op. cit.*, p. 11.

[86] Old Mambwe Mission Diary, 15 June 1895.

[87] Howell, *op. cit.*, p. 29.

[88] It is instructive that only a few weeks after Sampa had withdrawn permission for the White Fathers to establish a mission station in Mpanda, Makasa was asking Dupont for guns, probably in an attempt to resist the king's orders; Old Mambwe Mission Diary, 12 July 1895.

[89] *Ibid.*, 17 June 1895.

[90] *Ibid.*, 6 July 1895.

[91] *Ibid.*, 12 July 1895.

[92] Howell, *op. cit.*, p. 29; Old Mambwe Mission Diary, *loc. cit.*

[93] Howell, *op. cit.*, pp. 29–30.

[94] Mpashi, *loc. cit.*, p. 12.

[95] *Ibid.*, p. 13.

[96] Howell, *op. cit.*, p. 30.

[97] *Ibid.*

[98] Mpashi, *op. cit.*, p. 12.

[99] Howell, *op. cit.*, p. 31.

[100] *Ibid.*

[101] Mpashi, *op. cit.*, pp. 13–14; as translated by Daniel P. Kunene (1970), 'African vernacular writing—an essay in self-devaluation', *African Social Research*, No. 9.

[102] Howell, op. cit., p. 32.

[103] Howell, *loc. cit.*

[104] *Ibid.*

[105] Old Mambwe Mission Diary, 12 July 1895.

[106] Howell, *op. cit.*, p. 33.

[107] Roberts, 'A political history of the Bemba', p. 270.

[108] Gouldsbury and Sheane, *op. cit.*, p. 240.

[109] Old Mambwe Mission Diary, 30 July 1895.

[110] From the cairn at Kayambi mission church.

[111] Howell, *op. cit.*, p. 34.

[112] Old Mambwe Mission Diary, 1 December 1895.

[113] *Ibid.*

[114] *Ibid.*

[115] *Ibid.*, 31 March 1896.

[116] *Ibid.*, 6 April 1896; cf. Howell, *op. cit.*, p. 49.

[117] Howell, *op. cit.*, p. 50.
[118] *Ibid.*
[119] Old Mambwe Mission Diary, 20 May 1896.
[120] Roberts, 'A political history of the Bemba', p. 271.
[121] *Ibid.*, p. 272.
[122] Wills, *op. cit.*, p. 190.
[123] Bell to Major Patrick Forbes, Administrator for North-eastern Rhodesia, Blantyre, 16 January 1896, NER A8/2/2.
[124] Johnston to Rhodes, 31 December 1895, quoted in Roberts, 'A political history of the Bemba', p. 273.
[125] Bell to Forbes, 16 January 1896, *loc. cit.*
[126] *Ibid.*
[127] *Ibid.*
[128] Roberts, 'A political history of the Bemba', p. 274.
[129] Bell to Forbes, *loc. cit.*
[130] Bell to Forbes, 24 April 1896, NER A8/2/2.
[131] Extract from a personal letter quoted in *The Story of the Northern Rhodesia Regiment*, ed. W. V. Brelsford (Lusaka: Government Printer, 1954), p. 7.
[132] Bell to Forbes, 25 June 1896, NER A1/1/1.
[133] J. van Velsen, 'The Missionary Factors among the Lakeside Ngoni of Nyasaland', *R.L.J.*, XXVI (December 1959), pp. 7, 12.
[134] *Ibid.*, p. 12.
[135] Howell, *op. cit.*, p. 49.
[136] Old Mambwe Mission Diary, 31 May–1 June 1896.
[137] *Ibid.*, 1–4 July 1896.
[138] *Ibid.*, 11 July 1896.
[139] Howell, *op. cit.*, p. 50.
[140] *Ibid.*
[141] *Ibid.*
[142] Old Mambwe Mission Diary, 30 July 1896.
[143] Kayambi Mission Diary, 16 December 1896.
[144] *Ibid.*, 27 December 1896.
[145] *Ibid.*, 2 January 1897.
[146] Bell to Forbes, 16 January 1896, NER A8/2/2.
[147] Bell to Forbes, 31 May 1896, NER A1/1/1.
[148] Report by R. A. Young, 24 January 1897, NER A1/1/2.
[149] Bell to Forbes, 31 May 1896, NER A1/1/1.
[150] Brelsford, *The Succession of Bemba Chiefs*, p. 8.
[151] Chinsali District Note Book, p. 231.
[152] Report by R. A. Young, 24 January 1897, NER A1/1/2.
[153] *Ibid.*
[154] *Ibid.*
[155] Chinsali District Note Book, p. 231.
[156] Richards, 'The life of Bwembya', p. 35.
[157] Young to C. M. McKinnon, Collector, Chambeshi District, 8 March 1897, NER A1/1/2.
[158] *Ibid.*
[159] *Ibid.*

G

[160] Report by R. A. Young, Chinsali District Note Book, p. 241.
[161] *Ibid.*
[162] Young to McKinnon, n.d., NER A8/2/8.
[163] Chinsali District Note Book, p. 231.
[164] *Ibid.*
[165] *Ibid.*
[166] Gouldsbury and Sheane, *op. cit.*, p. 42.
[167] W. V. Brelsford, 'Shimwalule: a study of a Bemba chief and priest', MS, Institute of Social Research, Lusaka. Chimbwi was apparently also known by the name of Shinta; see White Fathers, *Ifya Bukaya* (Chilubula: 1932), p. 110.
[168] *Ifya Bukaya*, p. 110.
[169] Brelsford, 'Shimwalule'.
[170] *Ifya Bukaya*, p. 110. By custom, a Shimwalule was expected to relinquish his post after burying one Chitimukulu because only a new Shimwalule could bury the next Paramount; see Brelsford, *The Succession of Bemba Chiefs*, p. 41.
[171] *Ifya Bukaya*, p. 110.
[172] See Brelsford, 'Shimwalule'.
[173] Chinsali District Note Book, p. 241.
[174] *Ibid.*, p. 231.
[175] Gelfand, *op. cit.*, p. 85.
[176] Howell, *op. cit.*, p. 51.
[177] Roberts, 'A political history of the Bemba', p. 279.
[178] Howell, *op. cit.*, p. 53.
[179] Mpashi, *op. cit.*, pp. 30–31; interview with Chief Mwamba Nshika, 4 August 1967. It is worth noting that this episode is not referred to in either Howell's book or in the White Fathers' mission diaries.
[180] Howell, *op. cit.*, p. 58.
[181] Kayambi Mission Diary, 4 May 1897.
[182] Howell, *op. cit.*, p. 57.
[183] Gelfand, *op. cit.*, p. 19.
[184] *Ibid.*, p. 27.
[185] Roberts, 'A political history of the Bemba', p. 279.
[186] Howell, *loc. cit.*
[187] *Ibid.*, p. 58.
[188] Kayambi Mission Diary, 10 May 1897.
[189] Howell, *loc. cit.*
[190] Quoted in *ibid.*, p. 59.
[191] Kayambi Mission Diary, 14 July and 10 December 1897.
[192] *Ibid.*, 10 December 1897.
[193] *Ibid.*, 16 May 1897.
[194] *Ibid.*, 21 June 1898; Howell, *op. cit.*, p. 61.
[195] Mpashi, *op. cit.*, p. 33; Howell, *op. cit.*, p. 62.
[196] Quoted in Howell, *loc. cit.*
[197] *Ibid.*, p. 63.
[198] Quoted in *ibid.*, p. 64.
[199] *Ibid.*, p. 65.
[200] Brelsford, *The Succession of Bemba Chiefs*, p. 9.
[201] It is said that a Bemba chief's immediate relatives and henchmen were

killed at his death and not allowed to surround his successor 'so that they did not make mischief with the new chief'; Werbner, *op. cit.*, p. 34, n. 1.

202 Kayambi Mission Diary, 4 November 1898.

203 Howell, *op. cit.*, p. 65.

204 Gouldsbury and Sheane, *op. cit.*, p. 240. Roberts' account of this episode is broadly similar; 'A political history of the Bemba', p. 280.

205 Interview with Chitimukulu Musenga, 3 August 1967. The present Mwamba, Nshika, also agrees with the Paramount's account; interview.

206 Tanguy, *op. cit.*, p. 76. Literally translated, the quotation means: 'I am about to die; I know you love the Bemba; I leave my country in your hands; the people will seek refuge where you live; protect them against Ponde. My successor will be Kanyanta, my nephew; nobody else; you are his father.' Andrew Roberts comments: 'But Tanguy presumably got his information from a Bemba too; so this is not necessarily independent confirmation. Besides by that time the Fathers were anxious to show that they had never sought to usurp the Mwambaship, so that their testimony is hardly disinterested. Roberts to the author, 5 February 1969.

207 Werbner has observed that 'the Mwambaship became, and has continued to be, an office to which a prince advances from a lesser territorial post, until now the Nkolemfumuship': *op. cit.*, p. 38. Chitimukulu Musenga also stated that Nkolemfumu invariably became Mwamba on the death of the latter; interview, 3 August 1967.

208 Quoted in Howell, *op. cit.*, p. 74.

209 Dupont's Note Book, 20 October 1898, quoted in *ibid.*, p. 68.

210 Robert I. Rotberg, 'The missionary factor in the occupation of Trans-Zambesia', *N.R.J.*, Vol. V, No. 4 (1964), p. 332. See also his *Christian Missionaries*, pp. 34-36.

211 Assistant Administrator to Administrator of North-eastern Rhodesia, 6 March 1899, LO5/4/13, Salisbury Archives, quoted in Rotberg, 'The missionary factor', p. 332.

212 Wills, *op. cit.*, p. 204.

213 Rotberg, *Christian Missionaries*, p. 35.

214 Howell, *op. cit.*, p. 70.

215 *Ibid.*, pp. 70-71.

216 *Ibid.*, p. 70.

217 Rotberg, 'The missionary factor', p. 333.

218 Stokes and Brown, *op. cit.*, p. xxviii.

219 Chinsali District Note Book, p. 231.

220 During their first visit to Makasa, in January 1894, the White Fathers noticed, for example, that 'Bemba songs are very nice; but singers and drumbeaters are often mutilated'; Old Mambwe Mission Diary, 30 January 1894.

221 R. A. Young to Lt.-Col. S. Gore-Browne, 20 July 1914, reproduced in ' "Bobo" Young relates his exploits', *N.R.J.*, Vol. II, No. 2 (1953), p. 66; interview with Jean-Baptiste Mangara, 2 August 1967, Chitambi Village, Kasama.

222 Young to Gore-Browne, *loc. cit.*, p. 68.

223 *Ibid.*

[224] *Ibid.*
[225] *Ibid.*
[226] Interview with Moses Sikazwe, 29 July 1967, Mbala Local Court, Abercorn.
[227] *Ibid.*
[228] Young to Gore-Browne, *loc. cit.*
[229] Chinsali District Note Book, p. 231. According to Moses Sikazwe, Ponde had escaped long before the punitive party arrived at his village; interview, 29 July 1967.
[230] Young to Gore-Browne, *loc. cit.*
[231] H. T. Harrington, 'The taming of North-eastern Rhodesia', *N.R.J.*, Vol. II, No. 3 (1954), p. 10.
[232] *Ibid.*
[233] *Ibid.*
[234] Andrew Roberts, 'The history of the Bemba', *The Middle Age of African History*, ed. Roland Oliver (London: O.U.P., 1967), p. 69.
[235] *Idem*, 'A political history of the Bemba', p. 298.
[236] *Idem*, 'A political history of the Bemba', p. 69.
[237] Young to Gore-Browne, *loc. cit.*, p. 69; the italics appear in the original.
[238] *Ibid.*
[239] Gelfand, *op. cit.*, p. 86.

CHAPTER III

NEW WINE IN OLD WINESKINS

I. THE CHARACTER OF EUROPEAN RULE

It was perhaps natural that, after the dust of the so-called 'Awemba war' had settled down, and the whole of the Northern Province had been finally pacified, the Chartered Company Administration should have nursed a feeling of success and relief at the accomplishment of what had been a difficult task. Mwamba was dead, and Ponde and Mporokoso, who were the only remaining truculent malcontents, had been knocked out. In a word, all chiefs who had led the resistance against European intrusion had been defeated. R. A. Young, who perhaps more than any of his contemporaries has left on record much of his impressions about the march of events in the province during these early years, probably summed up the European view on African immediate reaction to European occupation when he wrote:

In 1901, the first year of taxation, the Awemba in the Awemba District alone paid without any bother or trouble over 14,000 taxes. The chiefs may not be satisfied with the new regime but there is not the least doubt that the Awemba people and all the surrounding tribes are greatly pleased that the old rule is ended. They have a freedom they never knew before and the state of terror and abject fear they lived in has been removed. The chiefs by their cruelty ruled their people through fear alone and now that this fear is removed the chiefs have lost all their former power.[1]

This was, on the whole, a fair comment on the state of affairs in the Northern Province on the morrow of the Bemba campaign. Tranquillity in the province was especially discernible among the hitherto intractable Bemba. A member of the Livingstonia Mission evangelistic band which reached the eastern Bemba heartland in 1904 wrote:

These Bemba are very ready to receive Christ as their king. I witness this because I was one of them [the missionaries] who went there [to Bembaland]. I and Samson were teaching and preaching in Chibeza

79

village; the Chief of the Biaza [Bisa] people and many people came round our preaching of Jesus crucified. They were also happy to hear that God loves them as well as ourselves.[2]

Three years later David Kaunda, the father of Zambia's first President, writing from Chinsali, echoed the same observations on the Bemba's receptivity and enthusiasm for Christianity:

Chinsali is growing and is now quite changed. . . . Many are coming searching school. . . . They are very much willing to hear the words of God preached among them. Many are crossing the Chambezi river in search of school. . . . There are many people and many villages— over 100 villages—east, west, south and north just in deep sleep.[3]

The White Fathers also noticed a marked willingness on the part of the Bemba to be Christians.[4] When Chilonga mission moved from the old site near Chief Luchembe's village to Pandafishala, its present site, in Chief Chikwanda's territory in February 1900, Chief Luchembe was unhappy, while the latter, glad that the missionaries were now in his country, moved his village nearer the mission station.[5]

But if, because of this apparent readiness to receive Christ and the generally quietist attitude among the African people after the Northern Province was pacified, the missionaries and Administration officials thought they had opened wide avenues for unfettered white control over a people supposedly grateful for its emancipation from the excesses of old tribal rule, they were soon to be disillusioned. For colonial rule brought with it certain changes which in many ways affected African societies adversely, and therefore Africans could not have readily acquiesced in it, even if such rule seemed to temper the rigours of the old order.

Of the many factors in the colonial situation which caused the people of the Northern Province constant disquiet, forced labour and taxation seem to have been the most potent and irritating. Both of them, as instruments of colonial rule, are indeed known to have been major causes of certain political upheavals elsewhere in Central and East Africa. In Angola forced labour was one of the main causes of the Bailundo revolt of 1902 against the Portuguese, which lasted for eighteen months and in which 'thousands of African lives' were lost;[6] in Tanzania both forced labour and tax were the major causal factors in the Maji Maji rising of

British South Africa Company administration, North-eastern Rhodesia, *c.* 1900. Earlier and later Government stations and missions are also shown. (District borders are as shown in *British South Africa Company Reports*)

1905-7;[7] and the unpopularity of the two was an important predisposing cause of the Southern Rhodesian rebellion of 1896-7 among the Shona.[8] Although in the Northern Province of Northern Rhodesia there was nothing like the Maji Maji rising or the Bailundo rebellion, forced labour and tax even there gave rise to considerable social unsettlement, as a result of which the local population put up various forms of resistance to colonial rule. But before discussing the reactions of the people of the Northern Province to these and other measures, it would be well to give some background to forced labour and taxation as instruments of white rule in Central Africa.

The rapid growth of the mining industry in South Africa and Southern Rhodesia at the end of the nineteenth century created so great a demand for labour that it could not be met from the local supply, and the labour supply situation seemed especially disconcerting in Southern Rhodesia. As the Chief Native Commissioner for Matebeleland wrote:

> The labour problem is one that requires the most serious consideration; there is not sufficient labour in Matabeleland to supply the various mines when they are at work; we must look to the outside provinces for our supply . . . Our best source of supply is from the north of the Zambesi . . . When once we establish a system whereby natives coming from the north to work are given fair and just treatment with reasonable remuneration for their services I do not fear any difficulty in the supply of labour from the north; and every year many natives from the north proceed to the Rand in search of work; it would be much more favourable for them to obtain the work here.[9]

The Matebeleland Chief Native Commissioner's plea probably became even more plausible and urgent when at the turn of the century many Europeans, including some ex-soldiers from the Boer War, took to farming in order to meet the increasing demand for agricultural products by an expanding urban population consequent upon the rise in the production of gold in Southern Rhodesia as well as South Africa.[10] Many of these men who went into farming had practically no experience in the occupation, and some of them lacked capital with which to set themselves up as modern farmers. The result was that they had to rely on African labour to develop and maintain their estates.[11] However, no labour from the local African population—the

Shona and the Ndebele—was forthcoming for the white farmers. Even in industrial centres, employers witnessed the same reluctance on the part of Southern Rhodesian Africans to engage in paid employment. In his report for the period 1900–2, Sir William Milton, the Administrator of Southern Rhodesia, revealed that 'out of a total of 7,500 labourers employed during a recent month on certain mines . . . less than 700 are aboriginal natives of Southern Rhodesia';[12] and a labour return on Africans working in the mines of Matebeleland at the end of 1902 showed that out of a total of 8,000 workers only 600 were Southern Rhodesians.[13]

Why was local African labour in Southern Rhodesia in such short supply? Various explanations were offered by the B.S.A.C. Administration authorities for this perennial problem. Some contended that the population of Southern Rhodesia, especially Matebeleland, was not dense enough to admit of large supplies of labour being drawn from the local population;[14] but others thought the cause of the problem was much more complex, that it was ecological and climatic and deeply rooted in the new social order, which had had a profound impact on the African traditional society in the colony. As William Milton commented in his report of 26 October 1900:

The supply of labour . . . has been worse and less reliable than before. The favourable position occupied by the native in this territory . . . is such as to render it unnecessary for him to improve his material condition and assist in developing the country. Blessed with a fruitful soil and climate, protected from pillage and exactions, and accustomed in hard times to be assisted by the Administration, no reason for work presents itself to him, and it is becoming increasingly obvious that the bulk of the labour which is urgently required for the prosecution of the principal industry [mining] will have to be obtained from outside sources.[15]

The effect of this popular indifference to work in farms and in the mines was to create what Southern Rhodesia's European employers of labour thought was 'an everlasting shortage of native labour', as a result of which the Chartered Company Administration between 1900 and 1905 'scoured the world from Aden to India, from China to Abyssinia' in an effort to remedy the situation.[16] Behind the Company Administration's efforts to recruit labour from such distant countries was the belief common among white employers that they would have, as Lewis Gann puts it, 'a "non-spasmodic" labour supply, . . . proletarians without a stake in tribal lands, men who would not wish to return to their villages after short spells of employment, but would depend entirely on their wage packets, and would therefore do more work'.[17] But over this scheme the Administration and employers alike experienced many difficulties. Many labourers who were recruited from Somalia, Ethiopia and other parts of north-east Africa deserted, while others rioted on board a ship at Beira in October 1900—causing what the Administration called 'a serious disturbance'—after they heard false rumours from sailors on the ship that they would be sold as slaves when they reached Southern Rhodesia and would work in chains on the mines there.[18] Furthermore, as a result of certain objections raised by the local British Resident to any systematic emigration from Southern Arabia and Aden, which had the support of the British government, no labourers could be recruited from these dependencies; the Indian government was opposed to any more of its nationals being signed on for work in Southern Rhodesia and South Africa because those who were already there were being discriminated against on grounds of race and fear of economic competition; and, additionally, no Chinese workmen could be recruited because European contractors and skilled artisans in Southern Rhodesia raised objections and fears that the yellow men would put them out of their jobs.[19]

In order to overcome the acute shortage of labour, which persisted after the Chartered Administration's abortive attempts to recruit north-east Africans, Arabs, Indians and Chinese, a determined effort was made to improve methods of recruiting labour from Northern Rhodesia, Nyasaland and the Portuguese territories so as to meet the competition for labour which Southern Rhodesian mines were facing from the wealthier Rand mines, competition which had grown fiercer after the Boer War.[20] Thus the Rhodesian Native Labour Bureau was formed in 1906, as a result of the recommendations of a committee which was appointed the previous year by Sir William Milton to enquire into the problem of labour shortage in Southern Rhodesia.[21] Earlier organisations—the Matebeleland Native Labour Bureau, formed in June 1899, and the Labour Board of Southern Rhodesia, which was formed a year later to serve the whole colony

—were found unviable, and incapable of competing with the recruiters from the Transvaal, who offered higher wages.[22] Under the Rhodesian Native Labour Bureau steps were taken to reduce the high mortality rate among labourers, most of whom died in transit from disease, starvation or from the hazards of travel from their areas of recruitment to Southern Rhodesia.[23] The Bureau provided labourers in transit with accommodation, blankets, warm clothing and other facilities, and saw to it that they received proper medical examination and adequate diet.[24] Africans from North-eastern Rhodesia were employed on contracts of twelve months, and those from North-western Rhodesia were taken on for six months, and in either case there was an option for renewal of contracts for another three months;[25] and in order to ensure that workmen returning to North-eastern Rhodesia would have money at home, the Bureau, through a system of deferred payments, handed over certain amounts of money to the Administration of North-eastern Rhodesia, which, unlike the North-western Rhodesia Administration, insisted on such an arrangement.[26] By 1912, the Rhodesian Native Labour Bureau had a chain of agencies throughout Northern Rhodesia.

Meanwhile, the Katanga mines, which were also experiencing labour shortage problems, had set up a similar organisation to obtain labour from North-eastern Rhodesia. Robert Williams and Company, a firm of consulting engineers to the *Union Minière du Haut-Katanga*, the company which took over the mines in 1906 from Tanganyika Concessions Ltd., engaged itself in supplying the *Union Minière* with most of its labour requirements,[28] with the result that the Katanga mines were worked in these early days largely by labour from the Northern and the Luapula Provinces of Northern Rhodesia.[29] So much did the Katanga depend on labour from these parts of Northern Rhodesia that, even when World War I broke out and the Chartered Company Administration's demand for porters increased tremendously? Robert Williams and Company were still allowed to recruit up to 4,000 labourers from the area.[30]

The problem of labour shortage was not confined to Southern Rhodesia or to South Africa alone. Even in certain parts of Northern Rhodesia, to which the South looked for its labour supply, there were instances when white missionaries and officials experienced a scarcity of unskilled labour. In October 1899, for example, the White Fathers at Chilonga mission in the Northern Province complained that 'it is difficult to find workers even for a salary';[31] and during the same year W. B. Chamberlain, a local sub-manager of the African Lakes Corporation, reported to John Gibbs, the manager of the company, that the B.S.A.C. was trying to obtain a monopoly of the limited labour supply on the plateau by forbidding the local people, under pain of death, to work for his company.[32] Eight years earlier, the African Lakes Corporation, in collaboration with the L.M.S. missionaries at Kambole mission, had deposed Chief Tafuna of the Lungu and sent him to prison in Blantyre, after burning two of his villages, for failing to meet the periodic demands of the missionaries and the Company for labour.[33]

Taking into account the fact that the Northern Province was a few years later to be a labour reservoir from which the Katanga mines, the Broken Hill mine and later the Copperbelt mines of Northern Rhodesia drew most of their workmen, it seems strange that there should have been a scarcity of labour in the area during these early days of colonial rule. It may well be that this inadequacy of the labour supply at this time was partly the result of depopulation of the province during the slave trade.[34] But it seems likely that this scarcity was caused, as seems to have been the case in Southern Rhodesia, by popular reluctance to take to remunerative employment. This unwillingness to become wage earners seems to have been common among most African communities, and the reason for its existence is not far to seek. As one authority has pointed out, its cause was partly sociological and partly economic.

The introduction of capitalist undertakings in Africa found a population that had little incentive to improve its subsistence by wage earning, and since it was inexperienced in the use of money it was slow to react to the stimulus of cash inducements. The entry of the African into the new economic field was therefore difficult and hesitating, all the more because those who controlled that field were Europeans or Asiatics. Native societies had their own system of economic organisation, the obligations of which were well recognised, but the discipline of labour in compliance with the orders of those who had no traditional authority was unfamiliar to them. The practice of slavery had also left a legacy which created suspicion against the new relationship of employer and wage earner.[35]

Clyde Mitchell, an anthropologist, also writes in much the same vein:

In spite of the conspicuous poverty of the tribal Africans and the apparent abundance of men with no calls on their time, the entrepreneur has not always been able to count on a steady and sufficient flow of labour for his needs. Wage labour was foreign to the tribesmen of the late nineteenth century and savoured to him somewhat of slavery.[36]

It was probably as a result of this awareness of the institutional and economic impedimenta which stood in the way of the African as a potential modern wage earner that the B.S.A.C. Administration, like other colonial governments, recruited labour through chiefs and used it on the strength of the custom of communal labour which seems to have been general among African societies.[37] But even with such methods, the Administration still encountered unwillingness and opposition to work among the African people of the Northern Province, and sometimes its officials resorted to brute force in order to get the labourers they needed, usually for work as porters or *tenga-tenga*, as the officials called them.[38] For example, Collector Charles McKinnon is said to have chained a number of chiefs and headmen at his district headquarters at Ikawa until their people turned up for work.[39] Apart from inflicting such punishment on African rulers for failing to supply the necessary labour, the Administration often burnt down the villages of recalcitrant chiefs and commoners who evaded forced labour.[40] Indeed, even as early as 1899 hut burning had become so frequent a phenomenon both in Nyasaland and Northern Rhodesia that Her Majesty's Government was moved to express great concern at the practice, which, as Lord Salisbury observed, sometimes made even the innocent suffer; and so the British government urged the Chartered Company Administration to apply less inhuman forms of punishment in every case.[41] But not even such coercive measures could afford the Administration all the labour it needed.

In 1901 hut tax was introduced in North-eastern Rhodesia.[42] Every adult African male paid three shillings each year for his hut; and those men who had grown-up unmarried daughters, old male relatives or widowed mothers or other female relations occupying their own huts paid tax for up to a maximum of six huts for such dependants.[43] The tax was paid in cash, but sometimes it was also paid in kind. The White Fathers at Kayambi reported in 1902, for example, that 'lots of hens are given and accepted as levy'.[44] But, as Gann has pointed out, although payment in kind was legally acceptable, the non-existence of markets for tax stock, grain or poultry so collected made the Administration averse to accepting such unsaleable commodities; and so by 1905 the payment of the hut tax in this way had ceased not only in North-eastern Rhodesia but also in the rest of the country.[45]

While it is true that taxation was generally regarded by the Administration as the African's contribution towards the cost of protecting him and towards a reduction of the country's financial reliance upon the coffers of the imperial government,[46] it seems equally true that it was also introduced as a means of forcing labour to centres of employment. 'The question of taxation . . .', writes Gann, 'was closely linked with the labour question, for the need to earn tax money was one of the most important incentives to induce Africans to take up paid employment.'[47] And Sheila T. van der Horst, commenting on African taxation in South Africa a few decades ago, has made an observation which seems equally pertinent to colonial taxation policies elsewhere in Africa and their effect on the local population:

Taxes [she writes] were levied for different reasons. Some were imposed in order to pay the costs of administration . . .; some because it was felt that the natives ought to contribute directly to the general revenue; and some with the definite object of forcing the natives to work for Europeans. For whatever purpose it was levied, the extension and increase in taxation had the effect of increasing the number of natives working for Europeans.[48]

It is, of course, true that as time went on, normal economic incentives became an influence of increasing strength in inducing the African people to engage in remunerative employment;[49] economic incentives were, for instance, sufficiently strong from 1931 onwards to ensure a regular and sufficient flow of labour into the Zambian Copperbelt.[50] But even then the 'tax incentive' continued to play a vital role in driving African labour to urban and other centres for work. In the Northern Province the tax incentive was, in fact, thought by the colonial authorities to be the main cause of labour migration for a long time, while among the Ngoni of Chipata (Fort Jameson) it was considered very important, although it was outweighed by economic incentives.[51] For the Administration, as Rotberg has observed, 'consciously set the rate of tax at a level that would successfully draw African males away from their homes to the usually distant centres of white agriculture and industry'.[52] Indeed, a plea made by one European member of the Northern Rhodesia Legislative Council in 1925 does illustrate perhaps even more clearly just to what extent tax was seen as a means of forcing African labour to centres of employment. Speaking during a debate in which the widespread shortage of labour in the country was generally deplored, Mr Clark, a nominated member of the council, urged the government to collect tax just before the planting and harvesting seasons, in order to ensure that European farmers had labour when they most needed it.[53]

The imposition of the hut tax in 1901 on the people of the Northern Province, together with the activities of recruiting agents, ushered in an era of labour emigration unknown during the province's two decades of European influence, and it appeared as if the Administration had achieved its objective of galvanising the supposedly indolent and indulgent African male population into taking up paid employment in white farming and industrial centres.[54] By the end of 1902, for example, the White Fathers at Kayambi had employed several men who wanted tax money;[55] and six months later, they recorded in the mission diary: 'Again people come back to work at the mission for their levy'.[56] In June 1904, their counterparts at Chilonga wrote: 'A group of young men leave Chilonga for work in the mines of Salisbury';[57] and two years later, Dr Robert Laws of Livingstonia could write of labour migration from the province, that young men were 'going by the thousands annually to Johannesburg, Salisbury, Broken Hill and Kambove'.[58]

Yet somewhat ironically, it was the imposition of the hut tax, and the labour migration to which it gave rein, which, as will be seen later, caused a widespread shortage of labour, not only in the Northern Province but also in North-eastern Rhodesia as a whole. The low wages paid by the Administration and private employers in the area as compared with the relatively high pay rates in Southern Rhodesia, or even in the railway belt of North-western Rhodesia, and later the Copperbelt, could retain only a few workers in the Northern Province.[59] For emigration even during these early days was apparently, as Lord Hailey has put it, 'primarily a proof of the low scale of pay available to the wage earning section of the people'.[60] This labour shortage and migration had profound consequences on the people of the Northern Province: it influenced their reactions to tribute labour for chiefs and to forced labour for the Administration, with all their political implications, and also adversely affected tribal economic and social life. Together with old and new grievances against white rule, it moulded African attitudes in the colonial situation, as will soon be seen.

A year before tax was introduced in North-eastern Rhodesia, the country was divided into nine districts for administrative and tax collecting purposes.[61] Two of these districts—Awemba District, with its administrative centres (bomas) at Kasama, Mpika and Luena (Luwingu), and Tanganyika District, with its bomas at Abercorn, Sumbu, Katwe and Mporokoso—and parts of a third district, the North Luangwa District, whose bomas were at Fife, Koka, Nyala and Mirongo,[62] covered the area known today as the Northern Province of Zambia. In charge of each district was a District Commissioner, under whom were Native Commissioners, who were responsible for divisions into which each district was divided, and D.C.s and N.C.s were usually also magistrates and assistant magistrates respectively, depending upon whether they passed requisite law examinations.[63]

Because white administrators were few, the B.S.A.C. Administration perforce relied on chiefs and headmen to govern the country. The traditional rulers were given power to try certain cases; they had powers of arrest and they were called upon to help the Native Commissioner in purchasing grain and collecting the hut tax,[64] and those of them who were 'loyal' were paid as agents for the Administration. In the Abercorn Division, for example, four chiefs were reported in 1904 as having been in receipt of subsidies from the local Native Commissioner, who authorised them to appoint their own headmen, subject to his approval.[65] Sometimes chiefs and headmen who were not in receipt of regular subsidies, were given presents for carrying out specific official instructions to the satisfaction of the Native Commissioner.[66]

Thus although the Native Commissioner for the Mpika

H

Division had stated that it was the policy of the B.S.A.C. Administration 'to work through and with chiefs'[67] this was a theory which was not realised in practice. The Chartered Company Administration, as Lemarchand has written of Belgian rule in the Congo during the same period, 'theoretically recognised the authority of the traditional chiefs, [but] in practice every effort was made to replace them with "trustworthy elements" whose only claim to authority was their personal loyalty . . .'[68] The traditional authorities in the Northern Province were, like others elsewhere under Company rule, little more than tools of colonial rule; they lost most of their former authority and influence, and at best, came to play the role of political brokers between their people and government officials. As one authority has observed:

the general effect of the policy [of direct rule] was to preserve the outward form of the indigenous systems, but to undermine the authority of the chiefs . . . by making them dependent on the administrative officer.[69]

This invidious position in which the chiefs found themselves under the Chartered Company's direct rule policy was observable even as early as 1903. In a report on native administration in his division, the Native Commissioner for Mporokoso wrote:

The chiefs complained that their authority was at an end, their position merely nominal, the people independent. They were then shown that as a means to regain some of their former powers, they must assist the government. To this they readily agreed, but it was sometime before they could understand what was expected of them. The natives were given to understand that they must acknowledge and listen to their chiefs.[70]

It is against this background of the B.S.A.C. Administration's policies—in regard to labour, taxation and the position of traditional rulers in the new political structure—that the reactions of the Northern Province's African population to colonial rule will now be examined.

2. THE FIRST STIRRINGS OF POPULAR DISCONTENT

The first signs of popular revulsion to European rule in the Northern Province came from those tribes, like the Lungu, the

Mambwe and the Namwanga, which had been under missionary and Company sway well before the Bemba were subjugated. It will be recalled that Chief Tafuna of the Lungu was exiled and imprisoned in 1891 for refusing to supply labour to the L.M.S. missionaries and the African Lakes Corporation. His was probably the first of the many cases of African resistance to the demands of European rule which were to characterise black–white relations in the colonial situation. The African people of the Northern Province, and more especially, the non-Bemba groups, may, in the words of Robert Young, have enjoyed 'a freedom they never knew before' under white rule,[71] and they may have felt grateful for the protection the union jack was giving them. But at no time did they forget that they were a colonised people—a people relegated to the status of second-class citizens in their own country by an alien and white elite, whose policies were as detestable and burdensome as old traditional rule was brutal—and throughout the colonial era, they strove to shake off the burdens of white rule.

Probably the first popular demonstration of African resentment to forced labour in the Northern Province was that put up in 1896 by the Namwanga people of Ilendela village near Ikawa *Boma* in the north-eastern corner of the province. Ikawa *Boma*, from which John Bell was operating, was hardly a year old from the time that it was opened by Major Forbes, the new Administrator for North-eastern Rhodesia, in 1895, and consequently a lot of work had to be done in order to develop the new station. One morning in August 1896, Bell sent out a few of his Makua police and a number of Ikawa villagers to recruit labour. The recruiting party went from village to village, taking on men as they went, until they reached Ilendela's village. There the headman refused to give them any men and his people took up guns, bows and arrows and fired at the party, who fired back, although hurting no one. The party then withdrew, but in retaliation, as they left, they drove off the goats and sheep of the village to Ikawa *Boma*, which was about seven miles away.[73] It was the first violent African reaction in the province to forced labour.

The incident was reported to the Collector by the party, and Bell hoped that Headman Ilendela would go and report the matter to him in accordance with established practice. But when it was clear that Ilendela would not go to the *boma*, Bell set off for the village with a few police. When he arrived there, the people ran out of their stockaded village into the surrounding bush. A few shots were exchanged, during which one villager was fatally wounded. Bell did not take kindly to this recalcitrance of the Namwanga, and took what he thought was the right punitive measure, explaining later that 'as the people had given evidence of some insubordination, I set the village on fire and returned to Ikawa'.[73]

The Ilendela incident had ramifying consequences which brought to the surface the hidden fundamental differences of attitude of the Administration on the one hand, and the local white missionaries on the other, towards Africans. A villager went to the Mwenzo mission of the Free Church of Scotland and complained to Rev. Alexander Dewar about the goats and sheep that had been taken away by Bell's police. Dewar felt so strongly about the incident that on 9 September he wrote to the Collector in most pungent terms, calling the Ilendela incident 'a case of pillage, incendiarism and murder, a poor man being shot down cruelly like a dog by one of your men', and added that 'the story is one of the most heartrending and pitiful I have heard on the plateau . . .' He urged the Administration to pay compensation to the father of the deceased.[74]

Although, when he replied to Dewar's letter on the same day, Bell assured the missionary that he had 'no objection whatever to natives complaining through you'[75], the Collector had in fact expressed the opposite view in his report of the incident to the Administrator. In the report he accused the Reverend Dewar of interfering in his administration of the district:

Dewar is exactly the type of missionary who considers it his duty to poke his nose into matters outside his province and make trumpery charges against officials and the administration. He has attempted it before, when the B[ritish] C[entral] A[frica] A[dministration] administered. I cannot have him interfere between me and the natives . . . There is no intimidation whatsoever, and I am particularly accessible to every native who wishes to see me. Dewar's mediation is immaterial to me.[76]

The Ilendela incident, quite apart from exposing the strained relations between the administration and the local missionaries, was a graphic representation of early African revulsion to European rule, the recurrent manifestations of which had been worrying Bell for some time. In the same report to Major Forbes, explaining further why he had burnt Ilendela village, Bell made mention of these repeated acts of defiance by the Namwanga people:

In several instances the Wanyamwanga in the neighbourhood have refused absolutely to obey me in any way and all along I have made it clear to them that if any serious case of this kind came to my knowledge again I would punish the offending village by turning the people out and destroying it.[77]

To what extent these instances of defiance of white authority were manifestations of xenophobia, and to what extent they were mere resentment of European administrative measures to which the Namwanga were unaccustomed, it is difficult to say. But it is clear that the relations between the Administration and the ruled had taken a new turn. The Administration officials were no longer looked upon as friends and allies in the age-old enmity between the Namwanga and the Bemba, as the latter were no longer a terror in the area, the last Bemba raid in their direction having been in the latter part of 1895, on Kameme's village in the Sengwe valley.[78] With the spectre of Bemba raids now removed, the Namwanga must have felt free to put their erstwhile white partners in the place to which they felt the latter belonged. They now looked to the missionaries for sympathy and mediation in their strained relations with their high-handed white masters.

In the Abercorn Division of the Tanganyika District, where white rule had also long been established, Africans were already questioning the intentions of the new regime and discussing their plight in the new situation. In August 1899, a group of Africans who met in a hut at a village not very far from Abercorn were airing their dissatisfaction at the conduct and activities of the whiteman. Their ring-leader was an alien—one Kalulia from Mtoa in German East Africa. Kalulia, who seems to have been involved in some unfortunate incidents with the Chartered Company officials, felt unhappy about the state of affairs in the district. His bitterness about the European moved him to say that 'the white men were behaving foolishly and that he was going to leave and return to his own country and turn rebel'.[79] This may well have been an empty threat by a frustrated man, but it was sufficient to alarm the Administration officials, who immediately charged Kalulia with 'using threatening language towards Europeans or concerning Europeans', and, although he was acquitted of another charge of wilfully having set fire to a store of the London Missionary Society at Nyamukolo, he was sentenced to six months' imprisonment and to twenty-five lashes by the Deputy Administrator, Robert Codrington. However, as his continued stay in the country—even whilst in prison—was considered too much of a security risk, he was deported to German East Africa long before the expiration of his prison sentence and, on the orders of Codrington, 'warned never to return to our territory'.[80]

The Ilendela incident and Kalulia case were only a few of the many similar incidents between the new rulers and the African people of the Northern Province. By the turn of this century, Africans were already brooding over grievances against the way the Administration was treating them. They were forced by Administration officials to work on roads and other projects even when they did not wish to engage in such employment, which was sometimes unpaid. They carried touring officials on hammocks, and if by some mishap the hammock bearers staggered and made the official fall off, they were flogged in retribution.[81]

For fear of being punished, the village communities had to draw water, collect firewood, provide free food and put up shelters for visiting white officials, even though more often than not the official spent only one night in them. The Rev. Mushindo, who himself as a young man had been a victim of B.S.A. Company coercion, describes the unhappy experiences of the African people during these early years of white rule:

The people were treated like slaves, and very often they would not be allowed to enter Native (or District) Commissioner's offices with their shoes on. The African messengers who were the Administration's employees also treated their own people with the same callousness as the white officials.

When tax defaulters were apprehended they were, more often than not, confined in a hut in which a big fire was made, producing a lot of smoke, while the door of the hut was closed. This was one form of punishment for the defaulters. While on tour, a white official sometimes rode a bicycle while an [African] attendant ran after him to carry the bicycle at points where the official was unable to ride it. This attendant, who had to run fast enough to keep pace with the cycling official, had also to carry his master's provisions for the day. Any remains of such provisions were given to the official's dog, and not to the attendant, however hungry the latter may have been.[82]

If the Rev. Mushindo's recollections are anything to go by, African attempts to evade taxation and labour recruitment, or to desert employers, and the tendency by the people to look upon Native Commissioners and their staff as enemies, then seem understandable.

In November 1899, just under two months after Kalulia's trial, there occurred what was probably one of the first strikes by an African rural labour force that was already conscious of its rights under the exacting demands of the white administration. Not far from Kayambi mission station a group of men who, like their kith and kin elsewhere in the country, were employed in road and bridge building by the Administration, walked home, taking with them their hoes and axes, in protest against low wages.[83] The background to the strike and the circumstances surrounding it are yet to be discovered. But an action of this kind, at that time, by an unorganised and rural labour force would seem very signifi-cant. Not only was it an assertion of an employee's rights, it was also a protest against exploitation by the Administration, which had put an end to slavery but had replaced it with forced, cheap labour.

Several such incidents took place later in other parts of the country. An Administration doctor, Dr Mackay, who was on an urgent medical journey, complained to H. C. Marshall, magis-trate and Civil Commissioner at Abercorn, that his (Mackay's) African carriers had refused to continue the journey with him. But all that Marshall could do for Mackay in the circumstances was to 'undertake to arrest and punish the natives',[84] two of whom he reported to Mackay two weeks later to have been 'in irons'.[85]

Marshall himself later had a lot of trouble with his own em-ployees in Abercorn, as a result of which he was forced to dis-charge them all. Writing to a certain Mr Miller, he commented: 'All the workers here are restless and somewhat troublesome, so I have promised to pay them off on the 31st inst.'[86] His assistant W. R. Johnstone, who had taken part in the skirmishes with

Mporokoso and Ponde in 1899, also came face to face with a situation similar to that with which Dr Mackay had earlier been confronted. Whilst on tour of the Abercorn Division in April 1904, the seventy-two men he had enlisted to build rest camps for his party as they went from village to village went on strike near Machiela village and went away without asking for their pay. Johnstone added that this was after the men had 'systematically loafed and have had to be driven . . . to make *bomas* ahead of my mob and each day I have had to use my carriers to help'.[87]

This haughty reaction to forced labour was widespread. In April 1906 in the Luwingu Division, J. H. W. Sheane, the Native Commissioner there, saw this resentment in its probably most expressive form. He was talking to Chief Chibanda at an *Indaba* (or big gathering of chiefs and commoners) where the latter had brought some 'volunteer' labourers for him, when one man, Chakulimba, intervened to urge the 'volunteers' to demand better pay and refuse to work if they were not given it. In a reasoned attack on the forced labour system and on the chiefs' undignified and selfish role in it, Chakulimba said to his friends:

It is all very well for those chiefs to say what we will do. You stick out for more money and refuse to work. Why should the chiefs get money by the month for sending us out as slaves?[88]

Chakulimba was rebuked by Chief Chibanda and later found guilty by Native Commissioner Sheane of 'seditious utterance'.[89] The other chiefs at the *Indaba* told Sheane that what Chakulimba had said was what other men in their villages were saying, and they expressed delight at the fact that the Native Commissioner had himself witnessed one of such cases with which they had to contend every so often.[90]

Like forced labour, the hut tax was a most unsettling factor in the lives of the African people. Indeed, these two instruments of colonial rule appeared synonymous, and equally invidious to the people. The Administration officials, as pointed out earlier, used the hut tax not only as the main source of revenue but also as a means of forcing men to go to labour markets where they were most needed. Some of those men who remained at home had either to engage in local employment, such as road building, with the Administration or the local missionaries, or to sell some of their meagre agricultural produce or poultry, in order to obtain the necessary money to pay their taxes. Others, from either sheer laziness or neglect, or, very often, from recalcitrance, made no attempt to pay tax. They ran into the bush at the sight of a white official or his equally detestable *boma* messengers, leaving their wives and children alone for as long as a week or until such time as the tax collectors were reliably reported to have left the area. Sometimes wives of runaway tax defaulters were taken away as hostages by the Administration officials, so that their husbands might give themselves up. And often village headmen or their representatives were flogged or made to pay extra taxes for those of their men who had run away, or whose whereabouts they could not account for.[91]

Thus although, early in 1930, Lord Passfield was to warn the Governor of Northern Rhodesia that 'Taxation is not meant to change the life of a people',[92] the hut tax had in fact already affected the life of the entire population. The people's attitude towards the tax collectors was of course not always docile or evasive. Sometimes they expressed their resentment of the Administration's exacting demands in physical violence. Most recorded instances of stubborn and protracted resistance to taxation, and to the population census and registration that went with it, are to be found among the Bisa and Unga people of the Bangweulu lake and swamp area, living as they did in an environment which made them insular in outlook, and almost inaccessible to Administration officials. Reporting on his visit to Unga country in January 1903, I. N. Leyer, Native Commissioner at Luwingu *Boma*, said that he had got a very strong impression that the Unga would certainly not pay any tax unless they saw 'a practical demonstration of force on the part of the Administration', and in anticipation of such an operation, he warned a meeting of villagers during his visit that the Administration would take strong measures against them 'in case of mass refusal, on their part, to pay hut tax'. He reported that such a demonstration of force was necessary because 'these people are a demoralising example in the way of disloyalty for the other parts of this [West Awemba] Division'.[93] Unlike the Bemba and another tribe in the area, the Chishinga, who were reported to have paid tax 'very well', the Unga were said to be notorious tax defaulters, and remained so, in spite of inducements by frequent messages and visits from the Native Commissioner and in spite of the fact that they were 'always profuse in promises and protestations of loyalty'.[94]

The Bisa were no less averse to white rule than the Unga. When, during the same tour to the lake and swamp area, Leyer visited Matipa, one of the most important Bisa chiefs, he heard a complaint from the chief that the Bisa and the Unga in the Chambeshi delta area, and on Chilubi and Mbabala islands on Lake Bangweulu, were angry with him (Matipa) for 'bringing the Europeans', that is to say, for supplying canoes to Administration officials, as a result of which they were able to get to these lacustrine people and tax them.[95] Matipa had continually been threatened by his people, and had lost his nerve, as a result of which he had to ask for, and subsequently obtained, two of Leyer's policemen to stay on and protect him for some time.[96] As a tactical measure to win the confidence of his critics, he suggested to the Native Commissioner that *The Kapopo*, which, according to Leyer, was the only canoe on the lake 'which is in any way fit for a European to use', should be sent to Luwingu *Boma*, so that Matipa might in this way shift the blame for 'bringing the Europeans' onto the Administration, while at the same time preserving his warm relations with the *boma* by saving the boat from possible destruction by some malcontents.[97] This was apparently the price he had to pay for the help he had been given by the Administration to accede to the much-contested chieftainship in 1902, and for what the *boma* had been doing since then to reinforce his tenuous reins of authority.[98]

A visit to Nbabala Island later in the year by J. H. Sheane, then Acting Native Commissioner at Luwingu, provoked an even more hostile reaction from the people. His camp was surrounded by Bisa men who, armed with bows and arrows, were dancing about, singing war songs and pouring insults on him. Sheane was only rescued from this 'somewhat awkward position', as he termed it, by the arrival at nightfall of his messengers, who had 'purposely kept behind in fear that the natives might come in on seeing them'.[99]

The incidents which have just been cited are but a few of the many instances of a violent show of resentment against the Administration by the lake and swamp people. On a number of occasions *Boma* Messengers reported instances of defiance to white authority by Bisa fishermen. On one occasion, Bisa men who brought sheep for sale to Chartered Company authorities and European private buyers at Chief Matipa's village were fired on by a group of young men from another village who told them that they should have nothing to do with the whiteman.[100] On another occasion, a headman was shot at with arrows by his own people because he had visited the Native Commissioner.[101] In such an atmosphere of strained black–white relations, the chiefs, whose support was courted both by the Administration and the people, found themselves in a very difficult position. Ideally, they were to serve two masters and please them equally, but in the rigours of the social change that was afoot and the emotional up-heaval that went with it, they very often found themselves falling in between two stools or leaning towards one side or the other. In either of these situations they inevitably incurred the dis-pleasure and wrath of one of the two sides to the conflict.

Chief Malongwe of Mbabala Island was only one of the many chiefs in the country who often found themselves in such an unhappy position. When a tax-collecting party of messengers arrived at his village, he, as was expected of him by the Admin-istration, gathered his people together for the touring messengers. However, this being one of the most odious moments in the lives of the people of the Bangweulu area, it provoked an ugly situa-tion which Mulongwe was only able to contain with the assistance of the Administration. Three of his men—Nkandu, Sikasumpe and Lufumpi—stepped out of the crowd and publicly scolded the chief for serving the whitemen and for making it possible for the hut tax to be introduced on the island. They minced no words in condemning the collaboration between the chief and the *boma*, and threatened:

When the messengers go away *my* [sic] friends will drown you, Mulongwe, and if the Mzungu [whiteman] comes we will drown him too.[102]

The three men were seized and bound up by the messengers on Mulongwe's instructions. When night fell, they tried to escape in Chartered Company canoes, but they were pursued and caught, in spite of a barrage of arrows they shot at the pursuers, and later, in court, Acting Native Commissioner Sheane sentenced them to four months' imprisonment each for threatening the chief and assaulting messengers and for their attempted escape.[103]

A *Boma* Messenger's duties, even more than those of an obliging chief, always earned him the implacable suspicion and hatred of the village people. When Messenger Peter Datton Musishya was sent out on a population census tour of part of the West Awemba Division some time in April 1905, he became an unhappy victim of this dislike of white rule among the people of the Northern Province. Arriving at one village, he found that all the men had run into the bush, having probably got wind of his coming.[104] However, when he saw one Chikunge, a youth of about sixteen years, skulking on the outskirts of the village, Musishya caught hold of him in an attempt to ascertain the whereabouts of all the men in the village. This provoked the boy's uncle, Konkola, who, from some hiding place, and apparently under the impression that his nephew was being arrested, immediately came and seized the boy by the hand and said to the messenger:

Why are you touching my nephew? You are bad messengers coming when the chief is absent and making a disturbance. . . . [If] anyone comes here about taxes we will beat him, and for your Bwana [master] I curse him too.[105]

In his report for the year ending 31 March 1904,[106] Leyer had attempted an analysis of the factors behind the recalcitrance of the Bisa people, then the largest single ethnic group in the West Awemba Division, followed by the Bemba, the Chishinga and then by the Unga. First, he said, the facility of flight in their canoes and hiding places in the marshes made any punitive or coercive action by the Administration against the Bisa difficult. Second, the Bisa, he said, had 'a natural idleness' which was 'much more engrained than among the Awemba'; and then, lastly, they seemed to have been infected by the bad example of the Unga, who had defied taxation for the previous three years, and whose chiefs—Mweshi and Kasoma—had been proselytising among the Bisa of Sumbu Island, taking half of the population to Unga-land.[107] Because of these factors, and because of the fact that the Bisa, by virtue of the gradual and peaceful European penetration of the lake and swamp areas, still had some measure of independence, it was difficult to bring them under effective white control.

That the Bisa were like the Unga in evading and resisting taxation had already been shown two years earlier, when there was an outbreak of smallpox in the area, as a result of which taxation was suspended because of the restriction on movement, which did not permit people to leave their home areas to seek employment elsewhere or to pay tax. At that time the Bisa openly asserted that even after the epidemic was over they would not pay tax, because, first, the Unga were not paying taxes and yet the Administration was taking no steps against them, and second, they said, because: 'We are burdened by this tax every year, one payment should be enough'.[108] A year later, when the epidemic was over, they insulted and threatened the touring Assistant Native Commissioner at Chief Mulongwe's village on Mbabala Island, and fired upon *Boma* Messengers at Mwinamweshi's village.[109] During the same period their allies, the Unga, had maliciously burnt grass to prevent a visit by the Native Commissioner,[110] and had deposed their chief, styled 'the friendly Kasoma' by the Administration, in order to evade tax.[111]

So far this account of the reactions of the Northern Province's African societies to the pressures of colonial rule has been confined to ethnic groups other than the Bemba. It seems necessary at this point to pay some attention to this tribe, which, up to the end of the last century, had put up protracted resistance to the establishment of European rule.

In his two works on the history of Northern Rhodesia, Gann has advanced the view that the tribes which proved the most 'difficult' once colonial rule was established in Northern Rhodesia were those, like the Lenje, the Bisa and the Aushi, which lacked a strong central political organisation; but those like the Ngoni, the Bemba and the Lunda of Kazembe, which had strong tribal organisation, were easier to rule once conquered.[112] There may very well be some truth in such a view; at any rate, the Bisa and their neighbours in the Bangweulu lake and swamp area appear, from several incidents which have been cited in this chapter, to have been 'difficult'. But until detailed studies are made at grass roots level of these societies, it would seem rather presumptive to take such a postulate at its face value. For the Bemba, at least, some modification of this view seems necessary. It would not be quite correct to regard them as having been pliantly submissive to the various demands that were made on them by the colonial regime; because, in fact, as will be seen later in this study, they proved not so easy to rule.

The first manifestations of Bemba resistance to colonial rule were in 1906, when an order was issued by the Administration that the *chitemene* system of cultivation should come to an end, and in order to understand clearly why the Bemba, who were reported by Robert Young to have paid the hut tax well when it was introduced in 1901, had turned a political somersault after some six years of colonial rule, it will be useful to give a brief account of the events that led to the abolition of *chitemene*.

The peace and tranquillity that followed pacification, as a result of which slave raids and tribal wars became things of the past, gave the people of the Northern Province a greater sense of security and more freedom of movement. The stockaded villages and the large settlements which used to be characteristic of the period before the establishment of *Pax Britannica* now fell into desuetude, as people scattered into *mitanda*, or small garden villages,[113] where, in the face of ravaging wild animals and birds, they lived *en famille* to tend their crops. Thus, although at the end of the nineteenth century villages with 200 to 500 huts were a common sight in the Mpika Division, for example, by 1904 such villages were nowhere to be seen, as the number of huts in each of the largest settlements had dwindled to no more than twenty.[114] In the Luena (Luwingu) Division, it was reported that between 1902 and 1905 a hundred *mitanda* had been formed, as a result of which a population of about 18,000 was scattered into smaller and less well organised groups, covering an area of over 4,000 square miles.[115]

If the formation and existence of *mitanda*, apart from being concomitants of the *chitemene* system of cultivation, were an expression of popular revulsion against the traditional authorities, they were, however, not necessarily an indication of the people's acceptance of white rule. If anything, they represented a popular desire to be independent, not only of the chiefs, but also of their high-handed new white masters. The political and administrative implications of this population dispersal were immediately apparent. Chiefs lost the little authority that they were still able to exercise over their people, as their spheres of influence were then confined to their capitals and could not embrace their wandering *mitanda* subjects. For the distances separating one *mutanda* from another were too great to be covered by the chiefs and headmen, who were generally elderly men.[116] The White Fathers, too, complained that 'villages are scattering in Mambwe area, as in Bemba area, which makes the spreading of our religion and contact with all the people more difficult'.[117] Out of reach, the *mitanda* dwellers attained a kind of independence which they fiercely and jealously guarded. When headmen tried to arrest offenders in *mitanda* they were often beaten, 'as Mitanda men brook no interference from subordinates [the headmen] and very little from the chief himself'.[118] Indeed, the *mitanda* folk acquired certain social and political peculiarities, which were described by J. H. W. Sheane, the West Awemba Division's Native Commissioner:

> In the Mitanda are collected the mass of malcontents who have renounced the authority of their chiefs and of the Boma. Here the fungoid growths of superstition flourish unchecked . . . the mitanda are the chosen haunts of the prisoner, the outcast and the adulterer.[119]

Both the chiefs and the headmen were very much aware of this social disruption caused by the garden villages; but they were helpless to remedy the situation. They lacked the necessary means to keep the disintegration of villages in check. Such manpower as could have been made available to them had to be paid for. But they had neither the money nor enough ivory or other goods with which to employ young men, who alone would have been able to withstand the hardships of constantly traversing the country to superintend the *mitanda* dwellers. The only choice left to the chiefs, who were naturally anxious to have district headmen who were both servile to them and acceptable to the people, was old men who, because of their limited mobility, remained mere figureheads outside their own villages.[120]

The chiefs themselves were naturally averse to this humble and ineffectual position to which they had been relegated in the new colonial situation. In 1903 the Native Commissioner of the Mporokoso Division reported that chiefs in the area were complaining 'that their authority was at an end, their position merely nominal, and their people independent'.[121]

The Administration soon realised that, in order to govern the country satisfactorily, it had to have the support of the traditional authorities, and consequently it did everything possible to uphold their authority and 'to try to regain, if possible, even a small proportion of their lost prestige'.[122] It was a formidable task and, in a sense, an absurd method of social reconstruction to which the Administration was applying itself. Acting Native Commissioner

J. H. W. Sheane had quite a good point when he questioned the wisdom of:

the attempts to reconstruct, from the top downwards through the Chiefs and District Headmen a solid fabric of state, whilst the foundations, the people themselves were allowed to crumble and sink into irreclaimable (?) obscurity and unseen anarchy of ever-increasing Mitanda.[123]

Only the passage of time proved to the Chartered Company officialdom that to strengthen the position of the chiefs and headmen whilst the social milieu upon which their authority rested was in a fluid state was like building a house on sand. When finally in 1906 the Administration abolished *mitanda* in order to achieve the social cohesion necessary for efficient administration, the people had grown so used to their *mitanda* way of life that political ferment of an unprecedented nature was caused by the abolition.

The problem of *mitanda*, combined with the violent reaction of the lacustrine tribes of the Northern Province to the Administration's policies and practices—which to some extent was a manifestation of the painful process of social and political adjustment to the colonial situation by a people who had hitherto been independent and almost secluded—awakened the Administration to the realisation that some changes in the social set-up of the Northern Province must be made if the Chartered Company's authority was to be effectively asserted. The old argument that some chiefs, like Tungati, Chibanda and Chipalu, were little more than retired servants of the 'old cruel Awemba civil service' and that for the *boma* to delegate the control of their own people to them would make them revive the old cruel methods of Bemba rule,[124] and the rationalisation about the formation of *mitanda*, to the effect that its concomitant population dispersal made easier the application of the principle of 'divide and rule', because collective resistance to authority by the *mitanda* folk was impossible,[125] seemed no longer tenable. The Administration felt that there was a need to redouble its efforts to strengthen the position of the chiefs, whom it now wanted to be a more effective medium of its conduct of affairs in the country. Although their traditional authority was far from restored, the chiefs were made to co-operate more closely with the colonial authorities in the collection of the hut tax, the apprehension of wrong-doers and in reporting anything affecting the welfare of their people to the *boma*.

One of the most far-reaching measures which the Administration took, in an effort to strengthen its hold on the running of affairs in the country and to boost the status and authority of the chiefs, was to abolish *mitanda* and *chitemene* in 1906.[126] The idea behind the abolition of *mitanda* was to bring the numerous small garden villages, which were littered all over the countryside, into bigger settlement units so that the Administration, using the enhanced authority of the chiefs resulting from such regroupings, would be better able to collect taxes and administer the country more efficiently. The abolition of *chitemene* was, however, motivated as much by the need to 'centralise' the administration as by the administrators' desire to change the agricultural methods of the Bemba to a less wasteful system of cultivation. As one report stated, *chitemene* was abolished 'in order to save the country from deforestation and to facilitate the control of natives and the collection of the hut tax'.[127]

As both *chitemene* and *mitanda* had become the basis of social and economic organisation, their abolition, sudden as it was, inevitably gave rise to serious and undesired consequences. Quite apart from the obvious economic consequences of the fact that people could not live or grow crops where they liked,[128] the social ills that followed the abolition seem to have been deplorable. The big new villages which were formed as a result of regrouping *mitanda* often lacked the unifying bonds of consanguinity and affinity which characterised the older settlements, and with the high mortality rate which seems inevitable when people come together in such large communities devoid of modern health facilities, suspicion, hatred and witchcraft became the curse of the day, just as adultery was rampant.[129]

The reactions of the peoples of the Northern Province to this social arrangement were soon apparent. To the Bisa, according to F. M. Thomas, the abolition of *chitemene* and *mitanda* 'came as a shock'.[130] Among the Bemba, these changes, coupled with a backlog of old grievances, gave rise to a situation which seemed so bad that in 1908 L. A. Wallace, the Administrator for North-eastern Rhodesia, directed that a special report be written on the menacingly changed attitude of this people.[131] For a few years, ever since their submission to white rule at the end of the nineteenth century, the Bemba, seemingly a tractable people, were now in the grip of an unprecedented political ferment. Perhaps because of their obliging disposition, which even R. A. Young had noticed,[132] the Administration, as the Native Commissioner for Luwingu commented later, had 'over-administered them'.[133] But there is little doubt that the abolition of *chitemene* and *mitanda* in 1906 precipitated a crisis which the Administration could not ignore.

The report on the attitude of the Bemba in the Mpika Division by Native Commissioner M. H. Melland seems to be the only recorded account of the state of affairs among this erstwhile warlike and intractable people at this time. But there is little reason to doubt that Melland's analysis of the situation in his division held true in other Bemba-occupied areas as well. Melland reported that there had been a marked change in the attitude to the *boma* of the Bemba, who, according to him, had hitherto been obedient and cheerful. But now he could notice

a great deal of discontent, which is on the increase, and that for the first time a tendency to grumble has arisen which is very noticeable coming from a people who have hitherto been conspicuous by their unquestioning and cheerful acquiescence in every rule. There has been a good deal of concerted action among chiefs which has spread to the people. This shows two things very clearly: (i) that the chiefs are able to work in unison, and (ii) that the people follow the chiefs.[134]

Melland's account leaves one with the impression that the Administration was startled by this apparent change of attitude among the Bemba. But considering the developments in the country since the Bemba threw up the sponge ten years before, this was probably not so much a change as a manifestation of a state of mind prevalent among the Bemba since the inception of white rule but which, until the abolition of *chitemene*, was only latent. It is instructive that the B.S.A.C. Administration had, until the shock rebellions of 1896–7 in Southern Rhodesia, also regarded the Shona and the Ndebele as having been too submissive to, and too quietist under, white rule to cause any trouble;[135] and it seems quite clear that its officials were under the same illusion even with regard to the Bemba. The chiefs had in the past differed among themselves and with their people, and no doubt their basic differences remained unresolved; but the critical situation precipitated by the prohibition of *chitemene* demanded at least a semblance of unity against the Administration. For it was quite clear to most people that the abolition of this old-time practice put the very essence of Bemba life in jeopardy. For the first time since the inception of colonial rule the traditional rulers and the ruled were able to put their heads together under one thinking cap, in an effort to achieve one common objective. It is significant in this connection to note, for example, that even factions of chiefs who had been mutually inimical over the years were able to come together and to form a deputation that went to see Native Commissioner Melland about *chitemene*. Early in 1908 the Mwamba party represented by Chiefs Mpepo and Luchembe on the one hand and the Chitimukulu faction represented by Chiefs Chikwanda, Changala, Kapoko and Lukaka on the other, sent a delegation to Mpika *Boma* to urge for the restitution of *chitemene*.[136] This was a clear illustration of the high spirit of co-operation that, in a moment of 'national' crisis, suddenly entered the minds of the African rulers. For, as Melland pointed out, prior to the formation of such a deputation, there must have been a great deal of co-ordination in the transmission of messages to and from each chief.[137]

While the chiefs were discussing the *chitemene* problem with the Administration officials at Mpika, the village people, for their part, could only show their resentment of the Administration's measures in some form of passive resistance. Whereas previously Native Commissioners on tours were warmly received, and given fowls and baskets of flour, or baskets of wild fruit in times of famine—with the customary apologies for giving the visiting officials so little food—this time things had dramatically changed. Melland noticed with perplexity during tours of his division that the people in the villages he visited had

systematically organised a boycott to which I have been subjected by the Awemba all the year. . . . On ulendo [tour] I have not in any Awemba village whatever received a single basket of flour, potatoes, etc., nor even a fowl. Formerly in such years as 1906 when the country was devastated by locusts, and there was no food, the chiefs brought up a fowl or two, and perhaps a basket of wild fruit, or mushrooms, and apologised for having no flour, but this year . . . no mention has been made of the customary presence, nor any reference to the lack of it.[138]

In a situation of this nature, where past grievances no doubt had a cumulative effect on the people, and combined with new ones to produce an even greater impact on their thinking, it is difficult to assign any specific degree of 'causal responsibility' to any one single factor. It may well be, for instance, as Melland's report suggests, that this attitude was also the result of the failure of the salt supply in the salt pans near the Bangweulu swamps and of the people's long-standing dislike of gathering wild rubber.[139] But while the immediate cause of this 'wind of change' was evidently the abolition of *chitemene* and *mitanda*, there is no doubt that other factors like the hut tax, game laws and forced labour played an important part in moulding this mood of disenchantment. As Melland commented:

Our interference with their liberty, the rigid collection of the hut tax, the abolition of 'fitemene' . . . and the prevention of free migration . . . pass regulations, game regulations, etc., etc., worry them and they never quite know what is coming next. All our acts and rules are questioned, though obeyed, and every innovation such as recruiting labour for the mines and collecting rubber is viewed with suspicion. All these things tend to aggravate the longing for the old days and discontent with present.[140]

This longing for the past appears to have been a mixture of emotions. While the chiefs were hankering after the power they had lost to the white man, the common people wanted to rid themselves of white rule, which had brought in its trail the new social and economic inconveniences they were now suffering. But this did not necessarily mean that white rule would be replaced by the old cruel rule of the chiefs. Melland's analysis of this nostalgia, although it appears in some respects a kind of rationalisation of the situation, is interesting. He was of the view that the ugly mood which the Bemba were in was the natural outcome of European rule forcing a warlike tribe to live in peace and on equal terms with their former subject tribes. It was, he said,

the inevitable result of a reign of peace and quiet coming to a land which was formerly held by a warlike tribe. The chiefs had great power and lost it. Is it not natural that they chafe under our rule? The people were the 'bosses' of the neighbouring tribes; is it not natural that they fail to see much advantage in a system which makes the Wawisa and other 'inferior' tribes equal in the eyes of the law with them? A new generation has arisen to which the cruelties of the old chiefs is but hearsay; is it not natural enough that they think the old days of raiding and conquering are superior to the present days of hut tax, pass and census regulations?[141]

Melland's pontifications about the pre colonial history of the Bemba and about the demands of white rule as the causes of their political ferment seems to have been a serious attempt on the part of the Company Administration officials to analyse and understand the thinking and attitudes of a people whose apparent docility they had taken for granted since the inception of Company rule a decade before. But like a Salisbury resident magistrate's realisation, after the outbreak of the Southern Rhodesian risings in 1896, that the Shona were not after all as content under white rule as they had hitherto been presumed to be by the Company officials,[142] Melland's report was little more than a 'post-mortem' —an attempt to explain a disconcerting *fait accompli*.

3. THE RESPONSE OF THE TRADITIONAL AUTHORITIES

What were the reactions of the traditional rulers to this cathartic situation brought about by the ill-advised policies of the Administration on *chitemene*? It will be recalled that reference was made earlier to the chiefs' concern at the abolition of their time-honoured system of cultivation and to the fact that they had made representations to Native Commissioner Melland at Mpika on the matter. This initiative on the part of the traditional rulers seemed to the Administration to be more than a mere coincidence of interests between the chiefs and their people. It seemed a definite, if subtle, revulsion against white rule, and the Company officials—or at least Melland—saw the traditional authorities as leaders of a popular movement against the *boma*. As Melland put it:

I feel certain, although it is hard to explain why, as most of the signs are so trivial in themselves, that there is growing dissatisfaction among the Awemba, and that the chiefs, who outwardly pose as friends of the boma and who still do all they can to assist us, and to see that our direct

orders are obeyed, are doing what they can to encourage this dissatisfaction, thereby tending to be the popular leaders of an 'anti-boma'
feeling. Some little trifle or other shows this tendency in every Awemba
village one visits though there is little to record.[143]

While holding the view that peace, and the egalitarian policy
of the Administration towards all tribes, were the 'principal cause
for the extraordinary speed with which the attitude of the
Awemba had changed', Melland also believed that this misguided
policy of the government which helped cause Bemba discontent
was 'partly one of system, and partly one of failure to comprehend
the native outlook, namely in the administration of justice'.[144] In
previous years, he said, Native Commissioners, in their relentless
efforts to make their authority felt, frequently visited every corner
of the country and thereby maintained very close contact with the
people. However, as officials became busier, as a result of increased administrative work, they toured their areas less frequently
and delegated some of their responsibilities to the chiefs, who, first
reluctantly, but later willingly, executed them, and when Native
Commissioners did go out into the country they tended to con-
centrate too much on checking tax papers and the census, and
rarely had time to speak to the people and listen to their complaints. At the *boma* they were often too busy to see the chiefs or
people who came to lay complaints with them, and consequently
few people went to the *boma* for help. This apparent remissness on
the part of the Administration, in conjunction with the amalgamation of villages following the abolition of *mitanda* and *chitemene*,
helped the chiefs recoup their lost power. The Native Commissioner, as Melland put it, became

in the eyes of the natives more of an unsympathetic foreign ruler, than
a 'guide, philosopher and friend'. They have ceased to confer with him
about their small troubles, because he is always too busy to listen. He
taxes, he fines, he imprisons, he represents the 'BOMA', but he has
ceased to help them in all their little worries, simply because he has no
time. When he visits them he is no longer able to sit and chat about the
village, the crops, the health, etc., he is absorbed in the taxes, the census book . . . When they visit him he is busy with transport, accounts
or mails. Who then has taken his place? To whom do the natives turn
when they find their bwana too busy? They have gone back to their
chiefs.[145]

Whether in fact a Company official was ever regarded by Africans as a 'guide, philosopher, and friend' is open to question. But Melland's argument that the unrest among the Bemba was the result of lack of contact between *boma* officials and the village communities was a hypothesis which colonial officials appear to have used from time to time to explain away virulent African reaction to white rule. It was, as will be seen later, to be used by P. J. Macdonell, a judge of the High Court, to explain the Watch Tower disturbances in the Northern Province during and after the First World War,[146] and by the Chief Secretary to the Northern Rhodesia government as one of the causes of the 1935 disturbances on the Copperbelt.[147]

The chiefs were, of course, far from being passive bystanders in this political catharsis. They were, as Melland observed, 'extremely intelligent men for the most part, and saw their opportunity'. The insistence by the Administration, in the face of increased pressure of work, that they should try minor criminal and practically all civil cases 'made them the real rulers of the country, or rather the real instruments of . . . [white] rule'. For they used their new powers to become popular by whipping up popular grievances against the *boma*. They were, as Melland observed, 'not the CAUSE of the present attitude of the Awemba, but they form the inspiration and encouragement to that discontented attitude'.[148]

As has been pointed out earlier, the dissatisfaction caused by the abolition of *mitanda*, let alone *chitemene*, was widespread among the Bemba. In the Luena (Luwingu) Division, where the Bemba population in 1908 was estimated at 6,000, it was also apparent that the Administration's interference with the Bemba's system of cultivation was causing great unrest. The Native Commissioner there reported that chiefs and headmen were always grumbling and 'openly stating that although they were tax-paying and law abiding, their food was taken away from them, and their women and children made to suffer'.[149] This unsettled state of affairs in Bemba country was naturally very disturbing to the Administration. Although the situation did not seem to pose any immediate danger, it was felt that it needed watching very closely because, as Melland argued, it had

undoubtedly an element of danger in it and it has developed with extraordinary rapidity in the past twelve months. We have caused that rapid development, though the rest of it was beyond our control. It rests with us to check the development.[150]

The question that the Administration had to ask itself was how this development was to be checked. Quite obviously a reversion to *mitanda*, as far as the administrators were concerned, was unthinkable. Melland suggested a 'go back to the people' campaign by officials, so that by resuscitating the old meticulous tour inspections Native Commissioners might win back the confidence of the people, and make them switch their loyalties from the chiefs to the *boma*. He proposed that chiefs should not be given any more powers; nor on the other hand should their existing powers be reduced. For he was anxious to see that the power to try those cases which in the past tended to cause friction between the people and the *boma* should remain with the chiefs. Particular stress was also laid on the importance of keeping close watch on certain chiefs who were considered subversive, and Melland recommended that any chiefs caught actually preaching sedition or spreading discontent should be exiled from Bemba-land. He drew special attention to the point that 'chiefs such as Ponde of Kasama district, or Luchembe of this [Mpika] Division, men with real power, are the greatest source of danger'.[151]

It is possible that if all these measures had been adopted by the Administration, their combined effect on the people would, from the point of view of the officials, have been salutary. But perhaps the most effective single factor to this end was the official authority for the re-establishment of *chitemene*, which was given at the beginning of 1909. In 1910, the Native Commissioner for Mpika Division reported that during the previous year everything in his division had proceeded 'very smoothly', because *chitemene* had been re-established and the Bemba's 'main grievance has vanished'.[152]

Melland's report, it will be recalled, had made reference to the Bemba traditional rulers chafing under colonial rule, because they 'had great power and lost it', and to a general longing for the past, when the burdens and indignities of colonial subjugation were unknown.[153] This nostalgia, this vain hope, which was also sensed by Cullen Gouldsbury during the same period, that 'the [white] strangers will eventually pass westward and leave him [the African] in peace'[154] was very clearly expressed by a Bemba headman named Tembwe during an incident in his village, just when popular discontent over the abolition of *chitemene* was at its peak.

Early in March 1908, a certain Kabutu, a *Boma* Messenger, was sent to patrol the eastern border of Chartered Company territory in the Mirongo Division. While he was at Tembwe's on his way to the border, he heard a certain Chilupe and other residents of the village ask a certain Malembeka from Mabanga's village for a pass. When Kabutu intervened to advise that as Malembeka had come from a village in the same area he did not need a pass, he (Kabutu), his wives and son were beaten up by Tembwe's people. Kabutu thereupon sent a message to a Mr Jossclin, a Company official nearby, for help, and in time, Levi, a *capitao*, and Mpepo, a constable, arrived on the scene to find all Tembwe's people gathered. A critical situation then arose, in which blood was almost spilt: the people threatened the *boma* officials with sticks, spears, bows and arrows and would have released the prisoners accompanying the officials had Levi and Mpepo not taken up their guns to face Tembwe's angry people.[155] Tembwe himself and his sons played a very active part in the riot, and what they are reported to have said then conveys the mood of a people entertaining hopes that whitemen would some day leave the country and its social and political integrity restored. Levi's evidence before Magistrate Robert Young on 26 March 1908 at Mirongo, gives an indication of this nostalgia and throws into bold relief the Bemba's deep-seated resentment to white rule and its African catspaws:

Daniel Son of Tembwe came and said Why do you stand there with guns? I said: What do all the men want with spears, bows and arrows and sticks? It looks like war. . . . Tembwe came to me and said: 'Take back this money to the whiteman (20s.) [which was probably an allowance paid to Tembwe as a headman by the Administration]. I don't want it. There is medicine on it. I refused to take the money and he threw it down. His son, Chitumbi took it up and said to his father: Why do you refuse the money now? Tembwe said: Why do you Levi come here always? Have I committed adultery with your wife or the Policeman's wife? I replied: I am doing what I am told by my master. Tembwe said: Some day the white man will go and you will be left and I shall kill you. One day when I catch you alone I will kill you. Constable Mpepo said: If you talk like that you won't get money from the Bwana. Tembwe said: It doesn't matter. I will stay here.[156]

After the restitution of *chitemene* in 1909 and the rearrangement in 1910 into smaller but manageable units of the big villages which were formed out of *mitanda* in 1906, the alliance against the Administration between the chiefs and the people broke down because the basis on which it had been established no longer existed. The feuds and the fissionary tendencies that characterised the relations between the ruled and their tradional rulers in the colonial situation once again came into play. The chiefs, as was the case in the past, again found themselves in the difficult inter-calary position of trying to avoid incurring the wrath of the Administration without at the same time falling out of favour with their own people. This difficult role was, of course, a reflec-tion of their relations with the colonial authorities on the one hand and their subjects on the other. The chief was, as one anthropologist has written of the position of the traditional rulers in more recent colonial situations,

an officer of . . . Government and should represent its interests and values to the African people; and yet he should stand on his people's behalf for the values and interests which they esteem. The chief thus takes on his shoulders the conflict between the authority of the colonial Government, and the aspirations of his own people . . . [157]

In trying to obtain the co-operation of the chiefs, the Admini-stration carried out a carefully worked out programme of social and political regimentation of the traditional rulers. This, in some cases, took the form of a psychological campaign of persuasion and intimidation, as was the case with Chief Milambo of the Unga, whose country had not until the end of 1908 been visited by a whiteman, and who until the following year, despite official pressures, had refused to recognise the government and to visit the *boma*.[158] In most cases, chiefs were exhorted to assume more responsibility in the running of the affairs of the country. For the experience of administrators in the lake and swamp area, for example, had shown that the direct use of force by the Admini-stration to make the people pay tax did not produce the desired results. The imprisonment in 1910 of some one hundred Bisa and

Unga tax defaulters, for example, tended to drive these lacustrine people back into the swamps,[159] which the government did not wish to see happen. Thus, rather than put the people under such direct hard-and-fast discipline, the Administration decided to foster the old tribal norms of discipline as far as possible by upholding, as much as it could, the authority of the chiefs and 'their approved headmen', and by encouraging the hearing of civil cases by chiefs.[160] Chiefs were made to understand that

if they behave as chiefs, and not as mere nonentities who give their names to pieces of country and receive a monthly pittance from the Administration, they are backed up by the Boma, and so their prestige and influence among their people increase.[161]

This was an ironical position, of which the chiefs were only too painfully aware. They were being enjoined and were expected to 'behave like chiefs', with all the powers of traditional rulers, at a time when they had lost their influence and had ceased to be the repository of all authority and were in fact little more than political middlemen, sandwiched between a stern and peremptory white administration and politically disenchanted and critical subjects. Indeed, it seems one of the contradictions inherent in the operation of colonial rule that the ruling class of a colonial people should have been expected to exercise fully its traditional functions and at the same time, without fear of prejudicing its own traditional authority, take orders from people outside the indigenous political framework, a framework within which such functions were best executed. For although there was an appreciable degree of co-operation between the traditional authorities and the white administration, there often were problem areas in which, because African norms and European values were in conflict, the chiefs' interests were at variance with those of the Administration.

It was no doubt due to the awkwardness of this ambivalent role they were called upon to play that certain chiefs did not take kindly to being used as instruments of white rule. Some, like the Bemba chief, Shimumbi, living near Lake Bangweulu, whom the Luwingu Native Commissioner once described as 'a cunning and calculating schemer ... apt to lose—and show the loss [of]—his temper',[162] were more forthright in expressing their resentment at European rule. Shimumbi was so intensely 'anti-*boma*' that the

Administration had to suspend him from the chieftainship in an effort to make him submit to Chartered Company authority.[163] And even after this was done, the Native Commissioner did not stop treating him as a dangerous character. He pointed out that 'were it not for the fact that he [Shimumbi] might be described as intensely unpopular among the people he would no doubt require to be carefully watched'.[164] Others, like the Bisa chief, Matipa, sought their way out of the impasse by being double-faced. Matipa appeared submissive to the *boma* and even zealous about the promotion of its interests in the presence of a white official; but once left alone, he was, as the Assistant Native Commissioner for Luwingu put it, 'a man of words only, not deeds'.[165] He was afraid of his people but wished the *boma* not to know this.[166]

There were, of course, a few chiefs like Tungati of the Bemba, and Mulongwe of the Bisa, who were outright collaborators with the Administration.[167] But these seem to have been a small category. For, as the Native Commissioner for Luwingu observed, it was generally those chiefs 'who have very little power [who] frequently visit the station [*boma*] or meet the Native Commissioner ...'[168] But, quite apart from the sheer desire to enhance their prestige and influence, such chiefs may have been drawn into co-operation with the Administration by the pecuniary benefits which usually went with such submission; or, as Max Gluckman has observed of the Zulu traditional rulers at about the same time, they may have sought co-operation with the colonial authorities out of conflict within their clans or tribes.[169] Most chiefs, however, seem to have assumed an attitude very much like that of Matipa, which was one of prevarication and double-dealing and which, under the circumstances, appeared the most reasonable to follow.

One of the problems over which the chiefs' sense of obligation to the Administration on the one hand, and to their people on the other, was often pitiably divided was the recruitment of unpaid labour for government road work and other projects, the onus of which fell squarely on chiefs and headmen. Chiefs were expected to supply free labour whenever the Administration wanted it, and if they failed to supply any labour at all they were punished. On the other hand, if they carried out their orders to the satisfaction of the *boma*, they stood the risk of being unpopular with their people.[170] This was an unenviable position, of which even the Administration was well aware, and which it tried to resolve. In 1912 the Native Commissioner for Luwingu complained that chiefs in his area were showing little appreciation of their responsibility to the *boma*, not only in regard to the supplying of free labour but in regard to the collection of the hut tax as well. He recommended, as a corrective measure for their shortcomings, that allowances paid to them should vary according to the extent to which they co-operated with the Administration.[171] Whether this was the best means of winning the co-operation of the traditional rulers remained to be seen. However, the real difficulty, as the Native Commissioner later realised, was that the chiefs felt that since the advent of white rule they had lost all their traditional power.[172] This sense of helplessness on the part of the traditional authorities tended to make them vacillate in the execution of the responsibilities vested in them by the Administration.

Not unusually, these vacillating tactics betrayed the chiefs' own sympathies before *boma* officials. The powers of arrest they were given in order to apprehend any of their people who disobeyed their 'lawful orders' did not seem to make their hold on the people any firmer. They remained unwilling to act as policemen for the Administration against their own people, because whenever they did so the only results they achieved were 'slights, insults, abuse and general unpopularity, and possibly a gradual dispersal of their people'.[173] It was pointed out to the chiefs that although the results of their efforts to assist the colonial authorities were bad, such set-backs would be circumvented if they promptly arrested those who interfered with the exercise of their powers of arrest and those who left their villages without permission. For, so the Administration argued, in this way the chiefs would acquire real influence and power.[174] But in spite of these exhortations they continued to pursue their convenient, but manifestly perilous, policy of 'discretionary alignment', which often meant siding with their people, at least tacitly, against the Administration. The Native Commissioner for Luwingu, after studying the workings of the new policy, observed that

the chiefs are fond of making vague and general complaints to the official of the intractability and disobedience and insolence of their people; when asked to name a definite offender and give details of his offence they cannot, and more probably dare not, for fear of unpopularity among their people . . . It does their influence less harm to ignore offences altogether than to have a man accused by them found not guilty and discharged.[175]

While this three-cornered warring relationship between the Administration, the traditional authorities and the people continued to characterise the mechanics of colonial rule, there were conflicts among the traditional rulers themselves. With the cessation of tribal wars and as European rule entrenched itself—emitting in the process some liberalising influence on the erstwhile strained inter-tribal relations—a new phenomenon developed on the African political scene which was to be a common feature during the inter-war years. Some chiefs and headmen—a few of them being of doubtful historical standing—began asserting their independence, recanting recognition of the suzerainty of their former overlords. They laid claim to pieces of territory which, they argued, were theirs by right but which were placed in wrong hands. Boundaries drawn up by the Administration were challenged and alterations sought. Certain existing chieftaincies took advantage of the presence of an ill-informed alien administration to expand at the expense of others, while decadent dynasties sought to reclaim their lost positions from the debris of the nineteenth-century tribal wars. 'Sub-imperialism'—if that is the right word to describe this new phenomenon of expansionist chieftaincies under white rule—was, however, until after World War I a rare development, since it seems to have burst into view after the traditional authorities had come to appreciate their new responsibilities, following many years of political regimentation by the Administration. What was common during the period before the war broke out was the resurrection of moribund chieftaincies, which were mostly non-Bemba dynasties wanting to assert their rights against their former Bemba rulers.

One of the most typical examples of these 'revivalist' dynasties is the case that was reported among the Lungu of the Mporokoso Division by the Native Commissioner there at the turn of the century. Chief Kaliminwa's authority was being challenged by another Lungu of royal parentage, Tomboshalo. Kaliminwa, son of Kalangu, and whose mother, Musanta, had tenuous connections with the Lungu royal family, was not generally regarded as a member of the Lungu royal family, and apparently owed his position to his prowess and successes during the Bemba wars towards the close of the last century, as a result of which Mwamba Mubanga Chipoya gave him his daughter, Nakabwe, for a wife.[176] Although there were some Bemba people in his area, the majority of Kaliminwa's subjects were Lungu. Freed from fear of the Bemba by the advent of the white administration, the Lungu made several attempts to regain the country for the Lungu royal family, which had been driven out during the Bemba invasions of the last century. Indeed, during the period 1901–2, having taken advantage of the fact that there was then no Administration official at Mporokoso *Boma*, they gained considerable ground.[177]

This caused Kaliminwa some concern, as his position was threatened. He immediately appealed to the Administration for help, and in 1903 the Native Commissioner toured the chief's area to hold meetings with dissident local chiefs and headmen. Although some of them, like Katila, chose to leave the country rather than submit to Kaliminwa, and others, like Mukumi and Kopeka, were persuaded to accept the *status quo*, men like Tomboshalo remained unflinchingly opposed to Kaliminwa's rule and considered the chief a usurper, and his dynasty a relic of Bemba rule. Tomboshalo gathered a band of men around him, armed with spears, bows and arrows, ready to defy Kaliminwa's authority as the latter went round the country with the Native Commissioner. At Ngoli's village, where they were found gathered by the touring party, Tomboshalo and his men impertinently refused to pay respects to the chief and walked away on the arrival of the Native Commissioner.[178]

His personal ambition apart, Tomboshalo seems to have been a bitter man. In his youth he appears to have been sold into slavery to the Ngoni by the Bemba, and when he was freed he lived in exile at the Nyamukolo mission of the London Missionary Society. In the meantime the territory that belonged to his late father, Chibwe, was being administered as part of Kaliminwa's country. It was therefore perhaps understandable that, after several years of lowly life, he should have made strenuous efforts to regain the comforts of an office which, he felt, rightly belonged to him. He was, moreover, given missionary encouragement in his struggle to oust Kaliminwa whilst he was at Nyamukolo, where,

as the Native Commissioner regretfully put it, 'he had unfortunately been backed by Mr Hemans, a black missionary of L.M.S.,
to attempt to re-establish himself in his father's land'.[179] His unbending determination was only tempered by the Native Commissioner's quiet, if ruthless, ingenuity. The headmen of surrounding villages who supported Tomboshalo's cause were called into
the Native Commissioner's tent individually one day and ordered
to go back to their villages and to desist from involving themselves in Tomboshalo's seemingly ridiculous claims; Tomboshalo
was thus left practically alone, and in the circumstances had to
acknowledge defeat, especially after his right-hand men were
punished following an all-night *indaba* at the Native Commissioner's camp. Tomboshalo agreed to recognise Kaliminwa's right
to the country, which the latter had won by conquest. On this
basis, the Native Commissioner considered that no punishment
should be inflicted upon Tomboshalo, and he was allowed to
retain his village under Kaliminwa.[180]

Later events were, however, to prove that Tomboshalo had not
in fact accepted the settlement reached at the Native Commissioner's nocturnal *indaba*. In May the following year he made
another effort to regain his father's country, and rather than face
the Native Commissioner of Mporokoso again, he went to lay
his claim before the magistrate at Abercorn (Mbala).[181] However,
as his trip to Abercorn coincided with that of the Native Commissioner for Mporokoso, he was unable to say anything against
the magistrate's order that he should go back to his village and
accept the suzerainty of Kaliminwa. But when he returned home
he again refused to recognise Kaliminwa, and told the local people
that his renewed defiance of his overlord's authority was given
rein by the Abercorn magistrate's findings in his case. Only after
a few weeks in prison at Mikomba in the middle of 1904 was he
made to live a quiet life.[182]

These attempts by the Lungu to divest themselves of the last
remnants of Bemba political control were not confined to the
Mporokoso Division alone. In the Abercorn (Mbala) Division,
owing to incessant boundary disputes between the Bemba and the
Lungu, the Native Commissioner was, in August 1911, forced to
call a meeting of chiefs in the area to discuss and delineate chief-
dom boundaries in the south-west of the Division. The Bemba
were represented by Chief Chilangwa and representatives from

Chiefs Chimbola, Fungo and Chisanga Ponde, and the Lungu by Chiefs Chitanga, Mungomba, Chundu and Kasongoleka.[183] After a protracted discussion, and on advice by Native Commissioner Henry C. Gouldsbury and magistrate C. P. Chesnaye, the two parties agreed that the Luombe and Luela streams should become the boundary dividing their people, the south of it being Bemba territory and the north Lungu. In consequence of this arrangement, it was found imperative that both Chief Mungomba, who had hitherto been living in Chisanga Ponde's area, and Chitangwa, whose village was situated in Chief Fungo's country south of the new boundary, should either move north or recognise the Bemba chiefs of the areas in which they lived. But both Lungu chiefs refused to do either, and only removed their villages after an ultimatum by the Administration.[184]

While the Lungu in the northern part of the Division were disengaging themselves from the waning clutches of Bemba influence, the Bisa in the south under Chief Nkuka were also remonstrating with their Bemba overlords. In 1911, and again in 1912, they complained to the Administration that Chief Chikwanda, who had in 1909 resigned the Nkulaship to return to his country in Mpika Division,[185] was continually worrying them and forcing them to run out to work for him. Furthermore, they said, he had once commandeered some of their salt. As a result of Chikwanda's high-handedness, the Bisa villages around Mpika *Boma*, like Chipelembe, Mwansabamba and Chipumba, were threatening to leave the chief's country. It was only after the Native Commissioner had punished Chikwanda and 'made him refund the salt and instructed him not to worry these people too much in the future' that the impending Bisa exodus was stemmed.[186] This incident was only the beginning of the protracted and tangled dispute between Chief Chikwanda and the Bisa chief, Nkuka (which will be discussed later in this study), and which is probably the most telling example of the ever-recurring attempts by representatives of tribes which were once under Bemba rule to gain chieftain rights over certain territories.

4. THE EFFECTS OF SOCIAL CHANGE: THE 'NEW MEN'

If popular resentment in the Northern Province against forced labour, the hut tax and other forms of colonial pressures had placed the traditional rulers in an embarrassing and helpless position, even in the exercise of their residuary traditional authority, migrant labour and its avowed illuminism certainly added more fuel to the simmering pot of African discontent with which the chiefs and the Administration alike were faced. The introduction of the hut tax in 1901 and, not unnaturally, the desire to earn money and acquire wealth drove hundreds of young men to places of employment outside their home areas. It will be recalled that only three years after the hut tax was introduced in North-eastern Rhodesia, the White Fathers at Chilonga Mission had reported that a few young men from around the mission area had left 'for work in the mines of Salisbury', and in 1908 they were again to report that 'several groups of men between 30 and 40 years of age' had left the area for Southern Rhodesia.[187] So engrained, it seems, was labour migration in the social and economic life of the Northern Province's population even before World War I that in 1913 the Native Commissioner for Mpika had complained that there were too few men left in his division to do the necessary *chitemene* work, and as a result, food production was at starvation level, and this in turn made even more men leave their villages in search of employment in industrial centres.[188] The Lungu and the Mambwe would probably have been in the same parlous position but for the fact they occupied grasslands on which women were able to make mounds to provide humus-rich gardens on which they grew crops.[189] In the Luwingu Division, where, owing to the outbreak of sleeping-sickness in the area in 1908, it was decided to stop labour migration for sometime in order to prevent the spreading of the disease, the Administration faced some kind of unrest.[190] The temporary stoppage of the flow of labour to Southern Rhodesia was, as the Native Commissioner put it, 'viewed with dismay by the surprisingly large numbers who have been there'.[191] The Bisa and the Unga, who, as the Native Commissioner recalled, had 'always been difficult to deal with', were now paying their taxes and no longer fled into the swamps at the sight of *boma* officials.[192] But the stoppage of labour migration seemed to have brought about a dramatic change in their attitude, much of which the Native Commissioner ascribed to 'these men [who] having thus gone far afield and recounted their experiences on their return' were turning the people against the Administration. Their influence, reported the Native Commissioner, was so infectious that as long as local employment was not available and people continued to go across the Zambezi for work, the people's confidence in the Administration would not grow any greater.[193]

The influence of migrant labour on local African political thinking was undoubtedly very significant. Commenting on Melland's report on the changed attitude of the Bemba towards the *boma*, the Native Commissioner for Luwingu argued that this change was partly due to different experiences of a number of young men who had served in the King's African Rifles, the Barotse Native Police, on the Rand and in other places of employment outside the Northern Province.[194] This, he said, was 'an unfortunate but necessary consequence of [their] having come into contact with [European] civilisation'.[195]

Not only did returning labourers, with their wealth of experience of living conditions in urban areas, question the moral and political integrity of Chartered Company rule in the province, but, with their pocketfuls of money and boxfuls of clothing, they also looked down upon the chiefs, who, although once the richest men in the country, were now the poorest, their only material advantage being the fact that they were exempt from paying the hut tax and were still able to demand free labour from their people.[196] The allowances they received from the Administration, which had not been increased since they were introduced at the turn of the century,[197] were too meagre to enhance their prestige among their subjects. With wealth—invariably the basis of power among the ruling class—lacking, the chiefs were unable to command the respect which their position in society deserved. Thus, as the Luwingu Native Commissioner observed, it must have been difficult for

an ordinary native who comes from the mines with several pounds in cash and a box full of clothing, and who, like some white people, is inclined to measure importance by material wealth, to pay much attention to their chief, whose only income, though sure, is very small.[198]

This contempt for authority seemed especially obvious after 1910. While previously labour recruits who returned home seemed 'comparatively unspoilt' to the authorities, repatriates after this period came back full of self-importance. The Native Commissioner for Luwingu reported that they appeared to have 'a contempt for all authority, and many complaints have been made by chiefs and headmen of their insolence and intractability'.[199] At a meeting of chiefs held by the Administration on 6 July, 1913, at Kasama, Chitimukulu Ponde complained that people had lost respect for chiefs, because few turned up, when called upon, to make chief's gardens.[200] From the Mpika Division, at this very time, the Native Commissioner reported that it was extremely difficult—even at exceptionally good wage rates like those offered by the Congo Pedicle Boundary Commission—to get the necessary number of men for local employment.[201] He recalled that whereas in previous years Africans had regarded it as a duty to oblige when called upon by the *boma* to work, they now seemed

to be growing a little more independent, be disinclined for work unless they actually need money. The money imported from the South must have something to do with this, as well as the engagement by the railways, the N[orth] W[estern] R[hodesia] mines, the Boundary Commission at higher than local rates of wages. . . . This spirit of independence need not yet be seriously marked but it seems to me important that we should check it within reason, where we can and as long as we can.[202]

It was not only the men who had been to Southern Rhodesia or to the Broken Hill mines who proved difficult to the *boma* or the traditional authorities when they returned to their villages; but even those who worked as carriers of government mail or goods, or porters for itinerant Administration officials within North-eastern Rhodesia were able to imbibe new ideas, and emulate the behaviour towards officials of people with whom they came into contact outside their own tribal societies. The behaviour of a group of young men in Chief Chiyalula's village in the Luwingu Division, who had just returned from Fort Jameson in the Eastern Luangwa (later called the Eastern) Province was very illustrative of this type of 'new men'.

Ponde, Mwansakombe, Mwansa, Musenga, Namansaka, Mwila and Katuta—all Bisa men of Chief Chiyalula's village—had just returned from Fort Jameson, when they made it clear to the chief that they would never give *Boma* Messengers accommodation when the latter came to the village on their usual tax-collecting errands. They considered that the Administration had no right to demand that chiefs and their people should provide accommodation for its officials. Ponde and Mwansakombe, bragging about their experiences in Fort Jameson, told Chief Chiyalula: 'The Angoni show but little respect to the police, so we, when the Messengers come, or police, shall beat them and refuse them our huts.'[203]

Not long after these words were said, four messengers visited Chief Chiyalula's village. The chief, in conformity with established practice, showed Messenger Kawimbe, who arrived ahead of the other messengers with two prisoners under his escort, Ponde's hut as the one in which Kawimbe and another messenger and the prisoners would spend the night. This signalled the beginning of a riot. Ponde, true to his word, strongly objected to the chief's decision and drove the prisoners out of his hut, beating them and reiterating that he would not lend his hut to the messengers. Messenger Kawimbe, all alone, was unable to handle the situation and decided to await the arrival of Messenger Saidi, who was not very far away from the village. But his decision to defer punitive action against Ponde did not save him from the latter's wrath. After beating the prisoners, Ponde turned on Kawimbe and beat him up, and in the meantime, Ponde's friend, Namansaka charged at Messenger Mukandala, who was just arriving, and bit him in the neck. The chief's intervention only earned him similar punishment at the hands of these Fort Jameson-inspired insurgents.[204]

With the arrival of Messengers Saidi and Mutemwa, the riot entered into a more critical phase. They joined in the fight, but the Messengers were overpowered. Ponde then decided on a *coup de grâce*. He told his men to go and fetch their spears, bows and arrows so that they could drive the Messengers out of the village. The men dispersed in different directions and each one of them later emerged from his hut armed with spears or bows and arrows, while bellicose Ponde was yelling: 'We will kill you, you Messengers who come to disturb us . . .'[205] It is said that bloodshed was only averted when Saidi, apparently the only armed Messenger, fired two cartridges over the heads of the rioters, which sent them scampering into the bush for cover. However, even after this successful show of strength, Saidi still felt unable to arrest the men; he preferred to leave this hazardous responsibility to Chief Chiyalula, whom he told: 'It is your business as a chief'.[206] When ultimately the men appeared in the Native Commissioner's

court, Ponde confessed: 'It is true we were a bit proud after returning from Fort Jameson with plenty of calico'.[207]

It was in these varying forms that Africans in the Northern
Province expressed their resentment of colonial rule in these early
days. When Company rule was established in the province, there
was, as pointed out earlier, a certain amount of complacency on
the part of the Administration; African acquiescence was for the
most part taken for granted. 'In Central Africa,' wrote one of the
architects of *Pax Britannica* in the province, 'there have always
been dominant tribes. For the moment we represent them.' The
African population, he said, 'for the most part appears placid and
contented enough'.[208] This was, of course, too superficial an
assessment as the political ferment over the abolition of *chitemene*
and the popular opposition to forced labour and tax have shown,
and, as will be seen, African opposition to white rule was in fact
to become even more articulate over the next three decades or so.

NOTES

[1] Chinsali District Note Book, p. 231.
[2] Quoted in Stone, *op. cit.*, p. 312.
[3] *Ibid.*, p. 313.
[4] Kayambi Mission Diary, 1 May 1900; 28 January 1903; 27 January 1904.
[5] *Ibid.*, 16 February–June 1900.
[6] Walter Rodney, 'European activity and African reaction in Angola',
Aspects of Central African History, p. 64.
[7] G. C. K. Gwassa and John Iliffe (eds.), *Records of the Maji Maji Rising, Part
One*, Historical Association of Tanzania, No. 4 (Nairobi: East Africa Publishing House, [1968], pp. 3–8.
[8] Ranger, *Revolt in Southern Rhodesia, 1896-7*, pp. 46–88.
[9] *Reports on the Administration of Rhodesia, 1897-8*, pp. 215–216.
[10] Gann, *The Birth of a Plural Society*, p. 78.
[11] *Ibid.*
[12] *Reports on the Administration of Rhodesia*, 1900-2; p. 18.
[13] B.S.A.C. *Directors' Reports and Accounts*, 31 March 1901 and 31 March
1902, p. 26.
[14] B.S.A.C. *Directors' Reports*, 31 March 1899–31 March 1900, p. 34.
[15] *Ibid.*, p. 14.
[16] Gann, *The Birth of a Plural Society*, p. 79.
[17] Idem, *A History of Southern Rhodesia: Early Days to 1934* (London: Chatto
& Windus, 1965), p. 177.
[18] B.S.A.C. *Directors' Reports*, 31 March 1899–31 March 1900, pp. 35–36;
cf. Gann, *A History of Southern Rhodesia*, p. 177.
[19] Gann, *A History of Southern Rhodesia*, pp. 177–178.
[20] *Ibid.*, p. 179.

²¹ R. R. Kuczynski, *Demographic Survey of the British Colonial Empire* (London: O.U.P., 1949), Vol. II, p. 441. Gelfand and Gann give the year for the formation of the R.N.L.B. as 1903; see Gelfand, *op. cit.*, p. 97, and Gann, *A History of Southern Rhodesia*, p. 179.

²² Gann, *loc. cit.*; Gelfand, *op. cit.*, p. 96.

²³ For a discussion of death rates among recruits from Northern Rhodesia and Nyasaland and the various hazards which befell them on their way to or from Southern Rhodesia and the Rand, see Gelfand, *op. cit.*, pp. 97–103.

²⁴ Gann, *loc. cit.*

²⁵ Kuczynski, *loc. cit.*

²⁶ Gelfand, *op. cit.*, p. 97.

²⁷ *Report of the Commission appointed to enquire into the Financial and Economic Position of Northern Rhodesia, 1938* (hereinafter referred to as the *Pim Report*), p. 29.

²⁸ *Ibid.*, pp. 29–30.

²⁹ E. A. G. Robinson, 'The economic problem', *Modern Industry and the African*, ed. J. Merle Davis (London: Macmillan & Co., 1933), p. 155.

³⁰ Gelfand, *op. cit.*, p. 104.

³¹ Chilonga Mission Diary, 9 October 1899.

³² Chamberlain to Gibbs, 1899, NER A1/4/4/8.

³³ Rotberg, *Christian Missionaries*, pp. 33, 60.

³⁴ At the beginning of this century, the estimated population of the whole of North-eastern Rhodesia was about 300,000—a density of barely three people per square mile; see *B.S.A.C. Directors' Reports and Accounts*, 31 March 1899 and 31 March 1900, p. 38; and Kuczynski, *op. cit.*, p. 415, n. 3.

³⁵ Lord Hailey, *An African Survey: a study of problems arising in Africa South of the Sahara* (London: O.U.P., 1938), pp. 603–604.

³⁶ J. C. Mitchell, 'Wage labour and African population movements in Central Africa', *Essays on African Population*, ed. K. M. Barbour and R. M. Prothero (London: Routledge & Kegan Paul, 1961), p. 199.

³⁷ *Ibid.*, p. 608.

³⁸ The term is a corrupted form of the Nyanja word *mtenga-mtenga* (plur., *amtenga-tenga*), which means a porter or carrier for an itinerant government official.

³⁹ Chamberlain to Gibbs, *loc. cit.*

⁴⁰ McKinnon to Capt. Daly, Acting Administrator for North-eastern Rhodesia, 12 July 1898, NER A1/7/1.

⁴¹ Lord Salisbury to the Secretary of the B.S.A.C. (London Office), 16 May 1899; NER A1/4/4/8.

⁴² Chilonga Mission Diary, June 1901.

⁴³ Mpika Division Report, 1904, IN 1/12.

⁴⁴ Kayambi Mission Diary, 29 May 1902.

⁴⁵ Gann, *The Birth of a Plural Society*, p. 83. According to one official report there was no hut tax being levied in North-western Rhodesia, but instead there was an annual poll tax of 10s. for all adult males and an additional 10s. for each wife or concubine a man had after the first one. The two systems of taxation continued until 1914, when the hut tax was abolished and replaced with a poll tax of 5s. and a tax on plural wives of the same amount: *Pim Report*, pp. 111–

112. But according to another report, the hut tax was also levied over a greater part of North-western Rhodesia: see *B.S.A.C. Directors' Report*, 31 March 1906, p. 8.

[46] Robert I. Rotberg, *The Rise of Nationalism in Central Africa* (Harvard University Press, 1966), pp. 39-40.

[47] Gann, *The Birth of a Plural Society*, p. 77.

[48] Van der Horst, *Native Labour in South Africa* (London: O.U.P., 1942), p. 111.

[49] Hailey, *An African Survey*, p. 1647.

[50] Mitchell, *op. cit.*, p. 205.

[51] *Pim Report*, p. 39.

[52] Rotberg, *The Rise of Nationalism in Central Africa*, p. 41.

[53] *Northern Rhodesia Legislative Council Debates* (henceforth to be referred to as *Debates*), p. 198, 27 May 1925.

[54] There was apparently a general belief among Europeans that African men 'lived a life of blissful idleness', 'drinking beer and watching their womenfolk work' and so, because of this belief, Europeans felt the African male should learn to work—for wages; Gann, *A History of Southern Rhodesia*, p. 122.

[55] Kayambi Mission Diary, 1 December 1902.

[56] *Ibid.*, 1 June 1903.

[57] Chilonga Mission Diary, June 1904.

[58] Quoted in Stone, *op. cit.*, p. 5. Kambove is near Jadotville in Katanga.

[59] Gelfand, *op. cit.*, p. 105.

[60] Lord Hailey, *Native Administration in the British African Territories*, p. 21.

[61] *Government Notice No. 1 of 1900*; see also *B.S.A.C. Directors' Reports*, 31 March 1890 and 31 March 1900, p. 37.

[62] *Ibid.*

[63] Wills, *op. cit.*, p. 223.

[64] Report on the system of Native Administration in the Mpika Division, Awemba District, 1904, IN1/12.

[65] Report on the System of Native Administration in the Abercorn Division, Tanganyika Province, 1904, in *ibid.*

[66] Report on the system of Native Administration in the Mpika Division, *loc. cit.*

[67] *Ibid.*

[68] René Lemarchand, *Political Awakening in the Belgian Congo: the Politics of Fragmentation* (Berkeley and Los Angeles: California University Press, 1964), p. 38.

[69] Lord Hailey, *An African Survey*, p. 452.

[70] Report on the system of Native Administration in the Mporokoso Division, Tanganyika District, 1903, IN1/12.

[71] Chinsali District Note Book, p. 231.

[72] Bell to Forbes, 31 August 1896, NER A8/2/2.

[73] *Ibid.*

[74] Dewar to Bell, 9 September 1896, NER A8/2/2.

[75] Bell to Dewar, 9 September 1896, in *ibid.*

[76] Bell to Administrator, 31 August 1896, in *ibid.*

[77] *Ibid.*

[78] Young, 'Awemba history as I have heard it'; *loc. cit.*
[79] Witness Musagala's evidence in the Abercorn Native Criminal Court, 22 August 1899, Tanganyika District Case Records, INH/3/1.
[80] R. Codrington's judgment, in *ibid.*
[81] Interview with Rev. P. B. Mushindo, 27 July 1967, Lubwa Mission, Chinsali.
[82] *Ibid.*
[83] Kayambi Mission Diary, November 1899.
[84] Marshall to Mackay, 1 November 1900, INH/2/2.
[85] Marshall to Mackay, 16 November 1900, in *ibid.*
[86] Marshall to Miller, 12 May 1901, in *ibid.*
[87] Johnstone's temporary journal, 11 April 1904, INH/4/1.
[88] Criminal Case Records, p. 34, Luwingu N.C.'s Court, KSZ/3/2/1.
[89] *Ibid.*
[90] Footnotes by Sheane in *ibid.*
[91] Interview with Chief Chikwanda Chitabanta, 24 July 1967, Mpika.
[92] Lord Passfield to Governor, 7 February 1930, ZA/1/12.
[93] Luwingu (Luena) Report, 1903, KSZ/7/3/1.
[94] Luwingu N.C.'s report for the year ending 31 March 1903, KSZ/7/1/1.
[95] *Ibid.*
[96] *Ibid.*
[97] *Ibid.*
[98] Luwingu N.C.'s report for the year ending 31 March 1908, *loc. cit.*
[99] Luwingu N.C.'s report for the year ending 30 September 1903, *loc. cit.*
[100] *Ibid.*
[101] *Ibid.*
[102] Criminal Case Records, p. 30, Luwingu N.C.'s court, 15 February 1904, KSZ/3/2/1.
[103] *Ibid.*
[104] Such desertions appear to have been common among the African people. An Acting Native Commissioner at Hartley in Southern Rhodesia reported in 1894 that the Shona were also 'in the habit of clearing away from their villages' on the approach of a *boma* official: Ranger, 'The nineteenth century in Southern Rhodesia', *Aspects of Central African History*, p. 146.
[105] Criminal Case Records, p. 30, Luwingu N.C.'s court.
[106] Luwingu N.C.'s report, KSZ/7/1/1.
[107] *Ibid.*
[108] *Ibid.*
[109] Luwingu N.C.'s report for the year ending 31 March 1904, KSZ7/1/1.
[110] The grass probably was to be used for building the N.C.'s camp.
[111] Luwingu N.C.'s report for the year ending 31 March 1904, *loc. cit.*
[112] Gann, *The Birth of a Plural Society*, p. 82; *A History of Northern Rhodesia*, p. 104.
[113] *Mitanda* (sing. *mutanda*), as opposed to normal villages, were settlements in gardens where people lived to protect their crops against vermin. They were usually far away from normal villages and moved as people changed gardens in the *chitemene* cycle. The practice appears to have been followed even in pre-colonial days, except that with the slave raids which increased with the Arab

slave trade during the nineteenth century residence in *mitanda* was, more often than not, very temporary: interview with Donald Siwale, 29 July 1967.

[114] Report on the system of Native Administration in the Mpika Division, IN1/12.

[115] West Awemba Division report for the year ending 31 September 1905, KSZ7/1/1.

[116] West Awemba Division report for the year ending 30 September 1903, in *ibid*.

[117] Kayambi Mission Diary, 4 January 1904.

[118] West Awemba Division report, 30 September 1903, *loc. cit.*

[119] *Ibid.*

[120] *Ibid.*

[121] Report on Native Administration in Mporokoso Division, 1903, IN/1/12.

[122] Report on the System of Native Administration in the Mpika Division, 1904, *loc. cit.*

[123] Acting N.C.'s report on West Awemba Division for the year ending 30 September, 1903, KSZ7/1/1.

[124] Luwingu N.C.'s report for year ending 30 September 1903, *loc. cit.*

[125] Luwingu N.C.'s report for year ending 31 March 1904, *loc. cit.*

[126] Chibonga Mission Diary, 16 August 1906.

[127] *B.S.A.C. Directors' Report and Accounts for the two years ending 31 March 1907*, p. 71.

[128] Chilonga Mission Diary, 16 August 1906. The siting of gardens, and therefore of *mitanda* as well, took into consideration the type and population of trees in an area, and consequently the new restrictions resulted in reduced food production. There was, in fact, partial famine: *Pim Report*, p. 24.

[129] Interview with Rev. P. B. Mushindo. No documentary evidence has been found in the course of this investigation to corroborate the Rev. Mushindo's account, but it seems true that such social ills existed in these villages, judging from their prevalence in *mitanda;* see p. 103 above.

[130] Thomas, *Historical Notes on the Bisa Tribe*, p. 51.

[131] 'Report on the attitude of the Awemba in the Mpika Division, 1908', KSD7/4/2.

[132] Chinsali District Note Book, p. 231.

[133] Report on Native Affairs, 26 March 1909, KSZ7/1/1.

[134] 'Report on the attitude of the Awemba'.

[135] Ranger, *Revolt in Southern Rhodesia*, pp. 26–40.

[136] 'Report on the attitude of the Awemba'.

[137] *Ibid.*

[138] *Ibid.*

[139] *Ibid.*

[140] *Ibid.*

[141] *Ibid.*

[142] Ranger, *loc. cit.*, p. 1.

[143] 'Report on the attitude of the Awemba'.

[144] *Ibid.*

[145] *Ibid.*

[146] Report by P. J. Macdonell to the Administrator, Sir Lawrence A. Wallace, on the Watch Tower movement with special reference to the High Court session at Kasama, 1919, ZA1/10.

[147] *Evidence taken by the Commission appointed to enquire into the Disturbances in the Copperbelt of Northern Rhodesia,* Vol. I (Lusaka: Government Printer, July–September 1935), p. 55.

[148] 'Report on the attitude of the Awemba'.

[149] Native Affairs Report for the year ending 31 March 1909, West Awemba Division, KSZ/7/1/1.

[150] 'Report on the attitude of the Awemba'.

[151] *Ibid.*

[152] Mpika Division Native Affairs Report for the year ending 31 March 1910, KSD/7/1/1.

[153] 'Report on the attitude of the Awemba'.

[154] Gouldsbury, *op. cit.,* p. 153.

[155] Native Court Case Book, Mirongo Station, KTP3/1.

[156] *Ibid.*

[157] Max Gluckman, *Custom and Conflict in Africa* (Oxford: Basil Blackwell, 1959), p. 52.

[158] Luwingu Division report on native affairs for the year ending 31 March 1909, KSZ/7/1/1.

[159] Luwingu Division report for the year 1911–12.

[160] *Ibid.*

[161] Luwingu Division report for 1912–13.

[162] Luwingu Division report for 1911–12.

[163] *Ibid.*

[164] *Ibid.*

[165] Assistant N.C., Luwingu to S.N.A., Fort Jameson, 26 May 1910, KSZ7/1/1.

[166] *Ibid.*

[167] Native Affairs Report for the year ending 31 March 1909, Luwingu.

[168] *Ibid.*

[169] Gluckman, *op. cit.,* p. 151.

[170] Luwingu Division report for 1912–13.

[171] Luwingu Division report for 1911–12.

[172] Luwingu Division report for 1912–13.

[173] *Ibid.*

[174] *Ibid.*

[175] *Ibid.*

[176] Report by N.C., Mporokoso, n.d., KSU/3/1.

[177] *Ibid.*

[178] *Ibid.*

[179] MS. by N.C., Mporokoso, n.d., in *ibid.*

[180] *Ibid.*

[181] *Ibid.*

[182] *Ibid.*

[183] Abercorn District Note Book, p. 92, KTN/1/1.

[184] *Ibid.*

[185] Dispute between Chiefs Chikwanda and Nkuka, ZA/1/9/27/7/1. According to Andrew Roberts, Chikwanda was never installed as Nkula: Roberts, 'A political history of the Bemba', p. 293.

[186] Dispute between Chikwanda and Nkuka, *loc. cit.*

[187] Chilonga Mission Diary, 23 October 1908.

[188] Gann, *The Birth of a Plural Society*, p. 86; *A History o {Northern Rhodesia*, p. 108.

[189] *Ibid.*, p. 109.

[190] Luwingu Division report for the year ending 31 March 1908, KSZ7/1/1.

[191] *Ibid.*

[192] *Ibid.*

[193] *Ibid.*

[194] Luwingu Division report for the year ending 31 March 1909.

[195] *Ibid.*

[196] Luwingu Division report for 1912–13.

[197] *Ibid.*

[198] *Ibid.*

[199] *Ibid.*

[200] Kasama District Note Book, p. 201, KDH/1/1.

[201] Memorandum for the Administrator's visit to Mpika, July 1913, KSD7/3/1.

[202] *Ibid.*

[203] Evidence by Chiyalula in the Luwingu N.C.'s court, 5 January 1905, Criminal Case Records, pp. 2–3, KSZ/5/3/1.

[204] *Ibid.*, pp. 4–5.

[205] *Ibid.*, p. 6.

[206] *Ibid.*

[207] *Ibid.*

[208] Gouldsbury, *op. cit.*, p. 153.

CHAPTER IV

THE POLITICS OF RELIGION:
THE WATCH TOWER MOVEMENT

When World War I broke out in 1914, a period of suspended animation seems to have intruded upon the panorama of African reactions to European rule—reactions which, as the last chapter has tried to show, were becoming increasingly articulate in their manifestation of African resentment against various practices and policies of the Administration. Owing to a lack of complete official records of African reactions to the war—a lack which could well be attributed to the Administration's preoccupation with the war itself—the first three years of the war appear to have been uneventful, and a gap remains unbridged in the history of the Northern Province's political evolution.

However, from a few available records, and from oral sources one is able to form an idea of what was happening in the province during this early period of the war. All available evidence seems to suggest that there was little African opposition to the war before 1917. Writing a year after the cessation of hostilities, Charles Draper, Acting District Commissioner for Tanganyika District, reported that everything had gone on well in his district throughout the war. Chiefs and headmen in the area had always gone to his office with unquestioning promptitude each time he summoned them to discuss matters of state, and they also invariably took his orders 'with expressions of loyalty [and] all volunteered any assistance it was in their power to give'. Draper further reported that although every able-bodied man was expected to turn out and do his share of work as a military porter, 'practically no undue compulsion became necessary'.[1] Another eye-witness of the state of affairs, who was, for a long time employed to recruit and superintend carriers, has asserted that 'there was no resistance or refusal by the African people to carry supplies to Abercorn, where the war was being waged. I gave them instructions and allocations to proceed to Abercorn and there was no resistance to government orders'.[2]

If there was no apparent African resentment to military work for most of the war period, this was mainly due to the psychological and other means which the Administration employed to interest people to come forward for military work. In the first place, Africans were made to understand that they were not merely fighting a European war, but were—which was the most important thing—engaged in the noble task of defending their motherland against white imperialist aggressors. Africans knew Germans, from their limited experience and from hearsay, to be more cruel colonial masters than the English,[3] and the Administration was at pains to portray them as such, in order that the people might fight tooth and nail to avert a possible replacement of a less detestable English administration by a more ruthless German regime.[4] This emotional appeal must have had a profound impact on people living in places like the Abercorn and Isoka Divisions, where the fighting was taking place, and it probably explains the prevalence of the general co-operative attitude in Abercorn about which Draper wrote.

The second method which the Administration applied to attract the labour it needed for the war was the use of economic inducements. This methods was not at all peculiar to the Northern Province; it was also successfully being used in Malawi, where African opposition to the war was articulate from the outset.[5] While recruits were being enticed with these economic blandishments, the morale of the *askari*, the men in the battlefield, was, according to one eye-witness account, sustained, among other things, by promises that the rifles which the soldiers were using during the war would become their own property after victory was won.[6] No evidence has come to light from official sources that in fact the colonial authorities had made these promises, but it is certainly true that the Administration did later award guns to a few chiefs, headmen and ex-servicemen who had rendered loyal service during the war. However, such awards were confined to persons in what the Administration called 'the Districts chiefly concerned' in the war, namely Isoka, Abercorn and Chinsali Districts, which were in the war zone.[7] A general scheme for the rest of the country which the B.S.A.C. Administration had in mind and which would have cost approximately £30,000 was considered too expensive, and disallowed by the War Office in London, which in turn decided that only two hundred Martini-Henry rifles would be distributed to District Commissioners in

Northern Rhodesia for loan to selected chiefs and headmen.[8] But by such devious means the colonial authorities were able to get a measure of co-operation from the African people during the war —co-operation which they would have hardly been able to enjoy in normal times.

The people of the Northern Province perhaps had good cause to exercise such reticence for the greater part of the war. But they could not have for very long lived down the inconveniences and the resentment caused by the rigorous hardships which they were called upon to endure. The heavy loads they were made to carry and the long distances they had to trudge from sources of supplies to the battle line were too exacting even for a people resigned to the hazards of war. In the Abercorn Division, for example, where the total population was estimated at 76,150, with a taxable male population of 16,170, it is said that 'thousands of men and women were employed for carrying periods of from a few days to four months'.[9] Altogether, 11,390 men served as 'front line porters', while about 6,000 women were engaged in casual transport, and 1,000 others in grinding grain brought all the way from the railway line,[10] because food supplies in Isoka, Abercorn and Chinsali Districts were, as the Administration reported, drained to the utmost to feed soldiers and 'the natives parted with more food than they could afford'.[11] 'The percentage of [people] engaged on war work,' wrote Draper somewhat hyperbolically, 'cannot be computed, the numbers being far in excess of the entire population.'[12] So arduous, a contemporary has said, were the conditions under which military porters worked that several of them died during the war,[13] and the Administration also confessed that the strain of the war on the people of the 'North-eastern Districts has been severe'.[14] Thus, although the emotional and political fever to which the war gave rise does not seem to have approximated to that which in Malawi precipitated the John Chilembwe rising of 1915,[15] or to that which in Mozambique helped bring about the Makombe rising of 1917,[16] it had nevertheless such an unsettling effect on the people that they only needed a touch of daring leadership to make them turn against the authorities. It is against this background that the vicissitudes of the activities of the Watch Tower movement must be examined. For the startling and alarming success with which the movement took root, especially in the areas most affected by the war, could not be understood without reference to the circumstances in which the sect was operating.

It must, indeed, be testimony to the above postulate that the first outbreak of Watch Tower activity should have occurred in the Isoka and Abercorn Divisions, among the Mambwe, the Namwanga and their offshoot, the Iwa, who were most affected by the war. In October 1917 a party of six Africans—Hanoc Shindano,[17] Posa, Simuchimba, Leviticus Kanchele, Yapangwa, and Makomba—were deported from Southern Rhodesia because of their Watch Tower activities.[18] They were all natives of the Tanganyika District, and some of them, like Kanchele and Shindano, had been students of Donald Siwale at Mwenzo mission before they trekked south in search of employment.[19] On their way back home they preached their new gospel in the Mkushi and Serenje Divisions, before finally establishing themselves among the Iwa people of Chiefs Kafwimbi and Terefya and among the Namwanga under Chieftainess Waitwika in the Isoka Division. Later the movement spread to the Abercorn Division, where it was headed by Hanoc Shindano. With his headquarters at Tukamulozya's village, Shindano deployed deacons and preachers all over the district to make the Watch Tower movement so popular and belligerent that it immediately became a source of worry for the Administration.

Considering the circumstances surrounding their return from Southern Rhodesia, the six Watch Tower apostles were understandably very bitter men. But they were also fairly enlightened people, who learnt quite a lot during their terms of employment in Southern Rhodesia's industrial and agricultural centres. As well as suffering indignities at the hands of their European masters, they also saw how vast the opportunities to better material welfare were in the new economic order, but painfully realised that the same European order of things was not permissive of African advance, at least the advancement that was commensurate with their expectations. This basic dissatisfaction, coupled with the poisoned atmosphere of a European war, made them ready imbibers of the millenarian doctrines of the Watch Tower movement, which, under the fiery leadership of Elliot Kamwana, had by 1915 gained considerable ground in Nyasaland, and, through Nyasa migrant workers, had also filtered into Southern Rhodesia.[20] Hanoc Shindano, one of the most prominent leaders of the movement in the Tanganyika District, had travelled widely in Southern Rhodesia and had spent two years at what J. Moffat Thomson termed the 'Cape Town Watch Tower mission'.[21]

Like Kamwana, who had, about a decade before, also undergone a similar religious re-orientation course under Joseph Booth,[22] Shindano and his group returned home to find a disturbed social situation of which they were quick to take advantage. In the true Charles Taze Russell tradition,[23] they preached disobedience to all civil authority, African as well as European, and enjoined their followers not to work for Europeans or the chiefs, who were, like all non-converts, labelled devils. The adherents of the movement got baptised to prepare for a new government, because the existing one would, they said, come to an end when the Americans came to drive out the English.[24]

The movement spread rapidly in the northern parts of the province, and it was estimated that by the end of 1918 the number of adherents was about one thousand.[25] The majority of the members at the beginning seem to have been the Iwa and the Namwanga in the Isoka Division, with a few Bemba there and in Chinsali.[26] The Mambwe in Abercorn and in Kasama formed another major segment of converts.[27]

It is difficult to explain why the Bemba seem not to have been as ready converts of the movement as the Mambwe or the Namwanga were. But it seems possible that because the leaders of Watch Tower then were all members of former subject tribes most of the Bemba may have looked with suspicion at the movement, especially considering its apparently seditious doctrines, as another attempt at political assertion by their former subjects. It is significant, for example, that Chitimukulu and Mwamba, during the Kasama High Court trial of its leaders, called the movement a disturbance caused by 'mannerless slaves'.[28] It is also likely that, since the readiness with which the Mambwe and the Namwanga imbibed 'Watch-towerism' was to a great extent dictated by the war situation in which they found themselves and which made them ready believers of the movement's millenarian prescriptions for the cure of their own social and political ills, the Bemba, who were farther from the war front, may have not been as susceptible to the movement as their northern neighbours. But whatever the reasons behind this apparent inertia on the part of the Bemba population, the movement, taking into account the few

L

Bemba who were converted, was, to all intents and purposes, a pan-tribal organisation.[29] For the first time in the colonial history of the Northern Province, a congeries of ethnic groups, once engaged in incessant internecine wars, found common ground for unity against colonial rule. Those Administration officials who had had the chance to read Owen Letcher's book, published six years before, must have marvelled at the big game hunter's perspicacity and prophetic genius when, in a most dismal and negrophobic tone, he wrote:

It has been my experience that to christianise a native is often a most effective means of turning him into an absolute rogue. The Native Commissioner is the best kind of missionary for the African native, not the man who attempts to fill the brains of the black with the religions of Europe and the dangerous doctrine that all men are equal.

Those who teach the native of Africa to regard the white man as his brother are dangerous maniacs, for in Africa civilisation and Christianity do not make for greater happiness of the natives. . . . In their natural state the African natives are, now that slave raiding and the bloody conquests of dominant tribes have stopped, the happiest people under the sun; teach them Christianity and you generally succeed in upsetting their mental balance and turning them into rogues.[30]

If the evangelisation of the African continued unchecked, warned Letcher, the consequences to European rule in Africa would be disastrous:

One day there will be some great awakening unless missionary influence in Africa is checked—a day when the blacks, united to some extent by a common language and a common faith, will rise against the white man . . .[31]

For all its underlying ethnocentricism, Letcher's prognosis seemed especially pertinent to the outbreak of the Watch Tower movement in the Northern Province.

That the movement was a religious one cannot be doubted. This is readily apparent from the fervour with which adherents performed their religious ceremonies and the steadfastness with which they held on to one of their tenets—that the end of the world was at hand and, therefore, they should grow no more crops nor rear any more livestock. At congregations, as the Native Commissioner, Chinsali, once reported, they often sang hymns 'lustily and at times shouting prayers and exhortations', while a few of them 'indulged in a wild frenzy, rolling of eyes and contortions of their bodies, making unintelligible ejaculations'.[32] But it was the 'Ethiopianism', the desire for political and religious self-determination, by the attainment of which they hoped to cure their social and economic ills, that gave the movement the unity and the force which became a source of concern to the Administration. 'Watch-towerism' became, in effect, a political organisation garbed in the sanctimoniousness of a religious movement, and it did not take very long before the Administration realised this. In September 1918, in an effort to curb the propagation of the pernicious doctrine of Watch-towerism, the Administration arrested Shindano and Kanchele, two of the leading 'pastors' of the Church. However, they were later acquitted by the magistrate at Abercorn.[33]

The invasion of the Northern Province towards the end of 1918 by the Germans under von Lettow-Vorbeck seems to have exacerbated the situation. But as the Native Commissioner, Chinsali, commented, it is not clear whether the extraordinary growth of the movement was the result of German propaganda or of the state of unrest caused by the invasion.[34] Indeed, some leaders in the movement even claimed responsibility for the invasion,[35] a claim which suggests that they had looked to the Germans for allies against the British authorities. However, as Hugh C. Marshall, the Visiting Commissioner, said, this is impossible to prove.[36] But whatever the truth of the matter was, there is little doubt that the advance of the battle front into the province led to increased Watch Tower activity. The situation, according to the Administration, was made even more conducive to this growth by the fact that, owing to their preoccupation with the war over the previous years, officials were not able to tour their divisions, and this gave the Watch Tower preachers more than elbow room for winning more converts.[37] A tour of the Isoka Division by a certain Mr Williams elicited the fact that Watch Tower activity there was on the increase. After a visit to Sub-chief Terefya's area, Williams reported that increasing Watch Tower 'irresponsible' teaching was causing friction and disturbances in the area.[38] Upon receipt of this report, Charles R. B. Draper, Acting District Commissioner, Tanganyika District, accompanied by a few police, set off early in January 1919 for

Mweni Terefya's area, which was in Chief Kafwimbi's country, to see the affected villages. He camped near Terefya's village, and on the same evening of his day of arrival he was able to witness the strange rituals of Watch-towerism. The congregation mainly consisted of young women and children, most of whom were stricken with Spanish influenza, an epidemic which may well have contributed to the atmosphere in which individuals turned to the millenarian faith of Watch Tower.[39] The congregation embarked on a continuous hymn singing programme, as youths, reading from the Bible and preaching in an excited and hysterical manner, worked on the emotions of the rest.[40] After sunset, Draper heard a lad shouting loudly on the outskirts of the village more or less incoherent passages from the Bible. When the boy was arrested, another took his place. Both of them were detained for a night by Draper for making an 'infernal noise'.[41]

This dominance of youth activity in a movement which was supposedly widespread might strike one as odd, as it tends to suggest that the older people were not sympathetic to the Church. Certainly Terefya, like most traditional rulers, did not support it. The only chief who appears to have entertained Watch Tower sympathies was the Shimwalule of the Bemba, and this supposed involvement by the most important priest in Bembaland seems very significant, as it suggests that the movement had in it certain 'articles of faith' which were shared by traditional African religion. But he too left the movement not long after its inception.[42] For how else could chiefs have looked at the organisation when they, like white officials, were being abused and taunted by the Watch Tower adherents? But it would not be right to interpret this youth activity as a sign of lack of interest in the movement by older people. It may well be that, like later African independence movements, the Watch Tower leaders used the youth arm of the organisation as a kind of political and social barometer as well as a disciplinary organ to gauge and influence public thinking.

But as to the involvement of the older generation in the movement, Draper was left in no doubt during his tour that it was prevalent. Terefya told him that most of the people in his village were members of the sect, and he was unable to do anything to stop them making the 'infernal noise' which Draper had heard the previous night.[43] They had acquired certain social idiosyncrasies which chiefs found unpalatable. They slept together in the centre of the village so that if the end of the world came about during the night none of them would be left behind in the moral filth of the existing imperfect world.

It became clear to Draper in such an atmosphere that people no longer had any regard for chiefs, headmen or old men, and that the spirit of disobedience and defiance was spreading. As an expression of the contempt in which chiefs and headmen were held, Chief Kafwimbi was, for example, popularly said to have turned into a woman and given birth to a baby by the name of Mary, and headman Musamansi was insulted and assaulted by Watch Tower adherents while the Acting District Commissioner was in the area.[44]

The Musamansi case, which Draper decided to try 'on the spot',[45] sparked off a wave of violent reactions from the Watch Tower members. After convicting the offenders in the case, Draper tried to send them to Kasama under police escort. But their co-religionists intervened and released them, and when he tried to re-arrest the prisoners they defied him with impunity.[46] Draper then tried to remove the principal offender, but he failed to do so in the face of the angry mob. His police were threatened and assaulted, and when he intervened to try and put a stop to the melee by striking one man, as he put it, with 'a mild blow in the chest', his arm was seized instantly.[47] As he had earlier on purpose sent off all his carriers and disarmed his six policemen, in an attempt not to appear to want to provoke trouble, he was too helpless to do anything. His attempts to get at the nearest prisoner only provoked angry cries:

You will not take this man (Jacob Kasuya) today. If you take one you must take all, also when we go you must send us bicycles and motor cars. We will never be taken to another country, we will be killed in our own country. If you come back, bring a Maxim gun. Talk will not move us.[48]

Engrained in these words was a fanaticism which, as one eye-witness has aptly commented, can only be likened to that of the Lenshina uprising of 1963-4 in the history of Zambia.[49] They were words of a fearless people, determined to rid themselves of what they thought were excessive and godless demands of a white administration. There was, of course, a 'religious' touch to it all, for as Draper and his police were wrestling with the irate mob they could see that

there were constant outbursts of praying and several young men went into fits of frenzy . . . working themselves into a bath of perspiration, gibbering and shaking all over and directly at me.[50]

The scene must have been very much like the one which Peter Worsley cites in his study of millenarian movements in Melanesia in which it is said that at a meeting in 1914 of one of Melanesia's 'cargo' cults, called the Taro cult, which was led by Buninia:

Young men drummed, while the prophet [Buninia] sang his cult-songs . . . Then one individual after another became possessed by a shaking fit, jerking their heads, their bodies, trembling, often with clenched fists and contorted faces.[51]

Draper found the situation uncontrollable, for no amount of reasoning or argument could succeed in silencing the fanatics; nor were their leaders able to control them either.[52]

This intransigence, so characteristic of the movement, was apparently in part the result of certain beliefs which adherents had come to accept almost dogmatically—beliefs which, a contemporary says, sought to put the white man in a bad light in relation to the African.[53] They believed that Europeans did not make any cloth, but that it came from God. If only, as 'Watch-towerists', they prayed hard, cloth would emerge from the waters of Jordan —the movement's centre of baptismal activities in the Isoka Division. The whiteman's guns were believed to have stopped firing bullets, and were now emitting water instead.[54] The movement emphasised the contempt in which it held Europeans by preaching that its members should no longer use, or eat from, any utensils made by whitemen, but should use their own.[55] It was an aggressive spirit of independence which one might call, using the words of a Livingstonia missionary's comment on Kamwanaism in Nyasaland, a 'flush of mistaken nationalism'.[56]

The incident at Terefya's village was not the only show of strength by the Watch Tower movement which Draper encountered in his division. A few weeks before he went to Terefya's area he had visited Mwika's village, which was the headquarters of the movement in Isoka. There he interviewed some four hundred followers, all of whom, he noticed, showed 'a threatening and contemptuous attitude'.[57] There were faction fights at the meeting between Watch Tower adherents and chiefs and headmen. As a result of these fights he was not able to arrest any Watch-towerists, most of whom were young men of what he called the 'military porter class'.[58] They had arrived at the meeting singing hymns lustily and at times shouting prayers, while some of them worked themselves into the same hysterical state that he was to witness during the Musamansi incident.[59] Draper tried to advise the gathering that the teachings of the Watch Tower Church were wrong and therefore must be stopped. But the adherents would not listen. They would not even listen to Donald Siwale, their fellow African, who was then interpreter to Draper; they just told him that he 'was misled by the whitemen'.[60] In reply to Draper's orders that they should stop their irresponsible teaching, one Kosamu from Chilanga village, speaking for all, said that they would not do so.[61] So defiant was the attitude of the gathering that at one stage Chief Kafwimbi petulantly said to Draper: 'Kill them all'. But the District Commissioner, whose good-natured disposition Donald Siwale still upholds, dismissed the chief's suggestion as puerile and unrealistic.[62] The meeting ultimately ended amid shouting and singing of a triumphant nature, and Draper felt that the situation was getting out of hand. What seemed most disturbing to him was the fact that this restiveness was not the work of foreign instigators but was caused by a local educated elite, whom he referred to as the 'ex-mission teacher class'.[63]

Why ex-mission teachers should have been the leaders of the movement can only be surmised. It may well be, as one government official later argued, that most, if not all, of these men had been turned away from the 'mission' Church on account of drinking beer or 'living in sin', and so as outcasts they formed a Christian Church of their own whose teaching was in accord with African values, such as beer-drinking and polygamy.[64] It may be that, as Sundkler says in regard to the formation in 1892 of the 'Ethiopian Church' in Johannesburg by Mangena M. Mokone, an African who was formerly a Wesleyan minister,[65] and as Worsley observes with regard to the proliferation of millenarian religious movements in the South Pacific,[66] the mission-educated elite in the Northern Province formed or joined the Watch Tower movement as a protest against racial segregation in mission

Churches, which was itself a revulsion against the divergence between the Christian doctrines of equality and brotherly love, and actual practice on the part of white missionaries. It seems also possible that to the 'ex-mission teacher class' the Watch Tower movement offered many leadership opportunities for those of them who had aspired to occupy positions of responsibility in the mission Churches—positions to which they could only rise after several years of probation under white missionaries.[67] But for whatever reasons the African educated elite of the Northern Province joined African Watch Tower, the leadership role which they played in the movement seems to have been characteristic of other African independent Churches as well. The leadership role of ex-mission teachers and preachers in such Churches has been given exhaustive treatment by Sundkler in his study of African independent Churches in South Africa;[68] it is also evident in the 'African National Church' and 'The Last Church of God and His Christ', for example, which were founded in the 1920's in Tanzania;[69] it is also known that the man who founded the Kimbanguist magico-religious movement of the Congo (Kinshasa) in 1921, Simon Kimbangu, was a former catechist who was educated at the Protestant mission of Ngombe-Lutete;[70] and the founder of African Watch Tower in Nyasaland, Elliot Kamwana, was an intellectual who was trained at the Livingstonia Mission's Bandawe station and Overtoun Institute at Kondowe.[71]

The situation with which Draper was confronted at Mwika's seemed serious. As a contemporary testified about two decades later, Draper 'was rather badly treated, which was quite a new experience for us. They [the Watch Tower adherents] made remarks about his appearance, knocked his hat off and kicked him'.[72] In a telegraphic message to the Administrator the District Commissioner stressed the point that, although he was taking pains to avoid even a semblance of persecution, he nevertheless regarded the situation as 'serious, and a decided menace to quiet and orderly administration'.[73] Under such pressure, Draper was forced to ask for a company of the Northern Rhodesia Police to meet him at Chunga's village in the Isoka Division, from where, he said, he would billet them in various parts of the affected area. He suggested to the Administrator that the Visiting Commissioner, Hugh C. Marshall, would do well if he immediately left Livingstone for Tanganyika District in order to get the feel of the atmosphere in the district and possibly hold a conference of chiefs and headmen.[74]

If Draper had viewed the situation with grave concern, the Administrator, L. A. Wallace, who was able to study the matter with a coolness of mind and an emotional detachment which only a person not physically and emotionally involved in the situation could command, did not seem to appreciate the urgency and gravity of the state of affairs. He wired back to Draper on the 15 January, informing him that he had given orders to the Officer Commanding, Northern Rhodesia Police, Kasama, to send a platoon to Chunga village, which, he added, should suffice but should not as far as possible be quartered in villages.[75] Draper naturally found this arrangement most unsatisfactory. In his view a platoon would not be able effectively to meet the growing opposition of the Watch Tower movement, whose members were already congregating in anticipation of the arrival of the platoon. In a telegram to the Administrator the following day, he asked for at least a hundred policemen, with European officers and a Maxim, as he considered these necessary for a show of strength that would ensure a settlement of the situation without bloodshed. He also asked for a free hand in the matter.[76]

For some reason, Administrator Wallace remained unconvinced that anything more than a platoon was necessary to contain the situation. In his telegraphic reply of the 17 January he reiterated that a platoon of drilled men should be able to arrest men identified as offenders, even among a crowd. But, he warned, Draper should avoid calling a crowd together, as this would make the situation more explosive. However, if, in Draper's judgement and in that of the Officer Commanding, it was not possible to effect arrest without bloodshed, it would be prudent not to push matters to a crisis and any further action should await reinforcements. He warned Draper:

You cannot be given a free hand to take drastic measures without the authority of the High Commissioner [for South Africa] with whom I am in communication.[77]

If Wallace's instructions had the salutary effect of making Draper exercise more restraint in a situation where all rash action was to be avoided, they also seem to have lacked an understanding of the processes of mental strain, anxiety and anguish which

Draper and other white officials in the troubled area may have been undergoing. The Administrator's punctilious attitude, which history can commend only because the crisis at Mwika's was peacefully resolved, could well have resulted in loss of life, had the Watch Tower adherents completely got out of control. But thanks to the tact and cool-headedness of District Commissioner Draper, the situation was contained without a single shot being fired. On 25 January he wired the Administrator in Livingstone from Isoka that he had 'successfully and without resorting to force' arrested one hundred and thirty-eight of the Watch Tower leaders in the division.[78] The remarks made by P. J. Macdonell, a judge of the Northern Rhodesia High Court, on this *dénouement* could not have been more laudatory of Draper's performance: 'I would like to say very emphatically,' wrote Macdonell of Draper, 'that I find it difficult to speak too highly of the restraint and forbearance shown by him at the Mwika meeting.'[79]

While Draper was grappling with the explosive situation at Mwika's, the District Commissioner for Awemba District at Kasama reported that a prominent leader of the Watch Tower had been arrested and placed in Fife (Isoka) hospital, as he was suffering from influenza.[80] But no sooner was he admitted to the hospital than he was removed by his supporters and taken back to Mwika's village—an incident which, according to the District Commissioner, was a source of added inspiration to an organisation which had been shaken by the mass arrest of most of its leaders.[81]

Although after these arrests things were quiet in the Isoka Division, Draper resisted the temptation of assuming a complacent attitude too soon. He maintained a platoon of police in the area for some time just in case trouble should break out again. Indeed it was well that he did so. For while the platoon, under Lieutenant Castle, was patrolling the area, it was readily apparent that the people of Isoka were still in a restless mood. The lieutenant later reported to Draper that during his tour of parts of the division he was

treated with respect, but not with the respect that I had imagined an official should be treated. At some villages men practically ignored me until reprimanded by my native sergeant . . . I have seen less civilised natives in our territory bordering Portuguese W. Africa, but

I have never noticed the same lack of recognition of a white man, not to mention an official.[82]

Castle was not sure whether this supercilious attitude was due to the suspicion with which the local people looked upon a white-man in general or whether it emanated from sheer hatred and fear of white officials.

While Draper was engaged in his tremendous task of trying to suppress the Watch Tower movement in the Isoka Division—an exercise in which for the first time in the colonial history of the Northern Province military force, or the show of it, was used to suppress African anti-colonial aspirations—Native Commissioner Dewhurst was grappling with the same problem in the Chinsali Division. Although the movement did not seem to be as wide-spread in Chinsali as it was in Isoka, there was nonetheless a size-able population of adherents in the area who were causing the authorities considerable concern. The movement in Chinsali, which lacked the vigorous and enlightened leadership like that in Isoka and, as will be shown later, in Abercorn, drew its inspiration from the Isoka branch's centre at Mwika's village.

Probably because of the movement's relative weakness in his division, Dewhurst was prone to use rather ruthless means to stamp out the sect in Chinsali. When in January 1919 he learnt that about ten adherents at the nearby villages of Chilembo and Longwe, who had gone to Mwika's village in Isoka to see Shadrack Sinkala, had returned home in 'a mad and defiant state' he sent out a messenger to arrest them. But the messenger was beaten up, and two other messengers who were later sent to Chilembo's and Longwe's proved equally powerless. Consequently, Dewhurst decided that he should go to the affected villages himself.[83]

Leaving Chinsali Boma at eleven o'clock one night he reached the troubled area at 2 a.m. and arrested the men while they were in bed. Some of the prisoners were tied up and put in one hut, while others, not tied up, were put in another. The latter became 'absolutely mad' and armed themselves with sticks, blocked the narrow entrance to the hut and started breaking down the walls of the hut.[84] As he had not brought sufficient messengers with him, Dewhurst then had the verandah of the hut netted with game nets, with a view to arresting the riotous men one after another if they tried to escape. In the meantime the prisoners were yelling insults at the Native Commissioner and the messengers. The men said things which only went to show how resigned Watch Tower followers were to any fate that might befall them. They seemed even prepared to die for their religion —a religion which, they said, was richer and more enlightening than the half-truths they had been taught by white missionaries. They yelled:

Messengers! Come into the hut and we will beat you. White man! Come into the hut and we will beat you. Mr Draper was beaten at Mwika village, he is now dead at Mwenzo. The white man persecutes us, we are slaves, therefore we want the Askari to be called up to kill us. We want to die. The recognised missions of the country deceived us by withholding part of the truth. Now we know the truth. We want to die, we want you to kill us . . .[85]

These cries provoked the anger of sympathisers in the village, who came out during the night and removed part of the net around the hut, and thereby made it possible for five of the prisoners to escape to Mwika's village. The remaining ones were only rearrested after a fight in which several messengers were wounded.[86]

Dewhurst's handling of the Watch Tower leaders at Longwe's and Chilembo's, and the order he made to suppress the movement, without prior consultation with the legal adviser to the Administration, earned him a severe reprimand from the Office of the High Commissioner for South Africa. He was told that the order to repress what he called the Watch Tower movement's 'irresponsible teaching' was unreasonable and tantamount to religious persecution.[87] It was an unhappy state of affairs, which Draper had judiciously avoided, and for which Dewhurst was paying.

In self-defence, Dewhurst suggested that in order that the higher authorities might prove that what he had done was both necessary and reasonable there should be an official enquiry into the matter.[88] He contended that the passive resistance of the Watch Tower movement, combined with its end-of-the-world beliefs, and its preaching that the power of the chiefs and the authority of the *boma* was at an end, had caused 'administrative, tribal and domestic chaos'.[89] The whole population had got out of hand,

and the situation was deteriorating, he said. People had grown to believe in immunity from any kind of punishment. The baptised regarded themselves as members of a new order and were sleeping in the open together in order to avoid being taken unawares by the end of the world which, they believed, was at hand. The leaders of the movement, mostly mission teachers or ex-teachers, who had come to wield great power at the expense of the authority of the chiefs and headmen were, he said, now mere nonentities incapable of reporting cases of sedition to the *boma*. They had become subversive and elusive men.[90] Moreover, argued Dewhurst,

such preaching, coming at a time when the Germans were marching through the country destroying bomas, etc., was in my opinion seditious, if not treasonable. With the prestige of the Boma at a low ebb, doctrines inculcating the end of the present form of government and the advent of a theocracy cannot be considered mere religious propaganda. In my opinion the date of the end of the world coinciding with the German invasion cannot be dismissed as a matter of pure chance.[91]

The unhappy memories of the John Chilembwe rising just across the border in Nyasaland seemed still too fresh for Dewhurst to have allowed the disturbed state of affairs in his district to continue unchecked. He chose to repress the Watch Tower movement immediately instead of 'contenting myself with waiting for breaches of the positive law'. This was because the whole population was 'committing a nuisance' and it was almost impossible to prosecute hundreds of people committing the same offence. On the other hand, if a few individuals were arrested and punished they would have been considered by other adherents as Christian martyrs and accorded such honour.[92] Thus, because the whole population was offending in the same way and because the chiefs were too frightened to put up any show of authority, all attempts to get cases of sedition prosecuted were doomed to failure. Dewhurst, of course, conceded that the ideal procedure in the circumstances would have been for him to try and suppress the movement by constant travelling in his area and explaining the dangers of Watch Tower doctrines to the people, as Draper had tried to do in the Isoka Division. But the urgency and gravity of the situation made any delay in taking corrective measures most impolitic and that was why, he said, he had not consulted the government legal adviser beforehand.[93]

Dewhurst's anxiety about Watch Tower activity in his division, the heavy hand with which he handled the situation, and Draper's frantic telegraphic messages to the Administrator about the situation in Isoka, should perhaps be looked at against the background of European attitudes in Central and South Africa if they are to be properly understood. The time of the Watch Tower unrest in the Northern Province happened to have fallen within a period (1872–1928) which George Shepperson has called 'the classical period of Ethiopianism because', he says, 'it was at this time that it [Ethiopianism] exercised its greatest political influence and was most widely noticed in the European, American, and African press'.[94] There were during this period widespread outbursts of African independent Church movements which, although being of very complex causation, were seen by Europeans mainly as a threat to white rule in Africa; and the term 'Ethiopianism' was used, as Shepperson puts it, 'as a convenient whipping-boy for their anxieties about African aspirations'[95] and was, in the years immediately after World War I, beginning to be replaced by the term 'Watch Tower'.[96] It seems possible, therefore, that the B.S.A.C. Administration officials in the Northern Province were also infected by such fears about the Watch Tower movement. Indeed, Dewhurst's contention that the doctrines of Watch Tower 'inculcating the end of the present form of government and the advent of a theocracy cannot be considered mere religious propaganda'[97] seems indicative of these anxieties.

Of the activities of the Watch Tower movement in the Abercorn Division during the war there is apparently very little recorded in the files of the Administration. But from the few records available, and from oral accounts, a picture crystallises of the Watch Tower movement as an emotional safety valve through which the African people vented their frustrations under white rule, and solaced themselves with hopes that some day Providence would, through the leaders of the movement, put things right. Moses Sikazwe's eye-witness account thus portrays Hanoc Chimpungwe Shindano, the leader of the movement in Abercorn and 'son-in-law' to Sikazwe himself, as a man intent on increasing his personal power and status by using underhand methods to delude his followers and by appropriating church collections. A good-natured, quiet-spoken and sober man before he went to Southern Rhodesia, Shindano, according to Sikazwe, returned to his home in Abercorn not only a Watch Tower convert but also a man of bibulous inclinations, who from church collections bought himself several head of cattle, married two wives, and spent sizeable sums of money on bluffing his followers into believing that he was a biblical Moses.[98] By some surreptitious means, he was able to convince his followers that they need not toil in order to get their food; for, he said, all their food would come down from God in the same way that the children of Israel had manna from heaven. Before addressing a large Watch Tower congregation Hanoc used to call together a few of his most trusted followers, who would secretly arrange with the local people, a day or two before the meeting, to have enough thick meal porridge and a variety of meats and vegetables prepared for adherents attending the meeting. The food would then be deposited in a nearby bush, which would be sealed off from the congregation until the appointed time, when Shindano would interrupt the sermon and inform the congregation that, as they were hungry, it behoved him to leave for the bush to pray to God for food, with which to feed them. He would then rejoin the congregation, whom he would tell to go and help themselves to delicious dishes from heaven and the people would go and have their fill, apparently believing in all earnest that the food was from heaven.[99]

Moses Sikazwe's account of Shindano's pretensions seems to be borne out by other incidents which are cited in official records. An African detective, Robert Simpelwe, who was posted to Abercorn by the Administration to keep an eye on the activities of the Watch Tower movement, reported that Shindano was collecting money from his followers which was ostensibly meant for the Church, but which was in fact 'for his own use'.[100] In another report Simpelwe showed how Shindano had spent a sum of £5 which he had collected from a few of his followers and with which he had promised to buy them Watch Tower literature. Simpelwe reported that the Watch Tower leader had instead used ten shillings of the money to pay a fine to the Native Commissioner, Abercorn, and another ten shillings to pay his poll tax; he had also bought himself clothes worth thirty-eight shillings, and with the remainder he paid fines for those of his followers who had been convicted of various offences by the Administration.[101] Thus, as the Assistant Native Commissioner, Abercorn, later remarked, Shindano appears to have made a 'not inconsiderable living from payments made to him by Watch Tower followers . . .'[102]

It seems, however, unclear whether before he left for Southern Rhodesia Shindano was old enough to have shown the moral attributes of sobriety and good-natured disposition which Sikazwe accords to him. Indeed, it seems equally doubtful whether in fact the Watch Tower leader was resident in the Northern Province before his emigration. In a statement which he made after his return from Southern Rhodesia, Shindano said:

I am a Mambwe native and used originally to live at Malengela in the Mbozi District of German East Africa. In 1905 I went with two white men with cattle to Southern Rhodesia. I stayed four years at Enkeldoorn, one year at Que Que, two years at Gatooma and for a short period at lots of other Bomas. At first, as I was a youngster, I worked at herding fowls but afterwards as an underground miner. I entered the Church of Watch Tower at Que Que. Sandris Chilwa, Mwabokutzi, Adaleyo, Sam Yalenda and Andulu—all miners there—taught me. They were Tonga natives from Bandawe, Chinteche District of Nyasaland.[103]

But as to Shindano's pretensions to the powers and status of a Moses, of which Sikazwe's account makes mention, these are vindicated by the Administration's accounts of the Watch Tower leader's preachings and activities.

Operating from 'Jerusalem', a church[104] he had built at Tukamulozya's village in the Mambwe area, Hanoc Shindano was, probably more than any other leader of the Watch Tower movement in the country, best known for the eloquent constancy with which he preached what was perhaps the most alluring of the movement's tenets—the 'African millenium'. He would tell his congregation that their troubles under the existing order of things would be over when the whiteman went back to where he came from. The merchandise and other European manufactures which the whiteman had brought into the country, claimed Hanoc, belonged to the African people by divine right, but the Europeans had fraudulently converted all this property to their own selfish use. However, he said, all such goods would change hands when, with God's help, the whiteman was pushed out of the country. The evidence given for the Crown by Robert Simpelwe, an African detective, during the High Court trial of Watch Tower leaders at Kasama early in 1919 is illustrative of Shindano's millenarian prescription for the eradication of African political, social and economic maladies:

Long ago [Shindano is alleged to have said] Europeans did not know God same as we, but some other people came to their country and taught them, and God helped them and gave them wise [sic] and all things, the Europeans did not know about our country (Africa), but God made them know and sent them with goods and many things we see to come and give us free, and teach about God, and when they get into this country, they hide everything, and teach us very little about God, they teach us how to write but they did not tell us what God sent them here for, and they could not give us little for the work we have done to them, therefore if we pray to God very hard with all our hearts, God will hear our prayer and will clear all Europeans back to England and everything will be ours, we will be rich as they are.[105]

To some Administration officials these words must have been reminiscent of Elliot Kamwana's teaching in Malawi, where he too used to tell his followers that all whitemen would one day leave the country and Africans would be relieved of the exacting demands made on them by colonial rule and that there would thereafter be freedom and prosperity for his people.[106] But Shindano's words were of a wider import than this. Not only were they a protest against forced labour, which, as was pointed out earlier, contributed considerably to the shaping of African attitudes and resistance to white rule, and was in part responsible for the rapid growth of Watch Tower during the later part of the war, but the words were also an expression of a belief which was also commonly held among the equally millenarian 'cargo' cults of Melanesia,[107] that white missionaries had deliberately withheld the secret parts of the Christian message which favoured the Africans. It might be said, as Peter Worsley has argued elsewhere with reference to Melanesia's 'cargo' cults,[108] that Shindano's re-interpretation of Christian doctrines in this manner reflected not merely the general contrast in levels of knowledge and power between white and black in the country, but also limitations of

M

African education in the more formal aspects. And the fact that education was at this time entirely in the hands of European missions may have given even greater credibility to this cult of 'the hidden secret'.

Shindano's doctrine that the wants of his people could be satisfied by mere prayer was, as pointed out earlier, given practical demonstration by himself when at a meeting as already related by Sikazwe, he feigned feeding the congregation with 'food from heaven'. In a similar manner, he appears to have told his followers that he could also obtain money from heaven by prayer. At a meeting which was held in December 1919 at his headquarters, Hanoc had secretly placed seven shillings along a village path some distance away from where the congregation was gathered. After a short prayer in front of his followers in which he asked for money from God, he took a few members of the congregation along the chosen path and showed them the money, which he said, was sent to him from heaven, adding: 'If I with such a little prayer can get 7s., then if all the people prayed there would be much wealth.'[109]

Among a people exposed to the attractions as well as the hardships of industrialism, Shindano's sermons must have found a ready hearing. For his preachings were no mere religious propaganda for consumption by an ignorant public. They were, in effect, criticism of a social set-up in which Europeans were the 'haves' and Africans the 'have nots'. It was, one might say, a rudimentary economic critique on income distribution in a rural plural society. For millenarian movements, of which African Watch Tower was one, are, as Worsley has observed, 'particularly characteristic of colonial and plural societies where a sharp division exists between the native people and the foreign administration'.[110]

Shindano's teaching, with all its attractions for the rather credulous and innocent people of Tukamulozya's area, had an unhappy end, however. There was starvation in the country, and J. Moffat Thomson, then District Commissioner for Tanganyika District, decided that he must take decisive action against Shindano. He went to 'Jerusalem' and flogged the Watch Tower leader for misleading the people with his false claims, and a few of his henchmen were also fined.[111] Shindano, however, in an attempt to save his reputation, paid the fines on their behalf with the money he had amassed from church collections. Before the trials commenced, he would bury the money in a nearby anthill, to which he would periodically retire to take appropriate amounts as each one of his disciples was convicted, claiming each time that he had got the money from heaven after praying to God.[112] After these incidents Moffat Thomson had no alternative but to arrest him, and he was later tried at Kasama with other leaders of the movement.

There is apparently nothing available on record regarding the actual proceedings of the High Court mass trial at Kasama, from which one could have assessed better the temper and motives of the Watch Tower leaders in their protracted confrontation with the authorities. But Mr Justice P. J. Macdonell, before whom they appeared, makes an illuminating analysis of the factors relating to the outbreak and growth of the Watch Tower movement in his report on the Kasama High Court session to the Administrator, L. A. Wallace.

With considerable justification, Macdonell attributed the rapid growth and the truculence of the Watch Tower to the war, and especially to the German invasion of the Northern Province in 1918.[113] Owing to the war, the Isoka Division, for example, had not been toured by white officials for four years. This, coupled with the fact that there had been several changes of Native Commissioners during that period, which meant that District Messengers had to tour the division alone, spurred the spread of the movement by the absence of the deterrent of a white official. Furthermore, the guns of the fighting forces, cases of assault, robbery and rape by what Macdonell termed 'the meanest of mean whites' accentuated the heat of the movement.[114]

That the aggressiveness, defiance and mischievousness of the Watch Tower movement were a direct result of the German invasion was a view generally held even by local chiefs and white officials. At Kasama High Court, Chief Mwenichilanga of the Namwanga testified that after a certain date, which coincided with the German raid, the movement, then a year old in the province, changed from a passive to an aggressive force.[115] The African people, who had seen the coming of the whiteman's authority a few decades before, and with it the end of the slave trade and tribal wars, had submitted to British rule in the belief that the English were invincible masters. But with the outbreak of the war this faith in British rulers sunk to its nadir at the time of the German invasion. As Macdonell, who was known for his negrophile views, put it:

The natives saw the Enemy marching unopposed through the country, looting and burning, while the British officials fled . . . Many natives, chiefs, and commoners alike, thought the end of our rule had come . . . From this and because of this the Watch Tower movement altered and became noisy, mischievous and defiant of authority.[116]

Apart from the German invasion, the bad treatment which the local population received from government officials during the war appears to have been partly responsible for the mischievous and defiant mood of the movement and for its rapid growth. In reply to a letter from Edward S. B. Tagart, the Secretary for Native Affairs, in which he was asked to comment on Judge Macdonell's charge that officials had ill-treated the Africans of the Fife Division, which was one of the causes of the Watch Tower outbreak in 1918, Draper admitted that there were instances of rape, robbery and assault, and that on occasions the *askari* had commandeered foodstuffs from the local people.[117] And like everywhere else in Africa during the war, labour was forced, he said, and 'at Fife, on occasions, men were brought in on a rope'.[118] His account of the maltreatment of Africans during the war was supported by his opposite number at Kasama, H. Croad, who bluntly wrote to Tagart:

War will always I suppose collect the riffraff, and the G[erman] E[ast] A[frica] campaign has certainly had a very bad effect on the natives and our prestige has certainly gone down. The less said about the campaign, I should imagine, the better.[119]

This is not to say, however, that African receptivity to the movement was occasioned solely by the war or by the German invasion. The war situation was only leaven to the dough of African discontent, which had long been in existence and which found expression in the religio-political teachings of Watch Tower. Indeed, as Stevenson has commented on the appeal of Watch Tower, 'when people have been having a rough time in their personal lives, when adversity has struck hard, . . . the message of a New World in which poverty and injustice, war and oppression will be unknown is obviously most attractive'.[120] Evidence of old grievances has already been shown in this chapter by the statements made by the leaders of the movement; and Macdonell, who was possessed of the keen circumspection of a judge, was very much alive to these cumulative grievances. Writing with an air of disillusionment over the apparent change in African attitude towards white rule and with some pessimism about the future, he commented sourly:

The pity of the whole thing [the Watch Tower movement] was the youth of those who appeared before us. Nearly all were young, many were little more than boys. It was a disquieting thing for the future. As one listened to plea and evidence which showed that the old words, obedience to elders and headmen and chiefs, obedience to the Boma, had lost meaning, one realised the delicate, fragile nature of our hold over these people and at times one saw the abyss opening. Hitherto ours has been in the main a rule over a willing [sic] people, above all over a non-critical one. It may easily become a rule over a willing and highly critical people, sceptical of our intentions, distrustful of all we do.[121]

Macdonell felt that, unless something was done to remedy the situation, there was every likelihood of even greater trouble erupting in the future. Like Melland during the Bemba unrest of 1906–8, he believed that the fault lay not in the Administration's stars but within the administrative system itself. He contended that it was because Native Commissioners had lost touch with the people that most of this political disenchantment had come about. His remarks, which, coming from a man in his position, must have been made not only in self-criticism and from introspection but also as a reappraisal of white–black relations, are worth quoting at some length:

I said this movement is a matter for pity as well as blame. We have governed the native and overgoverned him. We have taken from him the power of self-determination and have hedged him in with a net-work of rules and permits, a monotonous, highly regulated and very drab existence. We save him from war and enslavement but do very little else for him; we cannot even save him from the annual risk of starvation, and in return for what we have taken away we have given very little in exchange . . . we have taken the interest and excitement

out of life . . . Now this Watch Tower movement was to its converts,
I am certain, one piece of colour and interest—of romance if you can
use the word—which they had known. It was their own, there was no
European to supervise or initiate; for once in their lives they had the
power of self-determination . . .[122]

Unlike Melland, however, Macdonell never saw in repressive
measures the answer to African resistance. The remedial measures
he suggested were directed at assimilating the African to the
administrative set-up and at promoting his welfare, so that he
might feel that the Administration was more of a friend than an
enemy to him. He suggested that a school of agriculture should
be built to compensate Africans for the excitement and self-
determination they had lost as a result of the campaign against
Watch Tower.[123] He further recommended that white officials
should tour their districts regularly so that, by so doing, they
could win back the people's confidence. In the past officials were
not able to do this because of pressure of work in their offices.
But, so argued Macdonell, this could be solved without much
difficulty. He suggested a measure which must have sounded
'revolutionary' to his contemporaries: clerical work should be
left to African clerks so that white officials could be free to tour
their areas and know the people. There was of course the danger
that sooner or later these African clerks would get discontented if
they were not made Native Commissioners; but, in Macdonell's
view, this was a problem which could be solved if or when it
arose. What was of immediate importance was to find a solution
to the problem on hand.[124]

Underlying Macdonell's report and its recommendations was,
of course, the presumption that with the mass trial at Kasama the
Watch Tower movement would not cause the Administration
any concern for a long time. It was a piece of wishful thinking
which Visiting Commissioner Hugh C. Marshall later echoed,
when in August of the same year he wrote: 'There is every reason
to believe that the sentences awarded in the [Kasama] High Court
will check the Watch Tower movement for a long time.'[125]
These were, however, forlorn hopes; for, the movement only
needed a few months to pass before it would burst into disconcerting prominence again.

At the beginning of January 1920 a certain Samuel Longwe

reported to the Native Commissioner, Fife, that he had been informed by the Mwenzo Mission evangelist, John Siame, that there were some young men who were boldly preaching 'Watchtowerism' at Chitambi's village, a few miles from Mwenzo. They were telling people to stop sending their children to school, because missionaries had not come to the country to teach the African people the word of God, but rather to earn money.[126] At the end of the same month, Father E. Peuth, Superior of Kayambi Catholic mission, reported increased Watch Tower activity in the neighbourhood of his mission station. Africans, he said, were refusing to fetch wood and water for Europeans. At Pumpa's village, where he had spent a night during a tour of this part of the Abercorn Division, he met one of Shindano's lieutenants, and in a conversation with the priest the Watch Tower disciple is reported to have admitted that his movement was political and to have said that a revolt against the Administration was being secretly planned.[127] While the priest was talking to the Watch Tower leader, young boys of eight to fifteen years old were preaching to his carriers. They appeared to have been sent to do this by a certain Dominico Patala, a former teacher at Kayambi, who had been dismissed for misconduct.[128]

Father Peuth's report is the only indication so far that the Watch Tower movement in the Northern Province ever planned open revolt against established authority. Whether in fact this was the case, it is difficult to say. But it seems curious, judging from the complete absence of official comment on his report, that the Administration should have taken no counter-measures on receiving such serious allegations. The impression one gets is that Peuth's report was ignored and considered unfounded. Indeed, there might have been some scepticism in official circles about the Catholic missionaries' reports on the Watch Tower movement. As one perceptive official observed a number of years after Peuth's report, the White Fathers were

perhaps rather intolerant of any religious movement in opposition to their own . . . They are hasty to believe anything derogatory about their opponents and mere suspicion is sometimes accepted as evidence of misbehaviour. Their attitude towards Watch Tower adherents is contentious and they endeavour to bring government into the conflict. I agree with the Provincial Commissioner [Tanganyika Province] that accusations against Watch Tower leaders by White Fathers should be accepted with caution . . .[129]

However misconstrued Peuth's observations may have been, they seem to have made a deep impression on his mind. Probably because of these impressions, he was moved to write an intelligence report in the middle of the following month to the Officer Commanding, Northern Rhodesia Police, Kasama, in which he reiterated his belief that a Watch Tower rebellion was in the making, as it was evident that the sect's preaching expressed discontent among the people against the Administration. 'The sect,' he wrote, 'is working for political ends; the religious teaching, which does not amount to much, comes in only to hide the real end, which is only politic[al].'[130] That the movement was political rather than religious was, he argued, adequately exemplified by the remarks adherents were wont to make even in the presence of Europeans:

There they are [the Europeans], they who overburden us with loads, and beat us like slaves, but a day will come when they will be the slaves. All they have was given to them that they might give us. If they do not give us all they have they are unjust towards us.[131]

Peuth, still peering into the misty war years, had probably not forgotten the manner in which Europeans were killed during the Nyasaland rising of 1915. Living as he was in one of the small pockets of isolated white settlements amidst a restless people, he naturally entertained fears of Ethiopianism, that something more or less on the scale of the Chilembwe rising could occur. For he felt that if the sort of militancy the Watch Tower sect had shown was going to spread, then a popular revolt would be inevitable. He attributed this possibility to what the adherents themselves used to tell him:

God only is to be respected and obeyed, nobody else on earth has any right to it: no more the Europeans than the native chiefs. The English have no right whatsoever in the country, they are committing injustice against the natives in pretending to have rights. When we are more numerous, the things will change, more so if a big chief like Nsokolo or any other paramount chief comes with us.[132]

The priest was overawed by these utterances, which, in his

view, were indicative of an inchoate rebellion. 'It is evident,' he wrote, 'that the whole thing points to open revolt.'[133] Such a revolt was even more likely if *Boma* Messengers and *capitaos* joined the movement. Consequently Peuth advised the *Boma* authorities that they 'should have an open eye on their employed natives and be careful not to give arms to the natives right and left'.[134]

Peuth was not unnaturally worried about the security of the Europeans who were living in the area, and was at pains to impress upon the government the importance of taking adequate and timely measures to ensure that their lives were not placed in danger as a result of some delay or neglect on the part of the authorities. Although he entertained no doubts that any possible rebellion would, like that in Nyasaland, be quelled sooner or later, he nevertheless feared that a lot of Europeans would be murdered before the Administration could intervene. He therefore urged that 'troops, and reliable troops' should be kept at Kasama and Abercorn in readiness for any eventuality. As an illustration of the Watch Tower threat the priest pointed out that, although there was no Bemba in the Abercorn Division who were known to be members of the movement, most of the Mambwe people were members. Of these, there were 500 to 600 in the Kawimbi area alone, and some sixty in the Kayambi area.[135]

What was even more disturbing to Peuth was the new element of foreign influence in the movement. In the Kasanga (Bismarck-burg) area in Tanganyika, Watch Tower leaders were frequently seen mixing freely with the 'Balungwana' people (or Swahili), who were known to be of Islamic persuasion. As the Balungwana were as a rule Moslem fanatics, said Peuth, such mixing could not be looked upon with equanimity. For, so argued Peuth, such contact was bound to introduce an even stronger political element in the Watch Tower movement. Although the leaders of the movement conducted no correspondence with Europeans, they were, he said, 'American-educated' and were 'the same kind as the famous John Chilembwe, who raised the natives at Blan-tyre'. For example, the leader of the movement in the area was Hanoc Shindano, who, added the priest, had been educated in South Africa and was operating in villages near the Saisi river.[136] It is noteworthy that owing to Shindano's activities the Administration had to direct the Post Office Controller to detain all mail and packages addressed to the Watch Tower leader for inspection.[137] This may well have been the only official reaction to Peuth's reports.

The foregoing brief account may not show that the Watch Tower movement was very active even after the High Court trial at Kasama, but it shows that it was far from extinct and that if there was any significant change, it was only in its tactics. From open and violent defiance the movement now seemed to have mellowed into a scheming and more circumspect organisation. No doubt the Kasama trial had something to do with this quiet and restrained militancy. But as to the spirit of Watch-towerism itself, it went marching on, although this time less millenarian in outlook. A song supposedly written by one Joni Silomba, a Watch Tower leader, in faulty but poetic English on the back of a slip of paper which was given to a certain Kachembele, a youth of Mwenikapanza's village in the Isoka Division (as a notice of the first tax to be paid by the latter), is very illustrative of this new spirit. The song sought to assure the leaders of the movement— Hanoc Shindano, Mishack, Shadrack, and Leviticus Kanchele— who were at the time immured in various prison cells in the province, that Watch-towerism would not falter in spite of the persecution to which the leaders and their followers were subjected. It was more than solace to a depressed leadership; it was, indeed, an exhortation to 'the dauntless spirit of resolution'. It ran:

Oh you poor kings [in prison].

Let us go and see them the Angels—the Angels with their wings.

Refuse [to stop preaching] Hanoc, Mishack, Shadrack and Leviticus, the Europeans are not really fierce.

Refuse [to stop preaching] Hanoc, Mishack, Shadrack and Leviticus, the Europeans are not really fierce.

You will be angels and Angels will receive you.

You speak good. The Administration officials speak bad. They speak bad [these] Aloma [Romans]. It is not bitter; it is not bitter.

It is not bitter, Aloma.[138]

Although after the Kasama High Court trial the Watch Tower movement seemed to have assumed a more sober attitude towards the Administration and the traditional authorities, it never abandoned its doctrines. Early in 1922 G. Stokes, Assistant Magistrate, Isoka, reported that although the fifteen members of the movement who had been deported in 1919 were now living in a peaceful manner, they had not abandoned the tenets of their faith. While not appearing to be making any progress in the conversion of adults, they were achieving great success among children. In the movement itself there were, in the words of Stokes, a number of 'semi-educated natives' in the area who had been to Southern Rhodesia and South Africa. These men, he said, dissatisfied with the prevailing conditions, argued that they were not getting sufficient benefits in return for the heavy taxes that they were paying. They pressed for secular schools and government medical services direct from the central government and not through any missionaries.[139]

The sect's insistence that all educational and medical facilities should come straight from the government and not channelled through European missionaries of any denomination was perhaps as much a movement for social betterment as it was a mark of separatist self-assertion, a determined demonstration of independence of the Watch Tower Church from the European-controlled sects. And Watch Tower agitation for secular schools was something that found favour with the Administration officials, albeit for different reasons. Stokes recommended the idea because he sincerely hoped that the introduction of properly supervised secular schools would remove the grievances over which Watch Tower was brooding, while the Secretary for Native Affairs, looking at the problem from a slightly different angle, considered the introduction of such schools as a means of removing dangerous propaganda material from the movement—material which might well be used to cause more trouble in the future.[140]

Three years after Stokes wrote his report the movement seems to have lapsed into comparative inactivity; for six years, at least, there were no reports of Watch Tower incidents by officials until the beginning of 1932. The Native Commissioner, Abercorn, reported in June 1926 that 'little is heard of the "Watch Tower" and there is some reason to think that the movement has lost ground';[141] the Native Commissioner at Isoka wrote that very little was heard of the Watch Tower leaders in his sub-district and that the few leaders that he had heard about occupied themselves with prayer meetings and bible readings.[142] And from Chinsali it was reported that the movement had no followers in the sub-district.[143] Indeed, this lull in Watch Tower activity would seem to have been country-wide: in June 1926 the Native Commissioner, Serenje, reported that the movement was dead in the area;[144] and in their respective reports for the same period and bearing the same date, the Native Commissioners for Lundazi, Broken Hill, Mkushi, Ndola, Mumbwa, Kasempa and Nalolo told the same story.[145]

Whether this lacuna should be ascribed to sheer dilatoriness and otiosity on the part of the movement or to a change of policy and approach on the part of the new (Whitehall-controlled) Administration which assumed the reins of power in Northern Rhodesia in 1924, remains a matter for speculation. However, before Watchtowerism was able to stir again the government found time to consider the question of whether or not it should recognise the sect—a question over which official opinion was divided for some time.

At a conference of Provincial Commissioners in 1931[146] the question of recognising the Watch Tower movement was discussed with cold suspicion and steadfast prejudice. Its only proponent was the Provincial Commissioner for the Mweru-Luapula Province, a lone voice which did not do justice to the official assertion that the attitude of the government towards the movement, at least as far as the Northern Province was concerned, was one of 'benevolent tolerance'.[147] The Provincial Commissioner, addressing his colleagues, said:

It must be admitted that we know very little as to the ultimate object aimed at by the Watch Tower, since their ceremonies are more or less kept secret from authority . . . That there are subversive elements at work I have not the slightest doubt, and for this reason and also in an endeavour to bring the movement above the ground, I would recommend some suitable form of recognition by the government.[148]

In support of this liberal policy he was advocating, the Provincial Commissioner warned the conference against the dangers of persecution. In the Belgian Congo, he said, severe government action against the movement had only resulted in swelling its numbers and instilling a sense of importance in its adherents, who began to feel that 'they were martyrs to a cause which the white government was trying to stamp out but would not succeed'. He believed the Northern Rhodesia government had a lot to learn from the Belgian Congo government's misguided policy towards Watch Tower, and could possibly avert its dire consequences.[149]

The Provincial Commissioner's views were put in even more vehement language by his District Commissioner at Chiengi, who reiterated the wisdom of the observation that 'religion tends to thrive under persecution and the subversive element will therefore have something to work for by simply distorting facts . . .' The District Commissioner, having observed that the leaders of the Watch Tower movement included 'a large proportion of ex-mission natives' who had been turned away from the missions for beer drinking or for 'living in sin', submitted that it was only reasonable and natural that these outcasts should want to form a Christianity of their own. For, he argued,

why should they not have a denomination of their own? Beer in moderation does no harm whatever, and it is very rare to find a Native who has got into the mental, moral and physical condition that other races get into as a result of excessive consumption of stronger alcoholic liquors . . . Polygamy is not inconsistent with Christianity . . .[150]

But these views were not shared by the people at the top of the official hierarchy. J. Moffat Thomson, the Secretary for Native Affairs, informed the Provincial Commissioner of Mweru-Lua-pula Province that the main reason why the government could not recognise the Watch Tower sect was that 'the movement is not that of a separatist Church'. The government, he said, had no objection to any African separatist Church which was entirely free from European missionary control, as long as such a Church had a committee or council which held itself responsible for the actions and teachings of its members.[151] For example, the African Methodist Episcopal Church was, he pointed out, 'a true native separatist movement in the true sense of the term',[152] and the Administration had accordingly given it recognition. It had a bishop and a council, and had regulations for the guidance of its members.[153] The Watch Tower movement, on the other hand, was, he argued, not so well organised or controlled:

The irresponsible and uncontrolled so-called Watch Tower teachers who wander in N[orthern] R[hodesia], in practically every district, are unconnected with any proper society. They preach and teach any-thing that comes into their heads and there are many instances of distinctly subversive teaching.[154]

This was the thinking that dominated the official attitude towards the movement for many years. It was no doubt influenced by certain security considerations; but the insistence by the government that the Watch Tower movement should be of the same organisational pattern as the African Methodist Episcopal Church can, with the benefit of hindsight, only be seen as a misplaced comparison of the two organisations. For whereas the latter was largely the result of African leadership self-assertiveness in clerical affairs, the former was a lot more than that; it was in effect an 'independence' movement. But the official argument against recognition raged on until September 1937, when at another annual conference of Provincial Commissioners it was recommended to the Governor that the Watch Tower movement should be recognised, provided the organisation would abide by the laws of the country and that it would exercise effective control over its members.[155]

While these arguments were going on in official circles on the fate of the Watch Tower movement, the organisation itself was again astir. At the beginning of 1932 the Provincial Commissioner for Tanganyika Province reported that the movement was 'quietly active' in his province; but it was, he said, a type of quiet activity which was giving rise to considerable concern.[156] There was 'an uncomfortable atmosphere' throughout all villages of Watch Tower persuasion, and what he called a 'veiled feeling of passive resistance against government authority'.[157] Although the rank and file were inclined to be 'sheepish', the movement nevertheless needed watching. For, the times seemed particularly propitious for Watch Tower increased activity:

Periods of famine, epidemics, lack of employment, trumped up tales as to the reason for movements into the reserves, form material to be seized upon for propaganda of a mischievous and seditious nature.[158]

Thus the effects of the world slump of the early 1930's and of the Reserves Commission of 1927, as a result of which land in the Northern Province was in 1929 alienated to the Chartered Company and other European concerns, appear to have added new fuel to the embers of discontent upon which the Watch Tower movement had always thrived. 'So,' as Stevenson has remarked, 'this is a religion that does well in times of adversity, and rather less well in times of prosperity. It thrives on bad news.'[159]

At this time, however, the movement appears to have lacked the emotion that had characterised it at the end of World War I and during the two years that followed. A visit in 1933 by G. M. Billing, District Commissioner, Abercorn, to Tukamulozya, the traditional headquarters of the movement in the district, revealed that Hanoc Shindano, who had already been in prison twice on account of committing 'breaches of the peace',[160] was not as strong a leader as he used to be, because, according to Billing, his following had dwindled to little more than ninety-six.[161]

But in spite of this apparent absence of popular enthusiasm in the movement—which may well have been due to disillusionment as to the political efficacy of the movement itself—it could not be said that Watch-towerism was in the doldrums. It became readily apparent to District Commissioner G. M. Billing that the movement was still in constant touch with its main headquarters in Cape Town. Hanoc Shindano showed Billing a typed circular letter from Cape Town which appointed 8–17 April 1933 as a week of prayer. Enclosed with the document was a letter from Judge Rutherford, the president of the movement, alleging that there was a conspiracy against Jehovah and his Anointed, and that the time of vindication and deliverance was at hand.[162] In the Abercorn district itself Watch Tower activity was noticeable. Leaving Chief Mwamba's village one evening, Billing came across a Watch Tower meeting of some six men and thirty women and children, which was being addressed by a certain Paulo, who was once a teacher at Kawimbe mission but had since been baptised by Hanoc Shindano.[163] This seemed to Billing to be an indication that the movement was gaining some ground and, although he had had no reports of seditious preaching, he feared that with a large percentage of the population unemployed the movement could take a dangerous turn.[164] Such a development was more likely, thought Billing, because Shindano himself, although hitherto well behaved, was preaching to his followers that aeroplanes had stopped bringing mail for Europeans, but only delivered mail addressed to Watch Tower preachers, and that women who were baptised as Watch Tower members should divorce their husbands, should the latter refuse to join the movement.[165]

If Watch Tower was 'quietly active' in the Tanganyika Province during this period, it was more than that in the so-called

Awemba Province. In Mporokoso District, District Officer A. Benson sentenced three leaders of the movement to two months' imprisonment each, on counts of insolence and insubordination to Chiefs Nsama and Puta of the Tabwa, Mukupa of the Lungu and the Nyamwezi chief, Nsemiwe.[166] In his tour report of 1935 Benson reported that the spread of Watch Tower enthusiasm was reaching 'serious proportions', and that a situation had arisen which seemed to him to be almost a revival of the 1918–20 disturbances.[167] The movement was devoting more attention to the conversion of youths rather than adults, and the numbers of young people baptised were so large that Benson thought they constituted 'grounds for alarm'.[168]

The sect was very active in the Tabwa areas of Chief Nsama and Chief Katele, and both chiefs felt very much troubled over it. Chief Katele at one time tried to ban the movement altogether by a Native Authority Order which forbade the leaders of the sect to preach without a permit from either the chief or from a local headman. He imprisoned a few leaders who infringed the order; but owing to the very strong pressure that was brought to bear on him by a large number of Watch Tower devotees, he was forced to sanction the movement's operations in some parts of his country.[169] Unlike Nsama, who, with an iron hand, managed to keep the movement in check, Katele apparently fell prey to the political quandary so common among the traditional rulers: he had to decide whether he should assert his authority and incur unpopularity among his people, or suffer the consequences of a conciliatory attitude towards the sect. As Benson put it, 'what Chief Katele says and what his people do are two very different things, and there is no doubt that the situation gives cause for uneasiness'.[170]

Towards the end of 1935, presumably as another effort to curb Watch-towerism, the District Commissioner, Mporokoso, sent District Messenger Mukupa and other messengers to call in a certain Sosteni Mutungu, a prominent Watch Tower leader in the Shila chief Mununga's area, who was believed to have a lot of Watch Tower literature. Messenger Mukupa and his party, on arrival at Sosteni's house, found a crowd of the movement's adherents, and it became immediately apparent that they would not be able to take Sosteni to the *boma*. They therefore decided to take Sosteni's books only. But even the mere seizure of the Watch

Tower leader's library earned the Messengers the wrath of the crowd, which tried to take the books away from them. Terms of abuse were thrown at them, calling the Messengers the white government's damnable puppets:

You are useless; you are nothing; you only worship idiots; Government is your god; the uniform you are wearing is coloured red like the fire which will burn you.[171]

The Messengers' attempts to obtain the use of a boat from Chief Mununga's son were resisted. The Watch Tower followers threatened to break the boat to pieces if it was lent to the *boma* party; and, put in such a precarious position, the Messengers had no alternative but to make a quick get-away on their bicycles, as the surging crowd vainly tried to take away Sosteni's books.[172]

A few months before the Sosteni incident took place, there was introduced into African Watch Tower in Northern Rhodesia a new element which was to be of considerable importance for the movement in the future. In March 1935 the government agreed to the idea of a European representative of the Watch Tower Bible and Tract Society (which in 1931 was renamed the Jehovah's Witnesses) residing and working in the country[173]—a measure which, in effect, gave official recognition to the sect after many years of official suspicion as to the movement's intentions. This decision followed three years of negotiations between the international Watch Tower's Cape Town headquarters and the government. In 1932 the Jehovah's Witnesses suggested to the Northern Rhodesia government that they post a European member to Northern Rhodesia so that he might control the adherents of African Watch Tower who had been causing trouble in the country. But this offer was turned down, and it was not until 1934 when another approach was made, pointing out that a similar arrangement had successfully been made with the Nyasaland government, that the Northern Rhodesia government gave the matter a sympathetic hearing. Before this, enquiries had been made of the Nyasaland government, which, in the words of C. C. Dundas, the Chief Secretary to the Northern Rhodesia government, confirmed that

the policy had proved satisfactory in that it had made possible better control of the activities of the Society, identification of recognised

N

adherents of the Society and control of the distribution of the Society's literature . . .[174]

Following upon this decision by the Northern Rhodesia government to bring the gallimaufry of African Watch Tower groups in the country under European control, Llewellyn V. Phillips was posted to Lusaka in 1935 as the sect's European representative. Whether his presence in the country made any difference to the character of the Watch Tower movement in the Northern Province, is a question which is now going to be examined.

In September 1936 Phillips visited Mumbwa and Mazabuka in the Southern Province, Serenje in the Central Province, Abercorn in the Northern Province, and Fort Rosebery and Kawambwa in the Luapula Province.[175] The reception he was given by the adherents of African Watch Tower at these centres, especially at Serenje and at Kawambwa, seems a clear indication of the gap in outlook and doctrine that existed between the local sect and the international organisation. At Serenje, reported District Commissioner C. J. Bowden, Phillips' address on the 17 September to ninety local Watch Tower adherents

was not enthusiastically received, in fact a cold silence prevailed, and after the meeting, a note was handed to Mr Phillips, stating that the interpreter was very bad, and that they had not understood his words.[176]

It may well have been true that the interpreter was not competent enough; but it seems possible that he had been used as a scapegoat for the non-acceptance, by the gathering, of the new policies and doctrines brought by the white leader. For even after the second meeting, which was later arranged to rectify the misunderstanding which had been caused by the supposedly incompetent interpreter, the adherents 'felt that their representative [Phillips] was more in the nature of a pretender set up by Government than a true member of their Society'.[177] Phillips' meeting at Abercorn on 14 September was significantly not so well attended as the Serenje one; only ten Watch Tower adherents turned up, Hanoc Shindano being one of them.[178] Probably the unacceptability of the new doctrines he was preaching—that no member of the Society should create disturbances or preach, in any way, opposition to all established authority; that tax must be paid and the law respected and obeyed; and that all preaching at large meetings should be replaced by hut-to-hut visits of small Bible study groups[179]—made most of the members of Watch Tower stay away. Certainly he does not seem to have made much impression on the Kawambwa branch of the sect. After his visit, the Provincial Commissioner for the Northern Province wrote that Watch Tower adherents in that district were 'an unruly, impertinent lot of people, and I am afraid that it will require someone of stronger personality than Mr Phillips, the Society's representative, to convince them of the error of their ways'.[180]

The prosecution of Sosteni and a few of his henchmen that followed soon after the confiscation of his books did not seem to deter Watch Tower adherents from indulging in their usual contumacious behaviour. The movement continued its acts of insubordination to established authority. Llewellyn V. Phillips, the accredited chief representative of the Watch Tower Tract and Bible Society in Northern Rhodesia, had, in the early part of 1937, to send Johnston Chitafingwa, a leading African member of the sect, from Livingstone to Mporokoso to go and pour oil on the waters. But in spite of the instructions he was given by the District Commissioner, immediately on his arrival in Mporokoso District, that he should, whenever he wanted to preach, obtain prior permission to do so from the local chief or headman, Chitafingwa did things the way he liked. His visit to the capitals of Chiefs Nsama and Nsemiwe in a way typified his own attitude and that of the rest of the adherents towards established authority. With an air of self-importance and assertiveness, Chitafingwa told the two chiefs that he had been authorised by the *boma* to preach in their areas, and proceeded to enjoin them to build shelters for him in various places so that he could use them as churches.[181] When he was asked to produce a letter of such authority, he simply threatened to take action against the chiefs with the *boma*. Chitafingwa, however, soon realised the folly of his high-handed behaviour, and when he did so he went back to his temporary headquarters at Mubanga's village. There he called together all adherents from the areas of Chiefs Katele, Nsemiwe and Nsama. What was discussed at this large gathering is unknown, but the chiefs viewed the event 'with suspicion and alarm'.[182] Not long afterwards, R. S. Hudson, the Acting Chief

Secretary, had to ask Phillips to either withdraw Chitafingwa or 'ensure that he behaves in a proper manner'.[183]

The Watch Tower movement's recalcitrant conduct and attitudes were not directed at the civil authorities alone; they were, as has been shown earlier in this chapter, also aimed at other religious movements in the province, which were led by whitemen. But if in Abercorn and Isoka Divisions the Watch Tower movement seemed to confine itself to denouncing white missionaries for teaching African half-truths about God and for refusing the children of its followers to attend mission schools, in Mporokoso District it assumed a kind of aggressive exclusivism in its attitude towards other religious institutions. In October 1938 H. J. Barnes, a representative of the London Missionary Society,[184] had to complain to Llewellyn Phillips of the obstructionism and what he called the 'studied discourtesy' of Watch Tower adherents, which he invariably encountered as he went round the villages, preaching.

I have for a long time [he wrote from a camp in Tabwa country] withheld taking any action with regard to the Watch Tower people, but I do not propose to remain passive any longer. Both they and the African Methodist Episcopal 'Church' people are seriously interfering with Mission work, but to a large extent [I] agree with Government's attitude in this matter. They [the government] rightly allow 'religious liberty'. The fallacy is that neither movement in these parts is properly to be styled 'religious'. So far as I have been able to glean information (and I have enquired pretty extensively) they are not far from being seditious.[185]

Barnes had been a victim of a few incidents which contributed to his loss of patience and reticence. He recalled that in October the previous year when he visited Koshima's village in Chief Katele's country, Watch Tower youths and women made 'as much disturbing noise as possible', just as he and his party were about to start their church service. A similar incident took place at the same village at the time he was writing to Phillips a year later. This time, a group of adherents, led by one Maliya Mwenya, gathered a few yards away from the place where Barnes was holding his service and began talking and arguing at the top of their voices. His repeated appeals to them to stop the noise failed.

When they eventually dispersed, the youths among them went into a nearby hut and there they 'laughed loudly for a long time in order to annoy us'.[186]

Such incidents and similar ones which Barnes witnessed at Chilambwe's village in Chief Nsama's area, and at Muchembe's village in Chief Mporokoso's country seemed to him to be more than manifestations of religious fervour or rivalry; they were sure signs of an anti-white feeling among Watch Tower adherents. It was antagonism which was a lot more political than theological, and which had to be stemmed.[187] Barnes not unnaturally, therefore, felt compelled to appeal to Phillips to put an end to what he called the 'clearly intolerable' Watch Tower practices. He warned: 'A serious situation would ensue if these methods were allowed to persist.'[188]

After these intermittent outbursts of Watch Tower enthusiasm in the Mporokoso District, the movement's thrust and belligerence in the Northern Province seem to have subsided. As a security problem, it does not appear to have attracted much attention by the colonial authorities till after World War II. However, it would be well at this point to attempt a brief examination of the vicissitudes of the movement from its first appearance in 1917 to the eve of World War II.

To what extent was the Watch Tower movement political? The 'political' character of the sect remains a moot issue even today in some countries of independent Africa, where the movement appears to the authorities to be eating away the fabric of good government. It is banned in Malawi; and in Zambia, where in March 1969 clashes between members of the sect in the Samfya area of the Luapula Province and members of the ruling party, the United National Independence Party, had just subsided, one senior Cabinet Minister called the sect a political party,[189] and another roundly put it down as an instrument of foreign subversion against Zambia.[190]

But drawing a parallel between the movement's activities in independent Africa and during the colonial era is something that should be done with caution, in view of the two very different social situations. In the colonial context, with all its multifarious economic, racial and political problems, the colonial authorities tended, as a matter of course, to regard Watch Tower as something more of a political movement than a religious one. One senior official of the Chartered Company Administration contended that the sect was primarily political in its nature and intentions, although this aspect was as far as possible kept in the background to give the movement a religious character. It was, he said, the only movement in the country which was akin to Pan-Africanism.[191] Another official called it 'the first clear manifestation of a dawning race consciousness'.[192] And the commission of enquiry, headed by Sir William A. Russell, which probed the disturbances on the Copperbelt of Northern Rhodesia in 1935 had this to say about the role which the movement supposedly played in the unrest:

The Commission find that the teaching and literature of the Watch Tower bring civil and spiritual authority, especially native authority, into contempt; that it is a dangerously subversive movement; and that it is an important predisposing cause of the recent disturbances.[193]

This seems to have been a misreading of the movement by men who were part and parcel of a white society which, as pointed out earlier, saw the Watch Tower movement as an embodiment of Ethiopianism—a continent-wide black sectarianism which seemed to spell doom for *Pax Europeana* in Africa. Apart from the literature published by the Watch Tower Bible and Tract Society, which various African Watch Tower groups shared, and which gave these groups a certain degree of doctrinal uniformity, there is apparently no indication that there was any functional or organic unity between them which one could, even in the loosest sense of the word, call Pan-African. It seems also doubtful whether African Watch Tower was, in fact, as important a causal factor in the Copperbelt disturbances as the Russell Commission made it appear to be. Some authorities have in fact argued that it was merely used as 'a readily available scapegoat' for the disturbances.[194] Indeed, even one or two of the government officials who appeared before the commission seemed chary of assigning much importance to the movement as one of the causes of the unrest on the Copperbelt. J. L. Keith, the District Commissioner, Ndola, for example, in his evidence stated that he did not think that the indigenous Watch Tower was against law and order or a political danger; nor did he consider that there was any evidence that the European-controlled Jehovah's Witnesses had taken an active part in the strikes.[195] E. H. Cholmeley, a member of the Legislative

Council and a man who was in government service as a District Commissioner at Fort Jameson in the early years after World War I, when the Watch Tower movement was considered more seditious, warned the commission that 'it would be rash to hazard the opinion at this juncture that Watch Tower or similar propaganda was the chief, or even an important contributory cause of the recent disturbances . . .'[196] And *The Golden Age*, the international mouthpiece of the Watch Tower Bible and Tract Society, called the Russell Report 'the most utterly shameless publication that ever found its way to print'[197] and roundly put down the Copperbelt disturbances to a 'pre-arranged Roman Catholic riot, typically "Jesuit", done with the definite intention to try to use the words "Watch Tower" in order to injure Jehovah's true and faithful witnesses'.[198]

To what extent Africans from the Northern Province were involved in the Watch Tower movement or the Jehovah's Witnesses on the Copperbelt, it is difficult to say. One comes across the names of preachers like Paison Bwembya, who was proselytising in Luanshya,[199] and Nathaniel Siwale, who was operating in the Nkana–Kitwe area.[200] But as to how many of their fellow tribesmen resident in the Copperbelt area were members of Watch Tower is unknown. Commenting on the supposed involvement in Watch Tower of the 'Bemba'—a generic term which used to include tribal groups speaking various languages similar to Bemba, like the Ushi and the Bisa[201]—E. H. Cholmeley remarked: 'I find it difficult to believe that they would readily lend themselves to any anti-European or subversive movement.'[202] However, as for the strikes, in which the northern tribes appear to have played a significant role, these will be examined later.

To question the official view that the Watch Tower sect was a Pan-African, political movement is not to deny the political character of the organisation. If it was not an organised political movement, it certainly was a highly politicised movement of belief, as the statements made by some of its adherents cited in the earlier parts of this chapter have shown. It was a 'liberation movement', sharing common aspirations and, in some senses, a common direction throughout Southern and Central Africa, by its Ethiopian and millenarian doctrines. A quotation of what one Congolese member of the sect, Emile Ilunga, said in 1937, like the utterances of his counterparts in the Northern Province, does illustrate the political nature and the liberatory aspirations of the movement as a whole:

We blacks are here in our country and what we want is to be considered as Europeans, for the Bible makes no distinctions between whites and blacks. Our Watch Tower Movement seeks to put an end to all this, for it is only here in the Congo that the government considers natives as slaves. We are fed up with this, and the new God of the Kitawalist doctrine is here to help us.[203]

It would thus be preposterous to say, as Bishop May of the Anglican Church in Northern Rhodesia argued in 1924, that if the religious element of African Watch Tower were removed the movement 'would make no strong appeal'.[204]

Yet in spite of its Ethiopian character, African Watch Tower, considered as a political movement, was not a great success in Northern Rhodesia's Northern Province and perhaps equally so elsewhere. The causes of its failure in this respect were probably as unavoidable as the movement's objectives appear to have been unattainable at the time. If it is conceded that Watch-towerism was a liberation or an 'independence' movement—as Hanoc Shindano's millenarian preachings that the whitemen would one day be driven out of the country, and Africans left alone to enjoy the riches which Europeans denied them, would seem to suggest —it will be readily apparent that the organisation could never have achieved its objective. Apart from the millenarian ideas which its leaders made the people imbibe, the movement does not seem to have had a social or political programme for the betterment of its people; nor did the leaders, as Gann has observed, attempt to infiltrate their men into local key positions: 'They left their Party Programme to the Almighty, and when Jehovah failed to intervene much of their enthusiasm evaporated . . .'[205]

Second, Watch-towerism, for all the eloquence with which it rightly condemned the social and economic ills endemic in the colonial situation, committed the unforgivable error of having alienated the traditional rulers in its unequivocal and vehement denunciation of all civil authority. For the first time in the history of Northern Rhodesia, as Gann points out, tribesmen opposed chieftainship as an institution, and not just the person of a chief, as was always the case in the past.[206] In a society where chiefs and headmen were still the centre of social as well as religious life, such an approach was most ill-advised. It had the effect of estranging not only the rulers themselves but also those of their people who were still loyal to the institution of chieftainship and who could not therefore conjure up the image of a 'republican democracy' or theocracy such as Watch-towerist teachings implied. Such support was something which the movement should not have allowed itself to lose, especially considering that its enemy was first and foremost alien rule.

Third, it seems one of the most unfortunate shortcomings of the Watch Tower movement that it had no central authority within the province. Although there are no reports of rivalry in its leadership ranks—a fact which could be explained by the Administration's possible nonchalance about relatively unimportant, though interesting, details in critical situations—it seems there was very little co-ordination of effort between the various segments of the movement in the country. While leaders like Shadrack Sinkala and Mishack were operating at their headquarters at Mwika's village in Isoka, Hanoc Shindano seems to have been holding his own at Tukamulozya in Abercorn. This lack of 'provincial' unity in the movement's activities robbed it of the effectiveness that it had striven to achieve, and also contributed to the quiet but fairly rapid decline of its political influence.

Lastly, the vicissitudes of Watch-towerism seem to have been a direct response to changes in the social and economic conditions in the country. The movement burst into a political conflagration at the end of World War I and spread rapidly when labour redundancy increased as the soldiers and military porters returned home to throw in their lot with a population resentful of the war and its after-effects. During the 1920's, when the anti-war fever and the war's social and economic 'fall-out' had subsided almost to oblivion, and when the traditional ruling class was slowly but surely equipping itself to look after the welfare of its people better, the movement was apparently in the doldrums. It was, so it seems, only rejuvenated from this moribund state by the economic conditions of the world slump and its after-effects.[207] If this postulate is something one can go by, it seems clear that the Watch Tower movement thrived on social and economic discontent, and as long as such popular discontent was at a low ebb, it tended to relapse into comparative obscurity.[208] This, perhaps more than any other single factor, determined the movement's political character and dynamism at any given time.

If the Watch Tower movement was a failure, it was so only in the political sense. But as a religious organisation—even if one called it a 'novel movement of religious anarchism', as Gann has somewhat unbenignly branded it[209]—it grew from strength to strength in Northern Rhodesia, especially as the European-controlled Jehovah's Witnesses gradually gained influence over African Watch Tower in the country. J. L. Keith, District Commissioner, Ndola, in his evidence to the Russell Commission, testified that Watch Tower had 'almost become part and parcel of native custom in the villages' and that 'nearly the whole country is affected now';[210] and a year before Northern Rhodesia became the independent sovereign State of Zambia in 1964, there were some 28,300 'active Jehovah's Witnesses' in the country.[211]

But if there is any sense in which the Watch Tower movement could be said to have left a mark on the Northern Province's political history, it is the lessons the civil authorities and the rising African elite had to learn from the movement. The Administration woke up to a new realisation that the African, in spite of his relative docility in the past to European rule, could not be taken for granted.[212] Something more than merely governing him must be done: he had to have something in return for his obliging attitude and services. This was the realisation which had dawned upon Macdonell after the mass trial of Watch Tower leaders at Kasama. To the chiefs, the movement was a parabolical lesson in one important sense: it showed them that unless they looked after their people well, they always stood the risk of losing the people's loyalty to any 'upstart' movement or persons. For the educated Africans, Watch-towerism was a great discredit to intellectual leadership in the local people's endeavours to better themselves under colonial rule.

The next chapter will try to show how the chiefs and the headmen, in the face of this experience, strove not only for political self-aggrandisement but also to give more sympathetic attention to the aspirations of their people. Similarly, the last chapter of this study will endeavour to show how the African educated elite in the province, in trying to claim what they considered their people should rightly have, assumed a more realistic approach to problems than Watch Tower had done.

NOTES

[1] Report, 2 May 1919, Abercorn District Note Book, p. 2.
[2] Interview with Jaisy Masandiko, 27 July 1967, Own Village, Chinsali Boma.
[3] Interview with Zakariya Mukosa, Choshi Village, Chief Nkula, Chinsali, 27 July 1967.
[4] Interview with Donald Siwale, Izunda Farm, Nakonde, 28 July 1967.
[5] G. Shepperson and T. Price, *Independent African* (Edinburgh University Press, 1958), p. 229.
[6] Interview with the Rev. P. B. Mushindo.
[7] Annual Report upon Native Affairs for the year ending 31 March 1919, p. 2.
[8] Administrator of Northern Rhodesia to Secretary, B.S.A.C. (London office), 23 June 1919, ZA1/10.
[9] Report by Charles R. B. Draper, Acting D.C., Tanganyika District, 2 May 1919, ZA1/10.
[10] *Ibid.*
[11] Annual Report upon Native Affairs for the year ending 31 March 1916, p. 2.
[12] Report by Draper, *loc. cit.*
[13] Interview with Moses Sikazwe; cf. Gelfand, *op. cit.*, p. 274.
[14] Annual Report upon Native Affairs for the year ending 31 March 1917, p. 1.
[15] Shepperson and Price, *loc. cit.*
[16] Terence O. Ranger, 'Revolt in Portuguese East Africa: the Makombe rising of 1917' in K. Kirkwood (ed.), *St. Anthony's Papers*, No. 15 (*African Affairs*, No. 2), London, 1963, p. 64.
[17] The name is variously spelt; some records have it as 'Hanoc Sindano' and others as 'Enoc Singano'. But the above spelling will be used here, as it seems, from oral sources, to be the correct one.
[18] Report on the Watch Tower movement in Tanganyika District, encl., Acting Administrator for Northern Rhodesia to the High Commissioner for South Africa, 6 February 1919, ZA1/10, Vol. 1.
[19] Interview with Donald Siwale.
[20] S.N.A. to Chief Secretary, 16 January 1932, KSU1/2; cf. Rotberg, *The Rise of Nationalism in Central Africa*, p. 136, n. 1.
[21] J. Moffat Thomson, S.N.A. to Chief Secretary, 16 January 1932, *loc. cit.*
[22] Shepperson and Price, *op. cit.*, p. 154.
[23] *Ibid.*, pp. 150-151.
[24] Report by the Visiting Commissioner, 15 August 1919, ZA7/7/2. The Watch Tower followers, it seems, drew a kind of political or moral difference between the British and the Americans, an attitude of mind which, no doubt, was the result of the American origins of the movement itself and of the anti-British feeling emanating from a popular revulsion against British colonial rule.
[25] *Ibid.*
[26] *Ibid.*

[27] *Ibid.*

[28] P. J. Macdonell's report, 1919, *loc. cit.*

[29] Gann calls it 'the first mass action of a non-tribal kind to take place in the Territory'; Gann, *A History of Northern Rhodesia*, p. 169.

[30] Owen Letcher, *Big Game Hunting in North-eastern Rhodesia* (London, 1911), pp. 229–230.

[31] *Ibid.*, p. 235.

[32] N.C., Chinsali to D.C., Kasama, 22 January 1919, ZA/1/10, Vol. 1.

[33] *Ibid.*

[34] *Ibid.*

[35] Report by the Visiting Commissioner, *loc. cit.*

[36] *Ibid.*

[37] *Ibid.*

[38] *Ibid.* The Visiting Commissioner's report does not state who Williams was, but he may have been one of the officials at Isoka *Boma.*

[39] Hugh Marshall in fact argued that the Spanish influenza was one of the causes of the rapid spread of the Watch Tower movement in Isoka; *ibid.*

[40] *Ibid.*

[41] *Ibid.*

[42] *Ibid.*

[43] *Ibid.*

[44] Draper to Administrator, 19 January 1919, ZA/1/10.

[45] *Ibid.*

[46] *Ibid.*

[47] *Ibid.*

[48] *Ibid.*

[49] Interview with the Rev. P. B. Mushindo.

[50] Draper to the Administrator, 19 January 1919.

[51] Peter Worsley, *The Trumpet shall sound: a Study of 'Cargo' Cults in Melanesia*, pp. 60–61.

[52] Draper to Administrator, *loc. cit.*

[53] Interview with Donald Siwale.

[54] *Ibid.*

[55] Interview with Jaisy Masandiko.

[56] Cited in Shepperson and Price, *op, cit.*, p. 158.

[57] Report on the Watch Tower movement in Tanganyika District, encl., Acting Administrator, N. Rhodesia to High Commissioner for South Africa, 6 February 1919, ZA/1/10, Vol. 1.

[58] *Ibid.*

[59] *Ibid.*

[60] Interview with Donald Siwale.

[61] Report on the Watch Tower movement in Tanganyika District, *loc. cit.*

[62] Interview with Donald Siwale.

[63] Report on the Watch Tower movement in Tanganyika District, *loc. cit.*

[64] D.C., Chiengi (Mweru-Luapula Province) to P.C., Fort Rosebery, 5 February 1932, KSU1/2.

[65] B. G. M. Sundkler, *Bantu Prophets in South Africa* (2nd ed., London: O.U.P., 1961), p. 39.

[66] Worsley, *op. cit.*, p. 43.

[67] David Kaunda, for example, did not become a minister until 1930, which was after twenty-six years of missionary work in Northern Rhodesia from the time he founded Lubwa Mission in 1904; Stone, *op. cit.*, p. 315.

[68] Sundkler, *op. cit.*

[69] T. O. Ranger, *The African Churches of Tanzania*, Historical Association of Tanzania, Paper No. 5 [1969], pp. 16–22.

[70] Lemarchand, *op. cit.*, pp. 169–170.

[71] Shepperson and Price, *op, cit.*, pp. 153–154.

[72] E. B. H. Goodall, P.C., Ndola in *Evidence taken by the Commission appointed to enquire into the Disturbances in the Copperbelt of Northern Rhodesia* (1935), Vol. I, p. 76.

[73] Draper to Administrator, 14 January 1919, ZA1/10, Vol. I.

[74] *Ibid.*

[75] Administrator to Draper, Abercorn, 15 January 1919, *loc. cit.*

[76] Draper to Administrator, 16 January 1919, *loc. cit.*

[77] Administrator to Draper, 17 January 1919, *loc. cit.*

[78] Draper to Wallace, 25 January 1919, *loc. cit.*

[79] Macdonell to Wallace, 5 May 1919, ZA1/10, Confidential.

[80] Report by the D.C., Kasama, 25 January 1919, ZA1/10, Vol. I.

[81] *Ibid.*

[82] Lieutenant of No. 1 Platoon of the N.R. Police to D.C., Tanganyika District, 24 February 1919, KSL.

[83] N.C., Chinsali, to D.C. Kasama, 22 January 1919, ZA1/10, Vol. I.

[84] *Ibid.*

[85] *Ibid.*

[86] *Ibid.*

[87] Cited in N.C., Chinsali, to D.C., Kasama, 17 March 1919, ZA/1/10, Vol. 11.

[88] *Ibid.*

[89] *Ibid.*

[90] *Ibid.*

[91] *Ibid.*

[92] *Ibid.*

[93] *Ibid.*

[94] G. Shepperson, 'Ethiopianism: past and present', *Christianity in Tropical Africa*, ed. C. G. Baeta (London: OUP, 1968), p. 250. Shepperson for convenience, divides Ethiopianism into four phases: (i) 1611–1871, when Ethiopian references in the King James version of the Bible were cherished by the negro populations of America and the West Indies as full of liberatory promise; (ii) 1872–1928; (iii) 1929–1963, when in addition to Ethiopianism 'Zionism' also came into prominence; and (iv) 1963 onwards, relating to African independent Churches under African governments; *ibid.*

[95] *Ibid.*, p. 251.

[96] *Ibid.*, p. 261.

[97] Dewhurst to D.C., Kasama, 17 March 1919, *loc. cit.*

[98] Interview with Moses Sikazwe, 29 July 1967.

[99] *Ibid.*

[100] S.N.A. to Secretary, Native Affairs Department, 4 April 1923, ZA1/10, Vol. 1.

[101] Simpelwe to magistrate, Abercorn, 26 May 1920, ZA1/10, Confidential.

[102] Abercorn Assistant N.C.'s quarterly report, 30 September 1926, ZA1/10.

[103] Shindano's statement to N.C., Fife, enclosed in S.N.A., Livingstone, to Chief Native Commissioner, Salisbury, 23 March 1920, RC 3/9/5/29, Salisbury Archives; cited in Ranger, *The African Churches of Tanzania*, p. 13.

[104] This and other references in the rest of this chapter show that African Watch Tower had churches or shelters in which followers of the movement worshipped. This was a significant departure from the practice of the international movement, the Watch Tower Bible and Tract Society (later called the Jehovah's Witnesses), which had and has no churches.

[105] Simpelwe to D.C., Abercorn, 18 May 1920, ZA1/10, Vol. 1. See also S.N.A. to Secretary, Native Affairs Department, 4 April 1923, *loc. cit.*

[106] Shepperson and Price, *op. cit.*, p. 156.

[107] Worsley, *op. cit.*, p. 43.

[108] *Idem.* 'Millenarian movements in Melanesia', *R.L.J.*, Vol. XXI (March 1957), pp. 25–26.

[109] J. Moffat Thomson, Acting D.C., Abercorn, to S.N.A., 22 December 1919, ZA1/10, Vol. 2.

[110] Worsley, *loc. cit.*, p. 29.

[111] Interview with Moses Sikazwe.

[112] *Ibid.*

[113] Report by Judge P. J. Macdonell to Administrator, 1919, *loc. cit.* W. C. Stevenson, who for fourteen years was a full-time member of the Jehovah's Witnesses, as the Watch Tower was called after 1931, has observed that the movement made phenomenal gains in countries which have been the scene of war and other troubles: *Year of Doom, 1975: the Story of the Jehovah's Witnesses* (London: Hutchinson & Co., 1967), pp. 30–31.

[114] Report by Judge P. J. Macdonell to Administrator, *loc. cit.*

[115] *Ibid.*

[116] *Ibid.*

[117] Draper, Acting D.C., Abercorn, to Tagart, S.N.A., 11 July 1919, ZA1/10, Confidential.

[118] *Ibid.*

[119] Croad, magistrate and D.C., Kasama, to Tagart, 23 June 1919, in *ibid.*

[120] Stevenson, *op. cit.*, p. 30.

[121] *Ibid.*

[122] *Ibid.*

[123] *Ibid.*

[124] *Ibid.*

[125] Memorandum by H. C. Marshall, 15 August 1919, ZA/9/2/2/2.

[126] Samuel K. Longwe to N.C., Fife, 12 January 1920, KSL.

[127] E. Peuth to Acting Magistrate, Abercorn, 26 January 1920, ZA1/10, Vol. II.

[128] *Ibid.*

[129] J. Moffat Thomson, S.N.A., to Chief Secretary, 2 August 1933, SEC/NAT/314, Vol. 1.

[130] Peuth to the Officer Commanding, N.R.P., Kasama, 19 February 1920, ZAI/10, Confidential, Vol. 2.

[131] Ibid.

[132] Ibid.

[133] Ibid.

[134] Ibid.

[135] Ibid.

[136] Ibid.

[137] Legal Adviser to Administrative Secretary, 29 March 1920, ZA/1/10, Vol. II.

[138] Quoted in N.C., Fife, to D.C., Abercorn, 31 August 1920, KSL.

[139] Cited in S.N.A. to Chief Secretary, 4 April 1923, ZA/1/10, Vol. III.

[140] Ibid.

[141] Abercorn N.C.'s quarterly report, 30 June 1926, ZA/1/10.

[142] Isoka N.C.'s quarterly report, 30 June 1926, in ibid.

[143] Chinsali N.C.'s quarterly report, 30 June 1926, in ibid.

[144] Serenje N.C.'s quarterly report, 30 June 1926, in ibid.

[145] Quarterly reports, 30 June 1926, in ibid.

[146] From 1930 onwards, what were previously called 'districts' under the B.S.A.C. Administration became known as 'provinces' and 'divisions' or sub-districts became 'districts'; similarly, the heads of these administrative units were called 'Provincial Commissioners' and 'District Commissioners' respectively.

[147] Watch Tower Movement; General, SEC/NAT/312.

[148] Confidential correspondence, 1915–1932, KSU/1/2.

[149] Ibid. In an attempt to forestall the expansion of Watch Tower, which was first introduced into Katanga in 1923 by a group of propagandists from Northern Rhodesia and Nyasaland, the Belgian authorities deported thousands of its adherents to other regions of the Congo; but instead of achieving its desired objectives, this action merely exported the influence of the movement to other parts of the country; Lemarchand, op. cit., pp. 171–172.

[150] D.C., Chiengi, to P.C., Fort Rosebery, 5 February 1932, KSU/1/2.

[151] S.N.A. to P.C., Fort Rosebery, 12 March 1932, in ibid.

[152] No evidence has been elicited to show that the African Methodist Episcopal Church existed in the Northern Province. Probably Thomson's remarks were made with reference to other parts of the territory where the sect existed. Taylor and Lehmann state that one Northern Rhodesian African minister of the sect ordained in 1933 near Johannesburg had gone back to Abercorn to start a branch; op. cit., p. 216. But there is no sign that his work had brought forth any fruit before World War II.

[153] S.N.A. to P.C., Fort Rosebery, 12 March 1932, loc. cit.

[154] Ibid.

[155] Minutes of Provincial Commissioners' Conference, August–September 1937.

[156] P.C., Abercorn, to S.N.A., 11 April 1932, SEC/NAT/393.

[157] Ibid.

[158] Ibid.

[159] Stevenson, op. cit., p. 31.

[160] D.C.'s tour report No. 3/1932, Abercorn, SEC/NAT/314.
[161] *Ibid.*
[162] *Ibid.*
[163] *Ibid.*
[164] *Ibid.*
[165] S.N.A. to Chief Secretary, 3 August 1933, SEC/NAT/314, Vol. 1.
[166] Notes by A. Benson, 29 October 1935, KSU/1/10.
[167] Mporokoso District tour report No. 4 of 1935, KSU1/10.
[168] *Ibid.*
[169] *Ibid.*
[170] *Ibid.*
[171] Testimony by Messenger Mukupa before the Mporokoso Magistrate, 7 November 1935, KSU/1/10. *Boma* Messengers then used to wear red shorts, shirts and fezzes, and the red colour of the uniform apparently looked like that of the fires of hell to the Watch Tower adherents.
[172] *Ibid.*
[173] *Debates*, col. 158, 8 May 1936.
[174] *Ibid.*
[175] A. F. B. Glennie, D.C., Abercorn, to E. N. Jalland, P.C., Kasama, 12 October 1936, SEC/NAT/314, Vol. II.
[176] Bowden to P.C., Kasama, September 1936, in *ibid.*
[177] *Ibid.*
[178] Glennie to Jalland, 12 October 1936, *loc. cit.*
[179] *Ibid.*
[180] P.C., Kasama, to Chief Secretary, 24 November 1936, in *ibid.*
[181] Mporokoso District tour report No. 4/1937, KSU/1/10.
[182] *Ibid.*
[183] Hudson to Phillips, 31 July 1937, KSU/1/10.
[184] Bolink, *op. cit.*, p. 213.
[185] Barnes to Phillips, 23 October 1938, KSU/1/10.
[186] *Ibid.*
[187] *Ibid.*
[188] *Ibid.*
[189] Mr M. M. Chona, Minister without Portfolio, quoted in the *Zambia News*, 9 March 1969.
[190] Mr S. Kalulu, Cabinet Minister for the Eastern Province, quoted in the *Times of Zambia*, 14 March 1969.
[191] S.N.A. to B.S.A.C. Administration Secretary, Livingstone, 4 April 1923, ZA1/10, Vol. III.
[192] Lusaka Resident Magistrate to S.N.A., 13 December 1926, ZA1/10.
[193] *Report of the Commission appointed to enquire into the Disturbances in the Copperbelt of Northern Rhodesia* (1935), Vol. 3, p. 49.
[194] Taylor and Lehmann, *op. cit.*, p. 229; cf. Wills, *op. cit.*, p. 233; and Bolink, *op. cit.*, pp. 117–118.
[195] *Evidence*, Vol. 1, pp. 152–153.
[196] *Ibid.*, p. 356.
[197] *The Golden Age*, Vol. XVII, No. 425 (January 1936), p. 204.
[198] *Ibid.*, p. 207.

[199] Criminal Investigation Department report, 16 September 1935, SEC/NAT/314, Vol. II.

[200] C.I.D. report, 2 November 1935, in *ibid.*

[201] Evidence to the Russell Commission by E. B. H. Goodall, Senior P.C., Ndola, *Evidence*, p. 301.

[202] *Ibid.*, p. 357.

[203] Cited in Lemarchand, *op. cit.*, p. 172.

[204] Cited in Bolink, *op. cit.*, p. 116.

[205] Gann, *A History of Northern Rhodesia*, p. 170.

[206] *Ibid.*, p. 169.

[207] According to Kuczynski, as a result of the depression in 1930 in the labour markets of South Africa, Southern Rhodesia and the Congo, several Northern Rhodesians working there were laid off and they returned home; *op. cit.*, p. 472. Thousands of other workers were laid off on the Copperbelt and forced to return to their villages 'disillusioned and disturbed'; Bolink, *op. cit.*, p. 119.

[208] Stevenson, *op. cit.*, pp. 30–31.

[209] Gann, *loc. cit.*

[210] *Evidence*, p. 152. Information on the actual growth of the movement in the Northern Province in the late 1930's is lacking. The government seems to have been preoccupied with the movement's activities in so far as they affected security but was apparently oblivious to its growth in numbers.

[211] Norman Long, 'Religion and socio-economic action among the Serenje-Lala of Zambia', *Christianity in Tropical Africa*, p. 397.

[212] Report by Judge P. J. Macdonell, ZA1/10, Confidential.

CHAPTER V

POWER AND POLITICS AMONG THE TRADITIONAL AUTHORITIES

I. THE BACKGROUND

Somewhat paradoxically, the African traditional rulers in the Northern Province seem to have emerged from World War I and from the turmoil caused by the Watch Tower movement more of a social force to reckon with than they ever were since the inception of colonial rule. This was probably in part due to the introduction, during the war, by the B.S.A.C. Administration of the Administration of Natives Proclamation No. 8 of 1916, which, among other things, defined the duties of the chiefs and required commoners to carry out their 'reasonable' orders, and which enabled chiefs to exercise a 'considerable amount of control over their people in exacting customary free labour . . . and even in the recruitment of paid labour for the government . . .',[1] something which they had been unable to do before.[2] Furthermore, the recruitment of labour for the war which the chiefs and headmen had to carry out on behalf of the Administration under the proclamation, afforded them the opportunity of exercising a measure of authority over their people which until now they had eschewed. The sobering effect of the war, which for the most part prevailed over a people who in the past had almost invariably shown a defiant attitude towards authority, indeed made even more possible the exercise of these powers, and in a way restored the sense of self-confidence which the traditional rulers seemed to have lost during the previous two decades of white rule.[3]

Moreover, the outbreak and the activities of the Watch Tower movement had alienated the chiefs to a point where they almost identified themselves with the colonial authorities, in defence of the little power they still had, against the first political malaise ever to threaten their hold on the people. Chitimukulu's and Mwamba's viewpoint on the movement was perhaps typical of the attitude of the Northern Province's African rulers towards Watch-towerism. During the Kasama High Court trial of the Watch Tower leaders, the two chiefs made it plain that they regarded the whole movement 'with disgust [and] as a revolt of mannerless slaves, and marvelled . . . at the Boma for being so patient and so long-winded about it all'.[4] Earlier, some chiefs and headmen in the Chinsali Division had spoken 'in grateful terms' of Native Commissioner Dewhurst's 'prompt action, [which had] brought the [Watch Tower] people to their proper senses and by insisting upon cultivation saved portions of the district from hunger'.[5] It was this intense dislike of the Watch Tower movement which made chiefs and headmen co-operate fully with the Administration in suppressing it, and it was in the process of their fervent endeavours to extirpate the movement that they were able to wield more power.

Another factor which enhanced the power and influence of the traditional authorities was the change of government in 1924. When in that year the imperial government took over the administration of Northern Rhodesia from the Chartered Company, deliberate efforts were made to bring the territory's native administration into line with the general policy operative in other British African tropical dependencies, and these efforts culminated in the passing in 1929 of the Native Authority Ordinance and the Native Courts Ordinance by the Legislative Council—a measure which followed a recommendation by a conference of Administrative Officers two years earlier that a system of indirect rule be introduced in the territory.[6] The Native Authority Ordinance, 1929, replaced the Administration of Natives Proclamation No. 8 of 1916 and amended Proclamation No. 6 of 1919, which, in the words of J. Moffat Thomson, the Secretary for Native Affairs, 'merely made use of the chiefs and headmen as mouthpieces of the government and did not take sufficient advantage of native institutions'.[7] In explaining what the government hoped the new legislation would achieve, Moffat Thomson told the Legislative Council:

The new Bill introduces a more advanced form of native administration, which gives to the chiefs the management of their own affairs within their tribal areas and it is hoped it will preserve and maintain all that is good in native custom and tribal organisation . . . This system of local self-government has many advantages. It will make the natives more contented. Chiefs will take more interest in their affairs, and there will be no place for the political agitator.[8]

The government's hopes that, as a result of these measures, Africans would be more contented and that there would be no room for political agitators were, of course, to be proved false by later events. But there is no doubt that the establishment of Native Authorities was a significant departure from the Chartered Company's direct rule policy, which used the chiefs merely as instruments of white rule. The new policy was even more significant because it instituted Native Courts as well. Although chiefs had, even under B.S.A.C. rule, continued to exercise jurisdiction, particularly in civil cases,[9] their authority and influence in this field were tenuous, since most criminal cases fell under the jurisdiction of the Administrative Officer, who was often not conversant with the African judicial process. Thus the Native Courts Ordinance was introduced because, as Moffat Thomson pointed out,

Chiefs are better able to judge of the credibility of native witnesses and are often in possession of information relative to litigation which is not obtainable by European officers. Again, many civil cases are so bound up with native custom that it is almost impossible for a district officer to acquire such a knowledge of all the circumstances as will enable him to deliver a fair and comprehensive judgement.[10]

But if indirect rule means, as Leo Marquard argued, almost the same thing as 'the theory of self-determination applied to Native tribes'—which, although not allowing chiefs to exercise independent sovereign powers, nevertheless invested the institutions of chieftainship and tribal councils with political, administrative and judicial powers and established tribal treasuries, so that as much responsibility as possible might be delegated to the chief and his council and the task of the Administrative Officer confined to 'the much more subtle one of guiding rather than of directly controlling'[11]—then these ordinances, which took effect the following year, were far from accomplishing it. The Native Authority Ordinance of 1929, as T. F. Sandford, the Senior Provincial Commissioner, confessed seven years later while introducing a Bill in the Legislative Council to bring about the Native Authority Ordinance, 1936, had 'ignored almost entirely the existence of native councils and native officials'.[12] Furthermore, until 1937 there were no Native Treasuries, and this lack of financial responsibility on the part of the traditional authorities left largely incomplete the system of African local self-government about which Moffat Thomson had spoken in 1929. Under such circumstances, and in the face of the difficulties which were being experienced by the traditional rulers in obtaining tribute labour (about which more will be said), it seemed clear to the government that Native Authorities would become, as Sandford put it, 'mere debating societies, unable to fulfil their functions . . .'[13] It was no doubt for these reasons that the Native Authority Ordinance, 1936, was passed: to give recognition to tribal councillors and court officials, and also to set up Native Treasuries,[14] even though Native Authorities under the new ordinance were still not empowered to collect poll tax, their sources of revenue being confined to court fees and fines, game, bicycle, dog and arms licences, and ten per cent of the poll tax collected by the government from their people living either within or outside their tribal areas.[15] Similarly the Native Courts Ordinance of 1929 was repealed, and replaced by the Native Courts Ordinance, 1936, which gave power to the Governor not only to appoint Native Courts but also to prescribe their powers and procedures, and to empower the country's white judiciary to re-try, quash, reverse, or vary judgements from Native Courts.[16]

If all these measures had the effect of restoring some of the authority and influence lost by chiefs and headmen during the previous decades of colonial rule, they also seem, as will be seen later, to have given even greater impetus to the tendencies (to which reference was made in Chapter III) among the leaders of former subject tribes of trying to regain territories or chieftainships which they had lost to their more powerful neighbours during the tribal wars of the previous centuries, and of renouncing any vestiges of political influence over them by their former overlords. The inter-war years in fact saw the traditional rulers in the Northern Province as a generally self-assertive and self-aggrandising lot, who also used their new powers to demand *mulasa* or tribute labour, not merely as a right by custom, but also as something that was enforceable under the colonial legal system. Moreover, in contrast with their relatively guarded, if diffident, political stance before World War I, they became outspoken critics of government policies over matters relative to land and tax and became, in effect, the leaders of the protest movement against colonial rule earlier led by the Watch Tower prophets. It would be well here, before the discussion which follows later in this chapter, to give a brief background to these vexed issues.

The 1920's witnessed the appointment of a land commission, for one purpose or another, in each of the three territories of British Central Africa. In Nyasaland, the Jackson Commission of 1920 was appointed to report on the protectorate's land policy and on the advisability of setting up native reserves in that country;[17] in Southern Rhodesia the year 1925 saw the appointment of the Morris Carter Commission, whose report was later to become the cornerstone of the self-governing colony's Land Apportionment Act of 1930;[18] and, in Northern Rhodesia, two Reserves Commissions for the East Luangwa District and for the Railway Belt were appointed in 1924 and 1926 respectively, both of them under the chairmanship of Judge P. J. Macdonell,[19] and a third one, headed by J. Moffat Thomson, was appointed in 1927 for the Tanganyika District.[20] The three areas in Northern Rhodesia which were subjects of enquiry by the Reserves Commissions appear to have had native reserves even before the commissions were appointed,[21] and together with Barotseland, which covered an area of approximately thirty-seven million acres, they formed a total of seventy-one million acres of African land, as compared with nine million acres which were set aside as European land and another eleven millions which comprised Crown land.[22] However, unlike in the East Luangwa area, where the task of the Reserves Commission of 1924 was to devise a formula which would solve the problem of overcrowding, which had become most acute in the native reserves there, while at the same time affording European settlers sufficient land to grow more cash crops;[23] and unlike in the Railway Belt, where the problem before the commission appears to have been how to allay fears of economic competition from the African peasantry there by adjoining European growers,[24] the task entrusted to the Reserves Commission of 1927 for the Tanganyika District was to make more land available to existing and potential European coffee planters, by making the B.S.A.C. relinquish parts of its Tanganyika Estate, and by resettling some of the local Africans in reserves.[25] The Chartered Company had acquired 4,310 square miles of land in the district from the African Lakes Corporation which formed the 'Tanganyika Estate', most of which lay in the

Abercorn Division, extending to parts of the Isoka Division,[26] but only the Abercorn portion of this had been alienated, to any considerable extent, to Europeans, whom the B.S.A.C. Administration persuaded to settle in the area and take up land.[27] These first settlers originally came as ranchers, but after World War I a few of them, and others who came to the district later, began growing cotton and coffee; and so it was with a view to promoting the growing of these new cash crops that the Reserves Commission of 1927 was appointed to recommend ways and means of alienating more land to European farmers.[28] It visited the Awemba and Tanganyika Districts in the middle of 1927, and everywhere it went it met with strong opposition from chiefs to the idea of bringing in more Europeans to settle in the area.[29] But in spite of all this opposition, the Crown Lands and Native Reserves (Tanganyika District) Order-in-Council, 1929, was passed, which created native reserves and Crown lands in the district, and which, unlike the other orders-in-council for East Luangwa and the Railway Belt, gave Africans a time limit—four years—within which to move into the reserves.[30]

One of the objectives which the government thought would be achieved by increasing the number of European farmers in these parts of the Northern Province was to give the local population the benefits of local employment and check labour migration, which was giving rise to socio-economic problems in the area. It was hoped that by such local employment and training on plantations and in associated industries, the local people would be able to earn money not only whilst in such employment or training, but even after they had left their European employers to manage their own farms. This role of the European settler as a potential employer and trainer, who would help arrest the drift of men from the Northern Province, had been strongly emphasised by E. H. Goodall, the Acting District Commissioner for Tanganyika District, two years before the Reserves Commission was appointed:

A system which drives a large proportion of the taxable males hundreds of miles from their homes in order to meet their tax obligations and clothe their families is unsound. In this connexion the Kambole Industries experiment deserves every encouragement. Mr. Ross' aim is to introduce and foster local industries such as cotton growing on a commercial scale. He has about 100 natives regularly employed on the cotton fields and thus getting practical training, and he hopes that next year the natives will have seventy acres of their own cultivation. . . . If the few who have had the enterprise to grow a little cotton this year obtain good prices for their crops a big development is sure to follow.[31]

Taking into account the economic conditions prevailing in the country at the time, Goodall's argument seems to have been little more than wishful thinking. While transport and communications remained bad between the Northern Province and the country's urban centres on the line of rail, where the province's agricultural produce could be marketed, it seems inconceivable that any development on the scale which Goodall had envisaged would ever have taken place. Indeed, it was this very lack of easy contact with the town centres which seems to have limited European demand for land in the province.[32] Although after World War I the B.S.A.C. Administration had successfully persuaded a considerable number of settlers to take up land in the Abercorn Division, various enterprises failed,[33] and by 1938— nine years after the enactment of the Crown Lands and Native Reserves (Tanganyika District) Order-in-Council, 1929—only 500 of the 33,000 acres of land alienated for European settlement were actually under cultivation.[34] This lack of a European settler-farming community in the Northern Province, which apart from bad communications was also caused by the bad terrain of the area, made labour migration inevitable. Moreover, labour migration itself was not simply a question of labour finding its way to the nearest place of employment, irrespective of the wages and other working conditions obtaining at such a place. In fact, as the money economy made itself felt in the rural areas, the price paid for labour there became increasingly exposed to competition in the labour market and labour migration became more and more a reaction to a market situation in which labour, as a matter of course, flowed from areas of low wages to centres where it fetched a higher price. This point was made clear in a speech made by the Governor, Sir James Crawford Maxwell, during the opening of the fifth session of the Second Legislative Council on 17 April 1928, when he said:

The native inhabitant of the Tanganyika Plateau today walks three hundred miles or more to find employment at sixpence a day rather

than be content with twopence nearer home, whether it be north-
wards to the sisal plantations of Tanganyika Territory, westwards
to the Katanga, or southwards to the mines at Bwana Mkubwa or
Broken Hill.[35]

Thus, as long as wage differentials between rural areas and other
centres of employment existed, other differences apart, labour
migration was bound to continue, and the result of such migration
was to create the general labour shortage in the country, to which
the Governor referred during the same speech.[36] That the forces
of demand and supply were behind labour migration was a point
which stood out in 1925, when some Unofficial Members agitated
in the Legislative Council for the institution of a pass system for
Africans, which would help employers in the country retain the
labour they needed. In answer to this importunity, F. S. B.
Tagart, the Secretary for Native Affairs, outlined to the council
the economics of labour migration, which, in a way, was an
adumbration of what Sir James Maxwell was to say three years
later. He said that the proposed system was not going to be the
panacea for the desertion of African employees, who, like all
human beings, wanted improved conditions of labour.[37]

Tagart's explanation for labour migration and the resultant
labour shortage in the country appears, like Maxwell's, to have
presupposed a free labour market, where the law of demand and
supply operated without any inhibition or coercion. But in fact,
as was pointed out in Chapter III, the supply of labour was forced
to respond to the ever-growing demand for it by fixing taxes at
such a level as would make taxable men leave their homes to
work on farms and in urban centres in order to earn tax money.
The abolition of the three shillings' hut tax in 1914 in North-
eastern Rhodesia and its replacement by tax on plural wives[38] did
not in any way ameliorate the position of the African tax-payer.
In fact his position deteriorated, as he was now made to pay poll
tax of five shillings per year for himself and the same amount for
each wife or concubine he had in addition to his first one.[39] The
tax was, moreover, increased to ten shillings in 1920,[40] and even
when it was reduced to seven shillings and sixpence five years
later, and tax on plural wives was abolished in 1929,[41] great
difficulty was experienced by the African tax-payer in meeting
his obligations, as the tax did not take into account his ability to

pay. An investigation carried out by the District Commissioner, Abercorn, into the incomes of fifty African males in the Lungu Reserve No. II showed that the average *per capita* income in the area was only £1 18s 3d per annum, 30 per cent of which was paid to the government in tax.[42] It revealed further that much of this income—69·5 per cent—was earned from work outside the Northern Province, mainly in Tanganyika, and that only 12·5 per cent was earned from remunerative employment within the district, while 18 per cent was from the sale of agricultural produce.[43] These figures suggest that the majority of Africans in the Abercorn District went to work outside the Northern Province in order to earn tax money, which in itself indicates that it was not possible to raise enough money within the province. Clearly, such a system, in which men were forced to trudge several hundreds of miles in order to earn a few shillings to pay their taxes and meet their barest family needs, was most unsatisfactory.

If the situation was so bad in Abercorn, where there were a few European settlers who employed considerable numbers of Africans, it must have been worse in other districts, where, apart from *bomas*, missions (and the Shiwa Ng'andu estates in the Chinsali District), which employed a few workers, opportunities for earning money locally were almost non-existent.[44] The only exception appears to have been Luwingu District, where the people of the Bangweulu area were engaged in a lucrative external trade in fish, meal, groundnuts and skins with the Congo through European traders like Bourgeois and Massart.[45] But, generally speaking, local employment opportunities in other parts of the Northern Province were practically non-existent, and labour migration there was even greater. In Mporokoso District, for example, so many men had left the district for work abroad that the names of nine hundred of them had to be deleted from the tax register in 1936, because they had been absent for too long;[46] some of these absentees seem to have removed with their families into the Congo, where taxation was lower.[47] This family migration was a phenomenon which added a new dimension to labour migration as a reaction to taxes. It was also reported in the Muyombe Division of Isoka District, where 50 per cent of 158 taxable males whose names were struck off the tax register were believed to have migrated to Nyasaland with their families in order to get away from high taxation in Northern Rhodesia.[48]

Not only did these migrations give rise to general labour shortage in the Northern Province, but they also created a situation where there were few men available to perform the customary *mulasa* duties for the chiefs, and those young men who returned home from work abroad became increasingly averse to the traditional calls on them to carry out such responsibilities. This state of affairs, as will be seen later, was detrimental to the authority of the traditional rulers; and at a time when government policy was, through the mechanics of indirect rule, to make the institution of chieftainship as effective an organ of native administration as possible, the colonial authorities found themselves in a position where, while intent on promoting the authority of the chiefs, they were at the same time treating as 'slavery' or 'forced labour' one of the main pillars upon which the institution of chieftainship traditionally rested. This was one of the rare occasions on which the colonial authorities appear to have championed the cause of the common people against what appeared to them to be the selfish interests of the traditional rulers, who were intent on increasing their authority and influence.[49]

2. THE TRADITIONAL RULERS IN THE COCK-PIT

Attempts at political self-aggrandisement among chiefs were sometimes marked by succession disputes over vacant chieftaincies, like the dispute in 1924 over the Chitimukuluship between Mwamba IV Kanyanta and Nkula IV Bwalya, which followed the death of Chitimukulu Ponde two years before and which was the subject of a protracted enquiry by H. G. Willis, District Commissioner, Awemba District;[50] but more often such attempts were made by some chiefs of smaller tribes asserting their independence against old claims of suzerainty over them by chiefs of bigger tribes. Probably the most notable example of the latter was the case between Nkuka of the Bisa and Chikwanda of the Bemba in Mpika Division to which reference was made in Chapter III. It was a long and tangled story which went on for two decades, and it is not proposed in this study to go into the labyrinth of its turns and twists.

Towards the end of World War I, Nkuka reopened his age-old claim to Kasenga country—an area in the Mpika Division which, he said, had been under the Nkuka royal house for generations, but which Chief Chikwanda was falsely claiming as one of his dominions by right of conquest. According to the evidence he gave before the Broken Hill magistrate,[51] in one of his relentless endeavours to retrieve Kasenga for the Nkuka chieftainship and to be independent of Chikwanda, Nkuka claimed that there was never a time when Kasenga fell under Bemba hegemony as a result of an invasion by Bemba armies. The position, as he put it, was that before the Europeans came to the country Chikwanda was driven out of Bembaland by his uncle Chitimukulu and his brother Mwamba, probably because he had committed adultery with the Paramount's wives. Chikwanda then sought refuge in Kasenga country and the reigning Nkuka at the time gave him the necessary protection even though some time later he (Chikwanda), together with Chief Nkuka himself, were killed by Chitimukulu's envoys—an assassination in which the Bisa chief, Kopa, a brother of the murdered Nkuka, was an accomplice.

After the assassination of the two chiefs the new Chikwanda, with his people, went to live with the Nkuka, who had just succeeded to the chieftainship of Kasenga (the complainant in this dispute). But later when Chikwanda heard that his brother Chief Nkula was dead, he went back to Bembaland to succeed him, leaving his people behind to continue exploiting the salt pans in Mpika. Chikwanda did not, however, occupy the Nkula-ship for very long. According to Nkuka, he was turned out by the Administration for ill-treating his people,[52] and went back to Mpika and settled on the southern side of the Luitikila river, while Nkuka and most of his people occupied the other side of the river, with all its salt pans. Chikwanda was made to understand that he was Nkuka's guest and could claim no rights to any territory. This, according to Nkuka's version of the story, was the position, and Frank Melland, the Native Commissioner of Mpika Division at the time, was reportedly aware of it.[53]

Nkuka's claims were not, however, borne out by Melland's own recollections of the case. According to Melland, Nkuka came back to Kasenga about 1901 from the Luangwa valley, where he had lived for many years since the Bisa were driven to the valley and to Lala country by Bemba invaders under Chikwanda. He was not a 'real chief', but owing to a misapprehension which had been created by his predecessor, Cookson, the previous year, Melland recognised Nkuka in 1902 as a sub-chief and allotted him a small subsidy.[54] At that time Chikwanda was still living in Chinsali and had no representative in Kasenga. When, however, in 1909 Chikwanda returned to Mpika, Melland made Nkuka understand and accept the fact that he was Chikwanda's protégé and to him, in conformity with established customary procedure, he would have to supply labour and pay tribute. But the unfortunate thing about it all was that Nkuka assumed the full outlook and authority of a chief, not under any other superior chief, but independent and autonomous.[55]

Melland's account in Nkuka's case was to all intents and purposes vindicated by the evidence garnered from extensive enquiries which Jelf made among certain well informed eyewitnesses, two of whom were Chief Luchembe and Chief Chikwanda himself.[56] The evidence appears to have established as a fact the moot point that Nkuka was an impostor—a pretender to a non-existent sovereign chieftancy. But unfortunately Jelf's one-man commission of enquiry seems to have delved into too much detail, and as a result could not see the wood for trees. The question of whether or not the Nkukaship had existed in the pages of history as a chieftainship seems to have been lost sight of, and instead the Administration occupied itself with proving that Nkuka and his people were once conquered by Chikwanda and his warriors. In so far as the recognition of some chiefs' claims of suzerainty over others by right of conquest was convenient for administrative purposes, this was all well and good. But Jelf's investigations should have gone a step further: he should have taken upon himself to prove whether Nkuka's claims to chieftainship could be sustained by the facts of history. For the Bisa claimant was at pains not only to assert his desire to be independent of Chikwanda but also to prove that he was a chief in his own right. Both facets of the case were necessarily pertinent to the solution of the problem. Probably the narrow view which Jelf's report took may have been the result of the fact that, with the exception of Chief Kopa, all the other nine informants interviewed were Bemba,[57] who naturally were prone to stretch their case in the quarrel.

The Jelf report's shortcomings apart, there is little doubt that Nkuka had taken advantage of the presence of a European government to vent his anti-Bemba feelings and to rid himself of what he considered to be the clutches of Bemba overlordship.

So adamant was Nkuka in his refusal to recognise Chikwanda as his overlord that, when Hugh C. Marshall, the Visiting Commissioner, in June 1918 and in the presence of all parties to the dispute, ruled the case in favour of Chikwanda, he told Marshall: 'I cannot obey any Awemba; I can only be advised by Kopa'.[58] After Marshall's ruling in the case, Nkuka went to Broken Hill to canvass the magistrate there and later on proceeded to see the Administrator at Livingstone, where he is said to have told 'garbled and untrue tales' regarding the actual position.[59] He made it clear before he left that he would not go to District Commissioner Croad at Kasama to complain because the latter 'lives among the Awemba and will favour the Awemba'.[60] At one stage, when it was decided to remove him from Kasenga to another area in order to put an end to the dispute between him and Chikwanda, Nkuka refused to move, and sent thirty shillings to Assistant Native Commissioner Jelf in an unsuccessful attempt to bribe him into rescinding the decision.[61] H. Croad, the District Commissioner at Kasama, wrote of Nkuka's case:

You have here a good instance of the usual Awisa methods—Nkuka, who had been found and brought back by Chikwanda and given a wife by him and settled down by him in his [Nkuka's] old country, as soon as the Boma comes in he refuses to recognise him and tries to get the Boma to declare him [Nkuka] separate from Chikwanda.[62]

In his consistent opposition to Chikwanda's authority, Nkuka was able to draw on a number of factors which appeared to further his cause. He seems to have enjoyed a considerable following among his own people and among a few Bemba men who were married to Bisa women, and he used this support, and the 'power vacuum' created by the constant changes of Administration officials at Mpika, to take up a consistently defiant attitude and passive resistance to Bemba suzerainty.[63] Nkuka's intransigence was further reinforced by two other forces. The previous Chikwanda, Chikwanda II, seemed on the whole to have been a weak chief who had probably exercised little authority in Kasenga and could not, therefore, cope with Nkuka's unrestrained self-assertiveness.[64] Second, after the weak Chikwanda's death Averay Jones, the Native Commissioner at Mpika at the time, made the unfortunate mistake of separating Nkuka's area from Chikwanda's country—a measure which had the undesired result of giving Nkuka the impression that he was in fact independent of his Bemba overlord.[65] These two factors, quite apart from everything else, coupled with the fact that during World War I the dispute fell in abeyance as official attention was diverted to the war effort, tended to strengthen Nkuka's position,[66] so much so that by 1918 he was generally regarded as a chief and treated as such by most people and local Administration officials alike.[67]

In the Mporokoso Division revulsion against Bemba political influence by local ethnic groups seems, from available sources, to have been rather guarded and indirect. Kaliminwa, the local Lungu chief, whose father had earlier appealed to the white Administration to thwart the overthrow of his authority by Tomboshalo, another outstanding political figure among the Lungu (see Chapter III), was now vying with the local Bemba chief, Mporokoso, for political superiority in the country. Although he had got to the exalted position which he was occupying because of his late father's fighting prowess as a general in the Bemba armies during the latter part of the nineteenth century, as a result of which the latter was awarded the chieftain-ship and a woman for a wife by Mwamba,[68] the young Kaliminwa withdrew recognition of both the ruling Mwamba's and Mporo-koso's overlordship. He refused to respect the two chiefs, as his father Chilangwa had done, because they were of 'a junior stand-ing'. Mporokoso, who was a son of Mwamba and the immediate supervising authority over Kaliminwa, bore the brunt of the Lungu chief's rebellious turn of mind, scolding him in public as a worthless person.[69]

Kaliminwa's impertinent behaviour provoked Mporokoso into demanding of the *boma* that he be deposed, so that Chief Mwamba might appoint somebody else to the chieftainship. After all, argued Mporokoso, Kaliminwa was not strictly speaking a chief, even though his father was of royal blood. The demand for the deposing of Kaliminwa had earlier been made to the Visiting Commissioner in 1918, but it was then considered that the matter was exclusively in Mwamba's province to solve. However, it was now apparent that the situation could not be allowed to remain fluid indefinitely, and the Administration would have, in one way or another, to intervene in an effort to resolve the problem. For if the local Native Commissioner remained indifferent or averse to the quarrel, Mporokoso would have no alternative but to go to Kasama and fight the matter out with the District Head-quarters.

This difficult position forced the Mporokoso Native Commissioner to carry out investigations into the political authenticity of Kaliminwa's refusal to pay respect and tribute to Mporokoso. On 9 July 1920 he called in thirteen of the twenty headmen in Kaliminwa's country for an enquiry. The fact that they were all Lungu and avowed relations of the chief appears to have prejudiced the case in Kaliminwa's favour. For they all subscribed to their chief's argument that if ever he was to pay any tribute to any Bemba chief—as his father had done and as he himself had done on occasions before the war—it was only to Mwamba, whose suzerainty they were still prepared to acknowledge as a fact of history.[70]

In one other respect, however, their assessment of the problem was apparently as confused as the main point at issue itself (the deposing of Kaliminwa) was touchy. While the headmen professed loyalty for Kaliminwa, they at the same time claimed that he was not of royal blood. Yet they were the same old men who, a few years back, had appointed him a successor in his own right to the Kaliminwaship. One might indeed ask, as Father Safelles of Kapatu French Roman Catholic mission asked, 'why then had they proposed him [as successor] to the Administration?'[71] The answer may well be that, although, as the Native Commissioner put it, the Lungu and their headmen were restless under the new Kaliminwa's exacting rule, they were, by custom, averse to expressing disapproval of a person in authority publicly, even though they abhorred his exercise of authority.[72] But whatever the reason for the apparent ambiguity in the headmen's reactions to the Mporokoso–Kaliminwa dispute, it seems clear that their answers were not very useful towards finding a solution to the problem. For, apart from probably going by Hugh Marshall's precept in the Chikwanda–Nkuka dispute that Nkuka and other representatives of conquered tribes should be made to understand that they would only be recognised as chiefs or headmen under the Bemba—so that further political fragmentation might be stemmed[73]—the Native Commissioner in the end found no reason upon which to base his recommendation for the dismissal of Kaliminwa other than that, as he put it, 'my experience of Mporokoso is that he is a chief whose opinions are worthy of consideration'.[74]

While the Mporokoso–Kaliminwa power struggle was going on in the Mporokoso Division there was another clash in the Isoka Division between Katyetye, a Tambo chief, and Chieftainess Mweni-Milongo of the Iwa tribe over the boundary separating their respective countries. It was another instance of a former subject tribe (the Tambo) wiping off itself the cobwebs of domination by another tribe (the Iwa). The quarrel was of such gravity that G. Stokes, the Native Commissioner and assistant magistrate at Isoka, was forced to call a meeting of chiefs on 20 January 1922 in order to settle it.[75] Apart from the parties in the dispute, there were also present at the meeting Chief Kafwimbi of the Iwa and several headmen from the two tribes.

In his submission at the meeting, Katyetye claimed that many years previously, when the existing official boundary (along the Mpando Plateau ridge separating his country from Mweni-Milongo's) was being drawn, he was called to Milongo *Boma*, where he was informed by Robert Young and de Jong that owing to a delineation of the Chinsali–Isoka division boundary, two of his villages would go to the Chinsali division, while he himself and the rest of his people would remain in the Isoka division. To comfort him over the loss of part of his country, the Administration, so he alleged, gave him £5, and assured him that although the two villages had been placed under Chinsali they would continue to pay tribute to him and to no other chief.[76] It is not known whether in fact the alleged pact was made and whether Katyetye did continue to receive tribute from the villages in question. But when the boundary between the two divisions was revised in 1920 he was quick to demand that the villages be put under his direct control. This was the immediate cause of the dispute.

From the point of view of Chieftainess Mweni-Milongo, however, Katyetye's version of the point at issue was garbled and his claim a fake. According to the chieftainess, the area in which the disputed villages were situated was, until the advent of the Administration, part of Chief Kafwimbi's country. It only fell under Katyetye's sphere of authority when Messrs McKinnon and Young made the Chinsali–Isoka boundary at the end of the last century.[77] In this argument Mweni-Milongo and Kafwimbi were all one. The latter informed Stokes that from the time his grandfather, Kafwimbi Sungwe, drove the Tambo people across

P

Mpando Plateau some time during the last century, the country to the west of the plateau was taken by the Iwa, and, as the Tambo people had no chief of importance, every successor to the Kafwimbi stool had consequently exercised rights over the whole of the Tambo country.[78]

It must have been clear to Native Commissioner Stokes that Mweni-Milongo, supported by her overlord, Kafwimbi, was intent on retaining under her sway a piece of territory which, by all available indications, was Tambo country but which by sheer right of conquest she was claiming as her own. But, as if oblivious of the precedent set by the Administration in cases of a similar nature in the country, the Native Commissioner took the unusual stance of supporting the claims of a ruler of a former subject tribe against those of a ruler tribe's representative. He upheld Katyetye's claim and rejected the Iwa chieftainess's ancient claims to Tambo territory—a decision to which his District Commissioner later lent his support.[79]

The establishment of Native Authorities and Native Courts in 1930 provoked a spectrum of reactions from chiefs and headmen; and it heightened, and added a new dimension to, the struggle for power that was going on among the African rulers of the Northern Province. Although it was far from being a complete restoration of old chiefly powers, the introduction of indirect rule was generally welcomed, and it was seen and used as an instrument of political power in a variety of ways by the traditional rulers. In a hierarchical polity like that of the Bemba, there were very few problems of adjustment; for the basis for a pyramidal political structure—superior native authorities and subordinate native authorities—upon which the new system was to rest, was already an essential character of the Bemba political system. The only problem among a people like the Bemba appeared to be that some chiefs who formerly wielded and exercised extensive powers over their subordinates did not readily let their sub-chiefs exercise the enhanced authority which the new ordinances gave them. Because, by the creation of subordinate authorities and courts, a paramount chief or a senior chief was made to relinquish a substantial degree of his authority over junior chiefs, there was a temptation on the part of some senior chiefs to try to assert their old powers over their former vassals. At the end of 1930, for example, it was reported that ever since the introduction of the

Native Courts and Native Authorities Ordinance, Chief Mporo-koso, traditionally the principal chief in Mporokoso District, had been causing 'a good deal of dissatisfaction among the Awemba sub-chiefs by interfering in the internal management of their sections'.[80] Thus although the Acting Provincial Commissioner for Tanganyika Province had argued in the same letter that 'the ordinances mentioned above do not alter his [Mporokoso's] position'[81] over the sub-chiefs, it seemed clear that the chief had lost some of his power and he was painfully conscious of that fact. For, as the Provincial Commissioner himself said (in obvious contradiction of his previous assertion), Mporokoso was 'merely on the same footing as the others, viz, that of a sub-chief'.[82]

The reactions to the application of the ordinances by chiefs belonging to politically segmented ethnic groups, where it was not clear who was king or paramount chief of the tribe, caused even more complex administrative problems, as some chiefs raised strong objections to being placed under other chiefs whom they had never recognised as their paramounts. Among the Bisa, for example, where the Administration had found it difficult to determine which chief was the head of the tribe—Chief Kopa or Chief Matipa—the appointment of Kopa as the Bisa Superior Native Authority aroused a lot of objection from Matipa and other chiefs. Chief Mulongwe, in a statement to the District Commissioner, Luwingu, gave two reasons for refusing to be placed under Kopa. First, he said, he belonged to the *Bena Ngumbo* tribe and to the *Bena Ngoma* totem, of neither of which Matipa was a member. Second, he wished to be under Chief Mwewa of Fort Rosebery District, who belonged to the same tribe and totem as himself.[83] Chief Mbulu, of Chishi Island on Lake Bangweulu, whose stool traditionally had succession ritual connections with those of Chiefs Mwewa and Mwansankombe of the Fort Rosebery District, objected to Kopa's suzerainty for the same reasons, although, because his island had been transferred to Luwingu District in 1922, he said he was prepared to be under Kopa for administrative convenience.[84]

To Matipa the government's decision to put him under Kopa must have been painful and derogatory. For in the past, either from sheer error of judgment or from genuine acknowledgment of the chief's high political standing, the Administration had more or less recognised him as a Paramount Chief of the Bisa,[85] and his relegation to the status of a second-class chief must have been a thunder-clap to his political image. Matipa, even more than the rest of the chiefs, did not therefore relish the idea of being subordinated to Kopa. In the Bisa polity, where each chief enjoyed an appreciable measure of autonomy, the implementation of the Native Authority Ordinance was thus bound to cause a great deal of political discontent. Matipa and the other chiefs regarded the new arrangement as an annexation of their territories to Kopa and took exception to having to perform the servile duties that went with it, of paying tribute and supplying labour to Kopa.[86] Above all, they feared that with his newly acquired political power Kopa might in future appoint men of his own choice to succeed them, irrespective of the wishes of their own people. They said that such a thing had happened only very recently when Chitimukulu appointed a man from another part of the country, who was not the choice of the local people, to become the new Chief Shimumbi, and the same thing might happen to their chieftainships when they died.[87]

The furore over the appointment of Kopa as Paramount Chief of the Bisa necessitated the calling of a meeting of government officials to explore ways and means of solving the problem. On 28 August 1930 the Secretary for Native Affairs, the Provincial Commissioner of Awemba Province and the two District Commissioners for Chinsali and Mpika therefore met at the *boma* of the latter district to review the situation. Efforts were made to find an alternative means of creating a Bisa Superior Native Authority, and it was suggested that a council of chiefs be formed to replace Kopa as the Superior Native Authority.[88] But after close study of the proposal it was considered that such an arrangement would make the Native Authority unmanageable, because it was clear that sub-chiefs would try to press for their independence again and jealousies among them would take root unless all were appointed to the council. Such a council would obviously be an unwieldy body and it was therefore ultimately decided that Kopa, who had earlier been invested with a first-class stave of authority as the most important Bisa chief, would remain the Bisa Superior Native Authority[89] These measures were, in the words of F. M. Thomas, 'the first steps taken to resurrect the Bisa tribe as a unit, instead of a number of groups of persons spread over three districts'.[90] But they did not go far enough to unite the Bisa. As the colonial authorities realised eight years later:

The efforts to unite the Bisa tribe under Chief Kopa have not yet proved entirely successful. Years of independence and isolation have naturally had their influence on Matipa, who had controlled that portion of the tribe which migrated to the swamp and mainland areas of Lake Bangweulu, and much tact will still be necessary in order really to unite these sections of the Bisa tribe into an administrative and financial whole.[91]

Apart from engaging in such wrangles over who would be what in the new political structure, chiefs sometimes sought to bolster up their positions, not so much by doing those things from which their people would derive benefits as by over-asserting their new powers, which was invariably to the detriment of their subjects. They promulgated orders prohibiting the brewing and consumption of beer, and restricting the movement of women— measures which though considered morally necessary could hardly be popular, and were consequently very often infringed.[92] Their frequent infringement meant more court convictions, and the money collected from such court cases easily found its way into the chief's pocket, as until 1936 there were no Native Treasuries. There was, on the other hand, an evident lack of orders on sanitation, for example, which made for the social well-being of the people. Those few orders that happened to be made were often, as a senior government official once observed, 'inserted in the list to please the District Officer'.[93]

In the administration of justice some chiefs acted with the same iron hand. In 1930 some of them, for example, had to be reprimanded by the Secretary for Native Affairs for wrongful prosecutions to enforce their demand for *mulasa*, and Kazembe, Paramount Chief of the Lunda in neighbouring Luapula Province, was blamed for putting minor offenders 'in stocks'.[94] Sometimes an alleged offender was found guilty and fined for no reason other than that the chief hated him. At the time when Native Authorities and Native Courts were still in their formative stages, the chief's verdict was often upheld by the District Officer, who was at pains to eschew any action that might be prejudicial to the stabilisation of the new 'indirect rule' edifice.[95] The Native Court thus assumed something of the unfortunate image of the notorious seventeenth-century English Star Chamber. It is difficult to explain why this travesty of justice should have come about at all. But the view of a contemporary, that this might have been due to the fact that the chiefs had lost their traditional sense of justice and responsibility after the many decades that had passed without exercising most of their traditional judicial powers, seems instructive.[96] To the colonial authorities, however, these malpractices on the part of the traditional rulers did not come as a surprise, because the Northern Rhodesia government had foreseen these developments sometime before the new system of indirect rule became operational:

It is realised by everyone that there may be difficulties and disappointments. Some of the chiefs who will preside over authorities and will exercise judicial functions are ultra-conservative. Some may prove to be insufficiently intelligent, others may prove to be grasping and dishonest, while some may find themselves invested with considerably more power than they have hitherto enjoyed and may show at first a lack of sense of proportion.[97]

But whatever the causes of this moral decay among the traditional authorities were, its consequences were very unhealthy, and it may have been partly responsible for the rise of political pressure groups by the educated elite (Welfare Societies), which became a common sight in the Northern Province and other parts of Zambia in the 1930's. Chief Chikwanda Chitabanta, who was at the time an interested young observer at court in the Northern Province, describes the situation thus:

They [the chiefs] tended to over-assert themselves by over-punishing the people they convicted of certain offences. This aroused some disaffection among their people to such an extent that Native Courts were, in the eyes of the people, an extension of the Administration's judicial arm, and not a resuscitation of the chiefs' traditional powers. There was a cleavage between the chiefs and their people, the interests of the former coming into constant collision with those of the latter.[98]

But it would not be quite correct to attribute this apparent miscarriage of justice on the part of the traditional rulers to sheer over-enthusiasm or to purposeful political self-assertion on their part. For it must be realised that the role they were being called upon to play under the new system of indirect rule must have appeared to them to be somewhat strange after many years of direct rule. This is a state of affairs of which some government officials, like J. Moffat Thomson, the Secretary for Native Affairs, were cognisant. In a minute to the Chief Secretary he commented:

The present generation of chiefs has no experience of law making or issuing orders for the good government of their people. This work has been done for them for the past thirty years by Government under the system of direct rule. Chiefs were merely being told that certain things were prohibited and few if any explanations were given for the necessity of the orders. Chiefs were seldom consulted as to whether a set of laws was likely to be in accordance with native tribal custom, if the people thought them desirable . . .[99]

This point of unpreparedness on the part of the chiefs was echoed five years later by Lieutenant-Colonel (later Sir) Stewart Gore-Browne, member for the Northern Electoral Area, in the Legislative Council during the debate of a Bill which amended the Native Authority Ordinance, 1929.[100] Gore-Browne in stressing the point also emphasised the importance of educating the traditional rulers if they were to be well equipped for their new role under indirect rule, and illustrated his argument by quoting an unnamed African from South Africa who, on being asked to comment on the establishment of Native Authorities and Native Courts in Northern Rhodesia, reportedly told him:

I think you are asking the chiefs to do something very difficult. They are capable according to their lights and according to the traditions of their time of administering their own laws. You have, for good reasons, interfered with those laws and you are now asking them to rule their people according to your laws, or very largely according to your laws. That is probably all right, but remember that you will not make a success of it unless you educate your chiefs.[101]

The promulgation of the Native Authority and the Native Courts Ordinance in 1929 seems also to have given rise to renewed attempts by chiefs of former subject tribes not only to sever all old connections of political subservience with their conquerors but also to claim back their lost lands. At an *indaba* addressed by Acting Governor C. H. Dobree at Abercorn on 28 July 1930, Tafuna, the Paramount Chief of the Lungu, took the opportunity to urge the government to remove Chief

Kaliminwa's Bemba subjects who were living in Lungu country
in order to make way for his people. Dobree's reply, that it would
have been unfair to turn out the Bemba people because they had
occupied the country long before the coming of the whiteman,
did not seem to impress Tafuna. He insisted that if it was not
practicable to remove the Bemba from his country then they
should be made to pay tribute to Lungu chiefs and not to their
Bemba overlords.[102] Mukupa, another Lungu chief, was to make
an even more far-fetched claim four years later, which the District
Commissioner for Mporokoso described as 'extravagant, ...
[and] a mere resuscitation of old claims long since and many times
disallowed by Government, and ... cannot be upheld'.[103] He
claimed part of the country under the Bemba chief, Sunkutu, the
son of Mwamba *wa Milenge*, as his own.[104] The territory once
belonged to the Lungu, but when they were beaten in war by the
Bemba in the middle of the nineteenth century they fled the
country, leaving Sunkutu and his people to occupy it. They only
returned to settle in their old country after the white administration was established. The Administration therefore felt disinclined
to support Mukupa's claim. 'Mukupa and other Alungu chiefs,'
commented Mporokoso's District Commissioner, 'were fortunate
in being allowed to return to their old homes and should be
thankful for getting anything.'[105]

In spite of the government's overt disregard and contempt for
all their territorial claims, the chiefs of the 'newly emancipated'
tribes did not feel deterred from attempting to regain their old
domains. The political advantages to be gained from having a big
country and a large population in the new Native Authorities
system were too obvious and too tempting for any of these chiefs
to ignore: the larger a chief's country and its population the
stronger he was politically and the more likely he was to rise on
the ladder of influence and power within the ruling class. It is
little wonder therefore that, quite apart from the sheer desire to
regain what they considered to have been their territorial rights,
chiefs of minority ethnic groups should appear to have been so
obsessed with these expansionist ideas.

Perhaps most illustrative of this assertive spirit among former
subject tribes was the claim laid in the mid-1930's by a Tabwa
royal clan to Isenga country, which was under Chief Mporokoso.
Isenga, before the Bemba invasion in the latter half of the nine-

teenth century, seems to have belonged to the Tabwa under Chief Nsama Kabobolo, who ruled the country bounded by the Lufubu and Mwita rivers on the east, the Luangwa and Kalung-wisi on the south, and the Luntomfu on the west, with Kamwafi as his capital, situated eleven miles east of modern Mporokoso *Boma*.[106] Because of the extent of his domains, Nsama Kabobolo had put his niece, Mpala, at Lupungu, and his nephews, Lukwesa and Mutangala, at Muchinshi and Kashinda respectively, to safe-guard his interests. None of these representatives, however, was given territorial rights or jurisdiction.[107]

Nsama Kabobolo's system of administration survived him and his successor, Nsama Chipili. But it broke down when, on the death of Chipili, one of the latter's three nephews, Katandula—probably disgruntled at the fact that his late uncle had not given him a position of responsibility like the other nephews—seized the throne and drove out Chipili's other two nephews. The two men found refuge with Chief Mwamba and implored him for help against their rebel brother, Katandula. Consequently Mwamba sent an army under Mporokoso and Sunkutu to help Kafwimbi, one of Chipili's nephews, against Katandula. The latter was sub-sequently killed in battle and Kafwimbi, in gratitude for the help he had received, gave Isenga country to Mwamba as a gift, receiving in return the latter's daughter, Chisela, as a wife.[108] In the meantime Mporokoso was living on the southern side of the Luangwa while Kafwimbi, as Nsama, had his capital built at Kakoma. Kafwimbi, however, soon died in a war against the Swahili under Chandalala. His brother, Mutuka Sichipate, who succeeded him, was a tactless political megalomaniac who quarrelled with Mporokoso and simultaneously started a civil war in which some members of the Tabwa ruling class, like Katele and Mukulu, turned against him and sought the help of the Swahili and the Bemba under Mporokoso and Sunkutu, as a result of which Nsama Sichipate was killed and most of Tabwa country taken by the two Bemba princes.[109] The Tabwa fled the country, leaving it empty and apparently giving up all right to it—a state of affairs which probably explains the fact that at the time when the Tabwa ruling class was making its claims to Isenga there were no Tabwa in that country or any subject tribes under Mporo-koso.[110]

These may have been the true facts of history. But they seemed irrelevant to the thinking of the Tabwa ruling class, who wanted their country, Isenga, back. One of them, Safeli Kalima Zimba, writing from Elizabethville (Lubumbashi), in the Congo, refuted a statement allegedly made by Chief Mporokoso that 'owners of this [Isenga] country are absolutely all dead' as being 'not true' and 'quite a lie'. He contended that the owners of the country such as Mutangala were still alive in Chief Kabanda's country in Kawambwa District.[111]

A few months later Zimba was to write even more challengingly on the issue, this time from Nkana on Northern Rhodesia's Copperbelt. He described a statement earlier made to him by the District Commissioner, Mporokoso, that Isenga, which, as Zimba put it, 'is now under the care of Chief Mporokoso', was given to Chief Mporokoso by Chitimukulu in 1890 as a distortion of the true facts. 'That country,' he said, 'is not the country of Chief Chitimukulu. It was [sic] belong to us, as we are called ourselves (Ba Zimba).'[112] He pointed out that the first princes who inhabited the area were Makungu and Mutangala, the latter having had a village after which Kashinda mission was named. The two men, however, later decided to go to Chishinga country across the Kalungwisi river, leaving behind only young persons— Nsama and Katele—even though Mutangala would have become a chief had he stayed on in Isenga. Zimba added that he and his people wished to return to 'our land and country of "Isenga",' and towards the end of his missive he deplored the existing tendency among all chiefs to acquire territories which did not belong to them.[113]

The Isenga problem, which like similar other cases received no sympathetic attention from the government, seems to have been the last of the ever-recurring territorial claims of minor ethnic groups in the Northern Province during the inter-war years. The persistence with which the Administration turned a deaf ear to the claimants may have done quite a lot to dispel the illusion under which most of the representatives of former subject tribes laboured—that they could, with the help of the whiteman, reconstruct the pre-European congeries of tribal states. Such a proposition, because of its disruptive nature, could not commend itself to the colonial authorities, whose administrative 'reforms' had already cut across tribal boundaries. The colonial government's attitude towards all these 'secessionist' or 'revivalist' territorial claims was roundly summarised by the Acting Provincial Commissioner for the Northern Province when, during the Isenga dispute, he wrote:

The intention of Government since the inception of the administration in this territory [Northern Rhodesia] has been to maintain the authority of conquerors over such tribes as they had successfully subjected by the time of our arrival.

These subject tribes within the Awemba areas of the Mporokoso, Mpika, Kasama, Chinsali, Isoka, Kawambwa Districts are being assimilated gradually by the dominant Awemba.[114]

No evidence of such assimilation in the province has, of course, been elicited in the course of this investigation, but by this policy the fate of these divisive elements was sealed, and the traditional rulers were ultimately made to accept the political *status quo* and to channel their energies in the struggle for power through other avenues.

3. THE TRADITIONAL RULERS AND THEIR PEOPLE

While the struggle for power was going on among the traditional rulers, several chiefs were engaged in another kind of power struggle in which they sought to harness to the full the labour resources of their subjects, as they had done many years before, so that in so doing they might consolidate their positions further.

The demand for *mulasa*—as free or tribute labour was popularly known—by chiefs seemed to have gathered momentum in the years after World War I, as the ruling class grew politically stronger and more confident in the exercise of their authority over the people. During the pre-war years, when their morale was still shaken by the intense resentment and the openly defiant attitude of their subjects not only to themselves but also to the newly established white government, the chiefs seemed too powerless to make their people work for them, as custom and tradition had always had it. Every so often the Administration had to intervene in order to assist chiefs to get the labour and tribute to which they were entitled by custom. In July 1912, for example, the District Commissioner of Awemba District, on a visit to Luwingu, had to tell a gathering of chiefs, headmen and

villagers at an *indaba* that *mulasa* was compulsory for every commoner, and that not even workers returning home from Southern
Rhodesia were exempt from this obligation.[115] He repeated this
warning two years later, and added that anybody who refused to
work for his chief would be arrested and punished by the Administration authorities.[116] This last stern warning was apparently a
sequel to a policy pronouncement made by the Administrator the
previous year at an *indaba* in Kasama, that the common people's
obligation to work for their chiefs would henceforth be enforced
by the *boma*.[117]

To what extent such compulsion succeeded in resuscitating
this almost moribund custom it is hard to say. But in the inter-
vening war period, during which African labour was deployed,
inter alia, to transport supplies to the war front, the debate on,
and agitation for, free labour by chiefs fell into abeyance. It was
not until about seven years after the war, when the tumult caused
by the Watch Tower movement had died down, and when the
traditional authorities had been sufficiently schooled in the difficult
art of discretionary co-operation with the Administration, and
had marshalled together the necessary reins of coercive authority
over their people, that the chiefs began to assert their traditional
right to free labour.

By this time, however, *mulasa* had become rather anachronistic.
The expanding cash economy, which over the years had driven
young men to South Africa, Southern Rhodesia and the Belgian
Congo in search of employment, and which now directed the
ever-flowing river of rural labour into the country's Copperbelt
and other urban centres, had intensified popular aversion to free
labour for chiefs, as most people expected to be paid for all the
work that they were called upon to do by either the chiefs or the
boma.[118] Moreover, traditionally, free labour for chiefs was, like
tribute, a practice that was meant to cement social euphoria
between the rulers and the ruled. It was rendered on a *quid pro quo*
basis: the people worked for the chief because, with his armies, he
afforded them protection from external attack and because as they
worked in the royal gardens or built grain bins for the chief, they
were also given liberal quantities of beer and food.[119] The food
produced by tribute labour was also a form of social security for
the tribe; the chief used it to feed his people whenever they called
at his court for one reason or another, and such hospitality added

very considerably to the chief's power and prestige. In a real sense, then, *mulasa* gardens and granaries belonged to the people.[120] Furthermore, although it cannot be considered as rent, if by rent is meant a fixed amount of work or goods given in return for the right to use a fixed amount of land,[121] *mulasa* was, in the words of Audrey Richards, 'part of a series of mutual obligations observed between subject and chief, of which the right to land is one of the gains to the commoner, and the right to service just one of a series of chiefly prerogatives'.[122] But even though these mutual obligations between subject and chief continued to exist to a considerable degree even under colonial rule,[123] *mulasa* was increasingly being undermined by the forces at work in the money economy which made free labour something of an oddity.[124]

It is not surprising therefore that under these circumstances chiefs should have met with a lot of indifference and, more often, with calculated defiance in their quest for tribute labour. Again and again they were forced to fall back upon the Administration for help in their desperate attempts to get *mulasa*. At an *indaba* addressed by E. S. B. Tagart, the Secretary for Native Affairs, at Mporokoso on 26 November 1926, Sub-chief Chungu of the Lungu complained bitterly that it was becoming more and more difficult for chiefs in the district to obtain free labour.[125] Although this was no new phenomenon—as it began many years before— the sub-chief seemed particularly disturbed at the rapid rate at which the situation was deteriorating. It appeared to him that the visit by the District Commissioner, Kasama, a few months back was the cause of the parlous state of affairs. For during the District Commissioner's visit a meeting of chiefs had been held behind closed doors, and at that meeting, when the question of *mulasa* was raised, the visiting official made it quite clear that the chiefs' demands for free labour would no longer be supported by the *boma*. This policy statement, which was made in confidence to the chiefs, filtered through the walls of the *boma* offices to the public ear, and people began saying that free labour for chiefs was now over.[126]

Perhaps even more illustrative of the critical shortage of free labour for chiefs was the sad story that Chief Luchembe of Mpika had to tell G. Stokes, the Assistant Magistrate of that district. On several occasions, Luchembe had called on each one of his headmen to supply him with three men for *mulasa*. But not only did the headmen ignore the chief's orders, they also failed even to communicate with him on the subject.[127] Whether their attitude was indicative of sheer neglect or of inability to get the necessary men from unwilling subjects, or whether it emanated from petty jealousies of the headmen about the privileges of the chiefs, from which they rarely derived any direct benefits, it would be instructive to know. But the consequences for the chief of the headmen's failure to supply him with free labour were dire. Quite apart from everything else, he suffered considerable loss as a result of damage to his crops, which, because he was unable to get labour to thatch the roofs of his grain stores, got wet in the rain and were sprouting.[128] It is little wonder therefore that Luchembe felt so aggrieved as to threaten to sue his headmen for contravening native customary law.[129]

It must be pointed out, however, that although popular resistance to *mulasa* was widespread, it was still possible in certain cases for some chiefs who were respected by their people to get free labour. But such 'respected' chiefs were rare. For, as Hugh Hill, the Native Commissioner for Mporokoso, once said, respect for a chief was very much akin to popularity, and popularity for a chief often meant 'not reporting crime [to the colonial authorities] and indirectly supporting his people against the Boma'.[130] But even this limited reservoir of free labour on which a respected chief was able to draw gradually dried up as the people who did *mulasa* got to realise that after all the custom did not meet with the full approval of the Administration. Thus more and more *mulasa* fell on the shoulders of the willing horse, with the chief resorting to threats in order to get more labour.[131] As matters were, the willing horses were more often than not elderly men, as young men were away at work or, on their return home with their new-fangled ideas about tribal control, refused to take part in the exercise.[132] It was not very unusual, therefore, to find chiefs who had to offer some sort of payment in order to get the labour they required. Chief Mporokoso, for instance, had to pay the taxes of the four men who carried him about and had to pay men to look after his barns and a small herd of cattle, while in the past he used to get these services free.[133] In 1934 Audrey Richards saw Chief Nkula pay court fines for two of his subjects who were unable to find the necessary money, and in return they were made to build a house for the chief; and Chitimukulu had to offer payment to two bricklayers in order to obtain their services, even though such payment was below the current rates.[134] What is more, labour migration had so reduced the labour supply in the Northern Province that it was difficult for chiefs to get even a minimum of *mulasa*. Chieftainesses Chandawcyaya and Mulenga, for example, complained that they could not obtain tribute labour without the support of the territorial chiefs;[135] Senior Chief Mwamba complained in May 1933 that he was unable to get sufficient tribute labour to build his new capital until the Copperbelt slump forced men to return to their villages; and even Chitimukulu is said to have always grumbled about his inability to obtain labour to make his gardens, as a result of which his band of personal followers and singers was very much reduced.[136]

In the conflict over *mulasa* the Administration played a vital role. Before World War I, it had supported free labour for chiefs, and was prepared to go to any length to preserve the custom. The official argument for its preservation was based primarily on the social and political function of the custom in African life as seen against its historical background. This *functionalist* view of *mulasa*, coupled with the advantages to indirect rule that would presumably flow from it if it were preserved, was held so highly by the Administration that it was stamped with the legalistic rationalisation of English jurisprudence. It was seen as one of those few examples of African customary law which were not repugnant to natural justice, equity and good government, because in the circumstances of the time it was, in the view of the colonial authorities, capable of making a positive contribution to the good welfare of the community or its members.[137] Consequently, *mulasa* could not be disallowed under the principles established by section 5 of the Northern Rhodesia High Court Ordinance which defined the legal acceptability, in the Western tradition, of certain aspects of African customary law, and so *mulasa* was considered capable of being enforced legally.[138]

But unlike laws in physical science, *mulasa* was a 'living law,' whose principles were not immutable or stereotyped for all time. It was bound to change as the social values and behavioural patterns of the people changed, and so the new economic and political facts of the inter-war years soon made the enforcement of the custom by the Administration palpably ponderous. It was

in recognition of these hard facts of the situation that, in supporting the statement made by the District Commissioner of Awemba
District at the secret meeting with chiefs of the Mporokoso
Division mentioned above, E. S. B. Tagart had to tell an *indaba*
at Mporokoso in November 1926:

I agree with the ruling of the District Commissioner. The British
government cannot force people to work for others without pay. All
natives know that they are entitled to wages for the work they do. The
government cannot fine or imprison a man for refusing to perform
work for someone else for nothing. The government cannot intervene
between chiefs and their people in this matter. Good chiefs get respect
from their people and are obeyed by them. It is not the government
policemen who can force the people to respect and obey their chiefs.
It is a matter for the chief himself.[139]

Few chiefs, naturally, took kindly to this scathingly frank talk
by the Secretary for Native Affairs, and it would not have been
surprising if one chief in the audience had stood up to lay a charge
of abandonment against the Administration. But in deciding to
abandon its long-standing responsibility to the traditional rulers
the government was merely taking cognisance of the pressing
wishes of the ruled. The District Commissioner for Tanganyika
District saw probably with even greater perspicacity the need for
the shift in the government's stance over the *mulasa* issue when
he wrote:

I think we should also consider the matter from the side of the people,
not only the chiefs'. Conditions have greatly altered since chiefs had
the power to enforce *mulasa*. Natives in those days were governed by
tribal laws; they looked to the chief for protection and for redress of
their grievances. For these benefits they paid tribute either in kind or
by their labour. Today they have greater security and a better system
of government, so they pay their tribute (tax) to the higher power.
As they now derive no benefits from their chiefs, is it fair to force them
to continue to pay or render free service as they did formerly? This,
I think, might be the people's side of the question.[140]

The District Commissioner may have stretched his point by
equating *mulasa* to tax, since they were two different things,

having an equally different function in the African society; but the logic of his argument—that *mulasa* had outlived its usefulness in the colonial situation—was compelling and empirical.

An anonymous letter, dated 6 December 1928, by one African, bearing as its postal address the words 'P.O. Mpika and Serenje Boma' but in fact posted at Luanshya, perhaps put in most expressive terms what popular thinking was about *mulasa*. Written in faulty English, but in a demanding tone, it read:

Please, tell us; it is lawful to us to give money to any native chief? Every tribe to give money to their chieftain? And it is lawful to work for them without give us nor food? How it would be better to us to cease to pay tax to you, that it is well to give money to every chieftain, How can we live in this great indigence? It is you who told them to put us in bad conduct and to grant them 10/- a week? if a man refuse they beat him with a whip? Soon the war is nigh to break out between the different tribes. Will you let us live in this bad manner?[141]

Whether the writer was a mere migrant labourer, or a disillusioned member of the educated elite, or whether he was a Watch Tower adherent (as the last sentence but one of the letter would seem to suggest), there is little doubt that *mulasa* and tribute on the one hand and taxation on the other were causing confusion and hardship to the people, and that they could not co-exist for long.

In refusing to enforce the observance of *mulasa* on the people, the Administration was in no way advocating its abolition, but was merely admitting that the old method of forcibly making people obey it was no longer tenable. For the colonial authorities knew only too well that *mulasa* was one of the few remaining social institutions upon which the power of the chief rested, and to abolish it would have meant a further undermining of his authority—a state of affairs which a colonial government that was becoming increasingly reliant on chiefs to govern the country did not wish to see come about. At a conference of all District Commissioners in Northern Rhodesia early in 1929, it was resolved that no active steps should be taken by the government to discourage *mulasa* wherever it existed, but at the same time no recourse to the courts by any official or chief wanting to enforce the custom should be allowed.[142] The Governor subsequently

Q

ordered that the resolution be observed as the regulation governing the administration of *mulasa*.[143]

The colonial authorities thus seem to have devised a double-edged policy towards *mulasa*: they were loath to take any measures which would have either preserved or destroyed the institution; and they were neither assisting the chiefs to exact tribute labour nor prohibiting them from doing so. But this ambivalent policy, in effect, amounted to a withdrawal of official recognition of the custom,[144] and, as a commission of enquiry commented eight years later, 'it seems unfortunate that it was considered necessary to withdraw recognition from this valuable communal institution, which if properly worked was valuable not only to the chiefs but to tribal life as a whole'.[145] For *mulasa* was the economic basis of tribal organisation; it provided a reserve of food for the tribe and afforded the chief the means to meet numerous calls on his hospitality.[146] From *mulasa* granaries he was able to feed not only *mulasa* workers but also his panel of advisers and councillors.[147] But as a result of the withdrawal of government recognition of *mulasa* the institution suffered a death-blow, and the chiefs, who 'in most cases' received 'miserable salaries',[148] were faced with critical problems of government. Their inability to obtain tribute labour meant that they were unable to get food with which to feed their subjects at court, and this dearth of food supplies made most of their people unwilling to come forward for work at the capital.[149] Audrey Richards, during her research in the Northern Province in the early 1930's, witnessed Chitimukulu grapple with the administrative and political problems engendered by scarcity of tribute labour:

I have seen Chitimukulu hear cases alone with his clerk, and during 1934 the *bakabilo* summoned by him on important matters of business invariably melted away before the end of the meeting because they had not enough food. It took a period of three months of alternately summoning the council and then dismissing it because of food shortage, before the work could be carried through.[150]

Audrey Richards further states that in January 1934 Chitimukulu was forced by circumstances to give up the traditional distinction between his *mulasa* granary and his personal one, and that he was feeding his wife and family on anything he could lay his hands upon.[151]

If the ambivalent attitude of the government towards *mulasa* only succeeded in destroying the custom, this was not intentional on the part of the colonial authorities. For the government was always mindful of the need to preserve and, if possible, promote the power of the chiefs, who were a much-needed link in the British colonial policy of indirect rule, which by this time had become the accepted policy of British administration in Africa north of the Zambezi. The apparently lukewarm attitude of the government was probably in the 1930's dictated by the observance of the Geneva Convention of 1930, which forbade compulsory labour, save in cases of emergencies or for 'minor services';[152] but as to the importance of *mulasa*, as means for promoting the authority of the traditional rulers, the colonial authorities do not seem to have been in any doubt. Some government officials, in fact, hoped that the dying custom might be preserved by increasing subsidies payable to chiefs in order to enable them to pay for their labour.[153] Indeed, even the commission of enquiry led by Sir Alan Pim advanced the same view in 1938, and went even further to recommend that councillors should also be in receipt of subsidies, because the chiefs had not got the means to entertain them while they transacted official business at court.[154] But it seems doubtful whether such an approach, which was essentially businesslike and devoid of the essence of *mulasa*, would have achieved the desired objective. Indeed, the suggestion that chiefs should be paid higher subsidies to enable them to hire the labour they wanted in the place of *mulasa* was turned down by some chiefs in Mpika District, who felt that they would derive no respect from such an arrangement; and one government official, commenting on the function of *mulasa* after this incident, remarked: 'It is a matter of prestige.'[155]

Whether the traditional authorities could have afforded to pay competitive wages to pseudo-*mulasa* workers from their increased subsidies it is difficult to say. But it seems unlikely that paid labour could have been an effective lever with which the government would prop up the position of the traditional rulers. At this time there was a growing feeling of social emancipation among the African people which, even after World War II, expressed itself in unwillingness to work for other Africans. Quite apart from other factors, this phenomenon seems to have made some officials doubt the efficacy of supplying paid labour to chiefs, through increased subsidies, as an instrument of political support in the way *mulasa* was. As one official argued:

I have very grave doubts as to whether the people would work for them [chiefs]. The government often enough finds it difficult to obtain the labour required, and in my experience a native seldom cares to work for another native.[156]

The Native Commissioner, by arguing in this tone, had somewhat overstated the case, but there was nonetheless some element of truth in the argument.

The foregoing account of the power struggle and power politics among the traditional rulers may leave one with the impression that chiefs were doggedly and perpetually pursuing the indulgent and mundane policy of consolidating their positions in the rapidly changing Northern Province society, without doing anything for their people. But in fact the traditional rulers were still concerned with the welfare of their subjects. Admittedly, they often tended to feather their own nests in most of their remonstrations with the Administration on behalf of their people, but it was not unusual for a chief or headman to act as an outspoken representative of his people, especially when his interests and those of his subjects were identical or were adversely affected by some of the Administration's undiscriminating measures. The chiefs, in fact, became, for the most part, more vocal than the common people, who in the years past had been the centre of the social and political turmoil that erupted intermittently before the war over forced labour and the hut tax, and expressed itself in the belligerent Watch-towerism of later years.

One of the points on which chiefly opinion seemed quite representative of popular sentiment was over the age-long problem of taxation. The hut tax, which was introduced in North-eastern Rhodesia in 1901 at 3s in cash or in kind per hut, rose as poll tax, to 5s in 1914 and to 10s in 1920. The last rise, coming as it did at the time when a lot of labour had been laid off after the war and was still in the process of finding its way to urban and European agricultural centres, caused some hardship, and a number of people who failed to pay their tax were imprisoned. The difficulties caused to the village people by the 10s tax were very obvious to the chiefs who, in receipt of a few pounds a year in subsidies, had little cause to complain. At an *indaba* in

Abercorn addressed by the Secretary for Native Affairs, J. C. C. Coxhead, on 24 May 1921, Chief Nsokolo of the Mambwe, asked if he had anything to say, complained to the visiting official: 'Certainly we must be taxed and we expect it, but the advent of the 10s [tax has] made it a great hardship for all.'[157] It was not the tax alone that was heavy, the chief argued, but the punishment meted out to tax defaulters was equally heavy. Instead of telling a defaulter to go and look for money, so that he might pay his taxes, the Administration arrested and imprisoned him for three months or more, and when he got out of prison he was still expected to pay his tax. This was absurd, and Nsokolo asked the Secretary for Native Affairs the pointed question: 'Where is he to get the money?'[158]

Coxhead's rationalisation about the situation—that Africans should expect to pay higher taxes because Europeans were paying even more heavily, and that the village people could easily earn the tax money by selling some of their produce to the *boma*—did not seem to cut any ice at all.[159] Chief Nsokolo was quick to point out to the Secretary that food sold to the *boma* was fetching a very low price. At threepence or sixpence for a basket of meal, he said, a man would have to 'empty his grain bin before he can get enough money to earn [sic] his tax'.[160] Not even Coxhead's tactical announcement that village food prices had been raised by the government to five shillings per 60 lbs load could evoke any favourable reaction from the chief. Nsokolo, with the support of the Lungu Paramount Chief, Tafuna, insisted that it was still impossible even after this rise in food prices, as long as tax still remained at ten shillings, for a man to pay tax for each one of his three or four wives without going either to the Congo or to Southern Rhodesia to work. It was this state of affairs, said the chief, which had contributed to the increasing loss of men from the countryside.[161] Owing, no doubt, to such protests from Nsokolo and other chiefs, and partly to a possible desire for novelty on the part of the new British colonial government, the first Governor of Northern Rhodesia, Sir Herbert James Stanley, had to announce at an *indaba* on 22 October 1925, at Kasama, that the poll tax had been reduced from 10s to 7s 6d.[162]

Even though tax was brought down to 7s 6d, it was nevertheless still too high in comparison with the standard of living of the people. The majority of the population were subsistence peasant farmers whose monetary incomes were extremely low, and not all of them could afford to raise money even for the new tax. Chief Tafuna was only too conscious of this fact when, at an *indaba* on 22 June 1928, at Abercorn, he parleyed with the Governor, Sir James C. Maxwell, on the ramifying problems to which the poll tax gave rise. Tafuna complained that the current wage rates, which stood at 5*s* per month, were too low to enable people to pay their taxes. Such low pay, while high taxes prevailed, inevitably made people leave the country to go and earn 'taxable' incomes elsewhere.[163] On this point Tafuna was supported by another veteran, traditionalist political figure, Chief Nsokolo. Nsokolo's remarks epitomised the feeling of helpless entanglement in which the ruling class found itself as a result of the demands made on it by the government, to facilitate the collection of tax. Speaking to the Governor at the same *indaba*, the chief, with an air of tactless candour, said:

The Boma say we hide people; we don't. They scatter to find money, as wages here are so low. We chiefs get very little subsidy money. We cannot therefore help our people when they are arrested for tax default.[164]

The hut tax impinged on the lives of the people even more, because a man was obliged to pay tax on the second and every other additional wife he married. The economic logic of such a fiscal policy is, of course, open to question. But the colonial authorities saw the accretion of wives around a man as a kind of economic investment, for which a man must be taxed. As Sir James Maxwell put it at the Abercorn *indaba* of 1928:

If a man marries a second wife it is only right that he should pay tax for her. A man would not marry a second wife unless he was going to gain by it—has more labour for his land.[165]

This was a policy whose only basis seems to have been the misconception that in the traditional African society a husband was a capitalist and his wife only a factor of production (labour) to be exploited. It is indeed doubtful whether by having more than one wife a man always became materially better off, when, in fact, with the growth, by arithmetical progression, of the extended family, he took on more responsibilities. Moreover, sometimes the women who became plural wives were widows who had been inherited by men who were already married. In that event, the question of a man getting more labour for his land was beside the point, because such women continued to till their old fields, and they in fact became a social and economic burden. This is a point which was later realised by government officials. Moving the second reading of a Bill to bring about the Native Tax Consolidation Ordinance, 1928, which empowered the government to fix native tax according to the availability of employment opportunities in any given part of the country, and which gave power to District Commissioners to exempt Africans from paying tax on second and other wives who were elderly or indigent, E. S. B. Tagart, the Secretary for Native Affairs, commented:

The possession of several wives by a native is some indication of his wealth in the ordinary way. But, as is well known to those who have lived in this Territory and studied native conditions for any length of time, natives, according to custom, have often to take as wives elderly women who are widows of their relatives and such women are an incubus rather than an asset to the person who takes them. There is no reason to depart from the custom. It is a good one and one to be upheld. Every woman has to have a protector, and the man who inherits these women has to look after them and see that huts are built for them in the village.[166]

The same argument was ventilated a year later by J. Moffat Thomson, Tagart's successor, in a debate of the Native Tax Amendment Ordinance, 1929, which repealed certain sections of the Native Tax Consolidation Ordinance of 1928.[167] But before this tax amendment the reactions of the African people were manifestly antipathetic. Some men shirked their customary responsibility for inherited widows; and some women led a life of deceit because their husbands denied that they belonged to them, and the result was an unnecessary number of divorces.[168] The collection of the tax itself was as distasteful to Africans as it was to government officials, because of the time and effort wasted in ascertaining and registering plural wives, the constant necessity of weighing pleas for exemption and the undesirable inquisitorial methods that had to be resorted to in trying to locate such women.[169] Moreover, the tax exacerbated the exodus of men from the rural areas into industrial centres in search of more remunerative employment. It was estimated, for example, that

30–50 per cent of able-bodied men in Awemba District and 40–50 per cent in Tanganyika District were away at work at one time.[170] This exodus meant that a lot of women were left without husbands for a number of years. It seemed only fair, therefore, as Chief Mporokoso argued at an *indaba*, that such women should be married without their new husbands having to pay tax on them.[171]

If the vexed question of taxation and all its social consequences had provided a rallying point for chiefs to take a united stand against the government, the move by the colonial authorities to alienate land in the province drew the traditional rulers even closer together to question the wisdom of a measure which was an evident threat to their political authority. The division of the Northern Province into native reserves and European areas cut across the powers of the chief as the custodian of the land, and introduced into the province modern farm units which drew away labour from the subsistence farming communities and in that way accentuated the social disruption of village life which was already afoot. The dire social and political consequences of all this were only too clear, and chiefs could not possibly take kindly to the dismemberment of their land.

When the Reserves Commission—composed of R. W. Yule, Captain J. Brown and J. Moffat Thomson, as chairman—visited the Awemba and Tanganyika Districts in the middle of 1927, it met with strong opposition from chiefs. At an *indaba* in Abercorn on 16 August 1927, after the commissioners had informed the people that the country would be divided into black and white areas, and asked the chiefs to say how much land their people wanted, one chief after another stood up to inveigh against the whole idea of bringing more Europeans into the province. There was, indeed, a difference in emphasis as to what each chief considered to be the most disturbing element of the proposed measure, but in rejecting the proposition the chiefs were at one.[172]

Chief Tafuna, opening the debate, expressed the fear that as whitemen always made big gardens, Africans stood the risk of suffering from land hunger in the end, especially if more Europeans came to open up farms in the province. There was, moreover, the other problem that once white people took up land in the area, Africans would not be allowed to cut timber near their farms. As the timber belonged to the people, it would, in the circumstances, be justifiable for the people to refuse to work for such white settlers.[173] Tafuna's argument was given weight by an example which Sub-chief Zombe gave about what he had experienced in his own area. A Mr Duigan was given land in Zombe's country by the Administration without the chief's knowledge. No sooner had Duigan cleared the piece of land allotted to him than a series of clashes between the people and the white farmer began.[174] On a number of occasions when Zombe's people wanted to make gardens near Duigan's farm they were turned away. This interference with the local population's old liberties was causing concern, and because of this, Zombe said, he would never again allow a European to settle in his country.[175]

While Tafuna and Zombe had rejected the objectives which the commission had set out to realise from the point of view of the common people, other chiefs opposed the proposition because it trespassed on their traditional authority. Chief Mwamba of the Mambwe opposed the alienation of any part of his land to Europeans because he was already sandwiched between a Mr Smith and a Mr Barnshaw, as a result of which he was constantly being told to remove but had consistently refused to do so. He said he was beginning to wonder whether he was still the chief of the country, and should not therefore accommodate any more such inconveniences.[176] For Chief Makasa, white settlers were a group of disrespectful individuals who recognised no chief, and therefore he would have none of them in his country. He would only deal with the white officials at the *boma* as these respected him.[177] As far as Chief Penza was concerned, the presence of white farmers in the country was a disruptive force which should not go unchecked. Villages were splitting up as men went to work and live on European farms, and as a result these farm workers were losing all respect for chiefs. Penza therefore requested the government to allow chiefs to post their own *capitaos* on these farms so that the people's loyalty to their chiefs might be maintained.[178]

In the Mporokoso Division the commissioners found the same degree of opposition to the government's intention to introduce a social system of racial segregation in the Northern Province when they addressed a meeting of chiefs and some 500 people at Mporokoso *Boma* on 15 September of the same year. Except for one or two Tabwa chiefs who compromised by offering portions of their areas to potential white settlers, all the Bemba and Lungu chiefs in the division made no secret of their bitter opposition to the proposal.[179] But perhaps the most noteworthy views aired at the *indaba* were those expressed in rather guarded terms by Chief Mporokoso. He began his speech by acknowledging the fact that the country had been taken over by the whiteman's government. But although the African people had no quarrel with the white Administration officials—who had been governing them well—it would be foolhardy, said Mporokoso, for the people to assume the same accommodating attitude towards the proposals the commission was making on behalf of the government. He said diplomatically:

We are afraid if Europeans come they may stop vitemene [sic]. If they want to come we cannot stop it if they do not stop vitemene. We do not want our country sold to whitemen but they may settle. We do not wish to decide the allocation of land now. If a white man comes we can settle the matter with the boma official.[180]

In arguing in this manner, Mporokoso may not have realised that the scheme to which he was opposed was the brainchild of a colonial government, of which the *boma* officials in whom he seemed to place so much trust were in fact part. But his cautious or *festina lente* approach to the problem seemed the most pragmatic in the circumstances. For the central point in the commission's enquiry was not so much to find out if chiefs would take kindly to having a European farming community in their country as to investigate how much land the government could safely allocate to white settlers without causing undue hardships and offence to the chiefs and their people. The colonial authorities had in fact made up their minds that alienation of the land was necessary; and in spite of strong African opposition to the scheme by the Crown Lands and Native Reserves (Tanganyika District) Order-in-Council, which was passed in 1929, the government carved out 5,030,340 acres from a land mass of some 12,998,910 acres for a European population of forty-three, eleven of whom were women and eight government officials. The remainder was what the native population of some 106,513 got, and this worked out at 74·8 acres per head, as compared with 116,984 acres per head in the case of Europeans.[181]

To what extent this monstrous imbalance in the allocation of land influenced future African political attitudes it is, in the absence of the necessary data, difficult to say. But one indication of immediate African reactions to land alienation was the complaint made to the Acting Governor, C. H. Dobree, at an Abercorn *indaba* on 28 July 1930 by Chief Nsokolo, that some of his people had no land in the reserve he was given and had consequently moved into Makasa's country, and that a Mr Gliemann of Itimbwe ranch was refusing to allow people to use an established crossing on the Saisi river, which was now part of this farm.[182] Another indication was the criticism of the native reserves system aired by members of the Livingstone Native Welfare Association who were of Northern Province origin. Moffat Sinkala, a committee member of the Association, complained at the annual meeting, held on 6 April 1931, that the establishment of native reserves made it difficult for chiefs and headmen who were settled in areas which were 'unfit for human habitation' to move to better places. This, he said, was 'a horrible position indeed'; and he urged the government to reconsider its policy on reserves.[183] Another Northern Province man, Robert K. Simpelwe, a detective, who, it will be recalled, was the Administration's intelligence officer in the Northern Province during the Watch Tower unrest which broke out soon after the war, was equally critical of native reserves. He asked the question whether in the event of a mine being opened in a reserve the chief of the area would have shares in such an enterprise and he wanted to know to whom money collected from game and trading licences in the reserves would be paid.[184]

It is important to point out here that the alienation of land in the Northern Province was not like the land apportionment in Southern Rhodesia, where the races were each allotted specific areas for occupation or farming.[185] Here non-reserve areas were not European reserves but Crown lands which could be sold or leased to anyone, black or white, who had the means to acquire such land.[186] However, few Africans, if any at all, had the money to buy land, and since, as was pointed out earlier in this chapter, very few Europeans settled in the area, the non-reserve lands remained largely unoccupied. This encouraged the spread of the tse-tse fly, and in a district like Mporokoso where there was no prospect of European occupation, it was reported that 'a large area is left vacant as an elephant run'.[187] Meanwhile, the native reserves became overcrowded and by the time of the Alan Pim Commission they had seriously deteriorated. In the Mambwe (Fwambo) Reserve No. IV, there was congestion and erosion; the situation was the same in the Mambwe (Nsokolo) Reserve No. V, whose population density of sixty-eight per square mile was too great for the *chitemene* system; the Namwanga Reserve No. X, the Mweni Mpanga Reserve No. XI as well as the Kafwimbi Reserve No. XII had also deteriorated seriously.[188] This overcrowding was partly responsible for the emigration in 1938 of a number of families from Isoka to Tanganyika.[189]

Yet in spite of the parlous condition into which native reserves deteriorated, the traditional rulers, apart from the lone voice of the Mambwe chief, Mwamba, seem to have pliantly acquiesced in the situation, as if the plight of their people did not matter to them. Why this should have been so it is difficult to say. It seems possible that their apparent indifference on the question of native reserves, once these were established, may have in part been due to the power struggle going on amongst themselves, which seems to have been intensified by the establishment of native authorities and native courts, and in the course of which they appear in some cases to have ruled their people with a heavy hand. But it seems unfortunate that they should have been silent over so important an issue; and it is even more so when one considers that even the welfare associations which were then in existence in the province had, by force of circumstances, confined their attention and activities to their respective townships, since they were not allowed to discuss what was going on in the reserves around them.[190]

NOTES

[1] Lord Hailey, *An African Survey*, p. 453; and in *Native Administration in British African Territories, Part II*, p. 83; cf. *Pim Report*, pp. 179–180.

[2] Extract from the Legal Department Circular No. 5 of 1914 on Native Customary Law, ZA1/9/27/3.

[3] *Ibid.*

[4] Report by P. J. Macdonell, 1919, ZA1/10.

[5] Report by Hugh C. Marshall, Visiting Commissioner, 15 August 1919, ZA7/7/2.

[6] Lord Hailey, *An African Survey*, p. 454.

[7] *Debates*, col. 235, 18 March 1929.

[8] *Ibid.*, cols. 235–256.

[9] Lord Hailey, *loc. cit.*, p. 456.

[10] *Debates*, col. 238, 18 March 1929.

[11] Leo Marquard, 'The problem of government', *Modern Industry and the African*, ed. J. Merle Davis (London: Macmillan & Co., 1933), pp. 251–252.

[12] *Debates*, col. 62, 4 May 1936.

[13] *Ibid.*, col. 64.

[14] *Ibid.*, col. 62.

[15] Gann, *A History of Northern Rhodesia*, p. 291; *Pim Report*, pp. 182–183.

[16] *Debates*, col. 59, 4 May 1936.

[17] Philip Mason, 'Land policy', in Richard Gray, *The Two Nations*, p. 73.

[18] *Ibid.*, pp. 49–55; Gann, *A History of Southern Rhodesia*, pp. 268–270.

[19] Gann, *A History of Northern Rhodesia*, pp. 218–224.

[20] Reserves Commission: Tanganyika District, ZA1/10.

[21] Mason, *loc. cit.*, p. 85. Robert Rotberg, however, argues that the three areas did not become reserves until 1928–29, fifteen years after the B.S.A.C. Administration had (in 1913) drawn up plans to create reserves in the areas in order to restrain Africans from permanently occupying lands suitable for European settlement; Rotberg, *The Rise of Nationalism in Central Africa*, p. 37.

[22] Mason, *loc. cit.*

[23] *Ibid.*, p. 86; Gann, *loc. cit.*, pp. 218–219.

[24] Gann, *loc. cit.*, pp. 221–222.

[25] *Ibid.*, p. 224.

[26] Lord Hailey, *Native Administration in British African Territories*, p. 84.

[27] *Ibid.*

[28] Gann, *loc. cit.*

[29] Reserves Commission: Tanganyika District, *loc. cit.*

[30] *Pim Report*, p. 72.

[31] Tanganyika District Annual Report for the year ending 31 March 1925, ZA7/1/8/8.

[32] Lord Hailey, *Native Administration in the British African Territories*, Part II, p. 85.

[33] Mason, *loc. cit.*, p. 87.

[34] *Pim Report*, *loc. cit.*

[35] *Debates*, col. 15.

[36] The Governor said that, apart from the Abercorn Division, which somewhat incredibly had a labour supply in excess of its requirements, the whole country was short of labour; *ibid.*, col. 16.

[37] *Ibid.*, pp. 138–139, 22 May 1925.

[38] *Pim Report*, p. 112.

[39] *Ibid.*

[40] *Ibid.*

[41] *Ibid.*

[42] *Ibid.*, p. 117.

[43] *Ibid.*

[44] *Ibid.*, p. 118.

[45] It is estimated that in 1936 they sold fish worth about £1,650 and 90,000 lbs of meal; *ibid.*

[46] *Report upon Native Affairs*, 1936, p. 45.

[47] Kuczynski, *op. cit.*, p. 431.

[48] *Report upon Native Affairs*, 1936, p. 15.

[49] D.C., Abercorn, to Assistant Magistrate, Mpika, 22 December 1926, ZA1/9/27/3.

[50] Willis Enquiry, KSU3/1. For a discussion of this episode, see Brelsford, *The Succession of Bemba Chiefs*, p. 10.

[51] Statement by Nkuka, 5 January 1917, ZA/1/9/27/7/1.

[52] It is, however, possible that Chikwanda returned to Mpika merely because he preferred that part of the country, with its salt pans, to Nkula's country in Chinsali. His love for Mpika may have been the cause for his resigning the Nkulaship. See Brelsford, *The Succession of Bemba Chiefs*, p. 8. On the other hand, it seems likely that Chikwanda was not properly installed as Nkula, even though he continued to be recognised as such by the Administration. It is said that the relics of Nkula I Mutale had been removed by Chimbuka Chewe, a member of the old lineage expelled by Chitapankwa, so that without the relics no proper installation of Chikwanda as Nkula was possible; see Roberts, 'A political history of the Bemba', p. 293.

[53] Statement by Nkuka, *loc. cit.*

[54] F. H. Melland to P. W. Jelf, Assistant N.C., Mpika, 28 March 1918, ZA1/9/27/7/1.

[55] *Ibid.*

[56] Encl. P. W. Jelf to D.C., Kasama, 28 February 1918, ZA/1/9/27/7/1.

[57] *Ibid.*

[58] Memorandum by Hugh C. Marshall, 7 June 1918, ZA/1/9/27/7/1.

[59] Marshall's notes, 1918, ZA/1/9/27/7/1.

[60] Nkuka's evidence to the Administrator, ZA/1/9/27/7/1.

[61] Jelf to D.C., Kasama, 28 February 1918, ZA/1/9/27/7/1.

[62] Croad to S.N.A., 25 February 1918, ZA/1/9/27/7/1.

[63] Marshall's notes, 1918, *loc. cit.*

[64] P. W. Jelf to D.C., Kasama, 28 February 1918, ZA/1/9/27/1.

[65] *Ibid.*

[66] *Ibid.*

[67] *Ibid.*

[68] See Roberts, 'A political history of the Bemba', pp. 175–176.

[69] Report on an Enquiry by the N.C., Mporokoso, into the Conduct of Chief Kaliminwa, KSU/3/1.

[70] *Ibid.*

[71] Salelles to N.C., Mporokoso, 12 July 1920; KSU/3/1.

[72] Report by N.C., Mporokoso, in *ibid.*

[73] Marshall's notes, 1918, *loc. cit.*

[74] Report by the N.C., Mporokoso, KSU/3/1.

[75] Boundary Disputes: Chiefs and Headmen, ZA/1/9/27/6.

[76] *Ibid.*

[77] *Ibid.*

[78] *Ibid.*
[79] D.C., Abercorn, to S.N.A., Livingstone, 17 August 1922, in *ibid.*
[80] Acting P.C., Tanganyika Province, to D.C., Mporokoso, 30 November 1930, KSU/3/1.
[81] *Ibid.*
[82] *Ibid.*
[83] D.C., Luwingu, to P.C., Kasama, 17 July 1930, ZA/1/9/27/5/A, Vol. I.
[84] *Ibid.*
[85] *Ibid.*
[86] *Ibid.*
[87] *Ibid.*
[88] Minutes of the meeting of officials held at Mpika, ZA/1/9/27/5/A, Vol. I.
[89] *Ibid.*
[90] Thomas, *Historical Notes on the Bisa Tribe*, pp. 51–52. There were then three main Bisa groups—the Mpika group under Chief Kopa, the Luwingu group under Chief Matipa and the Chinsali group under Chief Kabanda; *ibid.*
[91] *Native Affairs Annual Report for 1938*, p. 44.
[92] S.N.A. to Chief Secretary, 4 December 1931, KSU/3/1.
[93] *Ibid.*
[94] Gann, *loc. cit.*, p. 230.
[95] Interview with Zakariya Mukosa, 27 July 1967, Chinsali.
[96] Interview with Chief Chikwanda Chitabanta, 24 July 1967.
[97] *Report upon Native Affairs for the Year 1929*, p. 5.
[98] Interview with Chief Chikwanda Chitabanta.
[99] S.N.A. to Chief Secretary, 4 December 1931, KSU/3/1; cf. *Pim Report*, p. 183.
[100] *Debates*, col. 72, 5 May 1936.
[101] *Ibid.*, cols. 72–73.
[102] *Indabas* with the Governor, ZA/1/9/59/1/1.
[103] D.C., Mporokoso, to D.C., Abercorn, 16 September 1934, ZA/1/9/59/1/1.
[104] *Ibid.*
[105] *Ibid.*
[106] 'Brief history of Isenga country', encl. D.C., Mporokoso, to P.C., Kasama, 29 October 1937, KSU/3/1.
[107] *Ibid.*; cf. Roberts, 'A political history of the Bemba', pp. 178–179.
[108] *Ibid.*
[109] *Ibid.*
[110] D.C., Mporokoso, to P.C., Kasama, 29 October 1937, KSU/3/1.
[111] Zimba to D.C., Kawamba, 31 July 1936, KSU/3/1.
[112] Zimba to Chief Secretary, 20 May 1937, KSU/3/1.
[113] *Ibid.*
[114] Acting P.C., Northern Province, to Chief Secretary, 9 August 1937, KSU/3/1.
[115] Extract from Legal Department Circular No. 5 of 1914 on Native Customary Law, ZA/1/9/27/3.

[116] *Ibid.*

[117] *Ibid.*

[118] N.C., Mporokoso, to A.N.C., Abercorn, 12 December 1926, ZA/1/9/27/3.

[119] *Ibid.*

[120] Richards, *Land, Labour and Diet in Northern Rhodesia*, p. 261.

[121] *Ibid.*, p. 260.

[122] *Ibid.*

[123] *Ibid.*, p. 259.

[124] N.C., Mporokoso, to D.C., Abercorn, 12 December 1926, *loc. cit.*

[125] Minutes of a Meeting of Chiefs and Headmen held at Mporokoso, 6 November 1926, ZA/1/9/27/3.

[126] *Ibid.*

[127] Assistant Magistrate, Mpika, to Magistrate, Awemba District, n.d. ZA/1/9/27/3.

[128] *Ibid.*

[129] *Ibid.*

[130] N.C., Mporokoso, to D.C., Abercorn, 12 December 1926, ZA/1/9/27/3.

[131] *Ibid.*

[132] *Ibid.*

[133] *Ibid.*

[134] Richards, *Land, Labour and Diet in Northern Rhodesia*, pp. 259-260.

[135] *Ibid.*, p. 258.

[136] *Ibid.*, pp. 258-259.

[137] Legal Affairs Circular No. 5 of 1914 on Native Customary Law, ZA/1/9/27/3.

[138] *Ibid.*

[139] Minutes of a Meeting of Chiefs and Headmen at Mporokoso, 6 November 1926, ZA/1/9/27/3.

[140] D.C., Abercorn, to Assistant Magistrate, Mpika, 22 December 1926, ZA/1/9/27/3.

[141] Anonymous to the Magistrate, Kasama, 6 December 1928, ZA/1/5/1.

[142] Acting S.N.A. to D.C., Abercorn, 6 February 1929, ZA/1/5/1.

[143] *Ibid.*

[144] *Pim Report*, p. 187.

[145] *Ibid.*

[146] *Ibid.*

[147] Richards, *Land, Labour and Diet in Northern Rhodesia*, p. 263.

[148] *Pim Report*, *loc. cit.* As late as 1938 Chitimukulu was receiving only £60 p.a., Chief Kopa £36, while sub-chiefs received salaries between £12 and £24 p.a. Even Plateau Tonga chiefs, whose treasury was the richest outside Barotse Province, received an average of £11 6s. 8d. for each chief; *ibid.*

[149] Richards, *Land, Labour and Diet in Northern Rhodesia*, p. 263.

[150] *Ibid.*; cf. *idem*, 'Tribal government in transition' in the supplement to the *Journal of the Royal African Society*, Vol. XXXIV, No. CXXXVII (October 1935), pp. 19-20.

[151] Richards, *Land, Labour and Diet in Northern Rhodesia*, p. 263.

[152] Lord Hailey, *An African Survey*, pp. 617-618.

[153] N.C., Luwingu Annual Report for the year ending 31 March 1926, ZA/1/5/1.

[154] *Pim Report*, pp. 187–188.

[155] *Native Affairs Annual Report, 1935*, p. 48.

[156] N.C., Luwingu Annual Report for the year ending 31 March, 1926, ZA/1/5/1.

[157] Abercorn District Note Book, p. 53, KTN/1/1.

[158] *Ibid.*

[159] *Ibid.*

[160] *Ibid.*

[161] *Ibid.*

[162] *Indabas* with the Governor, ZA/1/9/59/12.

[163] *Indabas* by the Governor, B/1/3/937.

[164] *Ibid.*

[165] *Ibid.*

[166] *Debates*, col. 72, 18 April 1929.

[167] *Ibid.*, col. 26, 12 November 1929.

[168] *Ibid.*

[169] *Ibid.*

[170] *Report upon Native Affairs in Northern Rhodesia for the year 1928*, p. 6.

[171] Report on the Gathering of Chiefs of Mporokoso Sub-district to meet J. H. Venning, D.C., Tanganyika District, 28 July 1928, B/7/3/937.

[172] Report of the Reserves Commission, Tanganyika District, ZA/1/9.

[173] *Ibid.*

[174] *Ibid.*

[175] *Ibid.*

[176] *Ibid.*

[177] *Ibid.*

[178] *Ibid.* Interestingly, Chief Penza's proposal seems an anticipation of the establishment of the system of tribal elders on the Copperbelt, which sought to achieve the same objectives as Penza's system of *capitaos* on European farms. For a discussion of the status and role of tribal elders on the Copperbelt, see A. L. Epstein, *Politics in an Urban African Community* (Manchester University Press, 1959).

[179] Report of the Reserves Commission, *loc. cit.*

[180] Meeting of the Native Reserves Commission, 15 September 1927, KSU/3/1. 'Vitemene' is a corruption of *fitemene*, which means *chitemene* gardens.

[181] Native Reserves: Tanganyika District, B/1/3/366/28, c.f. speech by the Governor, *Debates*, col. 7, 28 February 1929, and *Pim Report*, p. 71.

[182] *Indabas* with the Governor, ZA/1/9/59/1/1.

[183] L.N.W.A. Secretary's annual report, 26 April 1934, SEC/NAT/321.

[184] *Ibid.*

[185] Mason, *loc. cit.*, pp. 49–60.

[186] E. A. G. Robinson, 'The economic problem', *Modern Industry and the African*, p. 235.

[187] *Pim Report*, p. 72.

[188] *Ibid.*, p. 71.

R

[189] *Report upon Native Affairs*, 1938, p. 48.

[190] S.N.A. to Chief Secretary, 4 December 1931, KSU/3/1; Circular from, D. M. Kennedy, Chief Secretary, to all P.C.'s, 4 September 1933 SEC/NAT/324.

CHAPTER VI

MODERN POLITICS IN EMBRYO

I. NATIVE WELFARE ASSOCIATIONS

The year 1923 could, with considerable justification, be said to have been the seed-plot of the thrustful African politics in post-war Northern Rhodesia. In that year the first Native Welfare Association in the country was formed at Mwenzo Mission in the Isoka Division by an embryonic African intelligentsia composed of former as well as practising evangelists and teachers of the mission. Although the association was to become defunct by 1929, its spirit, as will be shown later in this chapter, lived on to inspire and mould similar organisations in the country which, in the late 1940's, were to form the basis for a new and forceful nationalist movement.[1]

It seems paradoxical, however, that a forward-looking organisation of this nature should have first been formed in so remote a place as Isoka, and not in one of the country's town centres, where colour discrimination and the social effects of industrialism were poignant enough to have galvanised Africans into forming such a body. One finds oneself at a loss to explain this anomaly in the growth of the Welfare Association movement in Northern Rhodesia. But there is nothing necessarily unique about this development; Van Velsen has observed something similar in Nyasaland, where the first Native Welfare Associations were formed in the relatively peaceful north, rather than in the turbulent south, where the problems of land shortage and the insecurity of African 'squatters' on European farms were urgent and pressing.[2] To this apparent paradox in the development of Welfare Associations in Nyasaland an explanation could perhaps be found in the educational superiority which that country's northern peoples seem to have enjoyed over their compatriots since the foundation of Livingstonia, and on the strength of which they were able to assume political initiatives after the failure of the Chilembwe rising and when, after the First World War, the standard and availability of education, upon which they had depended to obtain jobs in Central Africa, appeared to have dropped.[3] But quite obviously, the same reason cannot be given to explain the birth of the Mwenzo Welfare Association; however, it seems necessary all the same to cast about for possible causative factors behind the formation of the association.

It will be recalled that the Isoka Division, like Abercorn and, to a lesser extent, Chinsali, was since 1917 the arena of Watch Tower political eruptions in the Northern Province, which were themselves largely a result of the First World War. The Watch Tower movement, as the last two chapters tried to show, had, by its own belligerent mood and actions, set chiefs and headmen against their people, and the involvement of some of the ex-mission teachers in the movement also made the traditional rulers look at their mission-educated subjects as men who could not be trusted. On the other hand, estranged by the social and political excesses of the Watch Tower movement, the more pragmatic educated African elite of Mwenzo found themselves not only kept at arm's length by the disgruntled teachers who were the leaders of the movement, but also bitterly opposed to the movement itself.[4] They were thus isolated, and it seems possible that in trying to escape their sense of isolation they formed an organisation like the Mwenzo Welfare Association, which also afforded them the opportunity to air their views about the state of affairs in the country.

However, the above explanation appears too much of an over-simplification and rationalisation of what may have been a very complex situation to be valid. Surely the conditions which have been described and are presumed to have caused the formation of the Mwenzo Welfare Association were not unique to the Isoka District? The Association could very well have been formed in the Abercorn District, for example, where these same social and political conditions prevailed, and where there were appreciable numbers of educated Africans at the London Missionary Society and White Fathers' mission stations. But the fact that no Welfare Association was formed in that district until 1932 suggests that Mwenzo Mission possibly enjoyed certain conditions which were conducive to the early formation of such an organisation, and it would be well here to essay an alternative, if complementary, explanation to the one postulated above.

Although the formation of the Welfare Association was no doubt dictated by certain local social and political needs, its moving spirit was of Nyasaland origin.[5] From 1894 when the Rev. Dewar established Mwenzo, the mission maintained close contact with its parent Free Church of Scotland station at Livingstonia. Not only did its clergy come from or through Livingstonia, but its own African students, like those from Lubwa Mission, which was founded in 1904 by David Kaunda, went there to finish off their primary education and to undergo training as teachers and evangelists.[6] Whilst at Livingstonia, Mwenzo students came under the political influence of men like Dr Robert Laws, with whose encouragement Malawi's first Native Association—the North Nyasa Native Association—was formed in 1912,[7] and whose activities, according to Robert Rotberg, 'provided the foundation upon which subsequent . . . nationalism was based';[8] and possibly they also imbibed some of the radical views of the Blantyre Church of Scotland missionaries to the south, who, in the words of Alfred Sharpe, were 'taking a course that makes them appear in the eyes of the natives of this Protectorate as an Opposition Party to H.M. Administration'.[9] Furthermore, Livingstonia happens to have been in the northern part of Nyasaland, which as pointed out earlier, was the birthplace of the Native Association movement in that country, and it seems therefore possible that the Mwenzo students, in their contacts with the intellectuals in these Associations, learnt something which they emulated—as the obtaining by Donald Siwale of a copy of the North Nyasa Native Association's constitution from Levi Mumba, his former school-mate at Livingstonia, would seem to suggest. It is little wonder therefore if, on their return to Mwenzo, the students seemed inclined to look critically at all that was happening around them.

Indeed, this critical attitude towards what the whiteman was doing in the country was already apparent, even as early as 1905, and was to provide the ethos from which the Mwenzo Welfare Association sprouted two decades later. The men of the moment —Donald Siwale, David Kaunda (the father of the first President of Zambia), Hezekiya Nkonjera Kawosa, Peter Sinkala, Hanoc Mukunka, Mathew Mpande, Nkhata and Ephraim Nyirenda— had as early as 1905 begun informal meetings to discuss the general attitude of Europeans towards Africans, and to question the practice, common among Europeans, of calling Africans 'boys', irrespective of their age.[11] Siwale and his colleagues had all been to Livingstonia Mission in 1904 to train as 'certified teachers', and on their return they were each given a school to run. Every year, in July, they attended refresher courses at Mwenzo, and during these courses they took the opportunity to exchange views on the state of affairs in the country. As Donald Siwale's own recollection has it:

We would meet Dr Chisholm, who was a very good man, and tell him about our feelings. When Dr Chisholm knew that we were not happy about something, he would call in Mr Waist-Sheane [J. W. West Sheane], D.C., Tanganyika District, and Mr R. A. Young to come and listen to our complaints. We would ask them questions, some of which they used to find very difficult to answer.[12]

These informal discussions continued until World War I, when, with the death in 1918 from Spanish influenza of Peter Sinkala, and with the resignation from teaching of Siwale to join the government as a clerk and of Mukunka and Nkhata to join the Northern Rhodesia Police, the group broke up.[13]

The disruption of this group of intellectuals was, however, short-lived. Donald Siwale, now back as a *Boma* clerk at Isoka, was, together with some of his old colleagues—David Kaunda and Hezekiya Kawosa—soon able to resuscitate the discussion forum in which they used to vent their grievances many years before. But this time they were determined to do more than just hold informal discussions: they decided to form a Native Welfare Association, and in this they had the blessings of Dr J. A. Chisholm, their old friend at the Mwenzo mission hospital.[14]

The idea of forming the Mwenzo Welfare Association was, like the spirit behind the old discussion group, again Nyasa-inspired. In 1923 Siwale wrote to Levi Z. Mumba, a Nyasaland Ngoni former school-mate of his during his school days at Livingstonia, for a copy of the North Nyasa Native Association constitution, of which he (Mumba) had been secretary since its formation in 1912.[15] Although slight alterations were made to the North Nyasa Native Association constitution to suit the local requirements of the Mwenzo Welfare Association, the new constitution remained, in its aims, very close to the original from the North Nyasa Native Association—liberal and accommodating, inviting 'educated chiefs and Europeans either to attend or join it as full members . . .'[16]

It may seem strange that the founders of the Mwenzo Association should, despite all the social humiliation and tax hardships they were suffering under white rule, have devised such charitable rules for their organisation. To an outside observer, sick of the human indignities of alien rule, their constitution must have appeared too compromising, if not subservient. But what the Mwenzo Welfare Association constitution reflected was more or less the mood of the African people during the period. After the intermittent outbreaks of violence against taxation and forced labour, as well as against white rule in general, in the period before the First World War, and after the misconceived and misleading millenarian teachings and the abortive stirrings for independence of the Watch Tower movement, it was becoming increasingly clear to most people that European rule had come to stay and that all hopes of driving out the whiteman were forlorn and unavailing. With this disillusionment came the realisation that it was most important and necessary to seek a formula by which peaceful co-existence between black and white could be achieved. It was not a defeatist approach, nor did it advocate African obsequiousness to European domination. It was nothing less than a down-to-earth reappraisal of the situation by which Africans sought their rightful position in the wider framework of human rights and justice, within the colonial machinery. The Mwenzo Welfare Association, like subsequent Welfare Associations in the country, was thus a participatory and not an independence organisation.

But in spite of their pragmatism and good intentions, the men who founded the Mwenzo Welfare Association aroused some suspicion in official government circles. The Association was, in its initial stages, suspected of being a subversive organisation, intent on wresting authority from the traditional rulers, in the same way the Watch Tower had tried to do. Even officials, like James Moffat Thomson, the District Commissioner for Tanganyika District, with a sprinkling of liberalism in their views, had for some time grave doubts as to how well intentioned the Association was. In a report written a year after the association was formed, he commented:

Some Natives of Mwenzo Mission held a Meeting and formed themselves into a Native Association and they drew up a series of questions and submitted them to the Administration. The Assistant Magistrate,

Fife, was asked to reply to the questions and did so. At first this was thought to be a movement for undermining the Authority of the hereditary Chiefs and Headmen by semi-educated natives but now I am of the opinion that such was not the intention of these people and that the characteristic of the Association is one of helpfulness to those they deem to be their less intelligent fellows.[17]

Convinced that the Association meant to play a constructive, and not a destructive, role in African society, Moffat Thomson was moved to suggest that if the organisation were put under the 'good guidance of the Missionaries and officials' and if 'with tact and sympathy' chiefs and headmen were included in the movement, 'good use might be made of this Association as a medium of expression of local native views'.[18] But in making such a suggestion, Thomson had somewhat misinterpreted the spirit of the Association. His suggestion, in effect, amounted to wanting to constitute special, regular *indabas*, at which the so-called 'semi-educated natives' might or might not take the lead. But this was clearly not the idea behind the formation of the Mwenzo Welfare Association. Indeed, the stipulation in the Association's constitution that only 'educated chiefs' could attend meetings or join as members, and that ordinary people had to be 'persons of good knowledge and character'[19] before they could be eligible for membership, suggests that the Association set out to cater for certain needs which neither chiefs, who were often identified with the Administration, nor the ordinary villagers, who did not know much about what was happening beyond the borders of their microcosm, were capable of appreciating or meeting. The Association catered for the special needs of men who, because of their wider knowledge of the outside world, looked at their problems against a wider social background and tried to find solutions to them on a correspondingly broader social scale. They thus aspired to be political leaders of the people in a way different from the sense and context in which traditional rulers were leaders. Thomson himself seemed cognisant of the unique position which this rural African intelligentsia occupied in the social structure of the Northern Province's changing society. He wrote in the same report of March 1924:

At the same time it must be remembered that the natives who received education from various Missions in the District have reached a stage when they hold communion among themselves to discuss Europeans, the Government and their own position in life. They draw comparisons of their lot with that of others whom they have met in the centres they have frequented for employment, with a result that a spirit of restlessness is being engendered. They do not consider that they are receiving from life what they believe they are entitled to. This impression is much more likely to increase than diminish and it seems to me that some method will have to be adopted to enable the natives to realise their ambitions socially, politically and materially.[20]

To say that the members of the Mwenzo Welfare Association had a wider view of problems in the country than the ordinary village people or that they had certain needs of their own, which they wanted met, is not to suggest that the Association was there to look after interests which were exclusively sectional. On the contrary, the Association was only too well aware of the problems that beset the people as a whole and it was mainly with a view to finding solutions to these problems that the Association was formed. There was, for instance, the problems of taxation, which had always caused untold hardship to village communities. The hut tax was raised from 7s. 6d. to 10s. in 1920, without commensurate employment opportunities being provided for people to earn the necessary money, and this weighed heavily on their scant economic resources, and engendered widespread discontent. 'With a 10s. tax liability,' as Thomson also noted, 'and no hope of earning it, the situation of the natives was a peculiar one and there is little doubt that at that time a spirit of discontent was prevalent in some of the villages amounting almost to a murmur.'[21] E. H. Goodall, Thomson's successor as District Commissioner for Tanganyika District, painted the picture of African discontent even more gloomily and wrote rather scathingly about the government policies which had brought it about:

The attitude of the Natives generally has been described as satisfactory. But there are sections of the population which cannot be called happy and contented. The 'Native Welfare' at Mwenzo and the Watch Tower movement are but manifestations, each in its own way, of the birth of a new spirit, a mental ferment caused by discontent with the present conditions of existence and a striving to better them. This is naturally one of the first results of education in all its forms: but it can only have been fostered by the unsatisfactory economic situation of the last four years. A system which drives a large proportion of taxable males hundreds of miles away from their homes in order to meet their tax obligation and clothe their families is unsound.[22]

It was this unhappy state of affairs which made the Mwenzo Welfare Association decide at one of its regular meetings in 1924 to protest to the Administration about the high taxes the people were being called upon to pay, and sent one of its members, the Rev. Jonothan Mukwasa, to go and lodge the protest with the Native Commissioner at Isoka.[23]

In addition to discussing problems of a political nature, the Association also expended some of its energies on tackling some of the social problems that faced African society. There were, for example, certain social ramifications of labour migration which were of concern to the Association. It was noted that certain men deserted their wives in the villages on the false pretext that they were going out to look for employment. This was condemned by the Association, and chiefs and headmen were urged to visit their people in the villages in order to help remedy the situation.[24] The Association also used to receive correspondence from interested persons who asked it for advice on, or for answers to, certain general problems. There was, for instance, a letter from Samuel W. Simukonda, a Namwanga working in the Belgian Congo, asking the Association a number of questions. Among the many issues Simukonda raised in his letter were two interesting questions he asked the Association to answer. He wanted to know why a man, having left his wife at home, should not take another 'wife' whilst working elsewhere. Then he asked why whitemen slept with African women with impunity, while African men who went to bed with white women, if found, always got into trouble.[25] These were topical issues which interested every member of a society which was undergoing rapid change, and the Mwenzo Welfare Association was naturally seen as a forum for discussing such issues.

But the Association did not last very long. Only five years from the time of its foundation it became defunct, when Donald Siwale resigned from government service in protest against a cut in his salary and became an adviser to Chieftainess Waitwika of the Namwanga, and when most of the leaders of the Association left

Mwenzo to work on the line of rail.[26] The death of the organisation was something which was regretted even by the Administration because, as one official report put it, the M.W.A. 'served a useful purpose by providing a means of expression for natives on social and political matters affecting the people'.[27]

This was not, however, the end of the Welfare Association movement. Some migrant workers from the Northern Province became leading apostles of the movement in various urban centres. On the fourteen member Committee of Northern Rhodesia's first permanent Native Welfare Association[28]—that of Livingstone—which was formed in 1930, four of the founder members, Lobati Kabinda, Philip Silavwe, Amon Chela and Moffat Simon Sinkala, were from Isoka District; two, Gideon M. Mumana and William Konie, were from Kasama and one, Andrew Sinyangwe, was from Abercorn.[29] Among the prominent members of the Ndola Native Welfare Association in the early 1930's were three northerners—N. Bweupe, G. Mukwasa and J. Mumba;[30] and on the Luanshya Native Welfare Association, Kenny Rain, a Bemba from Kasama, and John Lombe and Henry Chibangwa from Mporokoso seem to have played so dominant a role that the Association was refused government recognition partly because of their 'subversive activities'.[31]

What part did the men from the Northern Province play in these Associations?[32] Mention has already been made of the fact that the Luanshya Native Welfare Association was not granted recognition by the government, partly because of the 'subversive activities' of John Lombe, Henry Chibangwa and Kenny Rain and partly because, according to government officials, there were dissensions within the leadership of the Association itself. But it was for their so-called subversive activities against the colonial authorities that the three men were noted, and in this respect Henry Chibangwa seemed the ringleader.[33] At the Association's meeting held on 21 November 1931, Chibangwa moved a motion urging the government to give Africans what he called 'Equal rights', 'Better treatment' and 'Justice to we Native people of this colony?[34] He said that he quite appreciated the liberal policies of the imperial government towards Africans, epitomised only recently in the White Paper on the Native Paramountcy doctrine as the new British colonial policy towards East and Central Africa's plural societies, but he felt that this welcome

policy was vitiated by the pass system, which required Africans
to carry passes or permits in townships, and, therefore he urged
that passes be abolished.[35] His motion was 'carried unani-
mously'.[36]

Chibangwa reiterated his abhorrence of the pass system when,
accompanied by Kenny Rain and John Lombe, he went to Livingstone in January the following year and was interviewed by
J. Moffat Thomson, the Secretary for Native Affairs. Asked by
Thomson what he meant by 'equal rights' and the rest of the
slogans which he used at his Association's meeting a few weeks
before, Chibangwa retorted:

In the towns and in the compounds we have to carry a pass. In the
villages we do not have to carry passes, that is why I say we want
'Equal Rights'.[37]

To Thomson's explanation that passes were necessary for pre-
venting unemployed Africans from wandering about in urban
areas, he simply said: 'We want to be treated fair.'[38] Chibangwa's
interview with the Secretary tempered what appears to have been
a wrathful official reaction to his motion on human rights; for
after it Thomson advised against his expulsion from the Luanshya
Welfare Association, which had been contemplated, because such
action, said Thomson, might make the man 'a hero and in consequence urged on to higher flights of imaginary grievance'.[39]
Thomson argued that the best thing that the District Commissioner responsible for Luanshya should do would be to talk
to the members of the Association 'and to explain to them in a
calm and sympathetic manner the absurdity of Chibangwe's resolution', and those of them who were sensible would readily see
how ridiculous they had been to support it.[40]

The problem which was thrown into bold relief by Chibangwa's resolution was, not unnaturally, typically urban; but it
was also symptomatic of the racial tensions which were embedded
in a plural society where the whiteman was considered superior
to the blackman. What the African intelligentsia in these Associations apparently wanted was only a recognition by the colonial
authorities that the African was as human as the European, and
therefore he was entitled to the same human rights accorded to the
whiteman and that he should not be subjected to social indignities
such as the pass system. Thus, as political organisations, the urban

Native Welfare Associations were like the defunct Mwenzo Welfare Association, participatory and not independence movements.

Perhaps no Association was more articulate in this fight for social justice at the time than the Livingstone Native Welfare Association; and in this the 'new men' from the Northern Province seem to have played a big role. At a general meeting held on 15 July 1930, the Association's treasurer, Gideon M. Mumana, inveighed against the common practice by the police of arresting Africans for using footpaths when in doing so they were merely avoiding the danger of being run over by cars on the roads, which, at any rate, they were not allowed to tread; and he went on to condemn the frequent arrests of Africans for merely window-shopping at European stores.[41] Such treatment was seen as a miscarriage of justice based on colour—something which was even more obvious over cases of miscegenation which came before the law courts. Philip R. J. Silavwe, the Assistant Secretary of the L.N.W.A., in a joint letter to J. Moffat Thomson, the Secretary for Native Affairs, from him and the Association's Acting Chairman, Samuel K. K. Mwase, a Nyasa, a complaint was made that there was racial discrimination in the administration of the law in cases of miscegenation. They argued, as Samuel K. Simukonda had done in a letter to the Mwenzo Welfare Association, that the law was deliberately bent by the courts always to favour the European and to put the African at a disadvantage.[42] Even an appeal to the High Court against a European adulterer, they said, would be 'prejudiced and the case discharged without any careful investigations, whereas the same offence committed by a native to a white woman he is found guilty and sentenced to imprisonment for life!'[43] And like Henry Chibangwa of Luanshya, they deplored the fact that such injustice should have been meted out to Africans by a government whose proclaimed policy was to put the interests of the native population above those of the immigrant races and, if the two conflicted, to uphold African interests.[44] And in view of this conflict between theory and practice inherent in the government's policies, the two men, on behalf of the L.N.W.A., pressed for a commission of enquiry to be appointed to rectify the situation:

The native understands his position but depending on the British justice he cannot help feeling that injustice [sic] sentences imposed on him by rulers are selfish and he does not consider that eviction [the conviction of] natives [is just] to all concerned; therefore the only best method he considers to remedy his evil is an appointment of an impartial commission of enquiry on the administration of justice through out the Territory at an early date.[45]

While the intellectuals from the north were thus asserting their influence in the Native Welfare Associations on the line of rail, their counterparts at home were by no means dormant in this respect. Four years after the Mwenzo Welfare Association was dead and gone, two other Native Welfare Associations were formed at Kasama and Abercorn, and remained the only organisations of their kind in the Northern Province until the 1940's, when further associations were formed at such places as Luwingu, Shiwa Ng'andu and Chinsali, and the Mwenzo (then called the Isoka) Native Welfare Association was revived.[46] Unlike the Mwenzo Welfare Association and the urban associations, the Kasama Native Welfare Association (K.N.W.A.) and the Abercorn Native Welfare Association (A.N.W.A.), both of which were sanctioned by the government at the end of 1932, operated under slightly changed conditions. The existence of Native Authorities, the formation of which followed the passing of the Native Authority and Native Courts Ordinances in 1929, made the Associations appear, even more than the old Mwenzo Association, a great threat to traditional authority. The colonial authorities, in setting up Native Authorities, were attempting to bring about a prototype system of local government which would not only lighten their administrative burdens but would also, as far as possible, accommodate growing African interest to participate in the running of the affairs of the country. The operations of Welfare Associations in the midst of Native Authorities was therefore something that the government had to watch very closely, lest these organisations disrupt the orderly development of the new local government system. In the towns, where there was no control by chiefs, the situation was different. But in the rural areas, where the chief and his councillors were an important cog in the chain of gubernatorial control, closer supervision was considered necessary over the activities of Welfare Associations. Indeed, the fear that Native Welfare Associations would upset the new policy of indirect rule by becoming political rivals to Native

Authorities seems to have been generally entertained by the colonial authorities in British East and Central Africa.[47]

As early as 1931 Moffat Thomson, then the Secretary for Native Affairs, could recommend to R. S. Dickenson, the Chief Secretary, that 'Chiefs and Native Authorities should not be encouraged to associate with these detribalised elements' in the Welfare Associations.[48] The Chief Secretary put Thomson's ideas —which were by then official policy—even more clearly when fifteen months later he sent an instruction to the Provincial Commissioner, Tanganyika Province, in connection with the Abercorn Native Welfare Association. He wrote rather warily:

It must be clearly understood that membership of the Association must be confined solely to natives who, though residing in Abercorn, owe no kind of allegiance to any Native Authority there, and who engage in no sort of political activity. The Association can act as the mouthpiece of natives who are not within the ordinary organisation of native society, but there must be no question or possibility of the Association becoming either a rival to or a 'cell' within the Native Authority.[49]

This policy decision by the Administration to restrict the membership and activities of Welfare Associations in rural areas to townships was sourly received by the K.N.W.A., whose membership was in part composed of men from the precincts of Kasama. In a letter signed by Aaron Nkata and John Mulenga Makonde, the chairman and secretary of the Association respectively, the organisation criticised the government for wanting to circumscribe its operations. They pointed out that the decision was a death-blow to the association, because by restricting membership to Kasama township the government was making the body cease to be a viable organisation, as Kasama was not large enough to provide employment for the number of educated Africans sufficient to keep the Association going.[50] Nkata and Makonde further pointed out that if the government was, by its decision, implying that the Association could continue to function by absorbing alien Africans in the township, it was deluding itself. For, there was no question of entrusting the affairs of the Association to aliens who had not come to Kasama to stay; the organisation must continue to be run by the natives of the country.[51]

The implications, therefore, of the government's decision to hem in the K.N.W.A. seemed to the chairman and secretary of the organisation to be tantamount to the proscription of the Association. But once the Association was defunct, there would arise the question of how the interests of the African people in the township would be represented. The Administration might advise people to lodge their complaints with the chiefs and the Native Authorities. But this would not be acceptable to the members of the K.N.W.A. because, so said Nkata and Makonde, 'most of the ba-Bemba chiefs are now in a somewhat primitive life; they cannot pay attention to their people, who have learnt methods of things from the white men'.[52] Moreover, all K.N.W.A. members were employed, and it would be difficult for them to attend chiefs' courts.[53] There were clearly certain basic differences between the Association's interests and those of the traditional rulers, which made political symbiosis impossible. The Association itself welcomed, and was indeed engaged in some measure of, co-operation with the chiefs for the development of the country, but this was all that could be done in the circumstances. But for as long as chiefs did not understand the aims of the Association, argued the K.N.W.A. leaders,

We should go on carrying [out] the Association's functions by ourselves and without any regard to our Chiefs. In future, when our Chiefs learnt [sic] what the Association is, and the Government thinks it fit to associate us with them, we can accept it, but not now when they do not know what it is.[54]

In its struggle to retain its 'district' composition rather than be confined to the township, the K.N.W.A. seems to have enjoyed the support of government officials in the province. The District Commissioner, Kasama, agreed that the government policy decision in the matter was a death-blow to the organisation, which depended for its strength partly on the township residents and partly on people living in the environs of Kasama, with allegiance to Paramount Chitimukulu. He therefore recommended to the Provincial Commissioner that the ambit of the Association's membership should remain as it was, since he did not consider a clash between the K.N.W.A. and the nearby Native Authority possible.[55] The Provincial Commissioner, in endorsing his District Commissioner's recommendation said that the Association was 'merely a debating society and affords a means of recreation to a number of better educated natives who might be otherwise much worse employed'. On retirement to their villages, these men with such 'debating' experience could, moreover, he said, be of assistance to Native Authorities in the discussion of tribal affairs.[56] These ideas, however, evoked no sympathy in the top ranks of officialdom in Livingstone, where Moffat Thomson made sure that his point of view remained the official policy. He urged that the K.N.W.A. should, as directed previously, confine its activities to the needs of the Africans living in Kasama township, leaving all matters affecting Africans in tribal areas for chiefs and Native Authorities. There should be no usurping of the functions of the traditional rulers, as was insinuated in the Association's letter, signed by Nkata and Makonde, to the District Commissioner, Kasama.[57]

From the records available, it is not clear whether or not Moffat Thomson's view was finally adopted as government policy in respect of the K.N.W.A. If it was in fact adopted, there is reason to believe that it was not rigorously enforced. As late as the middle of 1937, Franklin Temba, Makonde's successor as Secretary of the Association, had to report that there was a general slackness by members—especially those living six to ten miles out of Kasama—to attend meetings.[58] However, in spite of opposition from some quarters of the Administration, the K.N.W.A. did its best to try and realise the objectives for which it was formed. At its meeting on 15th September 1934, the Association chose among its members three men to form a Local School Advisory Committee which would apprise the Superintendent of Education, Kasama, of what people wanted government to provide in the nature of educational facilities.[59] Six months later, with Aaron Nkata in the chair, a meeting of the Association registered its grave concern at the rough manner in which passengers and goods were treated on transport lorries owned by Messrs Smith and Kitchin. Women, it said, were treated like men and passengers in transit were not given proper accommodation whenever they had to spend a night on the transport routes. The association urged that special 'passenger only' lorries with rain- and sun-proof tops, and with good ventilation and seats, be substituted for the existing ones, which carried goods as well.[60] At yet another meeting under the chairmanship of Y. Silwizya, when G. E. Noad, the District Commissioner for Kasama, was present, James Luka, one of the members,

s

conscious of the need for news media to disseminate news and ideas among the African people, asked the District Commissioner and his Administration to start a paper on the lines of *The Mirror*, a paper published in Bulawayo by the Southern Rhodesia government for Africans in both English and the main local African languages.[61] The question of having an African paper in Northern Rhodesia on the lines of *The Mirror* or its Nyasaland equivalent, *Zoona*, was also discussed the previous year by the Ndola Native Welfare Association. The need for it as a medium of African expression seemed great; as E. H. T. Chunga argued during the discussion of the matter:

We have many things to talk about. We understand what Europeans are doing, but they do not know what we are doing and what we feel. We live together and therefore we must have some means to understand each other. We are not content without a paper because we do not say what we see, hear or think.[62]

Although when it was submitted to the government a month later the Ndola Association's proposal for an African newspaper was rejected as being too expensive a venture,[63] it was probably in response to such agitation that the government ultimately established *Mutende* in 1936.

The District Commissioner, Kasama, could not ignore the pressures which were being exerted on him by the Kasama Native Welfare Association. Before he left the meeting at which James Luka had enquired about the possibility of government setting up an African paper—to which he does not appear to have given an answer—the D.C. made a suggestion which appears to have been directed at diverting the critical energies of the Association into less troublesome channels. He suggested that the Association should start a debating society where members would discuss African history, and no more. After a considered speech in which he pointed out the advantages to African culture of such debates, he ended with a warning:

But I must mention to you that when such a society is organised, your Association should not discuss or debate upon politics. You know your Association is not a political one.[64]

What the D.C. had said was in fact the official attitude towards such organisations. But it was too narrow a view as far as the

Association itself was concerned. The various issues which it had raised at several of its meetings were surely too political to be merely social or cultural, and the District Commissioner was presumably so painfully aware of this that he was inclined to curb further political activity by the Association. For instance, he sought to stem the agitation for better passenger lorries with an economic argument which may well have received little appreciation in African circles. He said that if special lorries were introduced the fares would rise to such a prohibitively high level that passengers would be worse off.[65]

For all its assertiveness, the K.N.W.A. seems to have been haunted by a sense of weakness—weakness, that is to say, not of purpose but of numbers. Since its inception, this had been the deficiency dogging the Association's activities. Every year membership was decreasing as people left Kasama township either on transfer or resignation. Most people who remained in the township were considered by the remaining members of the Association to be 'illiterate natives whose opinion cannot warrant the required aims of the Association'.[66] This decline in membership was causing constant worry to the Association, as paucity of members inevitably robbed it of the effectiveness it so much needed to achieve its objectives. Franklin Temba was moved to write on the behalf of the association in May 1936 to the District Commissioner, Kasama, urging that the Association be made a district organisation rather than merely a township one. It was felt that if the organisation's 'sphere of influence' were to cover the whole of Kasama District, the Association would better be able to advise the government on the thinking of the people.[67] But it is doubtful if such territorial expansion of the Association's activities would have made it any more viable. For, as has already been indicated earlier, the K.N.W.A. was finding it difficult to conduct its meetings successfully, because very few of its members turned up. In their annual report for 1937, R. M. Siame and T. Simuchimba, the Association's chairman and secretary respectively, reported that the meetings of the K.N.W.A. had not been successful owing to a general remissness on the part of members (especially those living six to ten miles from the township) to attend meetings, and the majority of members attended meetings only if they heard that a government official was going to address the Association.[68]

Comparatively little is known about the workings of the Abercorn Native Welfare Association, which, like the K.N.W.A., was also founded in 1932, with Franklin Temba as its first chairman; he later became a veteran member of the Welfare Association at Kasama. But like every other welfare association, the A.N.W.A. was a socio-political organisation. At one of its annual general meetings in 1934, the chairman, M. B. Liabunya, in his opening remarks, summed up the aims and objectives of the Association. He told the members that the people of Abercorn should consider themselves lucky to have formed a welfare association as their counterparts in other *bomas* in the country had done. For, he said, the African residents of Abercorn township were now in a position to

meet and discuss matters which are of interest to ourselves and which affects [sic] the native community in the township, and I am sure the Government officials will assist correcting our difficulties ... You must also understand that this is the only way of approaching Government officers when we have something to talk about the Township, etc.[69]

Liabunya's words did not, however, quite accurately describe the limits of the Association's activities and intentions. Like its Kasama equivalent, the A.N.W.A. did not intend to confine its operations to Abercorn township. It wanted to stretch its activities far beyond the confines of the township, and the government's injunction to the contrary was naturally not well received.[70]

As elsewhere in the country, the office of the District Commissioner in Abercorn became the focal point of African complaints about what the government was doing or had failed to do. Not infrequently the District Commissioner was invited to discuss or advise on certain issues raised by the Abercorn Welfare Association. Sometimes points at issue were communicated to him in writing by the Association. One of the things the Association had to take up with him was the high rents which African traders in Abercorn were made to pay for their trading plots. The Association complained to the *boma* that the rents which were being paid for trading plots—which were, for that matter, on the outskirts of the township—were too high. It was intriguing, the members argued, that rents should be so high in a place like Abercorn, which was so far away from the railway line and where money was scarce. The A.N.W.A. therefore urged the government to give early consideration to reducing the onerous rentals which the poor African traders were forced to pay.[71]

Apart from the foregoing, there appears little else on record about the activities of either the A.N.W.A. or the K.N.W.A., which were the only welfare associations in the Northern Province before World War II. For organisations which set out, however modestly, to improve African life in the overlapping influences of a money and a subsistence economy, such information as is to hand is too scant to enable one rightly to assess the mark these associations may have left on the political thinking of the Northern Province's African population. Robert Rotberg has concluded that owing to official lack of interest and to the fact that their members were few, these associations 'became social societies and football and recreational clubs and, before World War II at least, contributed little to the political ferment of Northern Rhodesia'.[72] But, as James R. Hooker points out, these organisations, which had some resemblance to the nineteenth-century British workmen's associations, must have been 'rather underestimated protest bodies'.[73] If they had degenerated into social clubs, it was partly because the administrative centres of the Northern Province within which the associations operated lacked the grave social and political problems upon which urban organisations of the same type throve and which inevitably made these bodies channels of African discontent in the towns. The relative weakness of the welfare associations in the Northern Province could also be attributed to the Administration's policy restricting their membership and activities to townships, as a result of which they were unable to discuss matters relating to problems like native reserves and *mulasa* which were burning issues in the province. Indeed, it seems possible that these associations would have been more effective as 'instruments of accommodation' had they been allowed to operate in native reserves and to discuss subjects pertaining not only to their respective townships but also to the country as a whole, like Welfare Associations in Malawi had done.[74]

But to conclude, as Rotberg implies, that the Welfare Associations in the Northern Province were of little or no consequence as far as the political history of Zambia is concerned is to relegate

to the limbo of political impotence organisations which were
fairly effective. The colonial authorities, it will be recalled,
deplored the breaking up of the Mwenzo Welfare Association
because, they said, the Association had served the useful purpose of providing a means of expression for the local African
population on social and political issues;[75] and the K.N.W.A.,
which gave evidence to the Alan Pim Commission in 1937 is said
to have been controlled by 'men of moderation and sense', men
whose opinion was well informed and whose views 'were sought
by the Native Taxation Committee [of 1938], the [Rhodesia–
Nyasaland] Royal Commission and by the Government on
several issues'.[76] Furthermore, it was as a result of the defunct
Mwenzo Welfare Association, the K.N.W.A. and the A.N.W.A.
that similar organisations were formed at Shiwa Ng'andu, Chinsali and Mporokoso during the war,[77] and the Mwenzo Welfare
Association was revived by Ewan Siwale, Paul Sichizya and
Sidney Simpelwe during the same period.[78] It was also from these
associations that Africans of forceful political views, like the
Rev. P. B. Mushindo, were chosen to be members of the Northern Province's Provincial Council and the African Representative
Council after the war.[79] and it was these associations which
formed the nuclei of Northern Rhodesia's first African nationalist
party—the Northern Rhodesia African Congress—in 1948.[80]

2. THE NORTHERNERS AND THE COPPERBELT DISTURBANCES OF 1935

Somewhat surprisingly, the Copperbelt strike of 1935, which
a Zambian newspaper three decades later called 'the beginning of
the African mineworkers' long struggle against racist exploitation',[81] does not seem to have received any attention from the
Copperbelt Native Welfare Associations at Ndola and Luanshya
or from those which were in existence elsewhere in the country;
at least, there is no indication in the minutes of these organisations that they ever discussed the disturbances, which, in the
words of Robert Rotberg, were 'Northern Rhodesia's first important industrial unrest'.[82] Yet there is evidence, as will be seen
later, that the African elite on the mines—clerks who worked
either in *boma* offices or in compound offices—played a leading
part in organising the strike. That the welfare associations

appear to have been silent over this issue might be ascribed to fear of possible punitive action against them by the authorities, who no doubt regarded the disturbances as a grave security problem. It was probably this fear which made even the clerks behind the organisation of the strike operate underground, as will be seen presently. But whatever the cause, this is hardly the place for such a discussion. The purpose of dealing with the Copperbelt disturbances of 1935 in this study is to try and assess the role played in the strikes by the people from the Northern Province, or the 'Bemba' as they were all called by the authorities,[83] so that in this way more light may be shed on the responses of migrant labour from the north to urban or industrial environment in particular, and to white rule in general.[84]

On 5 April 1935 the mining authorities at Kitwe (Nkana) found a notice, which was written in Bemba, posted on the town's African beerhall which, translated later into English for A. T. Williams, the District Officer-in-Charge, Nkana, by N. Mafuleka, an African clerk in his office, read:

Listen to this all of you who live in the country, think well how they [the Europeans] treat us and to ask for a land. Do we live in good treatment, no; therefore let us ask one another and remember this treatment. Because we wish on the day of 29th April, every person not to go to work, he who will go to work, and if we see him it will be a serious case. Know how they cause us to suffer, they cheat us for money, they arrest for loafing, they presecute [sic] and put us in gaol for tax. What reason have we done? Secondly, do you not wish to hear these words, well listen, this year of 1935, if they will not increase us more money stop pay tax, do you think that they can kill you, no. Let us encourage surely you will see that God will be with us. See how we suffer with the work and how we are continually reviled and beaten underground. Many brothers of us die for 22/6, is this money which we should lose our lives for. He who cannot read should tell his companion that on the 29th April not to go to work. These words do not come from here, they come from the N'sers who are far away and able to encourage us.[85]

The writer, using the pseudonym 'G. Lovewey',[86] claimed that the views expressed in the letter were representative of those of 'all of the Nkana Africans—men and women'.[87]

This letter, which the Russell Commission later called 'the only previous sign of trouble',[88] was an important revelation of the mood of the African mineworkers on the eve of the disturbances. The catalogue of grievances in the 'Lovewey remonstrance' and the call for a general strike by all people who lived 'in the country' —which presumably referred to all miners in the country and not just at Nkana—is something which surely casts a very dark shadow of doubt on the validity of the Russell Commission's findings that 'the primary cause of the disturbance at Mufulira was the abrupt and incomplete manner in which the announcement that the tax had been raised to 15s. was made throughout the compound',[89] that the Watch Tower movement was 'an important predisposing cause of the . . . disturbances'[90] and that the ill-treatment of African miners by their European superiors was only 'an additional predisposing cause'.[91] What appears more probable from the letter is that the 'primary cause' of the strikes was there long before the new tax rate: grievances about pay, maltreatment, bad working conditions and even about the old tax rates had been smouldering in the compounds, and therefore, as one writer has commented, 'the bawling out of the taxation increase was not so much the cause as the spark setting off the conflagration'.[92] If the Watch Tower movement appears to have played a part in the disturbances it is probably because, owing to industrial discontent on the Copperbelt, there was a general receptivity towards the movement's millenarian teachings, and because, as pointed out in Chapter IV, Watch-towerism thrived on discontent and bad news. But what is perhaps even more important from the point of view of this study is that the Lovewey letter, apparently written by a Bemba-speaking malcontent, foreshadowed the role which the peoples from the Northern Province were to play in the strikes which began six weeks later.

Although the call for strike action by African miners on the Copperbelt was first made by 'G. Lovewey' at Nkana, it was in fact at Mufulira where the first strike occurred, triggered off by the introduction on 20 May 1935 of a higher poll tax of 15s. The new tax rate was introduced under the Native Tax (Amendment) Ordinance of 1935[93] which, in the words of E. B. H. Goodall, the Senior Provincial Commissioner, sought 'to make possible the more equitable distribution of the incidence of native tax by making residence the basis of the assessment [of an African's ability to pay tax] instead of domicile'.[94] The tax rates under

the new ordinance varied according to the availability of employment in each area; thus the rate for most rural areas, where
employment opportunities were scarce, was 7s. 6d. a head, while
on the Copperbelt, where there were more jobs and where wages
were generally high, poll tax was fixed at 15s., which was the
highest in the country.[95]

But much as the new tax rates were considered equitable by
the colonial authorities, they were not viewed in the same light
by the African mineworkers, who, as Lovewey's letter shows, felt
that even the lower tax rate which had been in force up to the
middle of May 1935 was already burdensome. Indeed, the
announcement of the 15s. tax on the evening of 20 May in Mufulira's African compounds occasioned a strike of African miners
the following day, almost all of whom, according to E. B. H.
Goodall, the Senior Provincial Commissioner, were Bemba-
speaking.[96] According to Mwansa Mulele, a Bemba from Sunkutu's village, in Chief Misengo's area, Mporokoso District, the
decision to go on strike had been taken at a meeting of African
clerks on 20 May.[97] The strikers gathered together in the compound and began making a disturbance, as a result of which
John Smith (later Sir John) Moffat, the District Officer in charge
of Mufulira, was forced to go to the compound to try and contain
the situation. But his attempts to speak to the crowd were
spurned.[98] 'They refused to work that day,' testified Goodall
before the Russell Commission a few weeks later, 'and succeeded
in deterring most other tribes from going to work too. They
visited points in the plant where other natives were at work, and
attempted, in some cases with success and in others not, to drag
them from their work.'[99] The following morning, Wednesday
22 May, a large crowd of strikers, led by one William Sankata,
a Bemba from Sumbi's village in Paramount Chief Chitimukulu's area, gathered at the boma, and although Moffat did his
best to explain the new tax policy and how it affected them and
their kith and kin in the rural areas, only a few of the strikers went
to work after the address.[100] Meanwhile another crowd of excited
strikers had gathered on a nearby football field and had turned
down an invitation from Mr Schaefer, the Mufulira mine compound manager, to remove to the compound office so that he
might speak to them, stating that any European who wanted to
address them should do so at the same football pitch.[101] Later,

Moffat, accompanied by Schaefer and Constable Abbot, went to address the recalcitrant miners, and in order not to provoke the crowd he decided not to take any policemen with him and merely gave orders that they be on stand-by, just in case there was trouble.[102]

At the meeting, one spokesman after another inveighed against the new tax and demanded a wage increase. But the crowd, noisy and angry, refused to listen to Moffat, and he and his party left for the compound office, followed by the strikers, who, according to him, 'gathered round the edge of the compound office verandah and began to appear truculent indeed'.[103] They still seemed unwilling to listen to him, but with tact he persuaded them to go to his office so that their problem might be resolved by peaceful discussion. At the meeting which ensued, Moffat handled the situation with admirable *savoir faire* and patience. As Clegg has put it, he 'allowed the Africans to talk away their anger, listening at great length to their grievances'.[104] The strikers, one after the other, complained about the system under which they were compelled to buy duplicate arm badges, duplicate tickets and duplicate identity certificates (*chitupas*) and Moffat, listening patiently, noticed that the speakers were the same people he had seen throughout the day, and some of them were armed with sticks, while William Sankata had an axe in his belt.[105]

They were [Moffat said] the people who were causing all the trouble. After they had their say other strikers started. They made complaints which were greeted with applause, and the temper of the whole meeting improved very greatly. The natives began to enjoy it. They gradually got off the point and began talking generally about beer and other matters and I encouraged this. I hoped that the whole trouble would fizzle out in the general talk. They began laughing and cheering, and I thought the strike was really over . . .[106]

Indeed, the strike was practically over, because the following day, 23 May, most miners returned to work.[107] That this should have happened so soon and without loss of life or property was undoubtedly due largely to Moffat's own adroitness. In its report the Russell Commission wrote: 'The Commission find that the handling of the disturbance at Mufulira by Mr Moffat was masterly.'[108]

Only a day after the strike at Mufulira ended, notices were

found at Nkana on Friday 24 May, threatening a strike and general violence as well as violence to people who would go on to work; and the men behind the threats were again thought to be 'Bemba'.[109] However, according to A. T. Williams, the District Officer-in-Charge, Nkana, the notices were prepared and put up by clerks of Nyasaland origin who, at a secret meeting held somewhere on the Kitwe farms—which was an area mainly occupied by Africans—had agreed to prepare such notices, after one of them had read a letter from a friend in Mufulira urging the miners at Nkana to go on strike too. The only 'Bemba' at the meeting refused to be a party to such machinations; he would not even be persuaded to go and tell his own tribesmen to go on strike, and consequently he left the meeting.[110] Of this apparent spread of the strike from Mufulira to Nkana, the commission of enquiry reported:

The Commission consider that the cause [of the strike at Nkana] is to be found in communications which had passed between the educated class of natives at Mufulira and Nkana, and in the notices which were put up calling for a strike. . . . The Commission believe that this was the impelling cause of the disturbance at Nkana.[111]

After notices calling for a strike were put up on Friday, 24 May, on Sunday evening 26 May, a large crowd of Nkana miners met on a soccer pitch, and two hundred of them ran to the concentrator and, like their Mufulira counterparts, drove out all the Africans who were then at work.[112] The 'Bemba', according to Williams, took out gelignite from the mines to blow up the huts of 'western natives [the Lozi, the Luvale, the Tonga, the Ila, etc.] who would not participate in the strike'.[113] And when night fell there was a great deal of noise and some stone-throwing in the compound, and some Africans let off detonators. There was a very loud noise in the compound which was thought to be an explosion of gelignite.[114] About half the miners who were on their way for the night shift were prevented from going to work, and police on patrol during the night were badly stoned, and it was not until two lorryfuls of policemen went through the compound that the situation was quietened.[115] Although on the following day, Monday, 27 May, some of the workers went back to work, a large number continued the strike; there was considerable intimidation of blacklegs, and stone-throwing became serious.[116] Consequently, police reinforcements were brought in from Ndola in the morning and, later in the day, a detachment of the Northern Rhodesia Regiment arrived from Lusaka. A display of force both by the police and the army appeared to have a salutary effect on the strikers; the night was reported 'quite peaceful' and on 28 May most workers reported for work.[117] According to Williams, the strike at Nkana was confined to the Bemba and kindred tribes. 'I,' he said, 'saw none of the North-western natives implicated.'[118]

As the strike at Nkana was fizzling out, Luanshya was becoming the stage for the third and last scene in the 1935 Copperbelt tragi-comedy. To the mining authorities of Roan Antelope this must have come as a surprise, because enquiries which had been made earlier by Cecil Francis Spearpoint, the compound manager, through the tribal elders in the town ruled out any possibility of a strike at Luanshya.[119] But with Nkana only a few miles away the 'strike fever' soon spread to the Roan Antelope mine through social contacts. An African from Nkana is said to have distributed pamphlets in Luanshya on 26 May urging African mineworkers there to go on strike,[120] and the following day 'Bemba workers attempted to incite Africans to strike'.[121] On Tuesday night, 28 May, a notice written in Bemba was found on the road between the mine compound and the African canteen, which, rendered in English, read: 'Nobody must go to work on the 1st Day. All tribes and people. We shall die. They will kill us on Friday.'[122] However, as Gann has pointed out, it seems impossible to establish how the strike was organised, but on 29 May African miners stayed away from work, and in this strike, like in the other strikes at Mufulira and Nkana, the 'Bemba' again seemed to constitute the leading element.[123] An angry crowd of more than two thousand later gathered at a football field, and waving sticks and singing Bemba songs they foiled all attempts by Bonfield, the District Officer in charge of Luanshya, to address them. Bonfield, who was accompanied by his assistant and by Spearpoint, the compound manager, and his assistant, had to withdraw to the compound office,[124] a situation which was in fact a repetition of what happened at Nkana and Mufulira. But here the atmosphere was much tenser. On their way to the compound office, Bonfield and his party were surrounded by a much more hostile crowd which, as the commission of enquiry later commented, was armed with sticks, and stones, who even beat the ground in front of the returning party. This was an alarming experience which is quite unknown in the ordinary administration of natives; and it was fortunate that none of the party appear actually to have been struck.[125]

It was probably in the heat of some emotional tension which he may have suffered as a result of this incident that Bonfield later asked Superintendent Fold, who was in charge of the police contingent at Luanshya, to send for rifles and ammunition from the Luanshya police camp.[126] But the decision to arm the police, together with the many acts of violence which the miners later committed, made a tragic end to the whole drama almost inevitable. The strikers stoned vanettes carrying the police; they drove pickets away from their posts and entered the power-house and the smelter and drove out Africans who were at work.[127] Later in the day, according to a report by Bonfield, '1,000 Wemba . . . charged the compound office with sticks and stones',[128] and as a result seventeen policemen were injured.[129] There was a stampede among the Europeans, the police, the tribal elders and clerks present as well as other Africans who were seeking protection, as they sought refuge in the compound office from the 'hail of missiles'.[130] In the tense moments which followed, the police, apparently in sheer excitement, and without orders from anyone, opened fire, first over the heads of the furious rioters and then into them—killing six of them and wounding twenty-two others.[131] 'The crowd,' later testified John Lucien Keith, the District Commissioner, Ndola, 'was very distressed and very angry, shouting against the government and saying that it had killed them; they were trying to talk with the government, and the government had killed them like cattle.'[132] In the afternoon of the same day, 29 May, the rioters had fallen back and were in a fairly good temper. During Friday 31 May work gradually resumed, and on Saturday 50 per cent of the miners were back at work. In a telephone conversation on the same day, Goodall informed E. A. T. Dutton, the Acting Chief Secretary, that 'practically all those still on strike are either Wemba or kindred tribes',[133] and looking back at the riot a few weeks later, he remarked: 'It was a typical Wemba display, the natives amusing themselves in hurling missiles at the police.'[134]

From this brief account of the 1935 Copperbelt disturbances, it seems clear that a great deal of responsibility for the unrest was laid by the authorities on the Bemba and other kindred ethnic groups. Even the Mbeni Dance Society, whose membership was practically all Bemba, was treated with suspicion as an organisation which was instrumental in bringing about the disturbances. A. T. Williams, the District Officer-in-Charge, Nkana, argued that the resemblance between the crosses on the uniforms worn by Mbeni dancers and those which appeared on notices calling for strike action was suggestive of the possibility that the Mbeni dancers were at least connected with the agitation for strikes.[135] Mateyo Musiska, a Henga from Nyasaland who was Schaefer's clerk, also testified that 'the members of the Mbeni took a big part in the disturbances . . .'[136] This apparently subversive image of the Mbeni Society may have been adduced from the evidently recalcitrant conduct of a man like William Sankata, who was king of the organisation at Mufulira.[137] But evidence as to whether the society was purposefully subversive seems inconclusive. Indeed, as E. B. H. Goodall, the Senior Provincial Commissioner at Ndola, who had known the activities of the organisation on the east coast of Africa as far back as 1919, and saw it spread from there to Old Fife, Abercorn and Kasama and then, with labour migration, to the Copperbelt, commented on its character:

I do not think that the Mbeni were a material cause of [Watch Tower] trouble in 1919. Nor have they caused trouble since . . . Before the recent trouble I had forgotten all about the Mbeni, and I was amazed to hear the name again. I do not think they are dangerous now.[138]

J. L. Keith, his District Commissioner, also testified that the Mbeni was 'primarily a dance society' and that its influence was not subversive or interested in economic conditions,[139] and Chief Munkonge's testimony was in the same strain.[140]

But the question that must now be asked, and to which little effort was apparently made to find answers during the commission of enquiry, is why the 'Bemba' should have been a dominant element in the disturbances. To Dutton, the Acting Chief Secretary, the unrest was simply the result of lack of official contact with the African mining community on the Copperbelt, who, in consequence, no longer felt the government's influence and prestige.[141]. But as for the preponderant role played by the Bemba-speaking peoples in the strike, John Smith Moffat saw it as essentially a result of detribalisation. There was, he argued, a gradual lessening of tribal control over the 'Bemba' on the mines; and he warned that

Unless we are very careful we are going to get an industrial community consisting mostly of Wemba boys who will in course of time lose contact with their own people, but will remain aggressively Wemba, and who will be a strange people in a strange land. A wholly industrialised Wemba is, I should think, a very unpleasant person indeed, and it will come when his generation grows up here. He will require very strong discipline . . . I think he will be a very difficult man indeed to manage, and his son will be worse.[142]

But perhaps a more cogent explanation than this could be found for the leading role played by the 'Bemba' in the disturbances. Lewis Gann has suggested two possible explanations: first, that the Bemba were the most numerous individual tribal group on the mines, and second, that as a group they had a small number of men in good positions, a state of affairs which made them discontented, and envious of their more educated Nyasa counterparts who generally occupied high positions.[143] Gann's hypothesis indeed seems to be supported by certain data and it seems appropriate here to discuss these very briefly.

First, the numerical strength of the 'Bemba' on the Copperbelt. In a letter to Sir William A. Russell, the chairman of the commission of enquiry, Jim James Besa, a Bemba from Lubwa mission in the Chinsali District then living at Luanshya, took pains to refute all allegations that the Bemba were the perpetrators of the 1935 disturbances, and attributed the belief—popular in official circles—that this was so to the Nyasa clerks and policemen, who maliciously told lies to the authorities in order to spoil the good name of his tribe. He argued that the Bemba were not more numerous than other tribes and therefore they could not be held solely responsible for events in which every other tribe was equally implicated. He wrote:

. . . we are very sorry to say that Aliens natives wants to spoiling our Awemba names for nothing, Said that Awemba makes all people to stop work in the Mines, Said that they fear Awemba to go to work because [the Bemba] are waiting on gates to prevent people to go to work. Sir, we may say to you does one tribe should make this big trouble do you think Awemba get big number in the Mine than others tribes and aliens and how many get shot by bullet and how many killed not another tribe.[144]

Yet, contrary to what James Besa thought about the numerical strength of his tribe, the Bemba, according to a schedule submitted to the commission of enquiry by Colonel Stephenson showing the tribal distribution of African employees on the mines, were in fact the largest single tribal group, followed by what Stephenson called the 'Barotse and Western' group.[145] Out of a total of 13,103 Africans employed by the copper mines, among whom were 1,703 men from outside Northern Rhodesia, there were in all 3,478 Bemba proper at Mufulira, Nkana and Luanshya.[146] And if one takes into account related tribes—like the Bisa, the Shila, the Mambwe and the Chishinga—the number of northerners (5,659),[147] which was just under 50 per cent of the mines' total labour force, becomes of even greater significance in estimating the role they played in the disturbances.

But if the numbers of the Bemba-speaking peoples on the Copperbelt were crucial to the turbulent nature or even to the very occurrence of the disturbances, the same thing could not very well be said about the comparatively slow advancement of these peoples in various jobs on the mines, because practically no evidence has come to light that their role in the strike of 1935 was dictated by discontent arising from any situational impediments to their advancement. However, there is some indication of such discontent which emerges from what two representatives of the Africans from the Northern Province at Luanshya said in evidence against amalgamation to the Bledisloe Commission in 1938. Lameck, and James Besa, who had earlier refuted claims that the Bemba were in the vanguard of the 1935 strike, gave as one of their reasons for opposing amalgamation the following evidence:

We are far back in ranks and wages, but our friends from other countries are better appreciated and given further ranks and wages . . . This thing [is] done everywhere in Northern Rhodesia, chiefly in mining companies. We have found difficulties to work together with Northern Rhodesians and Nyasaland natives because the Nyasaland natives keeps to report to Bwanas that Northern Rhodesia natives are no good and they do not understand any kind of work. When Bwana hears this he can drive away a Northern Rhodesia native leaving a place for [the

Nyasa] reporter's brother and if this will continue, when shall Northern Rhodesia natives be trusted by Bwanas?[148]

But although the Bemba-speaking ethnic groups appear to have been the dominant *dramatis personae* in the 1935 Copperbelt strikes, one should be cautious in accepting the evidence of the mining and government authorities to this effect. For it must be remembered that the Copperbelt area was traditionally inhabited by the Lamba, the Kaonde, the Swaka, and to a lesser extent by the Lala, who were all linguistically akin to the Bemba. Against such an ethnological background, and with dominant migrant labour from the Northern Province, and with the process of detribalisation, in the course of which even non-Bemba ethnic groups like the Nyasas had mastered Bemba,[149] there is a likelihood that the authorities may have branded everybody who spoke some kind of Bemba a 'Muwemba' and so stretched the role of the northerners in the disturbances. But the important thing about this lumping together of the northerners by the mining and government authorities as one ethnic group—the 'Bemba'—is that it is probably the only indication of the assimilation of the other Northern Province peoples by the Bemba, which government authorities claimed had taken place in the province, but for which they could show no evidence.[150]

3. THE FIGHT AGAINST AMALGAMATION

One other factor which, like the welfare associations and urbanisation, helped African nationalist sentiment in the Northern Province crystallise into a definite form was the question of amalgamating the Rhodesias and Nyasaland, the feasibility of which was the subject of an enquiry by the Bledisloe Commission in 1938. There were, of course, other related commissions of enquiry previous to this one. There was the commission led by Ormsby-Gore which came to investigate the feasibility of closer association between the East and Central African British dependencies in 1925, and then there was the Hilton Young Commission of 1928.[151] But neither of these seems to have gone to Africans and asked for their views on the issues at stake as the Bledisloe Commission did a decade later. According to Captain Thomas H. Murray, member for the Southern electoral area, the Ormsby-Gore Commission coming up from the south, never got any

T

farther than Livingstone;[152] and the Hilton Young Commission only 'spent two or three days in Livingstone, five hours in Lusaka, and . . . four hours in Broken Hill'.[153]

The issues involved in making the three Central African countries into one, under a single government, provided yet another of the rare occasions when the traditional authorities and the common people could band themselves together in a crusade against the malpractices of white rule. As one eyewitness later remarked, in contrasting the animosities aroused among the people by the ill-advised functioning of the Native Authorities in the early 1930's and the unanimity among the ruled and the traditional rulers in the rejection of amalgamation:

However, the Bledisloe Commission on amalgamation of the three Central African countries proved a focus upon which these clashing interests [of the chiefs and their people] converged with unprecedented and almost inexplicable unanimity. The chiefs and the people were in total agreement in the abhorrence of amalgamation, and it was perhaps the first time since the establishment of European rule that the interests of the people and of the chiefs fused.[154]

Chief Chikwanda's assessment of the total rejection of amalgamation by Africans must, of course, be accepted with qualification in view of the fact this was not the first time that the traditional authorities and their people had put their heads under one thinking cap; they had done this before, as was shown in Chapter V, on issues like taxation and land. But the importance of Chief Chikwanda's analysis lies in the emphasis which he places on the comparatively high degree of unanimity between the ruled and their traditional rulers in rejecting amalgamation.

Unlike in Nyasaland, where welfare associations were a powerful mouthpiece of African political opinion, and in Northern Rhodesia's urban areas, where similar organisations were a forum of enlightened African opinion which the government could not ignore,[155] the Northern Province's Welfare Associations do not seem to have contributed anything to the acrimonious debate on amalgamation. The only evidence to hand suggesting that the matter ever received the formal attention of the two Associations in the province are reports that the K.N.W.A. had given evidence to the Bledisloe Commission,[156] and that members of the Abercorn Native Welfare Association had, at one of their meetings, resolved that 'they are content with their present government and are not desirous of any closer link with Nyasaland and Southern Rhodesia'.[157] Most probably the relative weakness of these Associations was mainly responsible for their apparent inarticulateness. But in the towns, where there were more effective African associational mechanism, the people from the Northern Province rose to the occasion and made their views on amalgamation known to the authorities. In his submission to the Bledisloe Commission, Joseph Mwanakatwe, an interpreter in the Livingstone High Court, and a secretary of the Livingstone Native Welfare Association, argued that amalgamation was bad for the African people of Northern Rhodesia because it entailed radical constitutional changes, which were in every way detrimental to African interests. In Northern Rhodesia, he said, although the white Legislative Council passed laws, they were usually sent to London to receive the royal assent before they could come into force. This arrangement was, in his view, a priceless constitutional safeguard which did not obtain under Southern Rhodesian constitutional law, and which the Africans of Northern Rhodesia should not allow to be lost through amalgamation with the self-governing colony:

This [constitutional arrangement] shows us that we are more safely treated on the line of law than natives in Southern Rhodesia, but if this Territory amalgamates with Southern Rhodesia, reference of laws to the Colonial Office will cease and we will have our laws made in the Parliament of Southern Rhodesia and fear there might be partiality in such laws. We are happy with our present Government and well protected.[158]

For Robert Simpelwe, also a member of the L.N.W.A., amalgamation was detestable because it would introduce Southern Rhodesia's racial policies in the country: whites would supplant Africans who were employed as telegraphists, telephone operators and typists by the Northern Rhodesia government and by the private sector, and the stringent pass, game and forestry laws of Southern Rhodesia would be used to curtail even further the social freedoms of Northern Rhodesia's African population.[159]

On the Copperbelt, little or no evidence appears to have been submitted by the welfare associations there to the Royal Commission. This was probably due to the pattern of representation which was devised and in which the leaders were usually the compound tribal elders.[160] The disadvantage about this system, from the point of view of this study, is that it was the groups, rather than the individuals, who submitted evidence in the form of joint memoranda, and consequently it is difficult to pick out the threads of the opinion expressed by the northerners on the question of amalgamation. Even the views of their representatives like the Bemba tribal elder James Besa, who, it will be remembered, had castigated the Nyasas for occupying almost all the high posts on the mines and for being catspaws of their European employers, were presented in a joint memorandum. But all the same the northerners, like all Africans on the Copperbelt, were at one in rejecting amalgamation. In a memorandum signed by twenty-three African residents of Kitwe, more than half of whom were of Northern Province origin, the appointment of the Bledisloe Commission was welcomed as 'the first time on which Africans in this Territory have been asked to give their opinions on political matter that affects their welfare'.[161] The signatories to the memorandum rejected the proposed political scheme on the grounds that 'instead of benefiting by the anticipated change of government we shall be the greatest losers'.[162]

Back in the Northern Province, it was the traditional authorities, and not the commoners, who aired the most forthright and poignant criticisms of the proposed union of the three Central African countries. Interviewed by the local District Commissioners on behalf of the Royal Commission, the chiefs made no secret of their abhorrence at the idea of uniting their domains with a country like Southern Rhodesia, which they knew, either from personal experience or from accounts by some of their subjects who had worked there, to be a whiteman's country, and where Africans, even of their own status, had little or no say in the running of the country's affairs. It was quite obvious to the chiefs of the Northern Province, as it must have been to other chiefs in the rest of Northern Rhodesia and in Nyasaland who were under the protective umbrella of British trusteeship, that amalgamation with Southern Rhodesia, with its racially segregationalist policies, would entail political ruin and social eclipse for their land-centred chieftainships. They were indeed also alive to the general body of government policy measures to which Africans in Southern Rhodesia—chiefs as well as commoners—

were subjected. In setting their faces against the introduction of similar measures in their own country, they also aired the views of their subjects. In their opposition to amalgamation the chiefs of the Northern Province expressed the same views and fears as their opposite numbers in Nyasaland had done.[163]

At an *indaba* in Isoka District, Iwa chiefs and their people spoke vehemently against amalgamation as a great social and political evil, because it sought to introduce in the country the same system of government as that which obtained in Southern Rhodesia. They argued that they did not like to see an oppressive system of pass laws, restrictions on cultivation, tax on cattle and dog licences introduced in Northern Rhodesia. They were also opposed to any closer links with Nyasaland, not because the system of government in that country was as detestable as that in Southern Rhodesia, but because *lobola* (bride-price) there was exorbitant, and so they feared that amalgamation with Nyasaland would inflate the bride-price at home.[164] In their spirited opposition to amalgamation with Southern Rhodesia the Iwa were at one with the Namwanga. The only difference was that, probably owing to decades of social contact and intermarriage with the neighbouring tribes of northern Nyasaland, the Namwanga were well disposed to amalgamation with Nyasaland. 'We know Nyasaland,' said Chief Mchifungwe when speaking on behalf of the other Namwanga chiefs in favour of closer links with their Nyasaland neighbours.[165]

Probably the most comprehensive and best reasoned argument against amalgamation was that by a Tabwa chief, Mukupa Katandula in the Mporokoso district. At a meeting of several Tabwa and Bemba chiefs with some two hundred people which was convened at Mporokoso *boma* by the District Commissioner, Mukupa displayed a profound understanding of the political and constitutional dangers of amalgamation for the African's future. He told the District Commissioner:

We are afraid of amalgamation, because officials in this country are our friends and companions, but we do not want to see strangers with other ideas in their places. We like our present form of government, which looks after our interests and leaves us free. Our people who have been to Southern Rhodesia report that natives have a hard time there. The tax is too high and there are many restrictions. We here are content and do not want amalgamation. We would rather be governed by the King of England and by our officials than by a self-governing Parliament as in Southern Rhodesia. In a self-governing Parliament the whitemen make laws in their own interests. We do not believe that our interests would be safeguarded. We do our best at present . . . and we are slowly developing health and education. In time things will go well, and we cannot understand why any change should be contemplated. We hope we will be left alone.[166]

Running through Chief Mukupa's rejection of amalgamation was the African fear of perpetual white settler domination, and in the last three sentences of his speech quoted above one sees a gleam of hope which Africans may have cherished that some day, provided they remained British-protected persons, they would manage their own affairs as an independent people.

A similar view, if less elaborate, of the implications of amalgamation was expressed by another Tabwa chief. Chief Katele considered all talk about amalgamation, or any action, however minor, that went some way to bringing about even a semblance of it, as a betrayal of the African people by His Majesty's Government. 'If there is amalgamation,' he said charily, 'we shall feel that we have been sold. Even if there were only amalgamation of the departments, . . . it would seem to us to be the first step in complete amalgamation.'[167]

To one Bemba chief—Mporokoso—amalgamation was much more than just the loss of power and status by the traditional authorities. It rekindled the smouldering embers of Bemba–Ngoni antagonism, which had its roots in the tribal wars of the mid-nineteenth century. Mporokoso saw in amalgamation the unsavoury social implications of mixing the Bemba and the Ngoni in one State, and he did not hesitate to reject outright any closer links with Nyasaland:

Chiefs in Nyasaland [he told the District Commissioner] are not respected as they are here. . . . We do not like Nyasaland natives and do not get on very well with them. The Angoni are a bad lot, born thieves. Nyasaland natives are wanderers and do not sit still. . . . We do not want to have anything to do with Nyasaland.[168]

Opposition to amalgamation was widespread. In all the districts of the province, one chief after another inveighed against the whole idea. Some even dismissed the economic necessity upon which it was constructed. They contended that economic co-operation or even, in the extreme sense, economic union did not necessarily call for the political union envisaged in amalgamation. This view was first heard in Mpika District, where some chiefs argued that all that the colonial authorities needed to do in order to achieve the economic objectives they aimed at was not to amalgamate the three countries, but rather to promote economic co-operation between them.[169]

The Mpika chiefs further stated that they did not want amalgamation because, as their opposite numbers in Isoka said, they were under a good government, and therefore they did not wish to gamble their political future by entering into a close-knit political relationship with countries whose laws they did not know very well. This point was stressed by Chiefs Kopa, Matipa and Saidi in a joint statement they made at Mpika *Boma* before District Commissioner T. S. L. Fox-Pitt on 13 June 1938 for the Bledisloe Commission. It was risky, they said, for chiefs to accept amalgamation when they did not know the type of life the African people in the other two countries were leading. For although a lot of young men from the Northern Province had worked in Southern Rhodesia, they never had contact with the rural population of that country, and this did not, consequently, befit them to play the role of advisers to their chiefs on whether or not amalgamation with Southern Rhodesia would bring in its trail any social and other problems to the Northern Rhodesian Africans, who were relatively politically uninhibited.[170] It was because of this fear and uncertainty about the political and social consequences of amalgamation to the African people of Northern Rhodesia that Chief Kopa was moved to warn the government that if union was imposed on the African people, the Bisa would remain outside it, and continue to be ruled by their own chiefs.[171]

In the Chinsali District, where District Commissioner W. V. Brelsford met a number of chiefs to collect information on what they thought about amalgamation, the same fears and denunciations were echoed about the proposed Central African union. At a meeting of chiefs which he addressed on 15 June 1938 one of the chiefs—Mukwikile—supported by Chiefs Mwaba and Nkweto, dismissed the whole idea of amalgamation as both unnecessary and risky. He recalled that when the British took over the country at the end of the last century the African people feared that their colonial masters would wrest all the land from the chiefs. But surprisingly, he said, this did not happen, and instead the Administration strengthened the position of the chief and defended the people against the Germans during the First World War. This benevolence was very much appreciated by the people, and Chief Mukwikile said that he and his people preferred to maintain these good relations with the government rather than join hands with the other two governments whose laws they did not know. He suggested that any closer links between the three countries should be limited to technical co-operation; Northern Rhodesia could, for example, get artisans and shopkeepers in exchange for whatever she could give the other two countries.[172]

Chief Nkula, who because of bad health was not able to attend the meeting which Brelsford had convened, sent in a written statement through his clerk to the District Commissioner, in which he outlined his reasons for rejecting amalgamation. He informed Brelsford that, since hearing about the presence of the Bledisloe Commission in the country, he had been making enquiries among those of his people who had been to Southern Rhodesia as to what sort of life Africans there led under self-governing white settlers. He said he was convinced beyond all doubt that there could be no political union between the people of Northern Rhodesia and those of the other two countries because of the lack of harmony between their native policies. 'We chiefs are trusted better in this country than are the people in Southern Rhodesia and Nyasaland.' School fees were too high in Southern Rhodesia, and, with amalgamation, the people of Northern Rhodesia stood the risk of having the level of fees in their schools raised to the same level, which would inevitably mean greater hardship for them, as they had not got enough money. There was, moreover, a discordance between the land policies of Nyasaland and Southern Rhodesia on the one hand, and of Northern Rhodesia on the other, which could very well adversely affect the relatively liberal system of land tenure in Northern Rhodesia, at least in the native reserves and native trust lands:

All our country is our own here, but I have heard that in these other countries a man can buy land and make it his own. We do not want that here. All the land should be free.[173]

For these reasons Nkula threw the idea of a Central African amalgamation out and, like Mukwikile, suggested closer technical co-operation as a better alternative.[174]

The other Bisa chiefs—Chibesakunda, Mukungule, Chinkumba and Kabanda—whom Brelsford met on the same day, after talking to Nkweto and other Bemba chiefs, objected to amalgamation in the same vein. Chief Chibesakunda apprised Brelsford of the fact that he himself had as a young man worked in Southern Rhodesia for two years and knew from personal experience that the laws of that country were bad, especially in so far as they affected the Africans. Africans, he said, were 'paying tax on sheep, goats and fowls', and they were not allowed to walk about in town without passes. In his view this was inhuman and he urged that people be allowed freedom of movement from one country to another in search of employment without having to amalgamate the three countries.[175]

In these variegated but consistent terms was expressed what was a universal rejection of amalgamation by the African people in the Northern Province as well as in the rest of the country. This unrestrained and trenchant opposition to the scheme, in conjunction with that which the Bledisloe Commission encountered elsewhere in Northern Rhodesia and in Nyasaland, greatly influenced the commissioners. The commission reported that although amalgamation was, in view of the identity of interests of the three countries, a necessary and almost inevitable development, the diversities between the native policies of Southern Rhodesia and of the two protectorates made immediate amalgamation both imprudent and impracticable. It recognised further that

The average native is ill-equipped to form a proper appreciation of the effects of amalgamation, either on his own position or on the prospects of the Territories, and in his present stage of development even longer time for consideration would probably have made but little difference to his attitude. Nevertheless the striking unanimity, in the northern Territories, of native opposition to amalgamation based mainly on dislike of some features of the native policy of Southern Rhodesia, and the anxiety of the natives in Northern Rhodesia and Nyasaland lest there should be any change in the system under which they regard themselves as enjoying the direct protection of Your Majesty, are factors which cannot in our judgement be ignored. If so large a proportion of the population of the combined Territory were brought unwillingly under a unified Government, it would reduce the prospect of co-operation in ordered development under such a Government. We do not mean to suggest that amalgamation must necessarily be postponed until such time as a positive demand for it arises among the natives of all the Territories, but we are agreed in doubting the practical wisdom of such a step until, through longer acquaintance with the issues involved, the fears and suspicions at present prevalent amongst the natives have been substantially removed, and they are themselves in a better position to form a considered judgement on those issues.[176]

With the benefit of hindsight one can say that the commission's contention that if the proposed political arrangement were imposed on the Africans it would fail, was a remarkably accurate prediction of the fate of the Federation two decades later. But its hopes that one day the African people of Central Africa would accept amalgamation were, as the struggle against federation was to show later, ill-founded, and were a telling example of a general tendency among the colonial authorities to play down the African's understanding of how current official policies affected him. For such a political association merely sought to create and maintain a British bloc in Central Africa—as the Northern Rhodesia Executive Council once said was the main political advantage of amalgamation[177]—Africans would not accept such a white-dominated political grouping. But it was well that the Bledisloe Commission, from its empirical observations, advised against the immediate formation of a Central African union, because the formation of such a political unit would have probably been an irrevocable departure by Britain from her colonial policy of trusteeship in the two protectorates.

If the Bledisloe Commission had found the imposition of amalgamation injudicious, His Majesty's Government found even the acceptance of the very principle of amalgamation, which some members of the commission had recommended, too presumptive and impolitic. The Dominions Office and the Colonial Office said that no announcement of the acceptance of the principle of amalgamation could be made, because the vital questions of native policy, 'unless they can be reconciled, present a serious obstacle to the unqualified acceptance of the principle of amalgamation'. For this reason, and also because only three of the six members of the commission had recommended the acceptance of the principle of amalgamation, His Majesty's Government found it necessary for further enquiries to be made into the matter in order to

ascertain whether native policy in these Territories can be co-ordinated 'on a basis, which, in the event of amalgamation, would maintain the principle of trusteeship for the native population, and at the same time effectively safeguard the legitimate interests of all other sections of the population.[178]

The Northern Rhodesia government was no less aware of African opposition to amalgamation. While noting that this opposition was largely determined by African fear of change, the Executive Council dismissed as unfounded press statements that African views were influenced by the 'interpreter class'. For it was quite clear that, although the illiterate Africans, like most chiefs, could not be expected 'to reason the position out philosophically', it would have been quite erroneous for the government or anybody to regard their views as worthless, because large numbers of Africans had had first-hand experience of life in Southern Rhodesia.[179]

There were, however, a number of white settlers in Northern Rhodesia who thought that Africans did not comprehend what they were opposing. J. E. 'Chirupula' Stephenson, for many years a Native Commissioner in the country, whose home was near the Central Province's boundary with the Northern Province, was one of those Europeans who thought that an African was something of a child who did not know what was good or bad for him. This, he said, was merely a question of racial differences. Quoting an old Boer saying in a letter to the commission, he argued that

it was not a question as to whether a black man was a better man, or worse man than the white man; but the realisation of the fact that the black man was a different man from the white man . . .

Stephenson consequently concluded that 'to expect of such people [the Africans] an opinion on the merits or demerits of amalgamation, is as reasonable as imagining a yokel explaining Einstein's "relativity".'[180]

Stephenson's views were too extreme but they were representative of the opinion of some Europeans who, like himself, had over
the years cultivated a paternalistic attitude towards 'the poor
native'. Roy (later Sir Roy) Welensky, member for the Northern
Electoral Area in the Legislative Council, was also of the view that
'the average African did not fully understand what the question of
amalgamation really implied, and . . . that far too much point
was placed on the evidence of the Africans'.[181] And Sir Leopold F.
Moore's views were even more sceptical of the reasonableness of
African opposition to amalgamation:

We know what Native opinion is worth. There is not one intelligent
Native in this country. Their opinion is not worth anything at all.
In fact, they do not understand the problem, which was shown in the
evidence they gave. They do not know anything at all about it. They
[the British government] put it off on the grounds that Natives would
not like it. Well, the Natives have got no grounds for liking it or dis-
liking it; we are running the show and we shall be running it for at
least a generation and possibly two or three.[182]

But all this denigration of the African's ability to understand the
issues at stake made no difference to the fact that African opposition to amalgamation in the two northern territories was strong.
Whether Africans needed 'to reason the position out philosophically'[183] in order to form 'a proper appreciation of the effects of
amalgamation'[184] on their position, seems to have been beside the
point. Indeed, one might ask the question which Harry Franklin
later asked about the plausibility of the decision by the Conservative party's research department not to take note of African
opinion on the proposed Central African Federation purely on
the grounds that more than 90 per cent of the Africans were
illiterate: 'does one need to read or understand the structural
engineering problems of tunnelling the English Channel in order
to know the purposes of the tunnel?'[185]

NOTES

[1] Hall, *op. cit.*, p. 113.

[2] J. van Velsen, 'Some early pressure groups in Malawi', *The Zambesian
Past*, p. 378.

[3] John McCracken, 'African politics in twentieth-century Malawi', *Aspects
of Central African History*, p. 198.

[4] Indicative of this anti-Watch Tower feeling was a report to the Administration of the sect's activities near Mwenzo made by one teacher, Samuel Longwe, and an evangelist, John Siame, to which reference was made in Chapter IV.

[5] Hall, *op. cit.*, p. 114.

[6] Stone, *op. cit.*, pp. 313-314.

[7] Gray, *op. cit.*, p. 171.

[8] Rotberg, *The Rise of Nationalism in Central Africa*, p. 7. Robert Laws taught Charles Domingo politics before the Kunda tribesman broke away from the Free Church of Scotland in 1910 to lead his own Church—the African Seventh Day Baptist, *ibid.*, pp. 70-71.

[9] Sharpe to Lord Kimberley, 31 October 1894; cited in Andrew C. Ross, 'The African—a child or a man?', *The Zambesian Past*, p. 332.

[10] Hall, *op. cit.*, p. 113.

[11] Interview with Donald Siwale.

[12] *Ibid.*

[13] *Ibid.*

[14] *Ibid.*

[15] Van Velsen, 'Some early pressure groups in Malawi', p. 378

[16] Hall, *op. cit.*, p. 113; cf. van Velsen, 'Some early pressure groups in Malawi', pp. 380-381.

[17] Tanganyika District annual report for the year ended 31 March 1924, ZA/7/1/7/9.

[18] *Ibid.*

[19] Hall, *loc. cit.*

[20] *Ibid.*

[21] *Ibid.*

[22] Tanganyika District annual report for the year ending 31 March 1925, ZA/7/1/8/8.

[23] Hall, *op. cit.*, p. 113; Rotberg, *The Rise of Nationalism in Central Africa*, p. 124.

[24] Minutes of the M.W.A., 28 October 1925, A 950.

[25] Simukonda to the M.W.A., 2 March 1926, in *ibid.*

[26] Interview with Donald Siwale.

[27] *Report upon Native Affairs in Northern Rhodesia for the year 1928*, p. 4.

[28] Rotberg, *The Rise of Nationalism in Central Africa*, p. 125.

[29] Minutes of the L.N.W.A. general meeting of 19 April 1930, SEC/NAT/321; encl., S.N.A. to Chief Secretary, 3 March 1931, in *ibid.*

[30] Minutes of the N.N.W.A. meetings of 4 April 1932 and 30 April 1933, SEC/NAT/329, Vol. 1.

[31] Acting P.C., Ndola, to Chief Secretary, 6 March 1934, SEC/NAT/325.

[32] The discussion here of the role of Northern Province workers in the Welfare Associations on the Copperbelt and on other town centres in no way presupposes that they were any more active than other groups in these organisations; nor is it intended to suggest that the northerners were acting as a separate entity from the other ethnic groups. In fact, they were, like every other group, members of these non-tribal organisations, reacting to the same racial and urban environment and seeking answers to their common problems.

The aim of the discussion which follows is merely to show the reactions of the
Northern Province people to urban environment as part of their general
reaction to white rule.

33 S.N.A. to Chief Secretary, 12 January 1932, in *ibid.*
34 Minutes of the Lu.N.W.A. meeting of 21 November 1931, in *ibid.*
35 *Ibid.*
36 *Ibid.*
37 Interview with S.N.A., 11 January 1932, in *ibid.*
38 *Ibid.*
39 Moffat Thomson to Chief Secretary, 12 January 1932, in *ibid.*
40 *Ibid.*
41 Minutes of the general meeting of the L.N.W.A. of 15 July 1930,
SEC/NAT/321.
42 Mwase and Silavwe to S.N.A., 13 February 1931, SEC/NAT/321.
43 *Ibid.*
44 *Ibid.*
45 *Ibid.*
46 Hall, *op. cit.*, pp. 121–122.
47 See van Velsen, 'Some early pressure groups in Malawi', pp. 405–406.
48 Moffat Thomson to Chief Secretary, 4 December 1931, KSU/3/1.
49 Chief Secretary to P.C., Abercorn, 9 March 1933, SEC/NAT/327.
50 Nkata and Makonde to D.C., Kasama, 26 March 1933, SEC/NAT/326.
51 *Ibid.*
52 *Ibid.*
53 *Ibid.*
54 *Ibid.*
55 D.C., Kasama, to P.C., Kasama, 1 April 1933, SEC/NAT/326.
56 P.C., Kasama, to Chief Secretary, 3 April 1933, in *ibid.*
57 Moffat Thomson to Chief Secretary, 13 April 1933, Sec/Nat/326.
58 K.N.W.A. Annual Report for 1937, in *ibid.*
59 K.N.W.A. Minutes, in *ibid.*
60 K.N.W.A. Minutes for the meeting of 23 March 1935, in *ibid.*
61 K.N.W.A. Minutes for the meeting of 6 April 1935, in *ibid.*
62 N.N.W.A. Minutes for the meeting of 22 February 1934, SEC/NAT/329.
63 S.N.A. to Chief Secretary, 24 March 1934, in *ibid.*
64 K.N.W.A. Minutes for the meeting of 6 April 1935, *loc. cit.*
65 D. C., Kasama, to Secretary, K.N.W.A., 16 April 1935, SEB/NAT/326.
66 K.N.W.A. Annual Report for the year ending 31 December 1935, in
ibid.
67 Temba to D.C., Kasama, 6 May 1936, Sec/Nat/326.
68 K.N.W.A. Annual Report for 1937, in *ibid.*
69 A.N.W.A. Annual General Meeting, 14 April 1934, Sec/Nat/327.
70 Interview with Moses Sikazwe, 29 July 1967, Abercorn.
71 A.N.W.A. Annual Report, 1934, Sec/Nat/327.
72 Rotberg, *The Rise of Nationalism in Central Africa*, p. 131.
73 Hooker, 'Welfare Associations and other instruments of accommodation
in the Rhodesias between the world wars', *Comparative Studies in Society and
History*, Vol. IX, No. 1 (October 1966), p. 51.

[74] Van Velsen, 'Some early pressure groups in Malawi', pp. 382–406.
[75] See p. 243 above.
[76] *Annual Report upon Native Affairs for the year 1937*, p. 58; *ibid.*, 1938, p. 47.
[77] Interview with the Rev. P. B. Mushindo.
[78] Hall, *op. cit.*, p. 121.
[79] Interview with the Rev. P. B. Mushindo.
[80] Hall, *op. cit.*, p. 125.
[81] *The Patriot*, p. 6, 24 October 1968. This paper was launched by a company of Zambians in order to recount to the Zambian people the story of their struggle for independence; but since this, its first issue, the paper has not been in circulation again.
[82] Rotberg, *loc. cit.*, p. 163.
[83] *Evidence*, Vol. I, p. 301.
[84] As was the case in respect of their role in Welfare Associations on the line of rail, the people from the Northern Province did not take part in the Copperbelt strikes of 1935 as a disparate or organised group but as part and parcel of an urban community responding to the same socio-political phenomena in an industrial environment. For an analysis of social and working relationships between various ethnic groups on the Copperbelt, see A. L. Epstein, *Politics in an Urban African Community*.
[85] *Ibid.*, pp. 416–417. A slightly different version said to have been translated by an African policeman is quoted in Rotberg, *The Rise of Nationalism in Central Africa*, p. 161.
[86] A. T. Williams, the D.O.-in-Charge, Nkana, was unable to find anybody by that name in the town; Rotberg, *loc. cit.*, p. 162.
[87] *Evidence*, Vol. I, p. 417.
[88] Report of the Commission, p. 18.
[89] *Ibid.*, p. 16.
[90] *Ibid.*, p. 49.
[91] *Ibid.*, p. 17.
[92] Clegg, *op. cit.*, pp. 81–82.
[93] It seems that the introduction of the new tax rates at the time was not legal, because the law has not yet been enacted nor the new rates published in the *Gazette*. See Gann, *A History of Northern Rhodesia*, p. 302, and Rotberg, *The Rise of Nationalism in Central Africa*, p. 161, n. 13.
[94] *Debates*, col. 14, 2 May 1935.
[95] Clegg, *op. cit.*, p. 80.
[96] *Evidence*, Vol. I, p. 65.
[97] *Ibid.*, p. 246.
[98] *Ibid.*, p. 65.
[99] *Ibid.*, p. 258.
[100] *Ibid.*
[101] *Ibid.*, p. 259.
[102] *Ibid.*, p. 260.
[103] *Ibid.*, p. 261.
[104] Clegg, *op. cit.*, p. 81.
[105] *Evidence*, Vol. I, p. 262.
[106] *Ibid.*

[107] Rotberg, *The Rise of Nationalism in Central Africa*, p. 163.
[108] Report of the Commission, p. 17.
[109] *Ibid.*, p. 18.
[110] *Evidence*, Vol. I, p. 436.
[111] Report of the Commission, p. 20.
[112] *Ibid.*
[113] *Evidence*, Vol. I, p. 424.
[114] Report of the Commission, p. 19.
[115] *Ibid.*
[116] *Ibid.*
[117] *Ibid.*
[118] *Evidence*, Vol. I, p. 437.
[119] Report of the Commission, p. 21.
[120] Gann, *A History of Northern Rhodesia*, p. 301.
[121] *Ibid.*
[122] Report of the Commission, *loc. cit.*
[123] Gann, *A History of Northern Rhodesia*, p. 301.
[124] Report of the Commission, p. 24.
[125] *Ibid.*
[126] *Ibid.*
[127] *Ibid.*
[128] Testimony of E. B. H. Goodall, *Evidence*, Vol. I, p. 68.
[129] Testimony of John Cavan Maxwell, Inspector of Police, in *ibid.*, p. 17.
[130] Report of the Commission, p. 25.
[131] *Ibid.*, p. 27.
[132] *Evidence*, Vol. I, p. 144.
[133] *Ibid.*, p. 31.
[134] *Ibid.*, p. 71.
[135] *Evidence*, Vol. I, p. 420.
[136] *Ibid.*, p. 252.
[137] The leaders of the Society had given themselves titles like Doctor, King, Emperor; see testimony of Chief Munkonge in *ibid.*, p. 128.
[138] *Ibid.*, p. 77.
[139] *Ibid.*, p. 151.
[140] *Ibid.*, p. 128.
[141] *Ibid.*, pp. 29–30.
[142] *Ibid.*, pp. 281–282.
[143] Gann, *A History of Northern Rhodesia*, p. 301.
[144] *Evidence*, Vol. II, p. 827.
[145] *Evidence*, Vol. I, p. 649.
[146] *Ibid.*
[147] *Ibid.* In 1937 the pattern of tribal distribution of African workers on the three mines remained almost the same. Out of 4,326 employees at Mufulira, 3,001 were northerners; Nkana mine's labour force was 6,495 and out of these 3,319 were from the Northern Province, and Luanshya had 2,432 northerners out of a total of 6,307; *Pim Report*, Appendix VI, p. 362.
[148] Royal (Bledisloe) Commission: Native Evidence, SEC/EA/11.
[149] Rotberg, *The Rise of Nationalism in Central Africa*, p. 163.

[150] See Chapter V.
[151] Rotberg, *The Rise of Nationalism in Central Africa*, pp. 97–100.
[152] *Debates*, col. 29, 28 November 1927.
[153] *Ibid.*, p. 30, 18 November 1930.
[154] Interview with Chief Chikwanda Chitabanta, 24 July 1967, Mpika.
[155] For a comparative analysis of the roles played by Welfare Associations in Nyasaland and Northern Rhodesia in representing African opinion before the Bledisloe Commission, see Gray, *op. cit.*, pp. 175–178; 190–191.
[156] *Annual Report upon Native Affairs for the year 1938*, p. 47.
[157] Memorandum on the Views of the Native Authorities (Lungu and Mambwe) and of the Abercorn Native Welfare Association, 31 May 1938, SEC/EA/11.
[158] Royal Commission: Native Evidence, SEC/EA/11.
[159] *Ibid.*
[160] *Ibid.*
[161] Memorandum on Closer Union or Amalgamation of Southern Rhodesia, Northern Rhodesia and Nyasaland, SEC/EA/11.
[162] *Ibid.*
[163] Gray, *op. cit.*, p. 176.
[164] Royal Commission: Native Evidence, *loc. cit.*
[165] *Ibid.*
[166] *Ibid.*
[167] *Ibid.*
[168] *Ibid.*
[169] Rhodesia and Nyasaland Royal Commission: Summaries of Evidence from Natives in the Northern Province, ZP/2/2/4.
[170] *Ibid.*
[171] Chief Kopa to D.C., Mpika, n.d., ZP/2/2/4.
[172] Royal Commission, 1938: Summaries of Evidence from Natives in the Northern Province, ZP/2/2/4.
[173] *Ibid.*
[174] *Ibid.*
[175] *Ibid.*
[176] *Bledisloe Report*, p. 218.
[177] Minutes of the N.R. Ex. Co. meeting of 16 June 1939, SEC/EA/Vol. I.
[178] 'Joint Dominions Office and Colonial Office Draft "Formula"', SEC/EA/14, Vol. I.
[179] Minutes of the Ex.Co. meeting of 16 June 1939, in *ibid.*
[180] J. E. Stephenson to Secretary, Bledisloe Commission, 5 June 1938, SEC/EA/13.
[181] *Debates*, col. 496, 6 June 1939.
[182] *Ibid.*, col. 501, 6 June 1939.
[183] Minutes of the N.R. Ex. Co. Meeting of 16 June 1939, *loc. cit.*
[184] *Bledisloe Report*, p. 218.
[185] Franklin, *Unholy Wedlock: the failure of the Central African Federation* (London: George Allen and Unwin, 1963), pp. 78–79.

CHAPTER VII

EPILOGUE

The uproar to which the debate on amalgamation gave rise probably marked the climax of African protest in the Northern Province against the encumbrances of colonial rule before World War II. But in spite of the spirited manner in which the question of amalgamation was discussed, neither the chiefs nor the African intelligentsia of the Welfare Associations in the whole territory ever agitated for independence; nor indeed, were their actions and pronouncements on the issue particularly hostile to white rule. The independence movement in which the African population was organised to eliminate colonial rule altogether was something of the future. Until two decades or so after the end of World War II, there was little of the rumpus and stir that characterised the later crusade against alien rule. African politics in the Northern Province and in the country as a whole before World War II were politics of resistance to government measures which were considered prejudicial to African interests and of agitation for a wider range of social and political rights as well as economic opportunities within the colonial system. Indeed, this appears to have been generally the case in other parts of tropical Africa where local African populations, in the words of Robert Rotberg, also

sought, in every conceivable constitutional way, to better the colonial political, social, and economic order. In an implicit recognition of the fact that the governments of Europe had come to stay and that the imposed codes of law could not be removed easily, Africans tried to work within the colonial context. Using practical concepts and languages of their respective rulers, they successfully claimed the democratic right to participate in the governing process. At first they wanted to achieve no more than the right to have their collective voices heard in matters directly affecting the lives and actions of the indigenous population.[1]

This was the ethos running through the Northern Province traditional rulers' remonstrations with the colonial authorities about taxation, land alienation and about their own position in the new political order; it was also the dominant theme in the village people's reactions to taxation, forced labour and *mulasa*, and in the Welfare Associations' dealings with the colonial administration. Indeed, even the Watch Tower movement, whose rejection of civil authority and whose millenarian teaching about African 'independence' and self-sufficiency in European manufactures and money were perhaps little different from the totalitarian theocracy, and the political and social exclusivism of the Jehovah's Witnesses in later years,[2] could be said to have been basically an 'instrument of accommodation' within the colonial system. According to Arthur Wina, one of the leading personalities in the nationalist and independence movement in post-war Northern Rhodesia, the African protest movement in Northern Rhodesia, as distinct from agitation for independence, continued until the years of anti-federation struggle, when it reached its 'highest point' and when a 'nationalist movement [for independence] under a determined leadership' was born.[3]

Because the leaders of the African protest movement before World War II merely craved equality of opportunity within the colonial context, and hardly spoke of freedom or independence, it has been the practice among some scholars to draw a sharp distinction between early African opposition to colonial rule and the independence movement of the post-war period, arguing, in fact, that African nationalism is a phenomenon which suddenly burst into view after World War II, as if it had no roots from which it sprang.[4] Robert Rotberg traces the rise of nationalism in tropical Africa to African experiences during the war, to the influence of the stirring pronouncements on freedom during and after the war by men like Roosevelt, Winston Churchill and Charles de Gaulle, and to the influences of nationalist agitation in India and Palestine.[5] For David Mulford, the development after World War II of African resistance to colonial rule in Northern Rhodesia into 'a broader African identity which manifested itself in the political consciousness of being *African*, a Northern Rhodesia African . . . marked the emergence of African nationalism' in the country.[6]

Such a view of the development of African nationalism, at least as far as Zambia is concerned, must rest upon the assumption that African nationalism only came into existence with the formation of modern political parties, which fostered a 'territorial nationalism' and were later organised as a mass movement for

independence. This is clearly a misreading of a historical development which began with the establishment of colonial rule itself.
Such a misunderstanding would probably not arise if African
protest movements and later independence movements were
seen as only phases of the same historical phenomenon—nationalism, the difference between the two being one of scale and degree.
As van Velsen has observed:

the beginnings of the early nationalist movements were rebellious in
character rather than revolutionary. That is, they accepted the prevailing political structure but tried to obtain fairer opportunities within it.
They simply wanted a fairer share of the cake but there was no question
of wanting the whole cake and doing the sharing themselves; that came
later . . .[7]

It must, in any case, be clear, as Terence Ranger has pointed
out, that 'the environment in which later African politics developed was shaped not only by European initiatives and policy or
by African co-operation and passivity, but also by African
resistance'.[8] It was, indeed, from earlier African expostulations
and bitter past experience of colonial rule that the post-war
nationalist and independence movement in Northern Rhodesia
drew its impetus. The systematic boycotts in the 1950's by the
African National Congress of shops and other public places which
discriminated against Africans[9] was the culmination of African
resentment against the colour bar, under which the urban
Zambian population had been chafing for decades, as the remonstrations in the 1930's by the Livingstone Native Welfare Association had shown.[10] Moreover, the African National Congress itself
was born of the country's Native Welfare Associations (some of
which had existed well before World War II), which merged into
a Federation of Welfare Associations in 1946. Thus, as Rotberg
has remarked about such organisations in tropical Africa in
general: 'Associational activity . . . provided training for future
politicians. In many ways, associations may thus be considered
the logical progenitors of the nationalist-minded political parties
of the 1940's and 1950's.'[11]

Perhaps equally illustrative of the connections between the
protest movement before the war and later African politics in
Northern Rhodesia is what African leaders had to say on the
vexed question of amalgamation. When the agitation for amalga-

mating the Rhodesias was resuscitated in 1943 by European politicians, Harry Nkumbula, then a schoolteacher on the Copperbelt, sought to strengthen the African case for opposing the scheme by referring to the vehement manner in which before the war the African people of Northern Rhodesia had registered their dislike of political union with Southern Rhodesia.[12] Eight years later, in an address on federation to a working committee of the African National Congress in Kitwe, Nkumbula, then President of Congress, emphasised even more the influence of past grievances on current African political thinking:

We must tell the white settlers in our Protectorate and the British that we cannot trust them any more . . . We have suffered from the hands of our supposed partners. Perhaps this has been a blessing in disguise. There is now a rising tide of nationalism among our people. Our national spirit, now ripe, is an upthrust from our long suffering. There is no going back. We are a nation and like any other on earth we love to rule ourselves.[13]

Just how consistently opposed Africans in Northern Rhodesia were to amalgamation and to what extent earlier opposition to the scheme influenced later African thinking is a point which emerges quite clearly from a speech by a Bemba-speaking member of the African Representative Council. Edward Sampa, speaking on amalgamation during the first session of the council at Chalimbana, observed:

Forcing men to do something savours of slavery. Slavery has long since been abolished. We have been speaking about these [amalgamation] matters for many years . . . If a person doesn't eat beef because it makes him vomit, it is no use forcing him to eat beef and telling him that if he keeps on eating it it will no longer make him sick. We cannot understand why we should be forced to accept something we don't want. We have refused to let Northern Rhodesia and Southern Rhodesia amalgamate . . . I want to say that we like the way we are ruled in this country and we don't want to be ruled the way the people in Southern Rhodesia are ruled.[14]

By arguing that the Africans of Northern Rhodesia liked the way they were ruled, Edward Sampa was not in any way saying that he had resigned himself, or committed his people, to perpetual colonial rule. He was, in fact, choosing the lesser evil (alien rule with protected status) and rejecting amalgamation for the same political reasons which Joseph Mwanakatwe of the Livingstone Native Welfare Association and the Tabwa chief, Mukupa Katandula had so clearly enunciated.[15] A few years later Kenneth Kaunda, who subsequently became Zambia's first President, saw African opposition to federation in the same light. He said that one of the reasons why Africans were opposed to federation was that they feared 'losing their protected status, which could lead to national independence and self-determination'; and he called the African paramountcy doctrine, enunciated by the British government some three decades before to ensure such status, 'the African Magna Carta'.[16]

So, in many and infinitely complex ways, the memory and effects of old grievances against the various malpractices of colonial rule interacted with a number of other factors to influence African politics in post-war Northern Rhodesia, thus making a prelude to the politics of independence. And in this process the Northern Province, which had borne the brunt of World War I and seen the outbreak of Watch Tower disturbances thereafter, as well as the establishment of the country's Welfare Associations in an endeavour to find solutions to some of the human problems in the area, played no small part. Some of its people, like Donald Siwale, who were involved in the protest movement against colonial rule long before World War II, continued to fight for social justice even afterwards;[17] and others, of the younger generation, like Kenneth Kaunda and Simon Kapwepwe, helped turn the protest movement into a vigorous political crusade which won independence for their country, after seventy years of white rule.

NOTES

[1] Rotberg, *A Political History of Tropical Africa* (New York and Chicago: Harcourt, Brace & World Inc., 1965), pp. 341–342.

[2] For a discussion of the Jehovah's Witnesses as a self-assertive, exclusive and theocratic organisation, see Stevenson, *Year of Doom*, pp. 141–171.

[3] Quoted in David C. Mulford, *Zambia: the Politics of Independence, 1957–1964* (London: O.U.P., 1967), p. 47.

[4] A brief but interesting discussion of the views of some of these schools of thought is in T. O. Ranger, 'Connexions between "primary resistance" move-

ments and modern mass nationalism in East and Central Africa,' Part I, *op. cit.*, pp. 437–453.

⁵ Rotberg, *A Political History of Tropical Africa*, p. 348.

⁶ Mulford, *op. cit.*, pp. 332–333.

⁷ Van Velsen, 'Some early pressure groups in Malawi', *op. cit.*, p. 411.

⁸ Ranger, 'Connexions between "primary resistance" movements and modern mass nationalism', *op. cit.*, p. 440.

⁹ Hall, *op. cit.*, pp. 175–176.

¹⁰ See pp. 245–246 above.

¹¹ Rotberg, *A Political History of Tropical Africa*, pp. 342–343.

¹² Cited in Rotberg, *The Rise of Nationalism in Central Africa*, p. 215.

¹³ Quoted in Mulford, *op. cit.*, p. 20.

¹⁴ *Proceedings of the African Representative Council*, 4 November 1946, cols. 17–18.

¹⁵ See pp. 267, 269 and 270 above.

¹⁶ Thomas Patrick Melady (ed.), *Kenneth Kaunda of Zambia: Selections from his Writings* (New York and London: Frederick A. Praeger, 1964), pp. 26, 31.

¹⁷ Siwale became one of the leading and outspoken opponents of federation; see Mulford, *op. cit.*, p. 33.

SELECT BIBLIOGRAPHY

I. PRIMARY SOURCES

(a) *The public records of the Republic of Zambia*

These are kept in the national archives of the government of the Republic of Zambia in Lusaka and consist of various official as well as some private documents which have been collected from different parts of the country over the years. For the period before 1911 they are divided into two separate parts: one part for North-eastern Rhodesia and the other for North-western Rhodesia; but from 1911 onwards, with the merger of the two regions as one unit, they all come under one section.

African New Apostolic Church, 1928–1939, SEC/NAT/287.
Amalgamation—correspondence, proposals, memoranda and minutes, 1929–1937, SEC/EA/9.
Amalgamation—correspondence and memoranda, 1937–1939, SEC/EA/5.
Amalgamation—memoranda submitted by non-African persons and bodies; correspondence, 1948, SEC/EA/10.
Amalgamation—native evidence and memoranda, SEC/EA/11.
Amalgamation—official evidence and memoranda, SEC/EA/12.
Amalgamation—Rhodesia and Nyasaland Royal Commission, 1938, ZP2/2/4.
Amalgamation—Royal Commission (Bledisloe) Report, SEC/EA/14.
Amalgamation—Views of Stephenson, J. E. 'Chirupula', SEC/EA/13.
British South Africa Company—in letters from the London office to the Administrator for North-eastern Rhodesia, 1895–1910, on native affairs, police, land settlement, the hut tax and labour, A1/2/1–8.
British South Africa Company—out-letters from the Collectors, Chambeshi District, to the Administrator, January–September, 1896; 1897–1899, A1/1/1–2.
British South Africa Company—out-letters from the Administrator to the High Commission for South Africa, 1909–1911, A2/2/1–3.

British South Africa Company—out-letters from the Administrator to Her Majesty's Commissioner in Zambia, 1903–1908, A2/3/1.
British South Africa Company—out-letters from the Administrator to the London office, 1899–1911, A2/4/1–11.
Chiefs—Mporokoso sub-district, 1934, KSU1/1.
Chiefs, complaints against, 1931–1934, ZA1/9/8.
Chiefs, deposals of, 1929 1939, SEC/NAT/191 192.
Chiefs, disputes among, 1931–1935, ZA1/3.
Chiefs and headmen, 1924–1927; 1935–1937, C1/1.
Chiefs and headmen, Awemba District, 1916–1918, KSD2/2.
Chiefs and headmen, appointment and dismissal of, 1928–1929, B1/3.
Chiefs and headmen—cases of misconduct, 1929–1939, SEC/NAT/423.
Chief Secretary—private and semi-official correspondence, 1930–1934, B1/5.
Civil disturbances, 1918–1924—Governor's correspondence, P1/3.
Closer association—correspondence between East and Central African governors and memoranda, 1935–1938, SEC/EA/4.
Complaints, 1926–1931, ZA1/5.
Constitutional development in Northern Rhodesia—correspondence and memoranda, 1931–1938, SEC/MISC/10.
Criminal case records and books—Abercorn Native Commissioner's Court, 1897–1902, 1NH/3; 1904–1910, F3.
Criminal case records and books—High Court of North-eastern Rhodesia, F.
Criminal case records and books—Isoka Division, 1911–1929, KSL1/3.
Criminal case records and books—Kasama Division, 1907 1910, F3; Luwingu Division 1910, F3; 1904–1939, KSZ1/3.
Diary—Magistrate and Civil Commissioner, Tanganyika District, INH/2.
Diary—Abercorn Native Commissioner, 1902–1903, INH/4.
District Note Books, Abercorn (vols. I–II), 1893– , KTN/1.
District Note Book, Chinsali, KTQ2.
District Note Book, Insumbu island, 1917–1924, KTA1/5.
District Note Books, Isoka, 1901– , KSL1/5.
District Note Books, Kasama (Vols. I–III), 1902– , KDH/1.
District Note Books, Luwingu, 1902–1909, KSZ1/5.

District Note Books, Mporokoso, 1904– , KSU1/5.
Forced labour, 1921–1926, B1/2/A298.
Free labour for chiefs, Tanganyika and Awemba Districts, AZ1/1–10.
Governor's correspondence, 1924–1939, P1/1–3.
Governor's tours, Tanganyika District, 1927, B1/3/A937; general, 1925–1932, ZA1/60.
History of native tribes, ZA1/9/162.
Hut-burning—correspondence, 1935–1939, SEC/NAT/67.
Labour—Luwingu Division, 1912–1913, KSZ1/1.
Land: B.S.A.C. mineral rights in North-eastern Rhodesia, A3/8/1–3.
Land: London Missionary Society, 1895–1910, A3/8/1–3; 1899–1910, A3/10/3.
Land: North Charterland Exploration Company, 1905–1907, A2/5/1.
Letter Books of Hugh Charles Marshall, 1899–1902; 1900–1903, INH/2.
London Missionary Society, 1926–1927, B7/1/A863; 1899–1910, A3/10/3.
Native Authorities and Native Courts, ZA1/9–10.
Native Reserves Commission, 1924–1925; Governor's correspondence, P1/3.
Native reserves and European areas: Tanganyika District, B1/4/LS.
Native reserves: Reserves Commission (Tanganyika District), 1927, B1/1/A1129.
Native reserves: Tanganyika District, B1/3/A366; ZA1/9/74/8.
Native reserves: Tanganyika District—in-letters, evidence and report, 1927; ZP1/3–9.
Native Treasuries, 1933–1937, ZA1/9/116.
Native unrest, 1922–1926, B1/1/A533.
Native Welfare Association, Abercorn, SEC/NAT/327.
Native Welfare Association, Broken Hill, SEC/NAT/324.
Native Welfare Association, Kasama, SEC/NAT/326.
Native Welfare Association, Livingstone, SEC/NAT/321.
Native Welfare Association, Luanshya, SEC/NAT/325.
Native Welfare Association, Ndola, SEC/NAT/329.
Native Welfare Associations (Civil Servants), 1930–1939, SEC/NAT/311.

Native Welfare Associations, minutes of, 1926, B1/1/A950.
Racial discord: general, 1932–1933, ZA1/9/10.
Report on the attitude of the Awemba, 1908–1909, KSD7/1.
Reports, Administrators', 1903/4; 1904/5; 1907/1910, A8/1/2.
Reports, annual—Tanganyika District, ZA7/1/7/9; ZA7/1/3/8.
Reports—annual, half-yearly; quarterly; inspection, and tour, 1903–1924, Awemba District, KSD7/4.
Reports—annual, inspection and tour, 1913–1934, Awemba and Tanganyika Districts, ZA1/9/95.
Reports—annual, 1902–1904; half-yearly, 1913–1916; tour, 1902–1915, and quarterly, 1902, Luwingu Division, KSZ1/4.
Reports, district, 1932–1939, SEC/NAT/363–65.
Reports, District Officers', 1934–1938, C4/2.
Reports, district quarterly, 1931–1932, SEC/NAT/64.
Reports—native affairs, 1909–1910, A8/1/1/1.
Reports—native affairs, Isoka Division, 1913–1923, KSL1/1.
Reports—native affairs, Luwingu Division, 1907–1911, KSZ1/2.
Reports—native affairs, Mporokoso Division, 1903–1910, KSU1/6.
Reports, slave trading, 1896–1897, A8/1/1/3; ZA1/9/60.
Reports, tour—Isoka Division, 1921–1924, KSL1/4.
Watch Tower—activities in Barotse Province, SEC/NAT/317.
Watch Tower—activities of followers, SEC/NAT/314, Vols. I–III.
Watch Tower—confidential, ZA1/10.
Watch Tower—Isoka Division, 1918–1920, KSL1/2.
Watch Tower—literature and correspondence, SEC/NAT/313.
Watch Tower—Mporokoso Division, 1919–1939, KSU1/4.
Watch Tower mission, ZA1/10, Vols. I–III.
Watch Tower movement, 1917–1927, ZA1/10/1.
Watch Tower movement, 1934–1935, ZA1/9/60.
Watch Tower movement, 1937–1939, SEC/NAT/317–18.
Watch Tower movement—proceedings, 1928–1939, SEC/NAT/312 and 393.
Watch Tower movement—recognition of the Society, 1932–1939, SEC/NAT/316.
Watch Tower movement—Visiting Commissioner's correspondence, ZA1/9/98.
Watch Tower movement—Visiting Commissioner's report, ZA7/7/2.

Watch Tower movement—Western Province, SEC/NAT/318.
White Fathers' missions, 1934–1936, C1/7.
Young, R. A. (n.d.) 'Awemba history as I have heard it'. MS.

(b) *Government reports and published documents*
British Central Africa Gazette.
B.S.A.C. *Directors' Reports and Accounts . . . , 1895– .*
B.S.A.C. *Reports on the Administration of Rhodesia,* 1897–8; 1898–
    1900; 1900–02.
Debates of the Northern Rhodesia Legislative Council, 1924–1940.
Illustrated Handbook of North-eastern Rhodesia. Fort Jameson:
    Administration Press, 1906.
Native Affairs Annual Reports, 1916–1950 (Government Printer).
North-eastern Rhodesia Government Gazette. Fort Jameson: Admin-
    istration Press, 1903–1911.
Northern Rhodesia Government Gazette, 1911–1940.
Proceedings of the African Representative Council, 1946–1950.
*Report of the Commission appointed to enquire into the Disturbances in
    the Copperbelt, Northern Rhodesia.* Lusaka: Government Printer,
    1935.
*Report of the Commission appointed to enquire into the Financial and
    Economic Position of Northern Rhodesia,* Col. No. 145 (1938).
Report of the Commission on Closer Union, Cmd. 3234 (1929).
*Report of the Director of Census (of Northern Rhodesia) regarding the
    Census taken on 5 May 1931* (Crown Agents), 1931.
Report on Native Taxation. Lusaka: Government Printer, 1938.
Report on the Administration of North-eastern Rhodesia, 1900–1903.
    Fort Jameson: Administration Press.
Rhodesia–Nyasaland Royal Commission Report, Cmd. 5949 (1939).

(c) *White Fathers' mission diaries*
These are kept in the archives of the Bishop of Mbala (formerly
Abercorn).
Chilonga Mission Diary, 1899–1914.
Kayambi Mission Diary, 1896–1905.
Old Mambwe Mission Diary, 1891–1896.

(d) *Oral sources: informants*
All the notes on oral evidence are in the writer's possession and
are based on eye-witness accounts given by the following persons:

Chileshe, Anock; Kasama village, Chief Mwamba, Kasama District; interviewed on 2 August 1967. Anock Chileshe, who is the father of Safeli Chileshi, one of the first Northern Rhodesian African members of the African Representative Council and the Legislative Council, saw service in the First World War, and is very knowledgeable about the history of Ituna, whose capital is only a few miles from his village.

Chibanta, Chief Chikwanda; Mpika; interviewed on 24 July 1967. He occupies one of the traditionally powerful Bemba chieftaincies, and as a young man at court in the 1930's and 1940's saw the introduction of indirect rule and its effects. He has until recently been the President of Zambia's House of Chiefs.

Kasonka, Zakeya; Chitulika village, Chief Chikwanda, Mpika district; interviewed on 24 July 1967. A businessman, he saw service as a military porter during World War I.

Mangara, Jean Baptiste; Kasama; interviewed on 2 August 1967. Mangara is a Nyamwezi of Tanganyika who, according to his own account, was once taken slave by the Catholic missionaries to Zanzibar and then to France. He was brought to the Northern Province in the days of Bishop Dupont, where he became a catechist and subsequently a government clerk.

Masandiko, Jaisy, Own village, Chief Nkula, Chinsali; interviewed on 27 July 1967. A former government clerk who saw the establishment of colonial rule in the 1890's and became a capitao of military porters in the 1914–18 war.

Mukosa, Zakariya; Choshi village, Chief Nkula, Chinsali District; interviewed on 27 July 1967. He is a store-keeper who was serviceman in the First World War.

Musenga, Paramount Chief Chitimukulu; interviewed on 3 August 1967. He is a nephew (sister's son) of the famous Mwamba Mubanga Chipoya and was present during Bishop Dupont's visit to Ituna before Mubanga Chipoya's death.

Mushindo, Rev. P. B., Lubwa mission, United Church of Zambia, Chinsali; interviewed on 27 July 1967. He witnessed the establishment of colonial rule and the Free Church of Scotland in the Northern Province.

Nkamba, Lufila; Chitukila village, Chief Chikwanda, Mpika; interviewed on 24 July 1967. He was a military porter during the first world war.

Nshika, Senior Chief Mwamba; Kasama, interviewed on 4

August 1967. As a young boy he witnessed the establishment of colonial rule.

Sikazwe, Moses; Mbala (Abercorn); interviewed on 29 July 1967. He was formerly a clerk in the colonial government and witnessed the establishment of European rule in the Northern Province. He is now President of Mbala local court.

Siwale, Donald K., Isunda Farm, Nakonde; interviewed on 28 July 1967. He attended the Livingstonia Mission, where he trained as a teacher and taught at Mwenzo Mission, before he became a government clerk and then adviser to Chieftainess Waitwika. He was a founder member of the Mwenzo Association.

(e) *Books and articles*

Campbell, Dugald (1922) *In the Heart of Bantuland: a record of twenty-nine years' pioneering in Central Africa among the Bantu peoples*. London: Seeley Service & Co.

Chapman, William (1909) *A Pathfinder in South Central Africa: a story of pioneer missionary work and adventure*. London: W. A. Hammond.

Crawford, D. (1912) *Thinking Black: twenty-two years without a break in the long grass of Central Africa*. London: Morgan and Scott.

Duff, H. L. (1906) *Nyasaland under the Foreign Office*. London: George Bell and Sons.

Gouldsbury, C. (1912) *An African Year*. London: Edward Arnold.

— and Sheane, H. (1911) *The Great Plateau of Northern Rhodesia: being some impressions of the Tanganyika Plateau*. London: Edward Arnold.

Gwassa, G. C., and Iliffe, John (eds.) (1968) 'Records of the Maji Maji rising', part one. *Historical Association of Tanzania*, Paper No. 4.

Harrington, H. T. (1954) 'The taming of North-eastern Rhodesia'. *The Northern Rhodesia Journal*, II, 3.

Johnston, Sir Harry (1896) *British Central Africa*. London: Methuen and Co.

Jordan, E. Knowles (1964) 'Chinsali in 1920–22'. *The Northern Rhodesia Journal*, V, 6.

Langham, R. W. M. (1960) 'Thornton and Rumsey of Mbesuma ranch'. *The Northern Rhodesia Journal*, IV, 4.

Letcher, Owen (1911) *Big Game Hunting in North-eastern Rhodesia*. London: John Long.

Livingstone, David (1874) *The Last Journals of David Livingstone in Central Africa*, Vol. 1, ed. H. Waller. London: John Murray.

Mansfield, Charlotte (n.d.) *Via Rhodesia: a Journey through Southern Africa*. London: Stanley Paul.

Richards, Audrey I. (1935) 'Tribal government in transition: the Bemba of North-eastern Rhodesia'. Supplement to the *Journal of the Royal African Society*, *XXXIV*, 137.

— (1939) *Land, Labour and Diet in Northern Rhodesia: an economic study of the Bemba tribe*. London: Oxford University Press.

— (1936) 'The life of Bwembya, a native of Northern Rhodesia' in *Ten Africans*, ed. M. Perham. London: Faber and Faber.

Sharpe, Alfred (1957) 'Travels in the Northern Province and Katanga'. *The Northern Rhodesia Journal*, *III*, 4.

Stokes, George (1957) 'Memories of abandoned Bomas, No. 12: Old Fife (period 1900–19)'. *The Northern Rhodesia Journal*, *III*, 4.

Tanguy, François (1954) 'Kayambi: the first White Fathers' mission in Northern Rhodesia'. Trans. Clifford Green, *The Northern Rhodesia Journal*, *II*, 4.

Young, R. A. (1953) ' "Bobo" Young relates his exploits'. A reproduction of Young's letter dated 20 July 1914 to Lieutenant-Colonel (later Sir) Stewart Gore-Brown in which the former relates the part he played in the pacification of the Northern Province, in *The Northern Rhodesia Journal*, *II*, 2.

II. SECONDARY SOURCES

(a) *Books*

Baeta, C. G. (ed.) (1968) *Christianity in Tropical Africa: studies presented and discussed at the seventh International African Seminar, University of Ghana, April, 1965*. London: Oxford University Press.

Barbour, K. M., and Prothero, R. M. (ed.) (1961), *Essays on African Population*. London: Routledge and Kegan Paul.

Barnes, J. A. (1967) *Politics in a Changing Society: a political history of the Fort Jameson Ngoni*. Manchester University Press for Rhodes-Livingstone Institute, Lusaka.

Bigland, Eileen (1939) *The Lake of Royal Crocodiles*. Norwich: Hodder and Stoughton.

Bolink, P. (1967) *Towards Church Unity in Zambia: a study of missionary co-operation and church-union efforts in Central Africa*. Sneek: T. Wever-Franeker.

Brelsford, W. V. (1948) *The Succession of Bemba Chiefs: A guide for District Officers*. Lusaka: Government Printer.

— (ed.) (1954) *The Story of the Northern Rhodesia Regiment*. Lusaka: Government Printer.

— (1956) *The Tribes of Northern Rhodesia*. Lusaka: Government Printer.

— (1965) *The Tribes of Zambia* (second edition).

Brown, Richard (1966) 'Aspects of the scramble for Matabeleland' in Stokes, E., and Brown, R. (eds.) *The Zambesian Past: Studies in Central African history*. Manchester University Press.

Cairns, H. A. C. (1965) *Prelude to Imperialism: British reactions to Central African society, 1840–90*. London: Routledge and Kegan Paul.

Clegg, E. (1960) *Race and Politics: partnership in the Federation of Rhodesia and Nyasaland*. London: Oxford University Press.

Colson, E., and Gluckman, M. (eds.) (1951) *Seven Tribes of British Central Africa*. Manchester University Press for Rhodes-Livingstone Institute, Lusaka.

Creighton, T. R. M. (1960) *The Anatomy of Partnership: Southern Rhodesia and the Central African Federation*. London: Faber and Faber.

Davidson, A. B. (1968) 'African resistance and rebellion against the imposition of colonial rule' in Ranger, T. O. (ed.), *Emerging Themes of African History: proceedings of the International Congress of African Historians, Dar es Salaam, 1965*. Nairobi: East African Publishing House.

Davis, J. A., and Baker, J. K. (ed.) (1966) *Southern Africa in Transition*. London: Pall Mall Press.

Duff, H. L. (1903) *Nyasaland under the Foreign Office*. London: George Bell and Sons.

Epstein, A. L. (1958) *Politics in an Urban African Community*. Manchester University Press for Rhodes-Livingstone Institute, Lusaka.

Evans, I. L. (1929) *The British in Tropical Africa*. Cambridge University Press.

Fortes, M., and Evans-Pritchard, E. E. (eds.) (1940) *African Political Systems*. London: Oxford University Press.

Franklin, H. (1963) *Unholy Wedlock: the failure of the Central African Federation*. London: George Allen and Unwin.

Gann, L. H. (1958) *The Birth of a Plural Society: the development of Northern Rhodesia under the British South Africa Company*. Manchester University Press for Rhodes-Livingstone Institute, Lusaka.

— (1964) *A History of Northern Rhodesia: early days to 1951*. London: Chatto and Windus.

— (1965) *A History of Southern Rhodesia: early days to 1934* London: Chatto and Windus.

Gelfand, M. (1961) *Northern Rhodesia in the Days of the Charter: a medical and social study, 1878–1924*. Oxford: Basil Blackwell.

Gluckman, M. (1960) *Custom and Conflict in Africa*. Oxford: Basil Blackwell.

Gray, J. R. (1960) *The Two Nations: aspects of the development of race relations in the Rhodesias and Nyasaland*. London: Oxford University Press.

Hailey, Lord (1938) *An African Survey: a study of problems arising in Africa south of the Sahara*. London: Oxford University Press.

— (1950) *Native Administration in British African Territories, Part II, Central Africa*. London: H.M.S.O.

Hall, R. (1965) *Zambia*. London: Pall Mall Press.

Hancock, W. K. (1942) *Survey of British Commonwealth Affairs*, Vol. II, Part I. *Problems of Economic Policy, 1918–39*. London: Oxford University Press.

Hanna, A. J. (1956) *The Beginnings of Nyasaland and North-eastern Rhodesia, 1859–95*. Oxford: Clarendon Press.

— (1960) *The Story of the Rhodesias and Nyasaland*. London: Faber and Faber.

Hodgkin, T. (1956) *Nationalism in British Colonial Africa*. London: Frederick Muller.

Hole, H. M. (1926) *The Making of Rhodesia*. London: Macmillan.

Holmberg, A. (1966) *African Tribes and European Agencies: colonialism and humanitarianism in British South and East Africa, 1870–95*. Goteborg: Akademiforläget.

Howell, A. E. (1949) *Bishop Dupont: king of the brigands*. Franklin, Pa.: News–Herald Printing Co.

Keatley, P. (1963) *The Politics of Partnership: the Federation of Rhodesia and Nyasaland*. London: Penguin African Library.

Kuczynski, R. R. (1949) *Demographic Survey of the British Colonial Empire*, Part II. London: Oxford University Press.

Lemarchand, R. (1964) *Political Awakening in the Belgian Congo*. Berkeley: University of California Press.

Macnair, J. I. (ed.) (1954) *Livingstone's Travels*. London: J. M. Dent and Sons.

Mason, P. (1958) *The Birth of a Dilemma: the conquest and settlement of Rhodesia*. London: Oxford University Press.

McEwan, P. J. M. (1968) *Readings in African History*. Part II *Nineteenth-century Africa*. Part III. *Twentieth-century Africa*. London: Oxford University Press.

Meek, C. K. (1946) *Land, Law and Customs in the Colonies*. London: Oxford University Press.

Merle Davis, J. (*et al.*) (1933) *Modern Industry and the African: an enquiry into the effect of the copper mines of Central Africa upon native society and the work of christian missions*. London: Macmillan.

Mpashi, S. A. (1966) *Abapatili Bafika Ku Babemba*. Lusaka: Oxford University Press.

Mulford, D. C. (1967) *Zambia: the politics of independence*. London: Oxford University Press.

Oliver, R. A. (1957) *Sir Harry Johnston and the Scramble for Africa*. London: Chatto and Windus.

— (1967) *The Middle Age of African History*. London: Oxford University Press.

— and Mathew, G. (1963) *History of East Africa*, Vol. I. Oxford: Clarendon Press.

Omer-Cooper, J. D. (1966) *The Zulu Aftermath: a nineteenth-century revolution in Bantu Africa*. London: Longmans.

Osei, G. K. (1967) *The African: his antecedents, his genius and his destiny*. London: African Publishing Society.

Perham, Margery (ed.) (1936) *Ten Africans*. London: Faber and Faber.

Ranger, T. O. (1963) 'Revolt in Portuguese East Africa: the Makombe rising of 1911,' in K. Kirkwood (ed.), *St. Anthony's Papers*, No. 15 (*African Affairs*, No. 2), London.

— (1967) *Revolt in Southern Rhodesia, 1896–7: a study in African resistance*. London: Heinemann.

— (1968) *Aspects of Central African History*. London: Heinemann.

Robinson, R., Gallagher, J., and Denny, A. (1961) *Africa and the Victorians: the mind of imperialism.* London: Macmillan.

Rotberg, R. I. (1965) *Christian Missionaries and the Creation of Northern Rhodesia, 1880–1924.* Princeton University Press.

— (1965) *A Political History of Tropical Africa.* New York: Harcourt, Brace and World.

— (1965) *The Rise of Nationalism in Central Africa: the making of Malawi and Zambia, 1873–1924.* Cambridge, Mass.: Harvard University Press.

Shepperson, G., and Price, T. (1958) *Independent African: John Chilembwe and the origins, setting and significance of the Nyasaland rising of 1915.* Edinburgh University Press.

Spiro, H. J. (1964) 'The Rhodesias and Nyasaland' in Carter, Gwendolen M. (ed.), *Five African States: responses to diversity.* London: Pall Mall Press.

Stevenson, W. C. (1967) *Year of Doom, 1975: the Story of Jehovah's Witnesses.* London: Hutchinson.

Stokes, E., and Brown, Richard (eds.) (1966) *The Zambesian Past: studies in Central African history.* Manchester University Press.

Sundkler, B. G. M. (1961) *Bantu Prophets in South Africa.* London: Oxford University Press.

Tanguy, François (1966) *Imilandu Ya Babemba.* Lusaka: Oxford University Press.

Taylor, J. V., and Lehmann, Dorothea (1961) *Christians of the Copperbelt: the growth of the Church in Northern Rhodesia.* London: SCM Press.

van des Horst, Sheila (1942) *Native Labour in South Africa.* London: Oxford University Press.

Walker, E. A. (1957) *A History of Southern Africa.* London: Longmans.

Wallerstein, I. M. (1966) *Social Change: the colonial situation.* New York: John Wiley.

Watson, W. (1958) *Tribal Cohesion in a Money Economy: a study of the Mambwe people of Northern Rhodesia.* Manchester University Press for Rhodes-Livingstone Institute, Lusaka.

White Fathers (1932) *Ifya Bukaya.* Chilubulu Mission.

Wills, A. J. (1964) *An Introduction to the History of Central Africa.* London: Oxford University Press.

Worsley, P. (1957) *The trumpet shall sound: a study of 'Cargo' cults in Melanesia.* London: Macgibbon and Kee.

(b) *Pamphlets, articles, manuscripts, etc.*

Barnes, J. A. (1950) 'African separatist Churches'. *The Rhodes-Livingstone Journal, IX.*

Baxter, T. W. (1950) 'Slave raiders in North-eastern Rhodesia'. *The Northern Rhodesia Journal, I,* 1.

Brelsford, W. V., 'Shimwalule: a study of a Bemba chief and priest'. Unpublished manuscript collection, Institute for Social Research, University of Zambia, Lusaka.

— (1944) *Aspects of Bemba Chieftainship.* Rhodes-Livingstone, Communication No. 2.

Brown, R. (1960) 'Indirect rule as a policy of adaptation'. Unpublished manuscript collection, Institute for Social Research, University of Zambia, Lusaka.

Gann, L. H. (1954) 'The end of the slave trade in British Central Africa, 1889–1912'. *The Rhodes-Livingstone Journal, VI.*

Gluckman, Max (1954) 'Succession and civil war among the Bemba: An exercise in anthropological theory'. *The Rhodes-Livingstone Journal, XVI.*

Hering, Joseph, 'History of the Bemba tribe'. Manuscript, White Fathers' Cathedral, Kasama.

Hooker, J. R. (1966) 'Welfare Associations and other instruments of accommodation in the Rhodesias between the world wars'. *Comparative Studies in Society and History, IX,* 1.

Hopkins, A. G. (1966) 'Economic aspects of political movements in Nigeria and the Gold Coast, 1918–39'. *Journal of African History, VII,* 1.

Kunene, Daniel P. (1970) 'African vernacular writing—an essay in self-devaluation', *African Social Research* No. 9 Institute for Social Research, University of Zambia.

Lemarchand, R. (1961) 'The bases of nationalism among the Bakongo'. *Africa, XXXI,* 3.

Ranger, T. O. (1965) 'The "Ethiopian" episode in Barotseland, 1900–05'. *The Rhodes-Livingstone Journal, XXXVII.*

— (1968) 'Connexions between "primary resistance" movements and modern mass nationalism in East and Central Africa', Part 1. *Journal of African History, IX,* 3.

— (1969) 'The African Churches of Tanzania'. *Historical Association of Tanzania,* Paper No. 5.

Richards, Audrey I., 'Chieftainship: officials of the chief'. Unpublished manuscript collection, Institute for Social Research, University of Zambia, Lusaka.

— (1940) *Bemba Marriage and Present Economic Conditions*. Rhodes-Livingstone Paper No. 4.

Roberts, Andrew (1966) 'A political history of the Bemba (North-eastern Zambia) to 1900'. Ph.D. thesis for the University of Wisconsin. To be published by Cambridge University Press.

— (ed.) (1967) 'The history of Abdullah Ibn Suliman'. *African Social Research* No. 4.

— (1970) 'Chronology of the Bemba (North-eastern Zambia)', *Journal of African History*, XI (1970), ii, pp. 221–40.

Rotberg, R. I. (1964) 'The missionary factor in the occupation of Trans-Zambezia'. *The Northern Rhodesia Journal*, V, 4.

Sanderson, F. E. (1961) 'The development of labour migration from Nyasaland, 1891–1914'. *Journal of African History*, II, 2.

Shepperson, G. (1954) 'The politics of African Church separatist movements in British Central Africa, 1892–1916'. *Africa*, XXIV, 3.

— (1963) 'Church and sect in Central Africa'. *The Rhodes-Livingstone Journal*, XXXIII.

Stone, W. Vernon (1968) 'The Livingston mission to the Bemba'. *The Bulletin of the Society for African Church History*, vol. II, 4.

Tanguy, François, 'History of the Bemba'. Unpublished manuscript collection, Institute for Social Research, University of Zambia, Lusaka.

Thomas, F. M. (1936) 'The Matipas–Bawisa chiefs: some notes on their history'. Unpublished manuscript collection. Institute for Social Research, University of Zambia, Lusaka.

— (1958) *Historical Notes on the History of the Bisa Tribe of Northern Rhodesia*. Rhodes-Livingstone Communication No. 8.

van Velsen, J. (1959) 'The missionary factor among the Lakeside Tonga of Nyasaland'. *The Rhodes-Livingstone Journal*, XXVI.

Werbner, R. P. (1967) 'Federal administration, rank and civil strife among the Bemba royals and nobles'. *Africa*, XXXVII, 1.

Wilson, Godfrey (1941) *An Essay on the Economics of Detribalization in Northern Rhodesia*, Part 1. Rhodes-Livingstone Papers No. 5.

Wilson, Godfrey (1942) *An Essay on the Economics of Detribalization in Northern Rhodesia*, Part II. Rhodes-Livingstone Papers No. 6.

INDEX

Abercorn (administrative centre of Tanganyika District), 1, 19, 89, 93, 135
Abercorn Welfare Association, 246–7, 252–3, 266–7
African Lakes Company, 25, 86, 91
anti-slavery activities, 6, 10, 17
land transactions, 29–30, 190
trading posts, 19, 25
African National Congress, 284
African nationalism, rise of, 283–4
African Representative Council, 254, 285
Amalgamation of Rhodesias and Nyasaland, proposed, African attitude towards, 70–5, 264–9, 285
Arabs:
defeat of, 45–6, 48–9, 57, 71
hostility towards creation of administrative posts, 56
hostility towards Europeans, 32–3, 47–9, 55–6, 70
influence on Mwamba Mubanga Chipoya, 60
relations with the Bemba, 2–3, 5, 10, 32, 48–9, 56, 57
slave trade, 5, 28, 55

Bemba (people):
attitude towards amalgamation, 270
economic and political organisation, 9
end of resistance to white Administration, 70
geographical location, vi, 2
hostility towards creation of administrative posts, 56
kingdom of, 8–9
reactions to abolition of *mitanda* and *chitemene*, 105–7, 111
reactions to Watch Tower, 137–8, 175
relations with Arabs, 2–3, 5, 28, 32, 45–6, 48, 55
relations with neighbouring tribes, 2, 7–8, 208–11
resistance to colonial rule, 102, 113
role in Copperbelt disturbances, 255, 260–5

threats of violence by, in Copperbelt disturbances, 259
Besa, J. J., 263–4, 268
Bisa (people), 6–7, 29, 204–5
attitude towards amalgamation, 271–273
reaction to abolition of *mitanda* and *chitemene*, 105
relations with the Bemba, 8, 196–9
resistance to taxation, 97–101, 114–115, 124–5
resistance to white rule, 97–9
Bledisloe Commission, 264–8, 271–5, 285
British colonial policy, 16, 205ff., 245–249, 266
African paramountcy doctrine, 243, 286
attitude towards proposed amalgamation, 274–5
indirect rule, 8, 186–9, 202–3
Native Reserves, 190
British South Africa Company Administration:
administrative districts in Northern Province, 89
attitude to Chief Mukasa, 215–20
forced labour policy, 83–4, 88–90
policy, 89–90, 103
relations with Watch Tower, 139–143, 150, 164–6, 168, 173–4
taxation, 86

Chiengi (administrative post), 6, 19, 25, 165
Chimfwembe, Chitimukulu Makumba, 11, 15, 37, 53
relations with White Fathers, 62–4
Chipoya, Chief Mwamba Mubanga, 13–15, 50–58, 60–4
role in Anglo-Bemba conflict, 50–4
Chitemene, 4, 102–17
Chitimukulu (Bemba rulers):
Chimfwembe Makumba, 11, 15, 37, 53, 62–4
Musenga, 64–5; recollections of circumstances of Dupont's 'succession', 64

302